Retrieving the American Past

A Customized U.S. History Reader

Compiled by

Professor Lambert
History 151
Purdue University

PEARSON CUSTOM PUBLISHING

Director of Database Publishing: Michael Payne
Sponsoring Editor: Natalie Danner
Development Editor: Katherine Gretz
Editorial Assistant: Samantha A. Goodman
Marketing Manager: Nathan L. Wilbur
Operations Manager: Eric M. Kenney
Database Project Specialist: Zach LaRosa

Cover Art: Christie's Images, Long Island City, NY
Granger Collection, New York, NY

Printed in the United States of America

10 9 8 7 6 5 4 3 2 1

0536647038
BA 5567

PEARSON CUSTOM PUBLISHING
75 Arlington Street, Suite #300/Boston, MA 02116
Pearson Education Group

CONTRIBUTORS

Senior Editors
Michael Les Benedict
Mark Grimsley
Susan M. Hartmann
Margaret E. Newell
Carla Gardina Pestana
Leila J. Rupp
David L. Stebenne
Warren R. Van Tine

Managing Editor
John Day Tully

Assistant Managing Editor
Jennifer Walton

Copy Editor
Ann Heiss

Contributing Editors

Tyler Anbinder
Kenneth J. Andrien
Jean Harvey Baker
Michael Les Benedict
Mansel Blackford
Paul C. Bowers
Rowland Brucken
John D. Buenker
John C. Burnham
Joan E. Cashin
William R. Childs
Albert J. Churella
Steven Conn
Saul Cornell
Nick Cullather
Jeanette Davis
Merton L. Dillon
Daniel Feller
Charles Coleman Finlay
Emily Greenwald
Mark Grimsley
Bernard N. Grindel
Peter L. Hahn
James Hansen
Susan M. Hartmann
Mary Ann Heiss
Earl J. Hess
Michael J. Hogan
R. Douglas Hurt
Bruce Karhoff
Michael Kazin
Terence Kehoe
K. Austin Kerr
Frank Lambert
Valerie Mendoza
James McCaffrey
Allan R. Millett
Pamela J. Mills
Daniel Nelson
Margaret E. Newell
Josef Ostyn
Carla Gardina Pestana
Patrick D. Reagan
Randolph A. Roth
Hal K. Rothman
John A. M. Rothney
Leila J. Rupp
Richard D. Shiels
David Sicilia
C. Edward Skeen
Amy L. S. Staples
David L. Stebenne
David Steigerwald
Marshall F. Stevenson, Jr.
Warren R. Van Tine
Christopher Waldrep
J. Samuel Walker

Contents

The Causes of Bacon's Rebellion

Carla Gardina Pestana
and Charles Coleman Finlay

Introduction

By 1675, the royal colony of Virginia concentrated its agricultural efforts on growing tobacco for export. Tobacco cultivation demanded a large labor force, and the planters relied mainly on English, Irish, and Scottish indentured servants, some of them poor young men and women, others convicts sentenced to a period of labor in the New World. When their terms of servitude expired, they wanted land for themselves, which put them in competition with plantation owners (their former masters) who wanted to expand their holdings to replace land that had been depleted by the overcultivation of tobacco. New land was becoming scarce, because the colony was reaching the limits of its boundaries. Beyond those boundaries lived various groups of Native Americans who opposed continued English expansion onto their lands. The royally appointed governor, Sir William Berkeley, sought to avoid further conflicts with the Indians by reaching boundary agreements with them. These agreements primarily hurt the ex-indentured servants and the newly arrived planters, since these people would benefit most if additional lands were made available for settlement. Some of these people went to live on (or beyond) the borders of the colony, where their presence sparked the hostilities that Berkeley sought to avoid.

In 1675 and early 1676, a series of confrontations occurred along the Potomac River in the Chesapeake region, pitting Doeg and Susquehannock Indians against these English planters. Nathaniel Bacon, a well-born Englishman who had recently migrated to Virginia, sought official sanction for a general attack against the natives. After Governor Berkeley refused to authorize

Bacon's request, Bacon led a group of volunteers to massacre one of the friendly tribes. When Berkeley declared Bacon a rebel and moved to arrest him, the young man launched an attack on the governor, and the entire colony collapsed into civil war. The rebels burned Jamestown, the capital, to the ground, and a period of plunder ensued in which partisans on both sides looted the homes and property of their enemies.

For most of 1676 Virginia was engulfed by civil war. The uprising against Berkeley, led by Bacon and named after him, was the largest armed revolt against English authority in the American colonies until the Revolution a century later. It was only put down after King Charles II dispatched an expeditionary force to quell the rebellion. After they had helped Berkeley restore order to the colony, the king's commissioners replaced Berkeley and sent him back to England to justify himself to the king. After an extended career (1642–52, 1660–77) as governor in the first royal colony in America, Berkeley died in disgrace in England shortly after his return there.

Although Berkeley's handling of the crisis (along with some of the policies that led up to it) resulted in his fall from power, the rebels were judged yet more harshly at the time. Many of them lost their lives after the rebellion was put down. During the revolutionary era, however, it became popular to present Bacon as the heroic forerunner of later Virginian revolutionaries like George Washington and Patrick Henry. More recently, scholars have been less inclined to side wholeheartedly with Bacon. They now tend to study the rebellion for what it reveals about serious divisions within late-seventeenth-century Chesapeake society. Bacon's Rebellion was the only colonial revolt to involve Native Americans, Europeans, and Africans. As such, it offers a glimpse of the social and political development of early Virginia.

Scholars Debate Motivation

Ironically, Bacon's Rebellion "waited" almost one hundred years after it first erupted in 1676 to become an important historical event. During and after the American Revolution, people like Thomas Jefferson searched for examples of previous resistance to English authority in the American colonies and identified Nathaniel Bacon as a model for a later generation of Virginian rebels. Well into the twentieth century, this view that Bacon's Rebellion was an early example of Americans standing up against English tyranny continued to be widely accepted by historians. Over the last four decades, however, some scholars have questioned its accuracy and reconsidered the evidence to find alternative explanations. All three of the readings below focus on explaining what motivated the colonists to take up arms against their government.

Prelude to the American Revolution

Thomas Jefferson Wertenbaker defends the traditional interpretation of Bacon's Rebellion, explicitly comparing Nathaniel Bacon's revolt against a "tyrannical" Governor Berkeley with the American colonists' later revolution against King George. The excerpt below is abridged from Virginia Under the Stuarts, *which was reprinted as part of* The Shaping of Colonial Virginia *(New York, 1958), 115–16, 123, 127, 130–31, 133, 143–45.*

Never was a people doomed to more bitter disappointment [than the Virginians were after Charles II was restored to the throne of England in 1660]. The years which followed the Restoration were crowded with misfortunes greater than any that had befallen the colony since the ghastly days of the Great Sickness [malaria epidemics]. Charles II, far from showing gratitude to his Old Dominion, overwhelmed it with injustice and oppression. The Virginians were crushed with tremendous duties on their tobacco and with ruinous restrictions upon their trade. The titles to their plantations were threatened by a grant of the entire colony to two unworthy favorites of the King. Governor Berkeley, embittered . . . and growing avaricious and crabbed with advancing years, soon forfeited that respect and love which his former good conduct had gained him. His second administration [1660–1677] was marred by partiality, oppression and inefficiency. The people were deprived of their right of suffrage by continued prorogation [dismissal] of the Assembly. Local government fell into the hands of small aristocratic cliques, while the poor were ground down with unequal and excessive taxes. Two wars with Holland added to the misfortunes of the colonists. Even the Heavens seemed to join with their enemies, for the country was visited by a terrific hurricane which swept over the plantations, destroying crops and wrecking houses. These accumulated misfortunes brought such deep suffering upon the colony that hundreds of families were reduced to poverty and many were forced into debt and ruin. No wonder that the commons, finally driven to desperation, should have risen in insurrection against the Governor and the King.

First among the causes of distress during this unhappy period must be placed the Navigation Acts. . . . [A series of laws intended to force the colonists to trade with England rather than other European countries.] Can there be any doubt that the Navigation Acts and the futility of all attempts to escape their baleful effects, were largely instrumental in bringing on Bacon's Rebellion? As prosperity and contentment are the greatest safeguards of the public peace, so poverty, nakedness and distress are breeders of sedition. Philip Ludwell spoke of Bacon's army as "a Rabble of the basest sort of People; whose Condicion was such as by a chaunge could not admitt of worse". Had England been less selfish in her treatment of Virginia, there would not have been so many indigent men in the colony eager to join in this wild uprising against the government. Berkeley himself admitted, in 1673, that at least one third of the freemen had been rendered so desperate by poverty and debt that in times of foreign war their loyalty to England could not be relied upon.

The wars of 1664 and 1672 with Holland added much to the distress in Virginia. The bold Dutch mariners, angered at the injury done them by the Navigation Acts, preyed upon the English merchantmen in every sea. Woe to the tobacco ship that encountered a hostile privateer, in its journey across the Atlantic! The English vessels were not safe even in the Virginia rivers, under the guns of their forts. Twice the daring Dutch came through the capes and into the James River itself, where they wrought great damage to the shipping. . . .

Great as was the distress caused by the depredations of the Dutch, the planters suffered even more during these wars by the stagnation of trade. The great risk incurred in crossing the ocean necessarily brought an increase both in freight rates and in the cost of manufactured goods. In 1667 the Governor and Council declared that the planters were "inforced to pay 12 pounds to £17 per ton freight" on their tobacco "which usually was but at seven pounds". Conditions were even worse during the second war. In 1673 Berkeley complained that the number of vessels that dared come to Virginia was so small, that they had "not brought goods and tools enough for one part of five of the people to go on with their necessary labor". "And those few goods that are brought," he added "have Soe few (and these hard Dealing) Sellers and Soe many Indigent and necessitous buyors that the Poore Planter gets not the fourth part . . . for his tobacco which he usually has had in other times."

In this period, so full of suffering and misfortune, the year 1667 was especially noteworthy for its long series of [natural] disasters. . . .

Perhaps the people of Virginia might have borne patiently all these misfortunes, had their Governor ruled them with wisdom and justice. Certain it is they would never have turned in wild anger to strike down his government, had that government not done much to make their condition intolerable. Sir William Berkeley was accused of destroying the representative character of the Assembly, of initiating a notorious spoils system, of intimidating Burgesses, of winking at embezzlement of public funds. And, although most of these charges were brought by the Governor's bitter enemies, some of them were undoubtedly true. . . .

It would not be just to give credence to all the accusations made against Berkeley. The King's commissioners who conducted

Charles II (1630–85), King of England during Bacon's Rebellion, recalled his long-time governor, William Berkeley in its aftermath. (Painting by Peter Lely. Courtesy of The Library of Congress.)

the investigation into his conduct, were his enemies; while many of the charges were brought by those who had taken part in the Rebellion. Thus the testimony against him is in most cases distinctly partisan. Moreover those that were closely associated with Sir William often expressed extravagant admiration for his ability and energy, and love for his character. "He hath," wrote the Council in 1673, "for neare 30 years governed this colony with that prudence and justice which hath gained him both love and reverence from all the Inhabitants here." . . .

But whatever is the verdict of posterity upon the conduct and motives of Sir William Berkeley, the causes of the Rebellion stand out with great clearness:—England's selfish commercial policy, . . . the Dutch wars, storms and pestilence, inefficient if not corrupt government, excessive taxes. The only wonder is that the insurrection did not occur earlier. In fact two mutinies did break out in 1674, when the excessively heavy taxes of that year were announced, but the rebels lacked leaders and were suppressed without great difficulty. As early as 1673 the defection of the planters was so great that it was feared many might attempt to deliver the colony into the hands of the Dutch. Berkeley wrote that a large part of the people were so desperately poor that they might reasonably be expected upon any small advantage of the enemy to "revolt to them in hopes of bettering their Condition by Shareing the Plunder of the Country with them". A certain John Knight reported "that the planters there doe generally desire a trade with the Dutch and all other nations and would not be singly bound to the trade of England, and speake openly there that they are in the nature of slaves, soe that the hearts of the greatest part of them are taken away from his Majesty". Thus the downtrodden planters, alienated from England, angered at the Governor, even distrusting their own Assembly, waited but an occasion and a leader to rise in open rebellion. A new Indian war offered the occasion, and they found their leader in young Nathaniel Bacon.

Conflict on the Frontier

Historian Wilcomb Washburn refutes the consensus Wertenbaker and many others shared on Bacon's Rebellion. He rejects comparisons with the Revolution and argues that the uprising must be understood in the context of Bacon's hatred for Native Americans and his desire for their frontier lands. Excerpted from Wilcomb E. Washburn, The Governor and The Rebel: A History of Bacon's Rebellion in Virginia *(Chapel Hill, 1957), 153, 159–60, 162–63, 166.*

What was the "cause" of Bacon's Rebellion? What motivated the 400 foot and 120 horse who marched with Bacon into Jamestown on June 23, 1676? Romantic historians like to see the rebellion as "a revolt of the lower classes of whites against the aristocratic families who governed Virginia," as "the cause of the poor against the rich, of the humble folk against the grandees."...

The more prosaic interests of the rebels have rarely been inquired into. It has been assumed that they were selfless patriots fighting a tyrannical government. We are told that Bacon was "a champion of the weak, a rebel against injustice, the forerunner of

---

Washington, Jefferson and Samuel Adams." Others have compared Bacon to Patrick Henry, to Tiberius Gracchus, to Callimachus, and even to Leonidas at Thermopylae.

It is generally assumed, on the other hand, that the governor and his council were the "grandees" of the colony and that they possessed vast holdings of land while the rest of the colonists eked out a precarious existence on their small plantations. Like so many other assertions about Bacon's Rebellion, this one is not based on a study of the evidence. An investigation of the land holdings of the partisans on both sides reveals a surprising equality between them. The leaders on both sides had large holdings. The followers on both sides had more modest holdings. What is most significant is that the leaders of the rebellion against Governor Berkeley almost invariably owned great tracts of land on the frontier, frequently had a record of oppression and aggression against the neighboring Indians, and occasionally had been punished by Berkeley for their crimes against the natives.

Governor Berkeley strove throughout his career to restrain the aggressiveness of the frontier landowners. But his power was limited. For one thing he was not in control of the government from 1652 to 1660 when the most unregulated expansion took place. His ability to control expansion was further restricted when, in 1666, he lost the right to allow or disallow individual grants. The assembly successfully challenged his authority to limit the right to acquire land, and "henceforth it was recognised in practice that the Governor had no more power over land grants than that secured by his individual vote in the Council." . . .

The connection between the colonists' itch for land and the Indian "troubles" is a close one. Since the Indian troubles set off the rebellion, it would seem fair to blame the rebellion in great part on those who caused the Indian troubles. But it seems an inescapable conclusion that the English, and particularly the rebellious frontiersmen themselves, were responsible for the Indian troubles. It was the frontiersmen's continuing violation of Governor Berkeley's efforts to settle the Indian-white relationship with fairness to both sides that precipitated the rebellion.

Colonel Moryson, one of the commissioners [who investigated the rebellion for the King], was well aware from his period in the Virginia government of the propensity of the frontiersmen to push the Indians off their land. He wrote in 1676 that there had not been a war with the Indians for the previous twenty-five years that had not been caused by the English coveting their land. When, therefore, Moryson and his fellow commissioners were presented the "grievance" of Henrico County that no satisfaction had been obtained against the Indians, they commented: "These Complainants never consider that the breach of the Peace and occasion of Bloodshed has still been on the side of the English, which was publickly Justified and affirmed in open Court in the face of a very great Assembly, and denyed by none."

The one cause of Bacon's Rebellion that has been consistently overlooked, then, is the aggressiveness of the frontiersmen. The careful [Richard] Hildreth [a nineteenth-century historian] nearly stumbled onto this conception when he wrote, with unconscious humor, that "the Indian war, the immediate cause of all the late disturbances, seems to have subsided so soon as expeditions against the Indians were dropped." What has caused English and American historians to overlook the frontiersmen's aggressiveness? The reason lies partly in the white historian's unconscious immersion in his racial bias. According to the mythology of the white view of the world, the Indian is ever "primitive," "warlike," and "aggressive," while the "civilized" white man is constantly on guard against his attacks. But the aggressiveness of the frontiersmen has been overlooked for another reason, one based on our idea of our political beliefs. Most of the writers and historians who have dealt with Bacon's Rebellion have written from what they regarded as a "liberal" point of view, and it is part of the mythology of this view of history that the American frontiersman symbolizes America's freedom, democracy, and hatred of oppression. Actually the American frontiersman of the seventeenth century paid scant heed to such ideals. . . .

The causes of Bacon's rebellion are complex and profound. They cannot be explained in terms of Berkeley's "greed" and "oppression," Bacon's love of "liberty," the "savagery" of the Indians, or the "patriotism" of the frontiersmen; such explanatory descriptions are meaningless labels pasted on the actors by those who see all history as a morality play. Nor can the rebellion be explained in terms of the concealed identities and mysterious motives of a Gothic romance. Bacon does not change, with the hemispheres, from the spoiled son of a well-to-do English country squire to a dedicated democratic frontier hero. Nor does Governor

Berkeley, after being the "Darling of the People" for thirty-five years, suddenly reveal his true identity as their blackest oppressor. Both men remained true to the faults and virtues of their natures.

Nathaniel Bacon would be vastly amused to find himself the sainted hero of the guardians of the liberal traditions of western democratic government. No doubt he would receive the news with an expression of his profane amusement at the idiocy of men. "God damn my blood," he might exclaim; "how easily people are led!"

Exploitation of Labor

Edmund S. Morgan chooses to examine the motives of the masses of people who rebelled, rather than focusing on Berkeley and Bacon, the leaders on opposite sides of the rebellion. In the following selection, he places the uprising in a pattern of resistance by people whose labor was ruthlessly exploited throughout the first century of Virginia's history. Condensed from American Slavery, American Freedom: The Ordeal of Colonial Virginia *(New York, 1975), 253–61.*

When Berkeley heard that the Susquehannahs had been seen at the falls of the James, he called a special session of the assembly. It met on March 7 and adopted measures that added political grievances to the settlers' anxieties over the Indians. The legislators decided to build a fort at the head of each great river and to man the forts with a standing army of 500 soldiers drawn from the lower counties; the tributary Indians were to be enrolled against the enemy and rewarded with trading cloth, but private trade with the Indians was forbidden. To people in New Kent and the Southside, the act that was supposed to end the Indian menace looked like a prescription for profiteering. The frontier forts would contribute more to the wealth of the men who built them than to the security of the people they were supposed to protect. The new ones would doubtless be located on the unoccupied upriver lands of the "great men" who sat in the assembly and would thus help to raise the value of their speculative holdings. The soldiers, recruited in the lower counties, would be paid 1,500 pounds of tobacco apiece, more than a frontier farmer on poor land was likely to make in a year. There would have to be another huge levy to pay for the troops and the forts, and both would be useless against roving Indians who melted into the woods after every attack. It almost seemed that the assembly had wished to guarantee the ineffectiveness of the scheme, because they had included a provision that if the enemy was discovered, he was not to be attacked until the governor was notified and gave his approval, by which time, as every frontiersman knew, the Indians would have vanished. The provision may have arisen from Berkeley's anger at the reckless commanders who had murdered the Susquehannah chiefs at the fort when they came out to a supposed peace parley ("If they had killed my Grandfather and Grandmother, my father and Mother and all my friends, yet if

This image comes from a cartouche (an illustration that appeared on a map of Virginia) in the early eighteenth century. It shows a typical waterfront scene from a later era, when manual labor was performed almost exclusively by slaves. The casks contain tobacco. (Courtesy of M.P. Middleton.)

they had come to treat of Peace, they ought to have gone in Peace"), but it would scarcely reassure frontiersmen of the government's ability to handle the Indian danger. Among those not reassured was Nathaniel Bacon. . . .

One day in the following April [1676], Bacon and some of his neighbors, James Crews, Henry Isham, and William Byrd, got together for a sociable glass or two. Byrd had lost three servants killed by the Indians. Bacon had lost his overseer at the falls. They were all unimpressed by the measures the March assembly had taken and were "making the Sadnesse of the times their discourse, and the Fear they all lived in, because of the Susquahanocks, who had settled [i.e., encamped] a little above the Falls of James River." They were also uneasy about the tributary Indians who lived close by. It was said that these Indians were not planting corn, which suggested that they intended leaving their towns for the warpath. Bacon in particular believed the country must defend itself "against all Indians in generall for that they were all Enemies." "This," he told Berkeley later, "I have alwayes said and doe maintaine."

While Bacon and his friends were telling each other their troubles on the north side of the James, the less prosperous planters on the south side were doing the same. They were even more upset than Bacon about the assembly's measures and also about the assembly itself. The 150 pounds a day plus expenses that the burgesses allowed themselves was as much a grievance as the useless forts that would enrich the great men. And Giles Bland was apparently encouraging them to appeal to the king against the extortionary local magnates. Bland was ready to carry the message himself.

The immediate problem, however, was the Indians. The Southsiders were eager to march against them with their own arms and without pay, and had appealed to the governor to commission someone to lead them. When he declined to do so, they lost patience and began to gather on their own in an encampment at Jordan's Point, just below the mouth of the Appomattox. Hearing of the move, Bacon and his friends left their talk and crossed the river to see what was up. Bacon's feelings about Indians were evidently known. He was a friend of the governor, a member of the council; and his appearance in the crowd, doling out a supply of rum like a good politician, gave a semblance of governmental approval to the gathering. "A Bacon! a Bacon! a Bacon!" went the cry. The young man was evidently not displeased, and he agreed to lead them against the Indians, perhaps assuming that Berkeley would not deny a commission to *him*.

And, indeed, if Berkeley had been willing to follow the line of least resistance, he would have been well advised to grant the commission gracefully. In April of 1676, however, the Southsiders' proposed march on the Indians apparently looked more dangerous to the safety of the colony than the depredations of the Susquehannahs. For months Indian tribes up and down the continent had been restive. King Philip's War, a concerted attack on the New England settlers, had broken out at about the same time as the skirmishes on the Potomac, a fact that looked sinister in itself. It was rumored that the Susquehannahs were negotiating for assistance from tribes three hundred miles to the north. All in all, Berkeley was convinced that the Indians were "generally conspired against us in all the western parts of America." With a larger Indian war brewing, Berkeley thought it desirable to keep a firm but friendly grip on Virginia's tributary Indians, not only because they might be useful as spies against hostile tribes but also to prevent them from joining the enemy. Berkeley, knowing the frontiersman's contempt for all Indians and his greed for their lands, would not risk sending out an expeditionary force that might not differentiate between friend and foe any more carefully than the Westmoreland militia who had started the whole conflict with the Susquehannahs. Nor could Berkeley risk creating an armed force of his most disgruntled inhabitants, men who were even more likely to turn against him than those he had led against the Dutch. The assembly may have been swayed by this danger when voting to garrison the new forts with men from the downriver counties.

Although Bacon seriously differed with Berkeley about the way to deal with Indians, he fully appreciated the danger of rebellious freemen. Living in Henrico County, he was in a better position than Berkeley to sense their mood, and he was not likely to underestimate it. As a prosperous government official in an area surrounded by men angry with the government, he could anticipate a rough time if discontent turned to rebellion. By leading the discontented in their proposed expedition against the Indians, which he relished as much as they did, he would gain their good will and at the same time avert their anger from the governor and assembly. According to Bacon, his leadership at Jordan's Point had precisely that effect. "Since my being with the volunteers," he wrote to Berkeley, "the Exclaiming concerning forts and Leavys has beene suppressed and the discourse and earnestness of the people is against the Indians. . . ." Bacon was offering Berkeley a way to suppress a mutiny. The Indians would be the scapegoats. Discontent with upper-class leadership would be vented in racial hatred, in a pattern that statesmen and politicians of a later age would have found familiar.

Berkeley did not take the offer. Virginia needed the friendship of the local Indians, and he did not trust the freemen. Furthermore, he did not know whether to trust Bacon. . . . When Berkeley refused Bacon a commission, Bacon chose to proceed without one, but he issued a conciliatory "Humble Appeale of the Voluntiers to all well minded and Charitable People." The appeal recited the uselessness of the forts, the need for a "moving force," and the willingness of the volunteers to "become both actours and paymasters of this necessary defensive warr" without charge to the colony. It asked "the Enactours themselves of this late Act for forts," to judge in their consciences "whether our proffer be not wholly clear from any dregs of Rebellion, and mutiny, and be not rather to be esteemed an honourable purchase of our Countries quiett and benefitt with our owne hazard and charge." It closed with a denunciation of all Indians and their combination against His Majesty's good subjects, who were the only rightful inhabitants and possessors of Virginia. . . .

Whatever Bacon's intentions may have been in assuming leadership of the self-starting crusade against the Indians, he was guilty of a greater insubordination than Berkeley could tolerate. On May 10, in a public proclamation, Berkeley denounced him and removed him from the council. [Despite the Governor's orders not to, Bacon proceeded to march against the Indians and massacred the friendly Oaccaneechees.] . . .

The nature of those offenses was treason, and the proper punishment death. In order to make that plain, Berkeley issued a "Declaration and Remonstrance" in which he explained that the mightiest subject in the land, even a peer of the realm, would deserve death if he successfully protected the country against an enemy without authorization from the king. This was an unfortunate line of reasoning to a people who put preservation ahead of loyalty to a governor who was not, after all, quite a king. And among men who as a matter of course believed that all Indians were alike, Berkeley could not at this stage of the game start winning points by stating that he too was now against all Indians, especially when he added that earlier "I would have preservd those Indians that I knew were hourely at our mercy to have been our spies and intelligence to find out the more bloody Ennimies." He also misread the situation in stating that "Mr. Bacon has none aboute him but the lowest of the people." Those he had in plenty, but there were men of the better sort too who shared Bacon's racist hatred of Indians.

With Berkeley's Declaration not only Bacon but all his followers and supporters became, by definition, rebels. They undoubtedly retained their zeal for killing Indians, but they were now invited to save a share of their hostility for the governor and council, the biggest men in Virginia. In a colony where the level of discontent was already so high and the means of suppressing a rebellion were so scant, it required a degree of foolhardiness in the governing circles to adopt such a position. With the local Indians fleeing out of range, and the Susquehannahs too elusive to lay hands on, the dangerous young men of New Kent and the Southside might well consider attacking their rulers, especially if led by men who could themselves lay claim to high position. As Giles Bland had recognized some weeks earlier, a bona fide rebellion could easily develop out of the existing situation, precisely because the freemen were led "by persons of quality there, which was wanting to them in 1674 when they were suppressed by a Proclamation, and the advice of some discreet persons, that had then an Influence upon them; which is now much otherwise, for they are at this time Conducted by Mr. Nathaniel Bacon, lately Sworne one of the Councell, and many other Gentlemen of good Condition."

Questions

1. *In order to explain the cause of Bacon's Rebellion, these scholars examine the leaders of the rebellion, the people who rebelled, and the government against which they rebelled. Which method seems best?*
2. *Washburn criticizes certain aspects of Wertenbaker's explanation of Bacon's Rebellion. Are his criticisms persuasive? Why or why not? Does he ignore any aspects of Wertenbaker's argument?*
3. *Morgan explains the motivations of the poor freemen who rebelled even though he lacks access to any records or documents in their own words. How does he do so?*
4. *What do we gain by studying Bacon's Rebellion today? Do the lessons we draw from it depend on which causes we use to explain it?*

Contemporary Views of the Rebellion

Only a few of the participants left records about their roles in the rebellion, and those were mostly the wealthy men who served as leaders of either faction. While we know that several different groups of Native Americans were involved, that women participated actively in both the Bacon and Berkeley camps, and that the last rebels out in the field were mostly European indentured servants and African or African-American slaves, we have few, if any, records from these people to explain their actions. The motives of all parties can only be interpreted through the limited existing records. (Throughout these documents, archaic abbreviations have been silently edited for greater clarity.)

Tensions on the Frontier

In the aftermath of the rebellion, commissioners sent from England by the king interviewed people and collected information about the rebellion to discover why it happened. The following selection describes the conflicts with local Native Americans that sparked a desire for revenge in Bacon and other frontier dwellers. Taken from the commissioners' report entitled "A True Narrative of the Rise, Progresse, and Cessation of the Late Rebellion in Virginia . . ." in Narratives of the Insurrections, 1675–1690, *ed. Charles M. Andrews (New York, 1952), 105–7.*

Few or none had bin the Damages sustained by the English from the Indians, other than occasionally had happen'd sometimes upon private quarells and provocations, untill in July, 1675, certain Doegs and Susquahanok Indians on Maryland side, stealing some Hoggs from the English at Potomake on the Virginia shore (as the River divides the same), were pursued by the English in a Boate, beaten or kill'd and the hoggs retaken from them; whereupon the Indians repairing to their owne Towne, report it to their Superiors, and how that one [Thomas] Mathewes (whose hoggs they had taken) had before abused and cheated them, in not paying them for such Indian trucke [goods] as he had formerly bought of them, and that they took his hogs for Satisfaction [of the debt]. Upon this (to be Reveng'd on Mathews) a warr Captain with some Indians came over to Potomake and killed two of Mathewes his servants, and came also a second time and kill'd his sonne.

It happen'd hereupon that Major George Brent and Col. George Mason pursued some of the same Indians into Maryland, and marching directly up to the Indian Towne with a Party of 30 Virginians came to a certaine House and there killed an Indian King and 10 of his men upon the place; the rest of the Indians fled for their lives. . . .

The Indians persisting to Revenge themselves Inforted [fortified their position] in Maryland and now began to be bold and formidable to the English who Besieged them; their Boldness and daring behavior of late tymes and their promptnesse to Fire arms, being (indeed) wonderfull, over what they seem'd formerly indued with, which doubtlesse was of some advantage extraordinary to them considering their Small Body, [and the fact that] the Virginians and Marylanders that Besieged them being said to make neer a thousand men. The siege held 7 weekes, during which tyme the English lost 50 men, besides some Horses which the Indians tooke, and serv'd themselves to subsist on. But Provisions growing very scarce with them during this siege the Indians sent out 5 greate men to Treate of Peace, who were not Permitted to return to the Fort, but being kept Prisoners Some tyme were at last murdered by the English.

At length (whether through negligence or cowardize) the Indians made theire escape through the English, with all their wives, children and goods of value, wounding and killing some at their sally and going off. After which the English returning (as Report Saith), the Marylanders composed a Peace with the Salvages, and soe diverted the warr from themselves. . . .

But about the beginning of January, 1675–6, a Party of those abused Susquahanocks in Revenge of the Maryland businesse came suddainly down upon the weak Plantations at the head of Rappahanock and Potomaque and killed at one time 36 persons and then immediately (as their Custome is) ran off into the woods.

Berkeley Declares Bacon a Rebel

When Governor William Berkeley refused to authorize attacks against the Susquehannocks, Nathaniel Bacon, a wealthy planter, took matters into his own hands, leading a group of volunteers in a massacre of friendly Indians. In the selection below, Berkeley defends his own actions and declares Bacon a rebel. Originally printed in the Collections of the Massachusetts Historical Society, *4th Series, (Boston, 1871) 9:178–81.*

Since that time that I returned into the Country [as Governor of Virginia: about 1660], I call the great God, Judge of all things in heaven and earth to wittness, that I doe not know of any thing relateive to this Country, wherein I have acted unjustly, corruptly, or negligently, in distributeing equall Justice to all men, & takeing all possible care to preserue [preserve] their proprietys, & defend them from their barbarous enimies. . . .

And now I will state the Question betwixt me as a Governor and Mr Bacon, and say that if any enimies should invade England, any Councellor Justice of peace, or other inferiour officer, might raise what forces they could to protect his Majesty's subiects [subjects], But I say againe, if after the Kings knowledge of this inuasion, any the greatest peere [or nobleman] of England, should raise forces against the kings p'hibition this would be now, & ever was in all ages & Nations accompted [accounted as] treason. Nay I will goe further, that though this peere was truly zealous for the preservation of his King, & subiects, and had better & greater abillitys than all the rest of his fellow subiects, to doe his King and Country seruice, yett if the King (though by false information) should suspect the contrary, itt were treason in this Noble peere to p'ceed after the King's prohibition, and for the truth of this I appeale to all the laws of England, and the Laws and constitutions of all other Nations in the world. . . .

Now my friends I have lived 34 yeares amongst you, as vncorrupt and dilligent as ever [a] Governor was, Bacon is a man of two yeares amongst you, his p'son and qualities vnknowne to most of you, & to all men else, by any vertuous action that ever I heard of, And that very action which he boasts of [the massacre of the Occaneechee Indians], was sickly & fooleishly, & as I am informed treacherously carried to the dishonnor of the English Nation, yett in itt, he lost more men then I did in three yeares Warr [against an Indian uprising several decades earlier], and by the grace of God will putt myselfe to the same daingers & troubles againe when I have brought Bacon to acknowledge the Laws are above him, and I doubt not but by God's assistance to have better success then Bacon hath had, the reason of my hopes are, that I will take Councell of wiser men then my selfe, but Mr Bacon hath none about him, but the lowest of the people.

Yett I must further enlarge, that I cannot without your helpe, doe any thinge in this but dye in defence of my King, his laws, & subiects, which I will cheerefully doe, though alone I doe itt, and considering my poore fortunes, I can not leave my poore Wife and friends a better legacy then by dyeing for my King & you: for his sacred Majesty will easeily distinguish betweene Mr Bacons actions & myne, and Kinges have long Armes, either to reward or punish. . . .

Lastly my most assured ffriends I would have preserued those Indians that I knew were howerly att our mercy, to have beene our spyes and intelligence, to finde out our bloody enimies, but as soone as I had the least intelligence that they alsoe were trecherous enimies, I gave out Comissions to distroy them all as the Comissions themselues will speake itt.

To conclude, I have don what was possible both to friend and enimy, have granted Mr Bacon three pardons, which he hath scornefully reiected, suppoaseing himselfe stronger to subuert [the laws] than I and you [are] to maineteyne the Laws, by which onely and Gods assisting grace and mercy, all men must hope for peace and safety. I will add noe more though much more is still remaineing to Justifie me & condemne Mr Bacon, but to desier that this declaration may be read in every County Court in the Country.

The Queen of Pamunkey Negotiates for Her People

Once Bacon began attacking the frontier Indians, Virginia's leaders sought assistance from the Pamunkeys, the most powerful of the tributary, or "friendly," Indians. In the following passage, Thomas Mathew, an eyewitness, relates how and why the Queen of Pamunkey tried to keep her people from becoming involved. Taken from Thomas Mathew, "The Beginning, Progress, and Conclusion of Bacon's Rebellion . . .," reprinted in, Tracts and Other Papers, Relating Principally to the Origin, Settlement, and Progress of the Colonies in North America . . . *, ed. Peter Force, (Washington, D.C., 1836) 1:14–15.*

Our comittee being sat, the Queen of Pamunky (descended from Oppechankenough a former Emperor of Virginia) was introduced, who entred the chamber with a comportment gracefull to admiration, bringing on her right hand an Englishman interpreter, and on the left her son a stripling twenty years of age, she having round her head a plat of black and white wampum peague three inches broad in imitation of a crown, and was cloathed in a mantle of dress't deer skins with the hair outwards and the edge cut round 6 inches deep which made strings resembling twisted frenge from the shoulders to the feet; thus with grave courtlike gestures and a majestick air in her face, she walk'd up our long room to the lower end of the table, where after a few intreaties she sat down; th' interpreter and her son standing by her on either side as they had walked up, our chairman asked her what men she woud [would] lend us for guides in the wilderness and to assist us against our enemy Indians, she spake to th' interpreter to inform her what the chairman said, (tho' we believed she understood him) he told us she bid him ask her son to whom the English tongue was familiar, and who was reputed the son of an English colonel, yet neither woud he speak to or seem to understand the chairman but th' interpreter told us, he referred all to his mother, who being againe urged she after a little musing with an earnest passionate countenance as if tears were ready to gush out and a fervent sort of expression made a harangue about a quarter of an hour often, interlacing (with a high shrill voice and vehement passion) these words "Tatapatamoi Chepiack, i.e. Tatapatamoi dead["] Coll. Hill being next me, shook his head, I ask'd him what was the matter, he told me all she said was too true to our shame, and that his father was generall in that battle, where diverse years before Tatapatamoi her husband had led a hundred of his Indians in help to th' English against our former enemy Indians, and was there slaine with most of his men; for which no compensation (at all) had been to that day rendered to her wherewith she now upbraided us.

Her discourse ending and our morose chairman not advancing one cold word towards asswaging the anger and grief her speech . . . nor taking any notice of all she had said, . . . he rudely push'd againe the same question "what Indians will you now contribute, &c.?["] of this disregard she signified her resentment by a disdainfull aspect, and turning her head half aside, sate mute till that same question being press'd, a third time, she not returning her face to the board, answered with a low slighting voice in her own language "six,["] but being further importun'd she sitting a little while sullen, without uttering a word between said "twelve,["] tho' she then had a hundred and fifty Indian men, in her town, and so rose up and gravely walked away, as [if] not pleased with her treatment.

Bacon Justifies Rebellion on Behalf of "the People"

Within months, the colony divided into factions that supported either Berkeley or Bacon, and both sides took up arms. On 30 July 1676, Bacon issued "The Declaration of the People," in which he defended his actions and attacked the policies of Berkeley's government. Reprinted from the Collections of the Massachusetts Historical Society, *4th Series, (Boston, 1871), 9:184–85.*

1st. For haveing . . . raised greate unjust taxes vpon the Comonality for the aduancement of private favorites & other sinister ends, but [without having] . . . in any measure aduanced this hopefull Colony either by fortifications Townes or Trade.

2d. For haveing abused & rendred contemptable the Magistrates of Justice, by aduanceing to places of Judicature, scandalous and Ignorant favorites.

3. For haveing wronged his Majestys prerogative & interest, by assumeing Monopolony of the Beaver trade, & for haveing in that unjust gaine betrayed & sold his Majestys Country & the lives of his loyall subiects to the barbarous heathen.

4. For haveing, protected, favoured, & Imboldned the Indians against his Majestys loyall subiects, never contriveing, requireing, or appointing any due or proper meanes of satisfaction for theire many Inuasions, robbories, & murthers comitted vpon vs.

5. For haveing when the Army of English was just vpon the track of those Indians, who now in all places burne, spoyle, murther & when we might with ease have distroyed them who then were in open hostillity, for then haveing expressly countermanded, & sent back our Army, by passing his word for the peaceable demeanour of the said Indians, who imediately p'secuted theire evill intentions, comitting horred murthers & robberies in all places, being p'tected by the said ingagement & word past of him the said Sir Wm Berkeley, haveing ruined & laid desolate a greate part of his Majestys Country, & have now drawne themselves into such obscure & remote places, & are by theire success soe imboldned & confirmed, by theire confederacy soe strengthned that the cryes of blood are in all places, & the terror, & constirnation of the people soe greate, are now become, not onely a difficult, but a very formidable enimy, who might att first with ease haue beene distroyed.

6th. And lately when vpon the loud outcryes of blood the Assembly had with all care raised & framed an Army for the preventing of further mischiefe & safeguard of this his Majestys Colony.

7th. For haveing with onely the privacy of some few favorites, without acquainting the people, onely by the alteration of a figure, forged a Comission, by we know not what hand, not onely without, but even against the consent of the people, for the raiseing & effecting civill warr & destruction, which being happily & without blood shed prevented, for haveing the second time attempted the same, thereby calling downe our forces from the defence of the fronteeres & most weekely expoased places.

8. For the prevention of civill mischeife & ruin amongst ourselues, whilst the barbarous enimy in all places did invade, murther & spoyle vs, his majestys most faithfull subiects.

Edward Hill Explains His Opposition to Nathaniel Bacon

Colonel Edward Hill, a Berkeley loyalist, vigorously suppressed the rebellion in Charles City County where he lived. When other planters in the area criticized his brutality, he countered with a description of the treatment he and his family received from the rebels, which he clearly believed justified his own actions. The following excerpt is taken from the Virginia Magazine of History and Biography, *3 (1895–1896): 250.*

I must with trouble and sorrow say that I am grieved to see the spirit of rebellion soe strong and fresh in the hearts of these people that would make it a grievance of the County for to obey those just comands which I received from his honor [the governor], and I should think theire true grievance should be that they were soe active and mischievous as they were from the beginning of the rebellion to the end thereof, and were the first that against the King's Governor's comands went out upon the Occaneechees, were the very men to help Bacon to force his comission, and marched a hundred miles out of theire own country [county] as low as Lower Norfolk to fight the king's loyall subjects, and over into Gloucester, and indeed all over the country, and in fine were the first in armes, and the laste that opposed and faced the King's Governor's power, yet these noe grievances, And I bless God, and truely rejoice in the great goodness and mercey of our most gracious king that they are pardoned; but me thinks with modesty they mought [might] have given me leave to have had my grievances that my house was plundered of all I had, my sheep all destroyed, my hoggs and cattle killed, all my grain taken and destroyed, wheat, barley, oates, & Indian graine, to the quantity of seven, or eight hundred bushels, and to compleat theire jollity draw my brandy, Butts of wyne and syder [cider, a mildly alcoholic beverage] by payles full, and [toasting] to every health instead of burning theire powder [shooting off their guns], burnt my writings, bills, bonds, acc'ts to the true vallue of forty thousand pounds of tobacco and to finish theire barbarism, take my wife bigg with child [pregnant] prisoner, beat her with my Cane, tare [tore] her childbed linen out of her hands, and with her ledd away my children where they must live on corne and water and lye on the ground.

Indentured Servants and Slaves Resist Surrender

Along with poor freemen, indentured servants and slaves who had deserted their masters formed a large part of Bacon's army. As the rebellion collapsed, they still held the fort at West Point. As the passage below indicates, Berkeley and his supporters were not above lying to trick such people into putting down their arms. Thomas Grantham was a ship captain who helped Berkeley suppress the uprising. From "A Narrative of the Indian and Civil Wars in Virginia . . .," in Tracts and Other Papers . . ., *ed. Peter Force, 1:44–45.*

What number of soulders was, at this time, in Garrisson at West Point, I am not certaine: It is saide about 250, sumed up in freemen, sarvants and slaves; these three ingredience being the compossition of Bacons Army, ever since that the Governour left Towne. These was informed (to prepare the way) two or three days before that Grantham came to them, that there was a treaty on foote betwene there Generall, and the Governour; and that Grantham did manely promote the same, as he was a parson [person] that favoured the cause, that they were contending for.

When that Grantham arived, amongst these fine fellowes, he was receved with more then an ordnary respect; which he haveing repade, with a suteable deportment, he acquaints them with his commission, which was to tell them, that there was a peace concluded betwene the Governour and their Generall; an since himself had (in some measure) used his indeviours, to bring the same to pass, hee begged of the Governour, that he might have the honor to com and acquaint them with the terms; which he saide was such, that they had all cause to rejoyce at, than any ways to thinke hardly of the same; there being a compleate satisfaction to be given (by the Articles of agreement) according to every ones particuler intress; which he sumed up under these heads. And first, those that were now in Arms (and free men) under the Generall, were still to be retained in Arms, if they so pleased, against the Indians. Secondly, and for those who had a desire for to return hom, to their owne abodes, care was taken for to have them satisfide, for the time they had bin out, according to the alowance made the last Assembley. And lastly, those that were sarvants in Arms, and behaved themselves well, in their imployment, should emediately receve discharges from their Indentures, signed by the Governour or Sequetary of State; and their Masters to receve, from the publick, a valluable satisfaction, for every sarvant, so set free (marke the words) proportionably to the time that they have to sarve.

Upon these terms, the soulders forsake West Point, and goe with Grantham to kiss the Governours hands (still at Tindells point) and to receve the benefitt of the Articles, mentioned by Grantham; where when they came (which was by water, themselves in one vessill, and their arms in another; and so contrived by Grantham, as he tould me himselfe, upon good reason) the sarvants and slaves was sent hom to their Masters, there to stay till the Governour had leasure to signe their discharges; or to say better, till they were free according to the custom of the countrey [which meant finishing their indentures, plus serving extra time for being runaways], the rest was made prissoners, or entertained by the Governour, as hee found them inclined.

Mrs. Cheisman's Attempt to Save Her Husband

Mrs. Cheisman's husband was an officer in Bacon's army who was captured at the end of the rebellion. The selection below describes her effort to protect her husband from a death sentence by claiming responsibility for his rebellious actions. Assuming she honestly stated her views in this interview, she stands as one of the female supporters of the rebellion whom we can identify. If this account had not been recorded by an anonymous participant, we would not know today that Mrs. Cheisman existed (and we shall probably never know her first name). Her husband was never tried for his crime, dying in prison of "feare, griefe, or bad useage," as the author of this narrative put it. Excerpted from "A Narrative of the Indian and Civil Wars in Virginia . . .," in Tracts and Other Papers *. . ., ed. Peter Force, 1:34*

There is one remarkable passage reported of this Major Cheismans Lady [or wife], which because it sounds to the honor of her sex, and consequently of all loveing Wives, I will not deny it a roome in this Narrative.

When that the Major was brought into the Governours presence, and by him demanded, what made him to ingage in Bacons designes? Before that the Major could frame an answer to the Governours demand; his Wife steps in and tould his honour that it was her provocations that made her Husband joyne in the cause that Bacon contended for; ading, that if he had not bin influenced by her instigations, he had never don that which he had done. Therefore (upon her bended knees) she desired of his honour, that since what her husband had done, was by her meanes, and so, by consequence, she most guilty, that she might be hanged, and he pardoned. Though the Governour did know, that what she had saide, was neare to the truth, yet he said litle to her request.

Thomas Hansford's Execution

Thomas Hansford, who was a colonel in Bacon's army, was captured by Berkeley supporters as the rebellion collapsed. The excerpt below, describes his capture and death. Taken from the same anonymous "A Narrative of the Indian and Civil Wars in Virginia . . .," printed in Tracts and Other Papers *. . ., ed. Peter Force, vol. 1:33.*

[P]resently after that he [Thomas Hansford, a soldier] came to Accomack, he had the ill luck to be the first Verginian borne that dyed [meaning the first person of English descent born in Virginia to die] upon a paire of Gallows. When that he came to the place of

Execution (which was about a mile removed from his prison) he seemed very well resolved to undergo the utmost mallize [malaise] of his not over kinde Destinies, onely complaineing of the maner of his death. Being observed neather at the time of his tryall (which was by a Court Martiall) nor afterwards, to supplicate any other faviour, than that he might be shot like a soulder, and not to be hanged like a Dog. But it was tould him, that what he so passionately petitioned for could not be granted, in that he was not condemned as he was merely a soldier, but as a Rebell, taken in Arms, against the king, whose laws had ordained him that death. During the short time he had to live after his sentence he approved to his best advantage for the wellfare of his soul, by repentance and contrition for all his sins, in generall, excepting his Rebellion, which he would not acknowledge; desireing the people at the place of execution, to take notis that he dyed a loyal subject, and a lover of his countrey; and that he had never taken up arms, but for the destruction of the Indians, who had murthered so many Christians.

Questions

1. *Why did Berkeley believe it significant that only "the lowest of the people" supported Bacon?*
2. *Do you think that Bacon was really speaking on behalf of the "people" when he issued the "Declaration"?*
3. *What motivated the various individuals whose actions are described or whose words are quoted in these documents?*
4. *Do you think there was one rebellion or several rebellions, according to the accounts you have read?*
5. *How did the rebellion appear from the perspective of various Native American groups who fought against or refused to fight against Bacon?*

FURTHER READING

Thomas Wertenbaker's Torchbearer of the Revolution: The Story of Bacon's Rebellion in Virginia *(Princeton, 1940) and Wilcomb Washburn's* The Governor and The Rebel: A History of Bacon's Rebellion in Virginia *(Chapel Hill, 1957) are still the two most important full-length books on Bacon's Rebellion.* 1676: The End of American Independence (*New York, 1984), written by Stephen Saunders Webb, connects Bacon's Rebellion with other developments in English-Indian relations on the North American continent that occurred simultaneously. Warren M. Billings has re-explored the long-term economic and political conditions that led to the conflict in "The Causes of Bacon's Rebellion: Some Suggestions," an article in the October 1970 issue of the* Virginia Magazine of History and Biography. *Martha W. McCartney examines in detail the Queen of Pamunkey and her role in Virginia politics before, during, and after Bacon's Rebellion in "Cockacoeske, Queen of Pamunkey: Diplomat and Suzerain," an essay in* Powhatan's Mantle: Indians in the Colonial Southeast, *ed. Peter H. Wood, Gregory A. Waselko, and M. Thomas Hatley (Lincoln, Nebraska, 1989).*

Violent Crime in Early America

Randolph Roth

INTRODUCTION

The United States is today the most violent industrial society in the world. Its rates of murder, robbery, and assault surpass those of every other affluent, politically stable nation. Why remains something of a mystery. As Eric Monkkonen's statistics on New York City homicides indicate, America has been more violent since 1965 than at any other time in its history, even during the surge in violence that occurred in the mid-nineteenth century. Statistics also show that murder rates in the United States have varied from region to region. They have traditionally been high in the South and low in northern New England and the upper Midwest. Other studies reveal that rates of violent crime have differed by race, gender, and ethnicity, and that each group's propensity for crime has varied according to economic conditions, cultural change, and other factors.

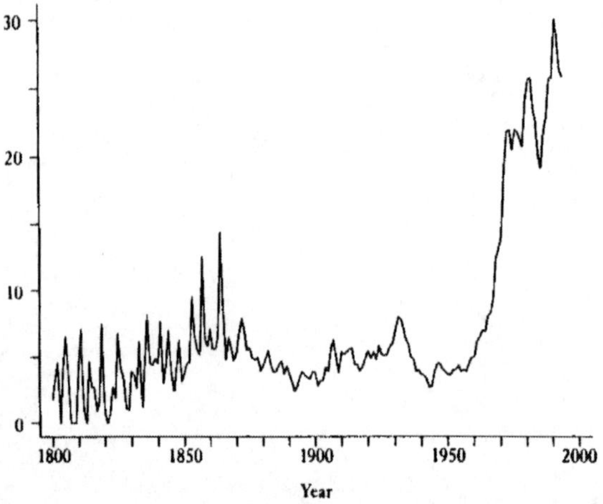

New York City homicides per 100,000 *(FBI, Uniform Crime Reports)*

America has thus not always or everywhere been a violent society. Historians must explain both the historic presence and absence of violence if they are to understand how and why America has become so violent.

The Historical Geography of Violent Crime

The following essays seek to understand why violent crime has been prevalent in certain times and places in American history and not in others. Elizabeth Pleck's Domestic Tyranny *asks why violence against spouses and children was relatively rare in colonial New England. It focuses on the role of religion in society. Edward Ayer's* Vengeance and Justice *wonders why Southern whites were the most violent nineteenth-century Americans. It focuses on the culture of slave society. Finally, Roger Lane's* Violence in the City *considers why black homicide rates rose and white homicide rates fell in northern cities after the Civil War. It focuses on the industrial revolution, which opened opportunities for whites and closed them for blacks.*

Puritans and Domestic Violence

The following selection looks at the efforts New England Puritans made to suppress domestic violence. Taken from Elizabeth Pleck, Domestic Tyranny: The Making of Social Policy Against Family Violence from Colonial Times to the Present *(New York, 1987), 17-22, 31, 33.*

The Puritans [of Massachusetts Bay] hoped that their "city upon a hill" would set an example of religious devotion for the rest of the world. The family was vital to their endeavor; it conveyed religious values and prepared the young for a pious life. It was also the foundation upon which a religious commonwealth was built. An institution so necessary to the Puritan mission could not become a sanctuary for cruelty and violence; family violence was "wicked carriage"—assaultive and sinful behavior—that threatened the individual's and the community's standing before God. . . . Moreover, family violence threatened the social and political stability of the Puritan's godly settlement. As a sacred institution, the family stood as a model for all other social relations. Harmonious family life helped to create a peaceful community, but a quarrelsome household endangered the social order. Any disturbance within the family, from verbal to physical abuse, was considered a failure to achieve domestic peace. With this view of the family, combined with advanced humanitarian ideas on the rights of women and children brought with them from England, the Puritans developed the concept of family violence as a public concern.

The Puritans attacked family violence with the combined forces of community, church, and state. In Puritan society meddling was a positive virtue. Neighbors informally but vigilantly watched each other for signs of aberration; church courts extracted confessions of sin from their errant members, and civil and criminal courts upheld the laws and punished wrongdoers.

They acted against family violence in ways without parallel in Western history. But they intervened in quarrelsome families only to correct the most severe abuses rather than to protect the rights of individuals. Despite their lack of a modern notion of family privacy, the Puritans regarded outside intervention as disruptive, justifiable only to the extent that it restored family order. Faced with the choice between preserving the family unit and permitting a victim of family violence to be removed from an abusive household, they invariably chose to preserve the male-dominated family.

The major form of protection for victims of domestic violence was the watchfulness over family life that Puritan communities provided. Neighbors were expected to watch each other so that the sins of a few would not jeopardize the standing of the entire community in God's eyes. . . . [The] Puritan religious leader Cotton Mather preached that for "a man to Beat his Wife was as

---

bad as any Sacriledge. Any such a Rascal were better buried alive, than show his Head among his Neighbours any more." Another Puritan minister castigated the wife-beating husband as a man who "shames his profession of Christianity, he breaks the Divine law, he dishonours God and himself, too." The husband-beating wife was "a shame to her profession of Christianity, she dishonours God and provokes the glorious God, tramples his Authority under her feet; she not only affronts her Husband, but also God her Maker, Lawgiver and Judge."

One suspects that in the majority of Puritan households, family life was harmonious, although by no means free of conflict or physical violence. . . . Yet in the midst of their devout settlement, the Puritans found "bad" and jealous husbands who drank heavily, frequented prostitutes, and took sexual advantage of servant girls; bad wives who cursed their husbands, flogged their servants, and stole their neighbors' pigs; and disobedient children and servants who lied, stole, and ran away from home.

Puritan neighbors regarded malcontents and deviants as disturbers of the peace, who needed to be put right. Thus they visited families suspected of moral lapses, praying with them for divine guidance. This neighborly surveillance encouraged at least the appearance of domestic tranquillity, carrying as it did the threat of public shame. . . . This Puritan domestic order is attested to by the low rate of family murder in Massachusetts Bay Colony or nearby Plymouth. Murder is the one form of disharmony in the home that least escapes the notice of authorities—the one instance of physical violence almost never considered reasonable or justifiable. There were only six indictments for family murder in the seventeenth-century Massachusetts Bay and Plymouth colonies among a population of about 6,000 inhabitants. On a per capita basis, the family murder rate was only 0.3 per 100,000 in Massachusetts Bay Colony between 1630 and 1692 and 0.1 per 100,000 if only husband-wife murders are included. The family murder rate was approximately the same in Plymouth Colony during the same years. By contrast, in Houston and Philadelphia about 1970, the family murder rate was 3.6 and 3.7 per 100,000, respectively, or about twelve times greater than in Puritan Massachusetts. . . . [I]t is likely that the modern American home is a far more dangerous place to live than its Puritan counterpart.

. . . With so much informal pressure to conform, only the truly recalcitrant had to be brought before a church court. . . . Church courts tried cases of spouse abuse, cruelty to children and servants, assaults, threats against parents, and child neglect; they also punished drunkenness, murder, adultery, fornication, and even lying. The procedure of a church court was designed to shame and disgrace the sinner. The ruling church elders investigated complaints and sought out two witnesses who would testify at a hearing convened before the entire congregation. The accused were given an opportunity to respond to the accusations of the witnesses. The goal of the hearing was not to determine innocence or guilt but to wring from the person on trial a confession of sin in the hope of securing for the wayward soul the promise of salvation. . . .

The total number of persons disciplined in various church courts never numbered more than a few dozen per year, in contrast to the several hundred cases of various kinds that appeared every year in the secular courts of Plymouth and Massachusetts Bay colonies. Accusations of family violence, incest, or rape were infrequent in church courts, as were complaints against masters for cruelty to servants or slaves. . . . Even when the rare instance of family violence was brought before the church court, the kind of justice meted out indicated a desire to preserve the family rather than to punish wrongdoing. The wife who was beaten was considered to be almost as much at fault as her husband. In the trial of Lemuel Phelps, an accused wife beater, his wife was called upon to confess that she had "transgressed the Rules and Duties of a Wife towards her husband in some of my past conduct in assuming too much authority over him and controlling him in civil and religious matters." She promised to reform. Then Phelps acknowledged that he had beaten his wife and had accused her of bearing a child not his own. He promised to behave "for the future as a kind and tender husband." Following the standard procedure in being restored to full church membership, Phelps stood before the entire congregation on Sunday, pleaded for their forgiveness, and read his confession. . . . Three years later Phelps was brought before the church court on the same charge; he again accused his wife of adultery. Presumably he underwent the same process of examination and confession as before.

In addition to church courts, the magistrates of the New England colonies—especially the colonies of Massachusetts Bay and Plymouth—enforced a criminal code that punished many types of family violence. Massachusetts Bay and Plymouth were the only two American colonies to pass laws against the beating of spouses; indeed, theirs were the first laws against spousal abuse enacted anywhere in the Western world. . . . [T]he Massachusetts *Body of Liberties* of 1641 provided that "Everie marryed woeman shall be free from bodilie correction or stripes by her husband, unlesse it be in his owne defence upon her assault." A few years later the law was amended to prohibit husband beating as well. The Pilgrims were probably following Massachusetts Bay in enacting a law against spouse abuse in 1672. This law punished wife beating with a five-pound fine or a whipping and husband beating with a sentence to be determined by the court.

The Massachusetts *Body of Liberties* also protected the "liberties of children." A provision that prohibited parents from choosing their child's mate included a clause that forbade parents from exercising "any unnatural severitie" toward children. If unnatural severity occurred, children were granted "free libertie to complaine to Authorities for redresse. " The *Body of Liberties* also forbade cruelty toward any creature "usuallie kept for man's use" and permitted servants to flee from abusive masters without penalty. . . .

In the last two decades of the seventeenth century, the tapestry of Christian morality that had woven together the interest of family, the state, and the church began to unravel, one thread at a time. The church courts no longer took an active role in punishing morals offenses. Indeed, by the end of the eighteenth century many churches had abolished their courts. . . . Moral laxity was also discernible in a small item of gossip entered in a clergyman's diary. He noted that several ministers were upset to learn that one of their own was repeatedly beating his wife. They discussed the matter several times but did not bring a legal complaint against the man or try him before a church court. Would Cotton Mather have allowed such wickedness to go unexposed? Public criticism of corporal punishment was beginning to have some effect. Boxing the ears was eliminated as a punishment at Harvard in the 1750s; the provision permitting it disappeared from the college's laws by 1767. The pillory was removed from the Boston Common in 1803, and the whipping post and stocks were taken down a decade later. . . .

What, then, was the significance of Puritan laws against family violence, if they were rarely enforced? Laws not only prescribe punishment for crimes; they also function as a guide to the community's moral principles. The purpose of the Puritan laws against family violence was less to punish abusers than to define the boundary between the saint and the sinner, demonstrate to each other and to God a vigilance against sin, and shore up proper authority in the household and in society. As a religious community gave way to a more pluralistic one, the state gradually relinquished its commitment to enforcing morality. Thus the campaign to eradicate wicked behavior yielded to tolerance and indifference.

Violence in the South

Edward L. Ayers explains the propensity of Southern whites for violence in Vengeance and Justice: Crime and Punishment in the 19th-Century American South *(New York, 1984), 9-14, 19-21, 23, 33.*

Southern violence had become legendary even before the nineteenth century began. Isaac Weld, after visiting the new United States in the 1790s, recounted stories of fighting and eye-gougings he had witnessed in Maryland and Virginia—stories that were already familiar features of Southern travel accounts. Weld had been "credibly assured" that in the Carolinas and Georgia "the people are still more depraved in this respect than in Virginia, and that in some particular parts of these states, every third or fourth man appears with one eye." Weld did not risk visiting these far reaches of the South to verify the troubling rumors, but Charles William Janson, an Englishman, did make the trip to Georgia and the Carolinas several years later and found the violence even more bloody and widespread than earlier writers such as Weld had led him to expect: "The eye is not the only feature which suffers on these occasions. Like dogs and bears, they use their teeth and feet, with the most savage ferocity, upon each other."

But not all Southern violence exhibited such unrestrained passion. While backwoodsmen brawled and disfigured one another, planters and politicians solemnly faced each other upon the dueling grounds. In 1826 a victorious duelist rushed to his fallen foe: "White, my dear fellow," he said quietly, "I am sorry for you." "I do not blame you," his bleeding opponent answered, and the two duelists clasped hands. The wounded man recovered, and the other was elected governor of Tennessee a few months later. Twenty-five years after this duel a student wrote home that college life in Virginia presented certain dangers: "challenges are continually passing; fights are had almost every day." Another student assured concerned faculty members that the bowie knife he carried would be used only "against a person who should insult him and refuse to give him honorable satisfaction."

Even after the South's fall in the Civil War, one thing remained constant. "Self-respect, as the Southerners understand it, has always demanded much fighting," a Connecticut native serving in the Freedmen's Bureau [an organization created by Congress in 1866 designed to protect the interest of freed slaves] explained to fellow Northerners. "A pugnacity which is not merely war paint, but is, so to speak, tattooed into the character, has resulted from this high sentiment of personal value." As in the colonial and antebellum period, all classes seemed touched with violence: "It permeates all society; it has infected all individualities. The meekest man by nature, the man who at the North would no more fight than he would jump out of a second story window, may at the South resent an insult by a blow, or perhaps a stab or pistol shot." . . .

Explanations for Southern violence have never been lacking. As early as the 1790s Thomas Jefferson observed that the unbridled authority wielded by slaveholders tended to breed impetuous behavior and shortness of temper, characteristics passed from one generation of masters to the next. . . . On the other hand, slaveholders enjoyed no monopoly of command over other people, and wealthy children raised by servants in other contexts have not been noted for their violence and lack of self-control. . . . Furthermore, an explanation of Southern violence based solely on the personality characteristics created by slaveholding does not explain either the apparent violence of the great majority of Southerners who never owned slaves or the persistence of Southern violence for more than a century after the end of slavery. There can be little doubt that slaveholders often seemed haughty and touchy, but there was obviously more than this alone to Southern violence. . . .

. . . Without condoning the killing, we should look at the South and its violence on its own terms and without censure of cultural habits we find abhorrent. In doing so we are led to reexamine white Southerners' own often-repeated explanation of why they killed each other with such frequency and regularity. They, of course, said they did it for honor's sake.

The mere word "honor," though, puts us on our guard and conjures up images of pretentious self-proclaimed aristocrats shooting each other in ridiculous displays of their own insecurity. That is because honor has no resonance, no meaning, in our culture today, where values antithetical to honor rule. Yet, just as they claimed, many Southern men recognized the dictates of honor: a system of values within which you have exactly as much worth as others confer upon you. Women, children, and slaves had no honor; only adult white males had the right to honor—and even they, if challenged, had to prove their worth through their courage. In a culture of honor, anthropologist Pierre Bourdieu explains, "the being and truth about a person are identical with the being and truth that others acknowledge in him." Thus, according to Charles Sydnor, in the antebellum South "it was considered as brutal and uncivilized to call a man a liar as it was to bruise or cut his body." . . .

In reconstructing the workings of Southern honor and violence, it is crucial to understand that Southern white men among all classes believed themselves "honorable" men and acted on that belief. Honor did not reside only within the South's planter class. All knew that the failure to respond to insult marked them as less than real men, branded them, in the most telling epithets of the time, as "cowards" and "liars." . . . Honor and "public opinion" came to seem synonymous, an overwhelming force that compelled men to wage fights for which they had little heart. Public opinion meant different things in different classes; to many poor men it meant the respect of a few drinking friends; to local luminaries it meant the judgment of nearby planters and professional men; to politicians it meant the verdict of the press. But to men of all classes, public opinion dictated that they not tolerate affront.

Just as men of different classes played to different audiences of honor, so the exact form of violence generated by conflicts between two unyielding claimants of honor varied from class to class. While some men faced each other under elaborate ritual on dueling grounds, many more combatants fought in obscure taverns and streets. Aggression flourished most democratically where gambling and drinking flourished. . . .

. . . [B]y the mid-nineteenth century the Northern United States had generated the core of a culture antagonistic to honor. This Northern culture celebrated "dignity"—the conviction that each individual at birth possessed an intrinsic value at least theoretically equal to that of every other person. In practice, of course, this ideal was qualified, violated, and undermined. Women, blacks, and Irish immigrants, to name the most obvious examples, were not treated as equals by native white men. Even those white men found their supposedly equal worth mocked by class distinctions. Nevertheless, from the perspective of world history few can fail to be struck at the public allegiance awarded dignity at every turn in the American North in the mid-nineteenth century. Dignity stood as the ideal, the goal, however often it was violated in practice. Deviations had to be explained away, rationalized.

In a culture of dignity, people were expected to remain deaf to the same insults that Southern men were expected to resent. "Call a man a liar in Mississippi," an old saying went, "and he will knock you down; in Kentucky, he will shoot you; in Indiana, he will say 'You are another.' Dignity might be likened to an internal skeleton, to a hard structure at the center of the self; honor, on the other hand, resembles a cumbersome and vulnerable suit of armor that, once pierced, leaves the self no protection and no alternative except to strike back in desperation. Honor in the Southern United States cannot be understood without reference to dignity, its antithesis and adversary to the north.

Both honor and dignity had roots in Old World cultures but developed new strains in the bracing environment of the New World. Almost from the very beginning a subtle and reinforcing sifting process created regional cultures in North America. Once British settlers arrived in America in the seventeenth and eighteenth centuries, they inevitably drew upon different elements of their diverse and changing culture as increasingly different economies led the Northern and Southern colonies further and further apart. Just as Northern settlers tried to reestablish the "English ways" of the counties and towns from which they came, so did the slaveholding gentry of colonial Virginia consciously adopt the culture of the English aristocracy. . . .

The Southern gentry of the colonial era adopted the values of a proud and domineering English ruling class, a class whose power and authority they planned to replicate in the New World. When, by the middle of the eighteenth century, the planting class in each of the major Southern colonies had assumed social, political, and cultural dominance, honor and its violence were a part of the culture they regarded as their own, as the only culture worthy of emulation. The style of the American colonial slaveholding gentry, argues Rhys Isaac, is "best understood in relation to the concept of honor—the proving of prowess. A formality of manners barely concealed adversary relationships; the essence of social exchange was overt self-assertion." Horses, clothing, and betting displayed this self-assertion, but so did the "conventional forms of aggression—in banter, swearing, and fighting."

Lower-class English and Scots-Irish emigrants carried their own experiences with violence to America, expectations and tendencies that soon combined with the aristocratic ideals of honor to spark violence on every level of colonial Southern society. Philip Vickers Fithian, a tutor from New Jersey who kept a journal of his sojourn in Virginia in the 1770s, described the forms honor took among the common folk. One combatant might have offended another when he "has in a merry hour call'd him a *Lubber*, or a *thick-Skull*, or a *Buckskin*, or a *Scotchman*, or perhaps one has mislaid the other's hat, or knocked a peach out of his Hand, or offered him a dram without wiping the mouth of the Bottle; all these, & ten thousand more quite as trifling & ridiculous, are thought & accepted as just Causes of immediate Quarrels, in which every diabolical Stratagem for Mastery is allowed and practised." . . .

. . . Without the disunity engendered by immigrant groups of widely varying background, without the social diversity generated by economic diversity, without any long-term challenge to its slaveholding oligarchies, the South maintained into the nineteenth century a pattern of local and personal power the Northern colonies and states did not, indeed could not, perpetuate. The formal written law never attained the weight it assumed in the North. Just as the apparent weakness of New England agriculture fostered the necessity for economic diversification in the North, so did early social tensions generate a tradition of a law that stood above society. The techniques of Southern agriculture, on the other hand, recreated themselves wherever Southerners went, and so did the Southern preference for personal rather than impersonal justice when honor was at stake. . . .

Southern honor did exist, did breed violence among men of every class, did cut against evangelical Christianity and the law of the state. Without the concept of honor, Southern violence remains inexplicable. Honor was the catalyst necessary to ignite the South's volatile mixture of slavery, scattered settlement, heavy drinking, and ubiquitous weaponry. Honor thus served to set the South apart from the North, and once established honor became an integral part of the Southern identity. But it was never more than a part. Southern honor, like Northern dignity, grew out of a historical conjunction of economic system and received culture. When these forces changed, honor and dignity changed. Honor increasingly came under attack from within and without the South that nourished it, incongruous and anomalous in the century of dignity's triumph.

Violence in the North

Roger Lane discusses the decline in white homicide rates and the rise in black homicide rates in the urban, industrial North, in Violent Death in the City: Suicide, Accident, and Murder in Nineteenth-Century Philadelphia *(Cambridge, Massachusetts, 1979), 116, 120-23, 128-29, 131-34.*

Before 1870 the homicide rates [in Philadelphia] move down but only erratically. Afterward, from the early 1870s to the end of the century, the drop is steady and pronounced, especially when considered in light of the changing threshold of tolerance. . . . Perhaps the professional police, and political realignment, in working to contain the worst effects of intergroup hostility, had some effect on the declining rate of homicide. But no such explanation can be stretched to cover the . . . rising levels of black violence, which countered the opposite trend among the majority. . . .

. . . [I]t is possible to find an explanation. In the nineteenth century Philadelphia's growth and that of America's urban population generally was largely the result of what is loosely called the industrial revolution. The changes associated with this process affected virtually every aspect of life in the city. Most directly they affected habits of work; much of the social history of the early industrial revolution (and indeed the process of development anywhere) can be written in terms of the transformation of a preindustrial into a modern work force. What has not been understood for the United States is the way in which that transformation affected ordinary behavior of all kinds, including—perhaps especially—the behavior reflected in the indices of violence.

What is most demanded of a modernizing society is "predictability in the behavior and relationships of individuals," or orderly cooperation at work. The rhythms of the agricultural year change continually, periods of intense activity alternating with long slack seasons, and except at harvest there are few chores that cannot be interrupted for an encounter, an adventure, or simply a distraction. The same is true of the older traditional urban economy organized around independent crafts and commerce. Few enterprises in early nineteenth-century Philadelphia employed more than a handful of workmen, each of them relatively unspecialized, their pace and hours of employment regulated by the variable flow of specific orders. The work force late in the century operated, in contrast, under a much tighter set of constraints. Bell, clock, and foreman enforced a degree of discipline that, if not harsher, was more nearly unremitting than earlier. The need to coordinate specialized individual tasks with those of large numbers of fellows in factory or office demanded synchronization and cooperation. The hours and the nature of the job prohibited the easy workaday consumption of liquor and put a premium on the ability to endure long stretches of frustration and boredom. . . .

For children in late nineteenth-century America, the requisite learning process often began in the growing system of public schools. It is not simply that the public schools operated as generalized agents of social control: quite specifically, the kinds of behavior they inculcated were those demanded by the changing economy. . . . [T]he drive for public schooling was strongest in communities in which there was a heavy demand for semiskilled manufacturing employment. Even apart from literacy, which had earlier been learned in a variety of less structured ways, the consciousness of bell, clock, and deadline, the self-discipline required to sit still, take turns, and mind the teacher, were well designed to prepare students for life in office or factory. Public education was in that sense fully relevant; the lessons of school and workplace naturally reinforced each other. . . .

The job listings for adult males indicted for first-degree murder, as available, indicate that these men were typically of lower status than . . . the general population. . . . [A]ccused murderers were less likely . . . to be white collar or skilled and more likely to be semiskilled, service, or unskilled workers. But it would be misleading to describe the nature of their work in more detail; what was found about jobs is less important than what was not found, for fewer than one-third . . . can be located in the directories at all. . . .

. . . Philadelphia's nineteenth-century murderers were typically marginal men, those left behind by or new to the demands for order and discipline. . . . The most violent group of all . . . was the one least touched directly by the industrial revolution, the one left farthest behind.

Even more than bureaucracy, more than schooling, industrial employment in the nineteenth century was reserved for white men. In Philadelphia as nationally, black men in the second half of the century were not only confined to the most casual and irregular work but were losing what foothold they had earlier secured in better-paying jobs. . . . By the late 1890s . . . [o]nly a little over 8 percent of blacks, as compared to nearly 47 percent of the city's working population as a whole, were "engaged in manufacturing and mechanical industries"; virtually none of these worked in factories but rather plied traditional trades, many threatened with obsolescence. . . .

It cannot be argued that the level of violence in the black community was wholly the result of patterns of employment or schooling. In every group a range of cultural patterns asserted themselves in many ways. . . . It appears, however, that this "subculture of violence" is almost wholly the product of American conditions and, both before and after the Civil War, of conditions experienced outside of slavery. Although the particular manifestations of the subculture . . . have been developed and transmitted inside the group, much of the explanation for its origins, and especially its continuance, must be sought outside, in the conditions of and opportunities for work.

The high rate of homicide among blacks may be explained up to a point in purely instrumental terms. . . . There was a clear need, very early, for members of Philadelphia's black community to carry weapons and be ready to use them. It is equally clear that this need was in turn related directly and indirectly to problems of employment. Commercial vice and crime, occupations found for want of better ones, not only created a routinely dangerous habitat for those surrounded by them but also reinforced the prejudices and hostilities of the dominant whites who repeatedly invaded black neighborhoods in gangs. If the black murder rate in the 1840s and 1850s was high, it was not dramatically higher than that among the Irish at the same time or the Italians two generations later. If the high rate was both produced by and contributed to a subculture that encouraged the violent expression of aggression, that too might be said of the Irish or Italians. What must be explained is not the initial level but the fact that this level continued to rise among blacks while it fell among white immigrants.

The rising rate of black violence may perhaps be explained partly by rising frustration, as the promise of freedom was never realized, as escape from bondage and tenantry in the South led only to discrimination and poverty in the North. It may also be explained, in part, . . . by the increasing availability of firearms. But the guns were equally available to all groups. And the point about anger or frustration, in terms of the suicide-murder ratio, is not just how intensely it was felt but rather how it was expressed.

Among other groups, over time, fewer individuals were inclined to the kind of reckless aggression of which homicide is the extreme expression. Only those newly arrived, perhaps, or the congenitally restless or resistant typically failed to meet the demands of the industrial age. The blacks, uniquely, were left behind as a group. They continued, uniquely, to express themselves in the old way in a new world. And without external checks to redirect it, the habit of violence continued to escalate as time moved them farther toward the margins of the industrial economy.

Questions

1. *Would Elizabeth Pleck agree with Edward Ayers that Northerners were less violent than Southerners because they embraced a "culture of dignity"? Would Ayers agree with Pleck that Southerners were more violent because they had never embraced Puritanism?*
2. *Would Pleck and Ayers agree with Roger Lane that a society's level of violence is determined largely by the nature of its schools and workplaces? Do they consider work or education?*
3. *Can the historical arguments of Pleck, Ayers, or Lane help us understand the surge in violence that has occurred since 1965, or that occurred in the mid-nineteenth century?*

Domestic Violence in Colonial New England and New Netherland

New England was distinguished in the seventeenth and eighteenth centuries for its low level of domestic violence. Elizabeth Pleck's Domestic Tyranny *attributes the region's nonviolence to the willingness of Puritan citizens, clergy, and magistrates to intervene in domestic disputes and to prosecute abusive parents and spouses. The three cases below from Plymouth County, Massachusetts, show how New England authorities dealt with husbands who beat their wives.*

Like the Puritan colonies of New England, the Dutch colony of New Netherland (renamed New York when the British seized control in 1664) was officially Reformed Protestant or "Calvinist." It too had state-supported "Puritan" churches and a well-developed network of courts, sheriffs, and prosecutors. But despite its religious and legal similarities to New England, New Netherland was marked by high levels of violence. According to New Netherland's surviving court records, the inhabitants of New Amsterdam (Manhattan) and the Hudson River Valley spent much of their time drinking, scheming, suing, cursing, fighting, and killing one another. Dutch magistrates, like their New England counterparts, were quick to intervene when people who were not related attacked one another. That did not stop the violence, but it encouraged victims and their families to seek legal redress. Dutch authorities approached cases of domestic violence differently, however, as three cases below from New Amsterdam and Fort Orange (Albany) reveal.

An important difference between New England and New Netherland is that New Netherland attracted a more rough-and-tumble and ethnically diverse band of settlers and traders. Many "Dutch" colonists were German, Swedish, Finnish, Walloon, English, or African, and those who were not members of the spiritually lax Dutch majority were as often Lutherans, Jews, Quakers, or Antinomians as members of English or Dutch Reformed churches. Most settlers prior to the mid-1640s were young unmarried men who, like the Dutch merchants who had founded the colony, were dedicated to the pursuit of profit, not to a spiritual or national ideal.

Violence in New England

The following cases of domestic violence in New England are from David Thomas Konig, ed., Plymouth Court Records, 1686-1859, *vol. 1 (Wilmington, Delaware, 1978), 194, 249, 267.*

General Sessions and Inferior Court of Common Pleas, Plymouth County, Massachusetts

March 1687/88: "Indian Sam, for abusing and Indeavoring to murder his squaw was sentenced to be whipt twenty stripes and to be sould to pay the court and prison fees," amounting to 25s.5d. (5s. to "Mr. Morton and the Clerk," 10s. to the sheriff, and 10s.6d. to the gaoler), "which was accordingly done."

March 1700/01: John Murdo (Plimouth) was fined 20s. for "striking his wife in the face with his foote."

March 1702/03: John Turner (Scituate) was fined 50s. and bound "to his good behaviour to all her Majestie's liege people and especially towards his wife" until next term for "abusing his wife and family and of several misdemeanors in his house." Ordered to pay fees and charges taxed at 1.15s. and stand committed, "but not finding surties [persons willing to post his bond] was committed to prison."

Violence in New Netherland

The following cases of domestic violence in New Netherland are from Charles T. Gehring, trans. & ed., New Netherlands Documents Series, vol. 6, Council Minutes, 1655-1656 *(Syracuse, 1995), 68-69 and Charles T. Gehring, trans. & ed.,* New Netherland Documents Series, *vol. 16, pt. 2,* Fort Orange Court Minutes, 1652-1660 *(Syracuse, 1990), 217, 257-58.*

[Note: Two of the men accused below of wife-beating, Jacob Hap and Jurriaen Teunissen, had been prosecuted and fined several times for assaulting other men by the time their assaults on their wives appeared in the court records.]

Interrogation of Pieter Jansen before the Council of New Netherland, July 1655

[several lines lost]

[ ] he [ ] and beat his wife [ ] responded [ ] because he was sitting there drinking [ ] made him mad [ ] cursing him as a scoundrel [ ] adulterer, so that he hit her on the head [ ] what he was doing with another man's wife [ ] touching her breasts and putting his mouth on them, he answered that it would never be proven, and if there were witnesses that he would then have to endure it; he said furthermore never to have done anything shamefull with Trijn in the tap room. Whereupon he evokes God as his witness.

Trijntjen Pieters van Toumgen in [from] East Friesland, housewife of the aforesaid Pieter Jansen Metselaer [mason], asked why her husband had hit her, answered that she had found her husband drinking at Poul de Guardiaen's and said, "well kid, you sit here eating and drinking, and don't want to eat with me." It was for this that he had hit her so. She went on to say to him, "I may well put up with your going out to drink a pint once in a while, but stay out of that house." Whereupon he said, "I won't stay out of that house." The wife requested that the saloon or house of Poul de Guardian be forbidden her husband; that otherwise she would have no pleasure with him; that when she came in here he didn't even greet her, kiss her or take her hand. All of which she offered to forgive him from the heart, and promised to bring him food and drink wherever he wanted it, just as long as it wasn't in a whorehouse like Paul de Guardiaen's.

Pieter Jansen was asked at the session, if he couldn't endure being in that house and in that barroom with Trijn, why didn't he then, in order to keep peace with his wife, stay away from there; and whether he had something against his wife; and why he did not want to eat or drink with her?

He said she was always full of smart words and carped at him.

Pieter Jansen is given notice that he is to live, eat, drink and sleep with his wife as is befitting an honorable husband, or he is to bring in sufficient reasons why he should not do so. Furthermore, he is to see to it that he earns a living by his trade and honestly supports his wife and children. *Ady ut supra.*

Interrogation of Jacob Hap before the Court of Fort Orange, February 1656

[Johan de Deckere, acting sheriff and prosecuting attorney,] plaintiff, against Jacob Hap, [a farmer,] defendant. He demands that the defendant be fined *f*100 [100 florins], plus expenses [court costs], for having last week scandalously beaten and bloodied his wife [Geertruyt Andriessen] and thrown firebrands at her, so that the sparks or embers flew through the partition door into the plaintiff's residence.

The defendant acknowledges that he beat his wife and drew blood.

The magistrates are of opinion that the defendant is not punishable because it happened between man and wife.

Interrogation of Jurriaen Teunissen before the Court of Fort Orange, October 1656

The officer, plaintiff, in a criminal case, against Jurriaen Glaessemaker (glazier), [and innkeeper,] defendant.

From Gehring, Charles T., *Fort Orange Court Minutes*, 1652–1660, 1st ed. (Syracuse: Syracuse University Press, 1995). By permission of the publisher.

The officer says that the defendant in the night of the 11th of October, coming from the watch to the door of his house [which also served as an inn and tavern], knocked on said door and after it had been opened by his wife, drew his sword from the scabbard and struck his own wife with it, saying "You damned whores and scoundrels," at which noise Cornelis Pietersen Hoogenboom, then lying asleep on a chest, woke up and fled to the garret, where he was followed by the defendant, who held a candle and his bare blade in his hand and finally, without exchanging words, cut and wounded Cornelis Pietersen in his right arm, as appears from the complaint of the said Cornelis Pietersen Hoogenboom, the report of Jacob De Hinsse, surgeon, and the testimony of Jan Barentsen Timmerman [carpenter], Jan de Graef, and Pieter de Backer [the baker] examined by the honorable magistrates upon interrogatories.

The defendant says that on knocking on his door, he heard a noise of someone climbing into his garret, whereupon he conceived a suspicion of theft or other mischief, which caused him to visit his garret and finding there Cornelis Pietersen Hoogenboom hidden under a bedstead, he thought himself justified in attacking him in his own house as a thief or criminal, considering that the sun had set.

The magistrates, having learned from the report of the surgeon that the wound is not dangerous, and having heard from the witnesses the circumstances of the case, order, in consideration of the circumstances, that the defendant shall settle with the officer, provided, however, that he compensate Cornelis Pietersen Hoogenboom for maintenance, medicine, and lost time.

Violence in the Mid-Nineteenth Century

The mid-nineteenth century was the most violent period in American history prior to 1965. Contemporaries often attributed the surge in violence to Irish immigration, urbanization, the Southern temperament, or the Civil War. Studies of nineteenth-century homicides have revealed, however, that the murder rate rose in the 1840s and 1850s, well in advance of the Civil War, and that it did so among the native born as well as immigrants, in the countryside as well as the cities, and in the North as well as the South. The homicide rate remained high through the Civil War into the 1870s and 1880s.

Whatever the cause, many Americans were quick to turn to violence when they felt crossed by neighbors, strangers, or family members. According to Roger Lane in Violence in the City, *the most common homicide in mid-nineteenth century Philadelphia "resulted from a brawl or quarrel originating in a saloon but reaching a climax in the street." A witness told the Philadelphia coroner of such a murder in 1876:*

> I heard Gallagher say to Madden "You are a sucker." Gallagher then grabbed a glass and threw it at Mr. Madden. McDonough also threw a glass. Mr. Geary made a grab for the men and then I heard a shot and Geary fell. Mr. Madden and Geary were good friends.

Roger Lane observes that the causes of such murders—"a spilled drink, a careless remark, an argument about the merits of different steam engines—almost always seemed tragically out of proportion to the aftermath." Most participants in such murders in Philadelphia were drunk. Note, however, that the per capita consumption of alcohol had dropped in the United States since the 1830s and that many societies with high rates of alcohol consumption did not have high levels of violence.

The documents below describe murders that occurred in the mid-nineteenth century in the nation's most violent region—the lower South—and in the nation's least violent region—northern New England. The testimony from the Inquest Book of Horry District, *South Carolina, tells of several murders that occurred in that county between 1849 and 1863. Some were about what Edward Ayers,* Vengeance and Justice, *calls questions of "honor": the defense of one's family and reputation against insult. Others, however, were about day-to-day matters, such as stray animals and slave discipline.*

The articles from the Burlington [Vermont] Daily Free Press *tell of a particular kind of murder that became common by mid-century in northern New England: feud violence. Between 1850 and 1890, middle-aged farmers and rural craftsmen were suddenly willing to kill neighbors to protect their property against seizure, damage, or trespass. Northern New Englanders put their lives at risk whenever they allowed their cattle to damage a neighbor's corn crop, or crossed a field without permission, or went to court over a boundary dispute. Young people did the same whenever they vandalized property, took an unauthorized swim in a stock pond, or pilfered fruit. Brothers killed one another over ownership of a clock or plow. Harsh words and physical assaults had been common in northern New England in property disputes since colonial times, but lethal and near-lethal violence in such disputes was restricted almost exclusively to the forty years that surrounded the Civil War. Feud murders usually occurred between 15 April and 15 September, from the first sign of spring to the beginning of the fall harvest.*

The testimony below tells of murders in Horry District, South Carolina. From a typescript of the Horry County Inquest Book, 1849-1874, at the South Carolinia Library, University of South Carolina. [Note: Slight punctuation corrections are included in some of these selections.]

An Inquisition upon the body of Willis Rabon, found dead in the woods near the plantation of Abraham Rabon, Sr. [September 1849]

[George H. Rabon sworn:] saith that on the fourth day of September 1849 he the said G H Rabon was in the woods and herd his brother Willis Rabon calling hogs and went to him. He had called up some hogs . . . [and] fed them and started to tolled [lead] them off. After we started off with hogs, Abraham Rabon Sr. [their uncle], Duke Rabon, and Abraham Rabon Jr. [their cousin] came to us in the woods near the path between Cooper Branch and Abraham Rabon's plantation and orderd us off and set his dogs on the hogs and cursed me and Brother Willis Rabon. Brother Willis Rabon said to him Abraham Rabon Sr. that if he did not stop his dogs that he would kill . . . the Dogs. . . . [Rabon Sr.] did not stop the dogs, and Brother Willis struck one of the dogs on the hog. . . . Abraham Rabon replied at the time that Willis spoke of killing the Dog that if he did we will Kill you.

They all three came at Willis. I saw Abraham Rabon Jr. with a Knife drawn in his hand making great speed toward Willis Rabon nearly in striking distance. I caught Abraham Rabon Sr. and said to him for Gods sake do not kill him, and he the[n] fought me. Struck me with a stick and Duke Rabon caught me by the legs and threw me down and Kicked me. When I got clear from them two I looked for Willis and I saw him near me standing with blood running down him. . . . I stept to him and said brother you are killed. He said yes Abraham [Jr.] has stabbed me. I then took him on my mare and went some forty y[ar]ds and he there stop[p]ed and got down and there Expired in or near fifteen minuttes after from the said stab.

Coronor's Jury Verdict: Abraham Rabon Jr. found guilty of manslaughter.

An Inquisition at Big Bay upon the body of Jack, property of John F. Sarvis, Sr. [December, 1851]

[William P. Jordan sworn:] Sayeth he saw John F. Sarvis Jr. stamp negro Jack and saw some marks on . . . Jack that . . . Sarvis said was dog bites and that he was sorry the dog bit the penis of Jack. . . . Jordan says the de[a]d body he believes to [be] Jack.

[John G. Lowrimore sworn:] John F. Sarvis Jr. said the dogs had bit Jack and saw marks like dog bites. This was sometime in November last and he saw young John Sarvis put [h]is foot on Jack's head and turn round on the negroes head, and that he the said Sarvis had a mind to kill Jack.

Coroner's Jury Verdict: Murder by some person or persons by some means to the Jurors unknown.

An Inquisition at Conwayboro upon the body of William Milligan [June 1852]

[James Stacy sworn:] He saw Absalom Causey inflict two wounds on William Milligan, one on his throat, and the other in his stomach. William Milligan went to said Causey after he (Causey) had stabbed Robert Milligan and struck him, witness believes about the face, at which time the said Causey having the knife in his hand stabbed William Milligan. . . . He saw Causey draw a pistol in the Grogshop [tavern]. Some one took the pistol from him and poked it out of the window and fired it off. After the pistol was taken from him, he [Causey] drew his knife while in the grogshop.

Coroner's Jury Verdict: William Milligan found guilty of manslaughter.

An Inquisition at the house of Edward T. Ricks upon the body of Edward Faircloth [March 1855]

[Edward T. Ricks sworn:] Says, Edward Faircloth came to house on Tuesday morning 27th February last, and said that Tilson, a slave, had stole his potatoes. He had sufficient proff [proof] against him, the said negro, and wanted sattisfaction of the negro Tilson. Ricks replied there is the negro at the negro house, you can whip him, or go to E. J. Parker [the Justice of the Peace]. Faircloth said he wanted sattisfaction now. Ricks and Faircloth stepted into the Negro House where the boy Tilson was. Tilson drew his ax and said to them stop. Faircloth advanced towards the boy Tilson. The boy Tilson struck Faircloth with his ax. They Faircloth & Tilson closed and fell. When Faircloth arose, he said I am a dead man, Called to Ricks to assist him. [Ricks] got Faircloth to his house. Remained there until he died, which was on the 1st day of March.

Coroner's Jury Verdict: Tilson, a slave, found guilty of manslaughter.

An Inquisition at Conwayboro near the residence of Samuel Bell on the body of Eli Thompkins [September 1860]

[Benjamin Thompkins Sworn:] Myself, my daddy [Eli Thompkins], & my brother started up from the Boro' on Sale [slave auction] Day in September to go home. We overtook Wm. R. Hughes & Wm. P. Hughes near Mr. Bond's work shop. I step'd on ahead with Wm. R. Hughes, talking about running over each other in a bragging friendly manner.

My daddy and my brother over took me. Brother and daddy was drinking very bad. They, my father and brother, commenced cursing the seed, breed, and generation of the Browns. I told him to curse them only in part, as I had some of the family in connexion with me. He still said damn me or God Damn me, at which time my father stept up and cursed me. I tried to apologize as I did not wish to fight them. My father step't up and shook his fist at me. . . . My brother walked round and kicked me. W. R. Hughes was near the path . . . . I struck my brother with a stick after he kicked me. He stop[p]ed and scratched his head then came back. We closed & went to the ground. I then said give me a fair fight. I heard my father cursing while I was down & heard him say turn me loose God damn you. My brother said take him off. My Daddy & Wm. R. Hughes then came up to me & pulled us apart. I then got up and turned on towards B. J. Singleton's Store. W. R. Hughes picked up his bundle and came on in the same direction. . . . I saw . . . my father advancing towards [W. P. Hughes, who] said don't you come on me or I will kill you 3 or 4 times distinctly. My father rushed at him and he W. P. Hughes snapped the Pistol at him. Father was saying nothing at the time. Hughes then jumped back and said he would kill him or words to that effect.

My father then said God damn you and all your weapons and my father then kicked him. . . . My father and Wm. P. Hughes then closed & Hughes threw him. Hughes had a knife. Saw my brother go up to them and heard a lick. I then told Wm. R. Hughes to go and part them. He went and I saw him part them. He went and I saw him take a knife from Wm. P. Hughes. My brother had no knife that I know of nor my father either. Wm. R. Hughes when taking the knife said Boys I am a liar if he has not killed your father or cut out his guts, or words to that effect. When W. R. Hughes took the knife, Wm. P. Hughes went off. My daddy got up and came towards the store house of B. J. Singleton & Co.

Coroner's Jury Verdict: William P. Hughes found guilty of manslaughter.

An Inquisition at Reaves' Mill Branch on the body of Absalom Causey [September 1863]

[William E. Todd sworn:] He heard Doctor Miles Gilmore say that he come his dore [arrived home] about the coming light [dawn]. Saw Causey git up out of bed with his [Gilmore's] wife. Saw Causey going out of dore. Knock him down with a large hick[o]ry stick with the intention of cutting his throat but finding his durk [dirk knife] missing repeated his blows at intervills till he (Causey) crost the fence. . . . [H]e heard Gilmore say that he had sent Causey word that if he ever cau[gh]t him in his [house] that he would kill him.

Coroner's Jury Verdict: Dr. Miles Gilmore found guilty of manslaughter.

Inquisition at Seth Belleme's on the body of Nancy Suggs [September 1863]

[J. J. Core sworn:] Says about two days after the death of Mrs. Suggs . . . he heard Arthur Suggs [her husband] say that he had bought ars[e]nick in Georgetown for the purpose of killing rats and before he got home the ars[e]nick got wet and that he flung it away.

[Meriah Thomas sworn:] Arthur Suggs came to her house about 12 Oclock A. M. and told her that his wife, Mrs. Nancy Suggs, . . . was very sick and that he had given her some medicine. . . . [A]bout six Oclock in the evening she (Mrs. Thomas) went to Suggs's. Found Mrs. Suggs very sick. Heard Mrs. Suggs say that the stuff that Arthur had given her was killing her.

[Henry Inmon sworn:] He heard Arthur Suggs say . . . in the presence of his wife, Mrs. [Suggs], that he (Suggs) wisht he had no wife and that Mrs. Suggs replide to him what have [I] done that you should wish so. Arthur answers never mind.

[Meriah Thomas recalled:] Says that about three weeks before the death of Mrs. Suggs that Arthur Suggs and one Mary Blanton came to her house about 4 O'Clock in the morning. Heard Mrs. Blanton say that they all thought she [Mrs. Suggs] had gone to hell but she had come back for satisfaction and she['d] be dam'd if she did not have it. At the same time, [Mrs. Blanton] pul'd a breast[pin] out of her pockett and said the pin was enough to sattesfy [convince] her who bust her clothing.

[Mary Stevens sworn:] Says that about two weeks before the death of Mrs. Nancy Suggs that she was at Arthur Suggs's. Heard Arthur Speake of difficulty between him and his wife. Heard him (Suggs) [say] to his wife Nancy you have brought me to what I am at. Mrs. Suggs says to him [Arthur] why should it be me. When I was at home minding my business you was running about. Arthur replide it is your fault and you shall be sorry for it the longest day you live. Witness heard Mrs. [Suggs] say that she thought her life was in danger.

Coroner's Jury Verdict: Arthur Suggs found guilty of murder.

A Murder in Vermont

The two newspaper articles below tell of the murder of Abial Chase by Jefferson Fulton in Fletcher, Vermont. Both men were farmers. Taken from the Lamoille Messenger; reprinted in the Daily Free Press, Burlington, Vermont, *14 September 1855.*

Shocking Murder in Fletcher [Vermont]

One of the most aggravated cases of premeditated murder that we have ever been called on to record was committed at Fletcher last Thursday [6 September 1855] by Jefferson Fulton upon the body of Abial Chase. It appears that there had been a controversy of long standing between the parties concerning a division fence. Sometime during the past summer by the consent of the parties the matter was left out to disinterested persons who brought in a decision in favor of Chase; and the controversy was considered at an end. The day previous to the fatal affray a son of Fulton, 12 years of age, together with another boy of about the same age was found in Chase's melon patch in the act of stealing melons. Chase in a kind manner reprimanded the boys. He told them that such acts were wrong, and would, if persevered in, lead to the States' prison, and if, hereafter, at any time they wanted any melons, to ask for them and he would willingly let them have them. Fulton's son replied, that he would take as many melons without leave as he wanted, that he was not afraid of him and he would like to see him help himself. Chase finding the boy so unreasonably saucy and impertinent seized him by the collar, pulled him off the rock on which he was seated, and told him to leave for home. The boy immediately went home and told his father that Chase had been abusing him most shamefully; that he had kicked, pounded and otherwise violently maltreated him.

The next day, (Thursday) he related to some of his friends what had taken place between his son and Chase, and remarked, "I don't know whether I'd better go and kill the d—n old cuss or sue him." He was advised to take the latter course; but Fulton filled a bottle with liquor, and proceeded to a short distance where his father was at work and producing the bottle said, "Father, take a drink with me, drink a good 'horn,' you will never have a chance to drink any more with me." He then hid the bottle in some bushes near by and proceeded on to where Chase and his son were making a rail fence. He approached toward them in an apparently laughing mood and when he had come quite up to Chase, remarked, "Old Jeff has come to see you." Chase said, "Well, what will Old Jeff have." Thereupon he drew a knife which he had concealed about his person and violently stabbed him in the side between the ribs. Chase turned to escape when he received another stab in the back. He ran a few steps and fell never to rise again. Fulton then gave chase after the boy, who at the top of his voice cried "murder," but being unable to overtake him returned, gave the lifeless body a kick or two for fear that his victim might not be dead, and made way for the woods and has not since been seen. . . . Chase is represented to have been a very peaceable and quiet man, and leaves a wife and five children to mourn his untimely death.

The End of the Tragedy

Since the above was written, we learn that Fulton has put an end to his own life by cutting his throat. On Monday about 5 o'clock in the afternoon he was discovered by one of those in search after him, about half a mile from the house in the woods seated on a log. Upon being discovered he immediately rose and ran. The man cried for assistance, and others who were but a short way off came up and gave chase. Fulton seeing that they were gaining upon him . . . concealed himself in some bushes. Those in chase arriving at the spot found that he was in the last agonies of death having cut his own throat with the very knife with which he took the life of his fellow man.

Feud in Vermont

The following newspaper articles tell of a feud between the Balch and Plumley families in Shrewsbury, Vermont. All involved were farmers. Excerpted from the Daily Free Press, Burlington, Vermont, *3, 4, 6, 14, and 15 August 1868; and the* Rutland County Court Records, *March 1869 session, Rutland County Courthouse.*

Desperate Affray and Homicide in Shrewsbury

RUTLAND, VT., August 2.

One of the most atrocious murders ever perpetrated in Vermont occurred in Shrewsbury . . . last evening. An old feud has for many years existed in that place between two families named Plunky [Plumley] and Balch. While appraisers were engaged in settling damages committed by horses of the latter on the property of the former who had impounded the horses, a dispute arose between them which resulted in the shooting and killing of John Gilman, Jr., a disinterested young man, by Horace R. Plunky [Plumley], a scion of the Plunky [Plumley] family. Gilman was first attacked with a pitchfork, and while defending himself was shot, three buckshot passing through his heart. Indiscriminate shots were then exchanged between the parties, resulting in the wounding of Plunky [Plumley] and John Gilman, Sr. Five of the principals in the affair, viz., Ziba Plunky [Plumley], Horace R., his son, the murderer, George Butterfly, his son-in-law, and two men named Abr[aha]m Winn and Napoleon Quartier, employees of Balch, have been arrested and are confined in the jail here [in Rutland] awaiting examination. Frederick Plunky [Plumley], another son of Ziba, and one of the contestants, is concealed in the woods at present, but will probably be delivered to the charge of the officers to-morrow morning.

Both the Plunky [Plumley] and Balch factions were evidently prepared for the fray, as they were all armed.

[5 August 1868]

The Rutland *Herald* gives the following fuller particulars of the fatal affray in Shrewsbury:

Some words took place between Balch and the Gilmans, in one side, and Butterfly on the other, as to the merits of the question under appraisal, which they seemed to settle. . . . Balch and Butterfly shook hands, the latter remarking that he was "willing to let by-gones be by-gones," and that he would "stand the drinks for the crowd." With this explanation Butterfly started for the house of his father-in-law [Ziba Plumley] to get a pint of rum with which to keep good his promise. He was absent, however, for about an hour, during which the appraisers had departed, but young Gilman remained in the field, within a few feet of the road, his father and Balch standing in the highway. At the expiration of the time mentioned, Butterfly returned, in company with Horace R. Plumley, Frederick Plumley, and Ziba, their father. Horace immediately approached Gilman, pointing a loaded shot gun at him, and ordered him out of the field, with which request Gilman expressed his willingness to comply, but the gun being in what he evidently regarded as too close proximity to him, he seized hold of the barrel of the same and attempted unsuccessfully to wrench it from the hands of Plumley. At this juncture Frederick Plumley approached Gilman and threatened to stab him with a pitchfork, with which he was armed, unless he quitted the field. Gilman turned to ward off the blow of the fork, and in doing so loosed his hold on the shot-gun in the hands of Horace, when the latter deliberately fired at him, the charge of shot taking effect in the region of the heart, making a hole about two inches in diameter, passing entirely through the body, and killing him instantly.

A couple of workmen in the employ of Balch, named Winn and Quartier, then came up, when cross-firing ensued between the belligerent parties, during which several volleys were discharged, resulting in inflicting a severe wound in the left leg of John Gilman, Sr., and a flesh wound in the right leg, as well as a scalp wound on the person of Horace R. Plumley, who fired the first shot.

[6 August 1868]
Vermont News

Daniel Balch was shot at on Tuesday evening [4 August 1869], while standing at the door of his father's residence, in Shrewsbury. The ball struck him in the forehead, but only inflicted a flesh wound.

[14 August 1868]
[Excerpts from the Public Hearing]

[Daniel Balch]: I heard Ziba Plumley, who was in the road, tell Horace [Plumley] to shoot him [John Gilman Jr.]. . . . He said to Horace, "shoot him, G—d d—n him;" I think these were his words. . . . [H]eard Ziba Plumley, when Horace was firing his revolver, say to him, "G—d d—n it, can't you shoot straighter than that."

[15 August 1868]

[Elam A. Clark]: I was going up east to Geo. Plumley's on business; when . . . I moved down to the scene, and soon after saw a man with a gun in his hand running through Ziba Plumley's lot, southwest of the cornfield; I then looked over the fence on the south side of the road and saw Isaac H. Balch there, in Dan. Balch's field, nearly opposite where young Gilman was killed; I started toward him and saw Simon Gilman, brother of the deceased, coming up the road; Napoleon Quartier and a woman were trying to stop young Gilman; . . . I asked him where he was going; he said he was going to shoot Horace Plumley; I said to him "no you are not," and he said he would; I took the pistol from him and him by the collar and commenced talking to him; he said they had killed "Johnny," and he would shoot them. . . . I then asked Balch what was the matter, when he slapped his hands together and said "I can lick any Clark who was ever in Cold River;" I saw he was intoxicated; he then called to his boys in the field and said "Rally up here boys and be ready; let's give 'em another round; let us exterminate every G—d d—n Plumley in Cold River;" I then said I had come to stop the fight and not to fight myself. . . . I asked Balch to go home; he refused, when . . . I turned and saw George Butterfly coming down hill, east, towards us; Balch then called to Butterfly, daring him to come on, saying he was ready for him; I then took a pistol from my pocket which I had taken from the Gilman boy and told Balch to go home, that there had been blood enough shed, and I would prevent more fighting. . . . I started for Butterfly and . . . I told him to hold on and took hold of him; he said "Let me go," but I did not; he said he had not been in the fight, and that Balch and Johnny Gilman had been to the cornfield and stumped him to fight; he said he knew they were armed and he had no show; but he had got like Holden's revolver, and now if they wanted to fight he was ready; he at the time had a pistol in his hand; I told him, "They say Johnny Gilman is killed, now this must be stopped where it is." . . . I told them (Plumleys') I would accompany them a piece if they would agree not to fight more; Geo. Butterfly gave me his revolver, and Horace Plumley his gun; we went down the road together, and met Deputy Sheriff Sanderson near where Gilman was killed; he arrested Horace. . . .

John Gilman: I heard Horace Plumley make threats against Quartier on the night of the hog suit at Cuttingsville; he said Quartier would "take it" for testifying against him on that suit; Napoleon Quartier's life was in danger at the time my son was killed . . . he [Plumley] was in the road before my son was shot.

[Abraham Winn and Napoleon Quartier, the Balches' hired men, were released on bond at the end of the preliminary hearing in August 1868, spending their appearance at County Court as witnesses for the State. At the March 1869 term of the Rutland County Court, George Butterfly was found not guilty. Ziba and Frederick C. Plumley were found guilty of manslaughter and sentenced to prison. Horace R. Plumley was found guilty of murder and sentenced to death. His sentence was commuted on 9 August 1869 to life in prison, perhaps in recognition of his service in the Union Army during the Civil War.]

Questions

1. *Did Dutch authorities have a consistent policy toward spouse abuse? Did they handle these cases the way authorities in Puritan New England would have? Were those differences responsible for the higher level of violence in New Netherland?*
2. *Based on the evidence from Philadelphia, South Carolina, and Vermont, consider the following questions: Why did the perpetrators commit murder? Can you detect any common themes in the murders that might account for the mid-century surge in homicides? Were tavern brawls and drunken violence a specifically urban problem? Was honor the primary motive for murder in the South? Were feuds peculiar to northern New England?*
3. *How might the surge in violence in the 1850s help us understand the causes and consequences of the Civil War?*

FURTHER READING

On the role that violence plays in American culture, see Richard Slotkin, *Regeneration through Violence: The Mythology of the American Frontier, 1600–1860* (New York, 1996) and *The Fatal Environment: The Myth of the Frontier in the Age of Industrialization, 1800-1890* (New York, 1985); and Daniel A. Cohen, *Pillars of Salt, Monuments of Grace: New England Crime Literature and the Origins of American Popular Culture, 1674-1860* (New York, 1993). Important works on violence include Roger Lane, *Murder in America: A History* (Columbus, Ohio, 1997); Philip Greven, *Spare the Child: The Religious Roots of Punishment & the Psychological Impact of Physical Abuse* (New York, 1991); Richard Maxwell Brown, *No Duty to Retreat: Violence and Values in American History and Society* (New York, 1991); and Altina L. Waller, *Feud: Hatfields, McCoys, and Social Change in Appalachia, 1860-1900* (Chapel Hill, North Carolina, 1988). On New Netherland, see Oliver A. Rink, *Holland on the Hudson: An Economic and Social History of Dutch New York* (Ithaca, New York, 1986).

Marriage in Colonial America

Randolph A. Roth

Introduction

Historians once viewed the eighteenth century as a simple time, when men and women married for practical reasons and expected less of each other emotionally. They have since discovered, however, that many eighteenth-century marriages were emotionally intense and that many couples did not think much about the future before they married and conceived children. Historians are no longer certain such marriages were less prevalent then than they are today.

Marriage worked best when husbands and wives agreed on how authority and responsibility would be divided. Nowhere in eighteenth-century America were women the complete equals of their spouses. But a few marriages, particularly among the Quakers, were relatively egalitarian. In many marriages, especially in Puritan New England, husbands and wives worked together on most economic and family tasks as partners.

Likewise, marriage worked best when husbands and wives had the same goals. Most people married someone of the same age, class, religion, and ethnicity, so couples often began married life with a good deal of common ground. But even compatible couples argued, and spouses could find themselves suddenly incompatible. One spouse might join a dissenting church, for example, or begin drinking too much or take up with new friends.

Finally, marriage worked best if husbands and wives handled their chores effectively. Couples had many more domestic responsibilities than they do today. They had to settle disputes, supervise laborers, educate children, house relatives, nurse the sick, and keep the family farm or business running. Because of this range of responsibilities it is likely that earlier historians were correct in their evaluation that people in the eighteenth century picked spouses for more practical reasons than romantic ones.

Marriage in New England and the Chesapeake

Historians have long debated the roles of married men and women in colonial society. Some historians claim that men subordinated women and restricted their activities to the domestic sphere, while others insist that women were often engaged in public life and were more independent than some historians have made them out to have been. Laurel Thatcher Ulrich, David Hackett Fischer, and Jack P. Greene separately arrive at a third conclusion: that marriages were unequal partnerships in which the roles of women and men overlapped and lines of authority were blurred. Greene argues that marriages in the Chesapeake were much like the marriages Ulrich finds in New England, although women's roles grew more circumscribed over time. Fischer argues that Chesapeake marriages were more patriarchal and less loving than New England marriages.

Women as Deputy Husbands

The following selection looks at the roles of wives in New England households. Abridged from Laurel Thatcher Ulrich, Good Wives: Image and Reality in the Lives of Women in Northern New England, 1650–1750 *(New York, 1982), 36–40, 42–43, 50.*

There is a revealing little anecdote in a deposition recorded in Essex County in 1672. Jacob Barney of Salem had gone to Phillip

Cromwell's house to negotiate a marriage. Although both Cromwell and his wife were present, Barney had turned to the husband, expecting, as he said, "to have their minds from him." But because Cromwell had a severe cold which had impaired his hearing, he simply pointed to his wife and said that whatever she agreed upon, "he would make it good." This incident dramatizes three assumptions basic to family government in the traditional world:

1. The husband was supreme in the external affairs of the family. As its titular head, he had both the right and the responsibility to represent it in its dealings with the outside world.
2. A husband's decisions would, however, incorporate his wife's opinions and interest. (Barney expected to hear their minds from him.)
3. Should fate or circumstance prevent the husband from fulfilling his role, the wife could appropriately stand in his place. As one seventeenth-century Englishman explained it, a woman "in her husband's absence, is wife and deputy-husband, which makes her double the files of her diligence. At his return he finds all things so well he wonders to see himself at home when he was abroad."

. . . As deputy husbands a few women, like Mistress Cromwell, might emerge from anonymity; most women did not. . . . To talk about the independence of colonial wives is not only an anachronism but a contradiction in logic. A woman became a wife by virtue of her dependence, her solemnly vowed commitment to her husband. . . .

One can be dependent, however, without being either servile or helpless. To use an imperfect but nonetheless suggestive analogy, colonial wives were dependent upon patriarchal families in somewhat the same way seventeenth-century ministers were dependent upon their congregations or twentieth-century engineers are dependent upon their companies. That is, they owned neither their place of employment nor even the tools of their trade. No matter how diligently they worked, they did not expect to inherit the land upon which they lived any more than a minister expected to inherit his meetinghouse or an engineer his factory. Skilled service was their major contribution, secure support their primary compensation. Unlike professionals in either century, they could

This woodcut illustrates the various tasks that colonial women performed as productive workers in the family. (Courtesy of Corbis-Bettmann.)

not resign their position, but then neither could they be fired. Upon the death of a husband they were entitled to maintenance for life—or until they transferred their allegiance (symbolized by their name) from one domestic establishment to another.

The skilled service of a wife included . . . specialized housekeeping skills . . . , but it also embraced the responsibilities of a deputy husband. Since most productive work was based within the family, there were many opportunities for a wife to "double the files of her diligence." A weaver's wife, like Beatrice Plummer, might wind quills. A merchant's wife, like Hannah Grafton, might keep shop. A farmer's wife, like Magdalen Wear, might plant corn. . . .

. . . Almost any task was suitable for a woman as long as it furthered the good of her family and was acceptable to her husband. . . . Under the right conditions any wife not only *could* double as a husband, she had the responsibility to do so. . . .

To explain fully the contradictions in such a system, we must return to the day-to-day behavior of individual husbands and wives, first examining the factors which enhanced the role of deputy husband and then exploring conditions which muted its significance for colonial women.

. . . [T]here was as much variation in seventeenth- and eighteenth-century families as there is today. Some wives were servile, some were shrews, others were respected companions who shared the authority of their spouses in the management of family affairs. Important conditions, however, separated the colonial world from our own. The most basic of these was spatial. . . . Male and female space intersected and overlapped. Nor was there the sharp division between home and work that later generations experienced. Because servants and apprentices lived within the household, a family occasion—mealtime or nightly prayer—could become a business occasion as well.

In June of 1661 a young maid named Naomi Hull described a discussion which took place in the parlor of the Samuel Symonds' home in Ipswich, Massachusetts, early in that year. The case concerned the length of indenture of two Irish servants. According to the maid, all of the family had gathered for prayer when one of the Irishmen asked if a neighbor's son was coming the next day to plow. *Mistress* Symonds said she thought so. One of the men asked who would plow with him. *Mistress* Symonds said, "One of you." When the two men announced that their indenture was up and that they would work no longer, both the master and the mistress questioned the servants. At one point Mistress Symonds interrupted her husband. "Let them alone," she said. "Now they are speaking let them speak their own minds." Because the involvement of Mistress Symonds was not at issue, this casual description of her participation is all the more impressive. Such an anecdote shows the way in which boundaries between male and female domains might blur in a common household setting.

Ambitious men in early America were often involved in many things at once—farming and running a gristmill, for example, or cutting timber and fishing. Because wives remained close to the house, they were often at the communications center of these diverse operations, given responsibility for conveying directions, pacifying creditors, and perhaps even making some decisions about the disposition of labor. On a day-to-day basis this might be a rather simple matter: remembering to send a servant to repair a breach in the dam after he finished in the field, for example, or knowing when to relinquish an ox to a neighbor. But during a prolonged absence of her husband a woman might become involved in more weighty matters.

Sometime in the 1670s Moses Gilman of Exeter, New Hampshire, wrote to his wife from Boston:

> Loving wife Elisabeth Gillman these are to desire you to speake to John Gillman & James Perkins and so order the matter thatt Mr. Tho. Woodbridge may have Twelve thousand fott [feet] of merchantable boards Rafted [logs tied in two large rafts and floated down river to the mills] by thirsday night or sooner if poseble they Can for I have Absolutly sould [sold] them to him & if John Clough sen [Senior] or any other doe deliver bords to make up the sum Give Receits of whatt you Receive of him or any other man and lett no bote [body] bee prest [for payment] or other ways disposed of untill I Returne[.] being from Him who is yos till death
>
> Moses Gilman

If Gilman had doubted his wife's ability to "order the matter," he could have written a number of separate letters—to John Gilman, James Perkins, John Clough, and perhaps others. But securing a shipment of twelve thousand feet of merchantable boards entirely by letter would have been complicated and time-consuming. Instead, Gilman relied on the good sense of his wife, who would be respected as his surrogate, and who probably had acquired some expertise in making out receipts for forest products and in conveying instructions to lumbering and shipping crews. A "loving wife" who considered herself his "till Death" was more trustworthy than a hired servant or business associate. As a true consort, she would know that by furthering her husband's interest she furthered her own.

Thus, a wife with talent for business might become a kind of double for her husband, greatly extending his ability to handle affairs. . . . But two cautions are in order. First, the biases of the twentieth century may tempt historians to give undue significance to what were really rather peripheral enterprises. Acting as attorney to one's husband is not equivalent to practicing law. To colonial women, it may even have been less desirable than keeping house. This leads to the second point. The value of any activity is determined by its meaning to the participant, not to the observer. In early America position was always more important than task. Colonial women might appear to be independent, even aggressive, by modern standards, yet still have derived their status primarily from their relationship to their husbands.

This is well illustrated in a New Hampshire court record of 1671. A carpenter named John Barsham testified about an argument he had heard between Henry Sherburne and his second wife, Sarah, who was the widow of Walter Abbott. Barsham had come to the house to get some nails he needed for repairing a dwelling he had rented from them. According to Barsham, Sarah became so angry at her husband's opposition that she "rose off from the seat where she was setting & came up to him with her arms akimbo saying we should have nayles & he had nothing to [do] in it." As if to add the final authority to her demand, she asked him "why he trode upon Walter Abbotts floor & bid him get out of doors, & said that he had nothing to do there." Sarah Sherburne was an experienced and assertive woman. She had kept tavern "with two husbands and none." The house in which she and Sherburne lived had been part of her inheritance from her first husband. But in the heat of the argument she did not say, "Get out of *my* house" or "Get out of the house *I* provided." She said, "Get out of Walter Abbott's house." Her identity was not as property owner, but as wife. To assert her authority over her husband, she invoked the memory of his predecessor. . . .

The role of deputy husband reinforced a certain elasticity in premodern notions of gender. No mystique of feminine behavior prevented a woman from driving a hard bargain . . . and under ideal conditions day-to-day experience in assisting with a husband's work might prepare her to function competently in a male world—should she lose her husband, should she find herself without a grown son, should she choose not to remarry or find it impossible to do so. But in the immediate world such activities could have a far different meaning. The chores assigned might be menial, even onerous, and, whatever their nature, they competed for attention with the specialized housekeeping responsibilities which every woman shared.

Marriage and Gender in the Chesapeake

David Hackett Fischer draws a sharp contrast between marriages in New England and the Chesapeake. Excerpted from David Hackett Fischer, Albion's Seed: Four British Folkways in America *(New York, 1989), 281, 283–87, 291–93, 295–97.*

Virginia and New England were alike in their ideas of universal marriage; both rejected the ideal of celibacy which was so strong in Catholic countries. But these two Protestant cultures of British America also differed in many ways as to their ideas of marriage, and their matrimonial institutions. In Massachusetts, . . . marriage was thought to be a covenant which could be terminated when its terms were not fulfilled. In Virginia, matrimony was regarded as an indissoluble union—a sacred knot that could never be untied by mortal hands. Divorce in the modern sense did not exist. Only permanent separation and maintenance could be obtained, and even that release was rarely granted. . . .

Children were rarely made to marry against their will, but neither were they left to decide the question for themselves. Parents and guardians entered into complex negotiations to settle the size of the marriage portion or "dot" which a couple needed to make its way in the world. . . . In both England and Virginia, many of these unions were cousin-marriages that had been arranged by elders. . . . The marriage of first cousins was condemned by New England Puritans as violating the law of consanguinity. But many an Anglican lady "changed her condition but not her name." [That is, married a close relative.] The same custom was common in Virginia, and fundamentally important to the cohesion of the tidewater elite. The culture of New England created a different set of matrimonial priorities.

One consequence of these customs appeared in the pattern of age at marriage. Male Virginians married at nearly the same age as in New England, twenty-five or twenty-six on the average. But brides in the Chesapeake colonies were much younger than in

---

Puritan Massachusetts. Before 1700, most Virginia girls found a husband by the age of seventeen. Mean age at marriage was a little higher—eighteen to twenty—but below the Massachusetts average. . . .

Other inequalities appeared in the proportion of Virginians who married at all. Though the ideal was universal marriage, the reality was very different in seventeenth-century Virginia, because so few immigrants were females. Nearly all women were able to marry, but for men the pattern was very different. One study of estate-inventories in southern Maryland from 1658 to 1708 finds that one-quarter of men died without ever marrying. A man's chances of finding a wife were a function of his social rank. Here was yet another system of inequality in this hierarchical society.

The Virginia pattern developed within a culture where marriage was regarded as something to be arranged between families, something that did not require love as a precondition, something that could never be dissolved, and something that joined husband and wife in an organic and patriarchal hierarchy. Given such an idea of matrimony, it seemed right and fitting in this culture that a typical Virginia marriage in the seventeenth century should join a man of maturity to a miss in her teens. These Virginia customs were very different from the marriage ways of Massachusetts. . . .

. . . In every culture there are happy marriages and unhappy ones. But historians of the family have remarked upon the extent of marital discord among the gentry of Virginia. . . . The trouble commonly arose from deep contradictions in the gender ways of Virginia. Perhaps the most common cause of trouble was money. Men were taught to believe that they were masters of their households. But women often possessed property of their own, and wished to make economic decisions independent of their husbands. An example was the disastrous marriage of Colonel John Custis of Arlington, one of the most powerful men in Virginia, and Frances Parke Custis. . . . The strife in this union seems to have arisen mainly from disputes over property. Mrs. Custis was a woman of wealth, which her husband had the right to manage as he wished. But he also had the duty to pass her property intact to her children. An elaborate marriage contract existed, but it became an invitation to struggle between husband and wife. So bitter was this strife that Col. Custis ordered that a record of his domestic misery should be carved upon his gravestone.

For years, this unhappy couple refused to speak to one another, communicating only through their slaves. Long silences were punctuated by outbursts of rage so wild and violent as to border upon madness. After one such tempest, Col. Custis surprised his lady by inviting her to go driving with him. They rode in sullen silence through the Virginia countryside, until suddenly the colonel turned his carriage out of the road, and drove straight into Chesapeake Bay.

"Where are you going, Mr. Custis?" the lady asked, as the horses began to swim.

"To hell, Madam," he replied.

"Drive on," said she, "any place is better than Arlington."...

Another cause of domestic conflict rose from the politics of family life.... A wife was bound by her marriage vows to obey her husband. An apparently male essayist in the Virginia *Gazette* laid down rules of "matrimonial felicity" for the instruction of wives: "Never dispute with him ... if any altercation or jars happen, don't separate the bed, whereby the animosity will increase ... read often the matrimonial service, and overlook not the important word OBEY."

But the unwritten customs of the culture encouraged women to demand more freedom and respect. In 1687, for example, a

In this eighteenth-century portrait, the mother is the prominent figure among the family. (Courtesy of Children's Television Workshop.)

spirited lady named Sarah Harrison married Dr. James Blair, the future founder of William and Mary College. When the minister recited the marriage vows, she startled the congregation by responding, "NO OBEY!" Three times the vows were repeated. Three times Sarah Harrison answered with increasing firmness "No Obey," until Dr. Blair finally agreed to take his chances and the wedding went forward without any promise of obedience. Their married life together proved to be deeply unhappy. Some years later, William Byrd noted in his diary:

> Went to the Commissary's, where . . . I was very much surprised to find Mrs. Blair drunk, which is growing pretty common with her, and her relations disguise it under the name of consolation.

Few women were as outspoken as Sarah Harrison. But many resisted by other means. Yet most were compelled to obey their husbands, often much against their will, in matters which they cared deeply about. Thus William Byrd compelled his wife to send her sick baby Otway to her mother-in-law, who lived at a plantation which was thought to be more healthy. The wife replied,

> I am very sorry you have limited Poor, sweet Otway, so that he has but a short time to stay with me. Poor dear babe . . . But Sir, your Orders must be obeyed whatever reluctance I find thereby.

Here was a fertile source of domestic strife.

A particular cause of trouble was the use of physical violence and verbal abuse by husbands against wives, and sometimes by wives against husbands as well. Here again the customs of the country were inconsistent. Men were expected to exercise authority over their wives, and were encouraged by custom to use moderate "chastisement" from time to time. But wife-beating was thought to be dishonorable and was punished in both England and America. . . .

Yet another tension in gender roles developed from ideas about love. Husbands and wives were expected to love one another—but not overmuch. Landon Carter complained of a Virginia lady who was "more fond of her husband perhaps than the politeness of the day allows for." Even in happy marriages, the love that men felt for their wives was not a love between equals, and sometimes it seemed to be less a love for a person than for a valuable piece of property. One gentleman wrote when his wife died:

> All grief will allow me to say of her is, that she was known to be a humble pious, virtuous, discreet woman, an ornament to her sex, and a crown to her husband. But woe is me the crown has fallen from my head.

A further source of conflict arose from a confusion of roles for women in Virginia. They were expected to be feminine, refined, delicate, gracious, modest, virtuous. At the same time, all but the most privileged of women were also expected to do farm work and even field labor as well as housewifery. Women of every estate were required to be resourceful but self-effacing. . . .

There were even theological disputes in Virginia on questions of gender. Some members of this culture shared a deeper sense of spiritual inequality between men and women than commonly existed in Massachusetts. At a rich planter's table as late as 1773, the northern tutor Philip Fithian was startled to hear an argument on the question of whether women had souls. That ancient conundrum had long since been laid to rest among the Puritans. But it still remained a topic of debate in Virginia.

All of these conflicts had a common denominator. In this society of English-speaking people, the rights which Christian Englishmen claimed for themselves were a standing reproach to the status of women in their society. A free-born English gentleman was in many ways the unfittest of all males to argue his wife into a condition of dependency. By an early date in the eighteenth century some of the ladies of Virginia were thinking of themselves as "She-Britons," and demanding a share of the rights that their husbands enjoyed. As early as 1736, the Virginia *Gazette* published an angry poem called "The Lady's Complaint," which captured the deepest contradiction in the genderways of Virginia:

> They plainly can their Thoughts disclose,
> Whilst ours must burn within:
> We have got Tongues, and Eyes, in vain,
> And Truth from us is sin. . . .
> Then Equal Laws let Custom find,
> And neither Sex oppress;
> More Freedom give to Womankind,
> Or give to Mankind less.

A Different View of Marriage

Unlike David Hackett Fischer, Jack P. Greene concludes that marriages in the Chesapeake were much like those in Britain's other colonies, although they had changed over time. Excerpted from Jack P. Greene, Pursuits of Happiness: The Social Development of Early Modern British Colonies and the Formation of American Culture *(Chapel Hill, 1988), 82, 94–95.*

[After 1680] improved life expectancy, a more equal sex ratio, and earlier marriages among creoles [native-born colonists] raised the birthrate, net reproduction nearly equaling deaths by the 1670s and exceeding them by the 1690s. In combination, these developments contributed by the end of the century to a total white population of nearly ninety thousand, a majority of whom were native-born. The same developments also led to a more settled and typically European nuclear family structure, more extended kinship networks, and considerably more compact settlements in all but the most newly occupied areas. . . .

In the private world of the family, quite as much as in the public world of politics and religion, the Chesapeake became far more settled—and far more like metropolitan Britain—during the eighteenth century. Despite improving demographic conditions, the genealogical depth of families remained shallow and the range of kinship connections relatively narrow during the early decades of the century. As in the previous century, this shallowness encouraged a broad conception of the family. Households tended to be open and associations with non-kin both intimate and extensive. With continuing increases in life expectancy through the middle decades of the century, however, the Chesapeake family became more susceptible to traditional definition. Parents began to live longer, typically into their mid-fifties and to have an average of four to five children who survived into adulthood. Grandparenthood, relatively rare in the previous century, became widespread and kinship networks much more extensive and intensive.

These developments may have turned Chesapeake families inward and made them more private, child-centered, nurturant, and affectionate and thereby brought them into close conformity with trends that were evident throughout the contemporary North Atlantic world. Much more important, they seem to have altered power relationships within the family. Just as an enlarging pool of older men lent strength to political and religious institutions at the local and provincial levels, so longer-lived fathers helped to bolster paternal authority within families. In the seventeenth century, higher survival rates for women had turned the Chesapeake into what one scholar has termed a "widowarchy" in which women, despite their disproportionately small numbers, enjoyed a role in family and economic life far more extensive than was usual among their counterparts in England. As disparities in survival rates among women and men dropped in the eighteenth century, however, husbands and fathers sought to transform the family into the well-ordered patriarchal units that had long been the ideal, if not necessarily always the norm, in metropolitan Britain. In consequence of these efforts, women found themselves more and more restricted to a domestic and ornamental role, and the Chesapeake, like Britain, became an even more male-dominated society.

Yet if Chesapeake fathers liked to think of themselves as patriarchs who presided firmly over deferential wives and children, the patriarchy they actually succeeded in establishing seems to have been a highly permissive one. They may have preached obedience to parents and encouraged passivity in daughters, but few of them, recent studies suggest, appeared to have tried to use their control over family land and other resources to establish a tight family discipline. Indeed, to enable their sons to function effectively in the fluid and competitive world of the Chesapeake, parents seem rather to have tried to inculcate in their offspring not obedience and deference but independence, self-assertiveness, self-confidence, and a reliance upon self-control. Not restraint but indulgence seems to have characterized parents' relations with their children, who enjoyed wide latitude in their behavior and were subjected to a minimum of parental interference in their lives.

Questions

1. *What tasks were reserved for women? men? What tasks were shared by men and women? What determined whether a task was "male" or "female"?*
2. *Are there signs that the marriages Ulrich describes were distinctively "Puritan"? that the marriages Fischer describes were distinctively "Anglican"? Did religious beliefs affect relationships between men and women?*
3. *How do contemporary marriages differ from those of colonial America? In what ways do they remain similiar? What broad forces that shaped marriage in the eighteenth century do not operate today? What new forces are at work shaping the nature of love and marriage?*

Fractious Courtships and Marriages

The stories of Samuel Sewall and Elizabeth Ashbridge show that couples in eighteenth-century America had as much trouble resolving their differences as couples do now. Men held the upper hand in courtship and marriage, legally and economically. But women asserted themselves. The result was a struggle to define the terms on which marriage would be based. The struggle led sometimes to violence, sometimes to love and friendship, sometimes to peaceful coexistence.

Samuel Sewall (1652–1730)

Samuel Sewall was a prominent Boston merchant who entered politics and rose to chief justice of Massachusett's highest court. From 1673 until his death, Sewall kept a diary, an extraordinary record of his thoughts, feelings, and spiritual progress. The passages below begin with the death of Sewall's second wife, Abigail, in May 1720. Sewall mourned for several months, but by October he had set aside his grief and begun his search for a new wife. Taken from The Diary of Samuel Sewall, *1674–1729, ed. M. Halsey Thomas, (New York, 1973), 2:950–51, 955, 957–67, 988–90, 993.*

[29 May 1720]

God having in his holy Sovereignty put my Wife out of the Fore-Seat [his second wife, Abigail, had died on May 26], I appre-

Excerpt from *The Diary of Samuel Sewall*, M. Halsey Thomas, ed., published by Farrar, Straus & Giroux, 1973, from the original manuscript at the Massachusetts Historical Society.

hended I had Cause to be ashamed of my Sin, and to loath my self for it; and retired into my Pue. . . . I put up a Note to this purpose; Samuel Sewall, depriv'd of his dear Wife by a very sudden and awfull Stroke, desires Prayers that GOD would sanctify the same to himself, and Children, and family. Writ and sent three; to the South, Old, and Mr. Colman's [churches]. . . .

[Tuesday, 31 May 1720]

Buried my dear Wife. . . . [H]ad a Comfortable day; though threatened with Rain. *Laus Deo.* I went into the Tomb: The good Lord prepare for me a House not made with Hands, eternal in the Heavens, and the Consideration of that will make the Grave a Lightsom place. My Son prays in his Sister's Chamber very pertinently, affectionatly. . . .

[5 September 1720]

Going to Son Sewall's I there meet with Madam Winthrop, told her I was glad to meet her there, had not seen her a great while; gave her Mr. Homes's Sermon. . . .

[Saturday, 1 October 1720]

I went to Madam Winthrop's just at 3. Spake to her, saying, my loving wife died so soon and suddenly, 'twas hardly convenient for me to think of Marrying again; however I came to this Resolution, that I would not make my Court to any person without first Consulting with her. Had a pleasant discourse about 7 Single persons . . . viz. Mad'm Rebekah Dudley, Catharine Winthrop, Bridget Usher, Deliverance Legg, Rebekah Loyd, Lydia Colman, Elizabeth Bellingham. She propounded one and another for me; but none would do. . . .

[3 October 1720]

Waited on Madam Winthrop again; 'twas a little while before she came in. Her daughter Noyes being there alone with me, I said, I hoped my Waiting on her Mother would not be disagreeable to her. She answer'd she should not be against that that might be for her Comfort. . . . By and by in came Mr. Airs, Chaplain of the Castle, and hang'd up his Hat, which I was a little startled at, it seeming as if he was to lodge there. At last Madam Winthrop came in. After a considerable time, I went up to her and said, if it might not be inconvenient I desired to speak with her. She assented, and spake of going into another Room; but Mr. Airs and Mrs. Noyes presently rose up, and went out, leaving us there alone. . . . I pray'd that Katharine *[Mrs. Winthrop]* might be the person assign'd for me. She instantly took it up in way of Denyal [denial], as if she had catch'd at an Opportunity to do it . . . could not leave her Children. I express'd my Sorrow . . . , pray'd her Consideration, and ask'd her when I should wait on her agen. She setting no time, I mention'd that day Sennight [one week hence]. Gave her Mr. Willard's Fountain open'd with the little print and verses; saying, I hop'd if we did well read that book, we should meet together hereafter, if we did not now. . . .

[6 October 1720]

A little after 6. p. m. I went to Madam Winthrop's. She was not within. I gave Sarah Chickering the Maid 2s. [shillings], Juno [Mrs. Winthrop's African American servant], who brought in wood, 1s. Afterward the nurse came in, I gave her 18d. [pence], having no other small Bill. After awhile Dr. Noyes came in with his Mother; and quickly after his wife came in: They sat talking, I think, till eight a-clock. I said I fear'd I might be some Interruption to their Business: Dr. Noyes reply'd pleasantly: He fear'd they might be an Interruption to me, and went away. Madam seem'd to harp upon the same string. Must take care of her Children; could not leave that House and Neighbourhood where she had dwelt so long. I told her she might doe her children as much or more good by bestowing what she laid out in Hous-keeping, upon them. Said her Son would be of Age the 7th of August. I said it might be inconvenient for her to dwell with her Daughter-in-Law, who must be Mistress of the House. I gave her a piece of Mr. Belcher's Cake and Ginger-Bread wrapped up in a clean sheet of Paper; told her of her Father's kindness to me when Treasurer, and I Constable. My Daughter Judith was gon from me and I was more lonesom—might help to forward one another in our Journey to Canaan. . . . I took leave about 9 aclock. I told [her] I came now to refresh her Memory as to Monday-night; said she had not forgot it. In discourse with her, I ask'd leave to speak with her Sister; I meant to gain Mad'm Mico's favour to persuade her Sister. She seem'd surpris'd and displeas'd, and said she was in the same condition! . . .

[10 October 1720]

In the Evening I visited Madam Winthrop, who treated me with a great deal of Curtesy; Wine, Marmalade. I gave her the News-Letter about the Thanksgiving; Proposals, for sake of the verses for David Jeffries. She tells me Dr. Increase Mather visited her this day, in Mr. Hutchinson's Coach. . . .

[11 October 1720]

I writ a few Lines to Madam Winthrop to this purpose: "Madam, These wait on you with Mr. Mayhew's Sermon, and Account of the state of the Indians on Martha's Vinyard. I thank you for your Unmerited Favours of yesterday; and hope to have the Happiness of Waiting on you to-morrow before Eight a-clock after Noon. . . .

[12 October 1720]

Mrs. Anne Cotton came to door (twas before 8.) said Madam Winthrop was within, directed me into the little Room, where she was full of work behind a Stand; Mrs. Cotton came in and stood. Madam Winthrop pointed to her to set me a Chair. Madam Winthrop's Countenance was much changed from what 'twas on Monday, look'd dark and lowering. At last, the work, (black stuff or Silk) was taken away, I got my Chair in place, had some Converse, but very Cold and indifferent to what 'twas before. Ask'd her to acquit me of Rudeness if I drew off her Glove [in order to hold her hand]. Enquiring the reason, I told her twas great odds between handling a dead Goat, and a living Lady. Got it off. I told her I had one Petition to ask of her, that was, that she would take off the Negative she laid on me the third of October; She readily answer'd she could not, and enlarg'd upon it; She told me of it so soon as she could; could not leave her house, children, neighbours, business. I told her she might do som Good to help and support me. Mentioning Mrs. Gookin, Nath, the widow Weld was spoken of; said I had visited Mrs. Denison. I told her Yes! Afterward I said, If after a first and second Vagary she would Accept of me returning, Her Victorious Kindness and Good Will would be very Obliging. She thank'd me for my Book (Mr. Mayhew's Sermon), But said not a word of the Letter. When she insisted on the Negative, I pray'd there might be no more Thunder and Lightening, I should not sleep all night. I gave her Dr. Preston, The Church's Marriage and the Church's Carriage, which cost me

6s. at the Sale. The door standing open, Mr. Airs came in, hung up his Hat, and sat down. After awhile, Madam Winthrop moving, he went out. John Eyre look'd in, I said How do ye, or, your servant Mr. Eyre: but heard no word from him. Sarah fill'd a Glass of Wine, she drank to me, I to her, She sent Juno home with me with a good Lantern, I gave her 6d. and bid her thank her Mistress. In some of our Discourse, I told her I had rather go to the Stone-House adjoining to her, than to come to her against her mind. Told her the reason why I came every other night was lest I should drink too deep draughts of Pleasure. She had talk'd of Canary [wine from the Canary Islands], her Kisses were to me better than the best Canary. . . .

[Monday, 17 October 1720]

In the Evening I visited Madam Winthrop, who Treated me Courteously, but not in Clean Linen as somtimes. She said, she did not know whether I would come again, or no. I ask'd her how she could so impute inconstancy to me. (I had not visited her since Wednesday night being unable to get over the Indisposition received by the Treatment received that night, and I *must* in it seem'd to sound like a made piece of Formality.) Gave her this day's Gazett. . . . Dr. Noyes and his wife came in, and sat a Considerable time; had been visiting Son and dâter [daughter] Cooper. Juno came home with me.

[18 October 1720]

Visited Madam Mico, who came to me in a splendid Dress. I said, It may be you have heard of my Visiting Madam Winthrop, her Sister. She answered, Her Sister had told her of it. I ask'd her good Will in the Affair. She answer'd, If her Sister were for it, she should not hinder it. I gave her Mr. Homes's Sermon. She gave me a Glass of Canary, entertain'd me with good Discourse, and a Respectfull Remembrance of my first Wife. I took Leave.

[19 October 1720]

Midweek, Visited Madam Winthrop; Sarah told me she was at Mr. Walley's, would not come home till late. I gave her Hannah's 3 oranges with her Duty, not knowing whether I should find her or no. . . . I went and found her there, with Mr. Walley and his wife in the little Room below. At 7 a-clock I mentioned going home; at 8. I put on my Coat, and quickly waited on her home. She found occasion to speak loud to the servant, as if she had a mind to be known. Was Courteous to me; but took occasion to speak pretty earnestly about my keeping a Coach: I said 'twould cost £100 per annum: she said twould cost but £40. . . . Came away somewhat late.

[20 October 1720]

. . . Madam Winthrop not being at Lecture, I went thither first; found her very Serene with her dâter Noyes, Mrs. Dering, and the widow Shipreev, sitting at a little Table, she in her arm'd Chair. She drank to me, and I to Mrs. Noyes. After awhile pray'd the favour to speak with her. She took one of the Candles, and went into the best Room, clos'd the shutters, sat down upon the Couch. She told me Madam Usher had been there, and said the Coach must be set on Wheels, and not by Rusting. She spake somthing of my needing a Wigg. Ask'd me what her Sister said to me. I told her, She said, If her Sister were for it, She would not hinder it. But I told her, she did not say she would be glad to have me for her Brother. Said, I shall keep you in the Cold, and ask her if she would be within to morrow night, for we had had but a running Feast. She said she could not tell whether she should, or no. I took Leave. As were drinking at the Governour's, he said: In England the Ladies minded little more than that they might have Money, and Coaches to ride in. I said, And New-England brooks its Name. At which Mr. Dudley smiled. Gov'r said they were not quite so bad here.

[Friday, 21 October 1720]

My Son, the Minister, came to me p. m. by appointment and we pray one for another in the Old Chamber; more especially respecting my Courtship. About 6. a-clock I go to Madam Winthrop's; Sarah told me her Mistress was gon out, but did not tell me whither she went. She presently order'd me a Fire; so I went in, having Dr. Sibb's Bowels with me to read. I read the two first Sermons, still no body came in: At last about 9. a-clock Mr. John Eyre came in; I took the opportunity to say to him as I had done to Mrs. Noyes before, that I hoped my Visiting his Mother would not be disagreeable to him; He answered me with much Respect. When twas after 9. a-clock He of himself said he would go and call her, she was but at one of his Brothers: A while after I heard Madam Winthrop's voice, enquiring somthing about John.

After a good while and Clapping the Garden door twice or thrice, she came in. I mention'd somthing of the lateness; she banter'd me, and said I was later. She receiv'd me Courteously. I ask'd when our proceedings should be made publick: She said They were like to be no more publick than they were already. Offer'd me no Wine that I remember. I rose up at 11 a-clock to come away, saying I would put on my Coat, She offer'd not to help me. I pray'd her that Juno might light me home, she open'd the Shutter, and said twas pretty light abroad; Juno was weary and gon to bed. So I came hôm by Star-light as well as I could. . . .

[22 October 1720]

Dâter Cooper visited me before my going out of Town. . . . Coming back, near Leg's Corner, Little David Jeffries saw me, and looking upon me very lovingly, ask'd me if I was going to see his Grandmother? I said, Not to-night. Gave him a peny, and bid him present my Service to his Grandmother.

[24 October 1720]

. . . [S]top't at Madam Winthrop's. . . . I told her, being encourag'd by David Jeffries loving eyes, and sweet Words, I was come to enquire whether she could find in her heart to leave that House and Neighbourhood, and go and dwell with me at the South-end; I think she said softly, Not yet. I told her It did not ly in my lands to keep a Coach. If I should, I should be in danger to be brought to keep company with her Neighbour Brooker, (he was a little before sent to prison for Debt). Told her I had an Antipathy against those who would pretend to give themselves; but nothing of their Estate. I would a proportion of my Estate with my self. And I suppos'd she would do so. As to a Perriwig [a type of wig], My best and greatest Friend, I could not possibly have a greater, began to find me with Hair before I was born, and had continued to do so ever since; and I could not find in my heart to go to another. She commended the book I gave her, Dr. Preston, the Church's Marriage; quoted him saying 'twas inconvenient keeping out of a Fashion commonly used. I said the Time and Tide did circumscribe my Visit. She gave me a Dram of Black-Cherry Brandy, and gave me a lump of the Sugar that was in it. She wish'd me a good Journy. I pray'd God to keep her, and came away. . . .

Samuel Sewall, a prominent judge in colonial Massachusetts, recorded both the grief he experienced over the death of his wife, as well as his careful search for another, in his diary. (Painting by John Smibert, 1729. Courtesy of the Museum of Fine Arts, Boston. Bequest of William L. Barnard [by exchange] and the Emily L. Ainsley Fund.)

[2 November 1720]

. . . [W]ent again, and found Mrs. Alden there, who quickly went out. Gave her about 1/2 pound of Sugar Almonds, cost 3s. per £. Carried them on Monday. She seem'd pleas'd with them, ask'd what they cost. Spake of giving her a Hundred pounds per annum if I dy'd before her. Ask'd her what sum she would give me, if she should dy first? Said I would give her time to Consider of it. She said she heard as if I had given all to my Children by Deeds of Gift. I told her 'twas a mistake, Point-Judith was mine &c. That in England, I own'd, my Father's desire was that it should go to my eldest Son; 'twas 20£ per annum; she thought 'twas forty. I think when I seem'd to excuse pressing this, she seem'd to think twas best to speak of it; a long winter was coming on. Gave me a Glass or two of Canary.

[Friday, 4 November 1720]

. . . I ask'd Madam what fashioned Neck-lace I should present her with, she said, None at all. I ask'd her Whereabout we left off last time; mention'd what I had offer'd to give her; Ask'd her what She would give me; She said she could not Change her Condition: She had said so from the beginning; could not be so far from her Children, the Lecture. Quoted the Apostle Paul affirming that a single Life was better than a Married. I answer'd That was for the present Distress. Said she had not pleasure in things of that nature as formerly: I said, you are the fitter to make me a Wife. If she held in that mind, I must go home and bewail my Rashness in making more haste than good Speed. However, considering the Supper, I desired her to be within next Monday night, if we liv'd so long. Assented. She charg'd me with saying, that she must put away Juno [let him go from her service], if she came to me: I utterly deny'd it, it never came in my heart; yet she insisted upon it; saying it came in upon discourse about the Indian woman that obtained her Freedom this Court. About 10. I said I would not disturb the good orders of her House, and came away. . . .

[Monday, 7 November 1720]

. . . I went to Mad. Winthrop; found her rocking her little Katee in the Cradle. I excus'd my Coming so late (near Eight). She set me an arm'd Chair and Cusheon; and so the Cradle was between her arm'd Chair and mine. Gave her the remnant of my Almonds; she did not eat of them as before; but laid them away; I said I came to enquire whether she had alter'd her mind since Friday, or remained of the same mind still. She said, Thereabouts. I told her I loved her, and was so fond as to think that she loved me: She said had a great respect for me. I told her, I had made her an offer, without asking any advice; she had so many to advise with, that twas a hindrance. The Fire was come to one short Brand besides the Block, which Brand was set up in end; at last it fell to pieces, and no Recruit was made: She gave me a Glass of Wine. I think I repeated again that I would go home and bewail my Rashness in making more haste than good Speed. I would endeavour to contain myself, and not go on to sollicit her to do that which she could not Consent to. Took leave of her. As came down the steps she bid me have a Care. Treated me Courteously. Told her she had enter'd the 4th year of her Widowhood. I had given her the News-Letter before: I did not bid her draw off her Glove as sometime I had done. Her Dress was not so clean as sometime it had been. Jehovah jireh! ['The Lord will provide!' With this exclamation, Sewall gave up his courtship.]

[9 November 1720]

. . . Dine at Bro'r Stoddard's: were so kind as to enquire of me if they should invite M'm Winthrop; I answer'd No. . . .

[Soon after Sewall gave up his effort to court Mrs. Winthrop, he turned his attentions to Mrs. Mary Gibbs, a widow who lived in

Newton, Massachusetts.]

[Copy of a Letter to Mrs. Mary Gibbs, Widow, at Newtown, January 12th, 1721/22]

Madam, your Removal out of Town, and the Severity of the Winter, are the reason of my making you this Epistolary Visit. In times past (as I remember) you were minded that I should marry you, by giving you to your desirable Bridegroom. Some sense of this intended Respect abides with me still; and puts me upon enquiring whether you be willing that I should Marry you now, by becoming your Husband; Aged, and feeble, and exhausted as I am, your favourable Answer to this Enquiry, in a few Lines, the Candor of it will much oblige, Madam, your humble Serv't. . . .

S.S.

[Friday, 26 January 1721/22]

I rode to Newtown in the Coach, and visited Mrs. Gibbs. Spake of the proposals I had intimated per Mr. H. Gibbs; for her Sons to be bound to save me harmless as to her Administration; and to pay me £100. provided their Mother died before me: I to pay her £50. per annum during her Life, if I left her a Widow. She said 'twas hard, she knew not how to have her children bound to pay that Sum; she might dye in a little time. Mr. Cotton, whom she call'd, spake to the same purpose, spake of a Joynture. I said I was peremptory as to the indemnifying Bond; Offer'd to take up with that alone, and allow her £40. per annum; Scolly's Tenement yielded but £33., and then I made no question but that there must be a Deduction for Repairs. She said she would consider of it: I said, I would also Consider. Afterward she excus'd her speaking to me. I suppose she meant the word Hard. Carried her a pound of Glaz'd Almonds, and a Duz. Meers Cakes; Two bottles of Canary. Visited Mrs. Cotton, wish'd her Joy of her young daughter Elizabeth. Gave little Mary 2s. Had a very good Legg of Pork, and a Turkey for Dinner. Mrs. Gibbs help'd me on with my Coat at Coming away; and stood in the Front door till the Coach mov'd, then I pull'd off my Hat, and she Curtesied. I had moved to be published next Thorsday; to carry in our names to Col. Checkley. . . .

[29 March 1721/22]

Samuel Sewall, and Mrs. Mary Gibbs were joined together in Marriage by the Rev'd Mr. William Cooper.

Elizabeth Ashbridge (1713–1755)

Elizabeth Ashbridge was an indentured servant when she married Mr. Sullivan, a teacher who loved singing and dancing. As it turned out, he was an alcoholic and had trouble holding onto a job. Ashbridge grew depressed as they moved from town to town along the mid-Atlantic coast. Lonely and miserable, she took a trip to Pennsylvania to visit relatives who happened to be members of the Society of Friends (Quakers). She was impressed by their kindness and devotion and gradually overcame her earlier prejudice against the Friends, who were generally despised for their pacifism, enthusiasm, and strange customs (which included silent meetings, simple dress, and preaching by both men and women). Her conversion angered her husband, who demanded that she abandon her newly pious ways; but Ashbridge, steeled by her faith, demanded that he be the one to change. Excerpted from Elizabeth Ashbridge, Some Account of the Early Part of the Life of Elizabeth Ashbridge . . . *(Concord, New Hampshire, 1810), 21–35.*

I now hired to keep a school, and hearing of a place for my husband, I wrote, and desired him to come. . . . Before he reached me, he heard I was turned Quaker; at which he stamped, [unreadable] said, "I had rather have heard she was dead, well as I love her; for, if it be so, all my comfort is gone.["] He then came to me; it was after an absence of four months; I got up and said to him, "My dear, I am glad to see thee." At this, he flew into a great rage, exclaiming, 'The devil thee, thee, thee, don't thee me.' I endeavored, by every mild means, to pacify him; and, at length, got him fit to speak to my relations. As soon after this as we were alone, he said to me, "And so I see your Quaker relations have made you one;". . . . He said he would not stay amongst them; and having found a place to his mind, hired, and came directly back to fetch me, walking, in one afternoon, thirty miles to keep me from meeting the next day, which was first day. He took me, after resting this day, to the place where he had hired, and to lodgings he had engaged at the house of a churchwarden. This man was a bitter enemy of Friends, and did all he could to irritate my husband against them.

. . . When my husband and he used to be making their diversions and reviling, I sat in silence, though now and then an involuntary sigh broke from me; at which he would say, 'There, did not I tell you your wife was a Quaker, and she will become a preacher.' On such an occasion as this, my husband once came up to me, in a great rage, and shaking his hand over me, said, "You had better be hanged in that day." I was seized with horror, and again plunged into despair, which continued nearly three months. I was afraid that, by denying the Lord, the heavens would be shut against me. I walked much alone in the woods, and there, where no eye saw, nor ear heard me, lamented my miserable condition. . . .

. . . At length, when he and his friend thought themselves too weak to overset me, he went to the priest at Chester, to inquire what he could do with me. This man knew I was a member of the [Anglican] Church, for I had shown him my certificate. His advice was, to take me out of Pennsylvania, and settle in some place where there were no Quakers. My husband replied, he did not care where we went, if he could but restore me to my natural liveliness of temper. As for me, I had no resolution to oppose their proposals, nor much cared where I went. I seemed to have nothing to hope for. I daily expected to be made a victim of divine wrath, and was possessed with the idea that this would be by thunder.

When the time of removal came, I was not permitted to bid my relations farewell; and, as my husband was poor, and kept no horse, I was obliged to travel on foot. We came to Wilmington, 15 miles, and from thence to Philadelphia by water. Here we stopt at a tavern, where I became the spectacle and discourse of the company. My husband told them his wife had become a Quaker, and he designed if possible to find out a place where there were none. . . . [H]e told them that I had been a good dancer, but now he could get me neither to dance or sing. One of the company then started up, and said, "I'll fetch a fiddle, and we'll have a good dance;" a proposal with which my husband was pleased. When the fiddle was brought my husband came and said to me, "My dear, shake off that gloom, and let us have a civil dance; you would, now and then, when you were a good churchwoman, and that's better than a stiff Quaker." I had taken up the resolution not to comply with his request, whatever might be the consequence; this I let him know, though I durst say little, for fear of his choleric temper. He pulled me round the room, till the tears fell from my eyes, at the sight of which the musician stopt, and said, "I'll play no more; let your wife alone." There was a person in company that came from Freehold, in East Jersey, who said, "I see your wife's a Quaker, but if you'll take my advice you need not go so far as you intend; come and live with us; we'll soon cure her of her Quakerism, and we want a schoolmaster and schoolmistress too." He consented, and a happy turn it was for me, as will shortly be seen. . . .

In our way to Freehold, as we came to Stony Brook, my husband turned towards me, and tauntingly said, "Here's one of Satan's synagogues, don't you long to be in it; I hope to see you cured of your new religion." . . . After walking nearly a mile, we came to a house, which proved to be a sort of tavern. My husband called for some spirituous liquors, and I got some weakened cider mulled, which rendered me extremely sick; so that, after we were a little past the house, being too faint to proceed, I fell down.—"What's the matter now?" said my husband, "what, are you drunk? Where's your religion now?" He knew I was not drunk, and, at that time, I believ he pitied me, although he spoke in this manner. After I was a little recovered, we went on, and came to another tavern, where we lodged. The next day, . . . we met a man riding full speed, who, stopping, said to my husband, "Sir, are you a schoolmaster?" He answered, "Yes." "I am come," replied the stranger, "to tell you of two new schoolhouses, two miles apart, each of which wants a master." How this person came to hear of us, who arrived but the night before, I never knew. I was glad he was not called a Quaker, lest it should have been thought a plot by my husband, to whom I turned and said, "My dear, look on me with pity, if thou hast any affection left for me, which I hope thou hast, for I am not conscious of having done any thing to alienate it. Here is an opportunity to settle us both, and I am willing to do all in my power, towards getting an honest livelihood." After a short pause, he consented to go with the young man. . . .

. . . We took a room, in a friend's house, one mile from each school, and eight from the meetinghouse. I now deemed it proper to let my husband see I was determined to join with Friends. When first day came, I directed myself to him in this manner: "My dear, art thou willing to let me go to meeting?" He flew into a rage, and replied, "No you sha'n't." Speaking firmly, I told him, 'That, as a dutiful wife, I was ready to obey all his lawful commands; but, when they imposed upon my conscience, I could not obey him. I had already wronged myself, in having done it too long;

and though he was near to me, and, as a wife ought, I loved him; yet God, who was nearer than all the world to me, had made me sensible that this was the way in which I ought to go. I added, that this was no small cross to my own will; but I had given up my heart, and I trusted that He who called for it would enable me, for the remainder of my life, to keep it steadily devoted to his service; and I hoped I should not, on this account, make the worse wife.' I spoke, however, to no purpose; he continued inflexible.

I had now put my hand to the plough, and resolved not to draw back; I therefore went without leave. I expected he would immediately follow and force me back, but he did not. I called at the house of one of the neighbors, and, getting a girl to show me the way, I went on rejoicing, and praising God in my heart.

Thus, for some time, I had to go eight miles on foot to meeting, which I never thought hard. My husband had a horse, but he would not suffer me to ride on it; nor, when my shoes were worn out, would he let me have a new pair; but, though he hoped, on this account, to keep me from meeting, it did not hinder me:—I have tied them round with strings to keep them on.

Finding that all the means he had yet used could not alter my resolutions, he several times struck me with severe blows. I endeavored to bear all with patience, believing that the time would come when he would see I was in the right. Once he came up to me, took out his penknife, and said, "If you offer to go to meeting to-morrow, with this knife I'll cripple you, for you shall not be a Quaker." I made him no answer. In the morning I set out as usual; he did not attempt to harm me. Having despaired of recovering me himself, he fled for help to the priest, whom he told that I had been a very religious woman, in the way of the Church of England, of which I was a member, and had a good certificate from Long Island; that I was now bewitched, and had turned Quaker, which almost broke his heart. . . .

. . . [He] got the horse and set off to fetch me, arriving just as the meeting broke up. I got on horseback as quickly as possible, lest he should hear I had been speaking; he did hear of it nevertheless, and, as soon as we were in the woods, began with saying, "Why do you mean thus to make my life unhappy? What, could you not be a Quaker, without turning fool in this manner?" I answered in tears, "My dear, look on me with pity, if thou hast any; canst thou think that I, in the bloom of my days, would bear all that thou knowest of, and much that thou knowest not of, if I did not feel it my duty?" These words touched him, and he said, "Well, I'll e'en give you up; I see it wont avail to strive; if it be of God I cannot overthrow it; and, if of yourself, it will soon fall." I saw the tears stand in his eyes, at which I was overcome with joy, and began already to reap the fruits of my obedience. But my trials were not yet over. . . .

. . . I joined the society. My husband still went to no place of worship. One day he said to me, "I would go to meeting only I'm afraid I shall hear your clack, which I cannot bear." I used no persuasions. When meeting-time came, he got the horse, took me behind him, and went. For several months, if he saw me offer to rise, he went out; till one day I rose before he was aware, and then, as he afterwards owned, he was ashamed to do it.

From this time, he left off the practice, and never hindered me from going to meeting. Though he did not take up the cross, yet his judgment was convinced; and, sometimes, melting into tears, he would say to me, "My dear, I have seen the beauty there is in the truth, and that thou hast followed the right way, in which I pray God to preserve thee." I told him, that I hoped He who had given me strength would also favor him, "O," said he, "I cannot bear the reproach thou dost, to be called turn-coat, and become a laughing-stock to the world; but I'Il no longer hinder thee." This I considered a favor, and a little hope remained that my prayers, on his account, would he heard.

We lived in a small house by ourselves, which, though mean, and though we had little to put in it, our bed being no better than chaff, I was truly content. The only desires I had were for my own preservation, and to be blessed with the reformation of my husband. He was connected with a set of men whom he feared would make game of him, which indeed they already did; asking him when he designed to commence preacher, for they saw he intended to turn Quaker, and seemed to love his wife better since she became one, than before. They used to come to our house, and provoked him to sit up and drink with them, sometimes till near day, while I have been sorrowing in a stable. Once, as I sat in this condition, I heard him say to his company, "I can't bear any longer to afflict my poor wife in this manner; for, whatever you may think of her, I do believe she's a good woman." He then came to me and said: . . . 'Come in, my dear, God has given thee a deal of patience: I'll put an end to this practice.' This was the last time they sat up late at night.

My husband now thought that if he was in any place where it was not known he had been so bitter against friends, he could do better. I objected to this, fearing it would not be for his benefit. Frequently, in a broken and affectionate manner, he condemned his ill usage of me. I answered, that I hoped it had been for my good, and therefore desired he would not be afflicted on that account. . . . My advice was for him to stay where he was, I was afraid he would grow weaker in his good resolutions, if he removed.

All I could say would not avail. Hearing of a place at Bordentown, he went thither, but was not suited. He next removed to Mount Holly, where he settled. We had each of us a good school; we soon got our house pretty well furnished, and might have done very well. Nothing seemed wanting to complete my happiness, except the reformation of my husband, which I had much reason to doubt I should not see soon. It fell out according to my fears. He addicted himself much to drinking, and grew worse than before. . . . I murmured not; nor do I recollect that I ever uttered any harsh expressions except on one occasion. My husband coming home a little intoxicated, (a state in which he was very fractious) and finding me at work by a candle, he put it out, fetching me, at the same time, a box on the ear, and saying, 'You don't earn your light.' At this unkind usage, which I had not been used to for the last two years, I was somewhat angry, and said . . . 'Thou art a vile man.' He struck me again; but my anger had cooled, and I received the blow without so much as a word in return. This also displeased him and he went on in a distracted-like manner, uttering such expressions of despair as, he believed he was predestined to damnation, and he did not care how soon God struck him dead. I said very little, till, at length, in the bitterness of my soul, I broke out into these expressions, 'Lord, look down on my afflictions, and deliver me by some means or other.' My prayer was granted, but in such a manner that I thought it would have killed me. He went to Burlington, where he got drunk, and enlisted to go as a common soldier to Cuba, in the year 1740. I had drunk many bitter cups, but this seemed the bitterest of them all. A thousand times I blamed myself for making such a request, which I was afraid had displeased God, who had, in displeasure, granted it for my punishment.

I have since had cause to believe that he was benefitted by his rash act, as, in the army, he did what he could not at home; he suffered for the testimony of truth. When they came to prepare for an engagement, he refused to fight; he was whipt, and brought before the general, who asked him, why he enlisted if he would not fight. 'I did it,' said he, 'in a drunken frolic, when the devil had the better of me; but now my judgment is convinced I ought not to fight, neither will I, whatever I suffer. I have but one life, and you may take that if you please, for I'll never take up arms.' He adhered to his resolution. By their cruel usage of him in consequence, he was so much disabled that the General sent him to Chelsea Hospital, near London. In nine months afterwards he died at this place, and I hope made a good end.

Questions

1. *What ambitions did Sewall and Ashbridge bring to courtship and marriage? Did their spouses or potential spouses understand their ambitions? share them?*
2. *Did Puritanism make Katherine Winthrop blunt, or did age and experience? Did Quakerism turn Elizabeth Ashbridge against her husband, or Was it discontent with a migratory life? Did religion shape marriage more than personality and circumstance?*
3. *Judging by the stories, what role did romantic love play in courtship and marriage?*

FURTHER READING

Most histories of marriage in eighteenth-century America cover marriages of a specific faith or region. See Edmund S. Morgan, The Puritan Family: Religion and Domestic Relations in Seventeenth-Century New England, rev. ed. *(Westport, Connecticut 1966); John Demos,* A Little Commonwealth: Family Life in Plymouth Colony *(New York, 1970); Daniel Blake Smith,* Inside the Great House: Planter Family Life in Eighteenth-Century Chesapeake Society *(Ithaca, 1980); Joan M. Jensen,* Loosening the Bonds: Mid-Atlantic Farm Women, 1750–1850 *(New Haven, 1986); and Barry Levy,* Quakers and the American Family: British Settlement in the Delaware Valley *(New York, 1988). An exception is Marylynn Salmon,* Women and the Law of Property in Early America *(Chapel Hill, 1986).*

The Role of Religion in the Coming of the Revolution

Richard D. Shiels

Introduction

The American Revolution occurred at a time in which nearly all white Americans considered themselves Christians, clergy held high status positions in society, churches were among the only communal institutions and pulpits had little competition as the source of public information and indoctrination. Official church membership was lower than in other periods and yet the influence of religion was pervasive. Religious issues and affiliations often affected political developments. What was the role of religion in the coming of the Revolution?

Three answers will be considered in this chapter. First, political issues with religious implications were among the points at issue between England and the colonies. Second, a person's allegiance to a particular religious community may have influenced his or her position on whether to support or oppose the revolutionary struggle against Great Britain. And third, the struggle seems to have been understood in spiritual terms by many colonists, regardless of their specific religious orientation.

At least two explicitly religious controversies contributed to the alienation of Britain from its colonies. For many years, Anglicans (members of the Church of England) had tried to establish a bishop in the colonies. Whatever the Anglican motives, Dissenters (those who belonged to some other Protestant church) considered this a blatant effort to increase the power of the king, since the king was the head of the Anglican Church. Then in 1774, Parliament passed the Quebec Act, and the second controversy began. The Quebec Act provided government for the colony of Canada, which England had recently taken from France; it also established the Roman Catholic Church as the official church in Quebec. The

Quebec Act changed little—since the French colonies in Quebec were already Roman Catholic—but it fed the long-standing suspicions of English Protestants, who had an abiding fear of Catholicism. The bishop controversy and the Quebec Act were two of many issues and incidents, starting with a series of taxation measures, such as the Stamp Act and Townshend duties, that drove England and its colonies apart.

American Christians were on all sides in this war: some were "Whigs" (the name given to those who supported independence), others "Tories" or "Loyalists," and still others were in the middle. None of the churches in colonial America was sufficiently centralized to commit its members to one side or the other. The leaders of the Anglican Church, officially called the Church of England, were generally Tories. This position is not surprising given that the king himself appointed the highest officers of the Anglican Church and that every Anglican priest was required to pray for the king in public worship. Moreover, the Anglican Church imposed a hierarchy upon its members and expected a deferential obedience from them. Perhaps what is surprising is that large numbers of Anglican laymen defied their priests and supported independence.

Quakers were also associated with loyalism in the public mind, but that judgment was not fair. Quakers (and also the Amish, the Mennonites, and the Dunkers) were pacifists, whose religion discouraged them from participation in any war. Baptists were a diverse group with no central hierarchy, and the result was that Baptists divided over the war. Baptist opposition to the values of an elite culture may have driven them to be democratic in some ways but their status as a minority may have caused them to fear majority rule. Congregationalists and Presbyterians were overwhelmingly Whig. In fact, so many Congregational and Presbyterian clergy were visible Whig spokesmen that, at least in the northern colonies, they were called "The Black Regiment." These were the predominant religious groups at the time; other groups could claim only small percentages of the population.

Religious ideas and affiliation were only two of the factors that determined any individual's stance on the war, of course. Further, even among those clergy and laymen who supported independence, the ideas they used to make sense of the issues were varied. The official reasons for resisting the Stamp Act, Townshend Duties, and other British actions are preserved in documents such as the Declaration of the Stamp Act Congress and the Declaration of Independence. These documents reveal an ideology—that is, a set of ideas about government, society, and human nature—that a line of British thinkers (called the "Whigs" in Britain) had developed over more than a century. Whig ideology was well-known to the educated American elite but may not have been familiar to every colonist. What was well-known to nearly every white colonist (perhaps not to all slaves or Native Americans) were the stories and the teachings found in the Christian scriptures and the ideas taught in various Protestant churches.

The ideas that Whig clergymen preached reflected their religious heritage as well as Whig ideology. The central concept of liberty was both a religious and a political term. The Reverend Jonathan Mayhew was typical, for instance, when he wrote "where the Spirit of the Lord is, there is Liberty." Similarly, the notion that England was corrupt and America must resist moral contamination drew upon centuries of preaching as well as generations of political controversies. The ideal of the "virtuous citizen" could be found in both the scriptures and the political writing of English Whigs. The concept of a social compact, associated with Whig theorist John Locke, was similar to the Puritan doctrine of the covenant.

Perhaps no simple summary of the role of religion in the coming of the Revolution can be made, and yet religion clearly had a role. Religious people were not united on one side or the other, and yet nearly everyone on both sides was influenced by religion. Revolutionary ideas clearly drew upon a long-standing political tradition, yet many Americans found similar ideas in their religious upbringing.

Historians Disagree

In the selections that follow, historians of American religion disagree over the role of religion in the coming of the Revolution. In part the disagreement results from looking at different groups of Christians and even different geographical areas. Residents of New England were more likely to support independence by the mid-1770s than were residents of other colonies. New England's Congregational clergy have been studied more thoroughly than the leadership of any other region or denomination. Moreover, published sermons are much more accessible to historians than those that remained unpublished—and it was sermons delivered on political occasions in New England that were most likely to be published. As you read, take note of various groups of Christians and where each stood on the issues of the day.

The Clergy, the People, and the Patriot Cause

Historian Patricia U. Bonomi finds religion central to everyday life in colonial America and an important factor in the coming of the Revolution. In the following excerpt , Bonomi focuses upon the contribution of clergy in the Congregational, Presbyterian, and Anglican churches. Note her use of the Pastoral Letter from the Synod of Philadelphia and New York and of the official efforts of William Tennent and others to recruit the Carolina backcountry to the Patriot cause. The second excerpt in this chapter uses some of the same material but draws very different conclusions. Taken from Paul U. Bonomi, Under the Cope of Heaven: Religion, Society, and Politics in Colonial America *(New York, 1986), 3–5, 209–14, 216.*

The skylines of our eastern cities in, say, 1760 were in their way just as striking as they are now, perhaps more so. But what drew the eye then, and gave the horizon its definition, was a very different sort of edifice from those that mark it today—not skyscrapers but church spires—and beneath that contrast lies a fundamental shift in the spiritual perspective of the American population during the more than two centuries that have intervened. The seaboard cities of colonial America, though relatively small, were amply supplied with places of worship. You walked no distance at all, in any of them, without passing a meetinghouse, and you were never beyond earshot of church bells. The sights and sounds of today's cities are not primarily symbolic of religion. But in eighteenth-century America—in city, village, and countryside—the idiom of religion penetrated all discourse, underlay all thought, marked all observances, gave meaning to every public and private crisis. . . .

[S]ermons, devotional writings, catechisms, pious legends, and theological treatises formed by far the biggest category of printed matter in colonial America. Up to 1765 more literature of this sort was published than were writings on political science, history, and law combined, and even during the Revolutionary era devotional works comprised the largest single classification. Moreover, this reflected the reading of all ranks. Religious books dominated the libraries of such southern gentlemen as Edmund Berkeley, William Fitzhugh, Richard Lee II, and many others. The Pennsylvania Quaker James Logan owned thirty versions of the Bible. Among commoner readers the variety may not have been so great, but the degree of specialization was even more striking. It is true that by the time of the Revolution there was a considerable awareness in America of the writings of British libertarian political theorists. Nevertheless, when one farmer who had fought at Concord Bridge was asked years later whether he was defending the ideas of such liberal writers, he declared that for his part he had never heard of Locke or Sydney, his reading having been limited to the Bible, the Catechism, Watts's Psalms and Hymns, and the Almanac. . . .

When in December 1775 the Continental Congress sought to persuade the alienated Carolina Regulators to join the patriot cause, it turned to the Presbyterian clergy for help. "The education of most of these men [the Regulators] have been religious," observed the North Carolina delegation. Since they "look to their Spiritual pastors with great respect . . . truths from their mouths come with redoubled influence" upon the Regulators' minds. Clearly it was not only in New England that clergymen molded political opinion by discussing public issues from the sacred desk. In all parts of America preachers declaimed against absolutism and episcopacy until the people "fancied they saw civil and religious Tyranny advancing with hasty Strides." As Ambrose Serle informed the Earl of Dartmouth from New York City in 1777, "your Lordship can scarcely conceive what Fury the Discourses of some mad Preachers have created in this Country."

Patriots never doubted the influence of the clergy in forming public opinion, generally agreeing with John Adams that instilling high principles in civil as well as religious conduct was fully compatible with spiritual leadership. New Englanders, of course, were accustomed to hearing election sermons, artillery-day sermons, and solemn orations from the pulpit during fast and thanksgiving days, many remarkably political in tone. Preachers in colonies outside New England . . ., also used their pulpits as drums for politics. John Adams was delighted to discover in 1775 that the Philadelphia ministers "thunder and lighten every sabbath" against British oppression. When the House of Burgesses appointed a day of fasting and prayer in 1774 to rouse Virginians against the closing of Boston's port, Thomas Jefferson recorded that the pulpit oratory ran "like a shock of electricity" through the whole colony. Landon Carter's minister "did very Pathetically exhort the people in his sermon to support their Liberties . . . and in the room of God save the king he cried out God Preserve all the Just rights and Liberties of America."

Nor was the ministers' influence limited to sermons. The Reverend John Elder of Paxton, Pennsylvania—still politically active at the age of sixty-eight—sat on his county's committee of correspondence, as did many middle-colony preachers. The Synod of New York and Philadelphia sent a pastoral letter to be read from all Presbyterian pulpits on June 29, 1775. It urged elders to maintain discipline over their congregations, parishioners to repent of their sins in order to deserve God's mercy in the coming conflict, and unity, fasting, and prayer. The letter's influence extended at least as far as Virginia, where it was reprinted in the *Virginia Gazette*. . . . Anglican clergymen in the southern colonies were far more likely to take the patriot side than were their northern colleagues. Many of them served actively on committees of safety and as chaplains, officers, and even common soldiers in the army. South Carolina was distinguished for the number of ardent patriots among its Anglican clergy, three-quarters of whom supported the Revolution. A similar proportion of the Anglican rectors resident in Virginia in 1776 favored the American cause.

The New England clergy's opposition to British measures is well documented. The quiet efforts of Dr. Samuel Cooper of Brattle Street Church and the more public patriotism of Charles Chauncy added significantly to resistance activity in Boston. The Reverend Jonas Clark of Lexington was the Revolutionary scribe of his town, writing up petitions and instructions on political subjects throughout the era and making his house a center for political gatherings. Two fiery young Congregational ministers converted entire towns in western Massachusetts from tory to whig by haranguing the people in town meeting and Sabbath convocation alike. Many New England parsons served on committees of correspondence and safety, and it was alleged that some threatened to withhold communion from loyalists. The Reverend John Cleaveland of Ipswich is said to have preached all the young men of his congregation into the army and then, accompanied by four of his sons, marched off himself to war.

Along the frontier preachers played an especially critical role as missionaries for the Revolution, carrying the whig gospel to hamlets and homesteads beyond the reach of newspapers and committees of correspondence. The Continental Congress subsidized a four-month tour by two Presbyterian ministers to the North Carolina backcountry in an effort to woo settlers to the patriot side. John Witherspoon addressed a special plea to recently arrived Scots, many of whom were settled on the frontier, to support the Revolution. The Congress also asked other ministers in western regions to "use their pastoral Influence to work a change in the disposition of the people. . . . [who were] not accustomed to speculate politically." They were especially gratified when the Pennsylvania Lutheran and Reformed ministers agreed to write pastoral letters "to set their Brethren in North Carolina right."

The Reverend William Tennent and William Henry Drayton of the provincial congress were dispatched by the South Carolina Committee of Safety in 1775 to persuade that colony's backsettlers to sign the Association [committing them to resist British measures]. Tennent enlisted the aid of Presbyterian and German preachers in the region and frequently preached two- or even three-hour sermons to their assembled congregations. Sometimes he succeeded spectacularly, as at Congaree where he converted the people from loyalism to the Association and then saw them form into volunteer companies. Philip Fithian toured the Virginia-Pennsylvania frontier in 1775 with considerable success. He preached mainly to New Light Presbyterians, noting that they "thronged" into the church at Sunbury, Pennsylvania on the continental fast day. . . .

For all their involvement in secular politics, the patriot clergy influenced public opinion primarily through preaching. The sermon literature of the 1770s—north and south, evangelical and rationalist—shows a striking uniformity of language and belief. Nearly every sermon addressed the political crisis, and did so in the idiom of the radical whigs. Preachers in all sections agreed that Great Britain was falling prey to vice and corruption. A power hungry ministry and venal Parliament, declared the Massachusetts New Light Samuel Langdon, had promulgated "new invented maxims of policy" that threatened to reduce the colonists to slavery. The most wicked maxim, commented on with remarkable consistency everywhere, was Parliament's assertion that it could bind the colonies "in all cases whatsoever." Such a claim, according to the Baptist preacher Samuel Stillman, denied that government was a compact based on the consent of the people as explained by the "justly celebrated Mr. Locke." The Virginia Anglican rector, David Griffith, thought the notion that Americans were represented in Parliament to be as absurd as the doctrine of transubstantiation.

A few preachers apologized for the excessive political content of their sermons, but most simply pointed to the widely accepted belief that human liberty was of divine origin. Since "liberty, traced to her true source, is of heavenly extraction," declared the Anglican Jacob Duché of Philadelphia, "we are bound to stand fast in our civil as well as our spiritual freedom." The New England Calvinist Nathaniel Whitaker, citing Richard Price on civil liberty and Locke on natural law, concluded that "liberty is the cause of God and truth"; thus submission to British claims "to bind us in all cases whatsoever" would be sinful in the eyes of God. Griffith of Virginia proclaimed in almost identical words that "the cause of truth and justice is the cause of God." Could Americans faced with British oppression "conform to the once exploded, but again courtly, doctrines of passive obedience and non-resistance"? asked the Massachusetts Congregationalist William Gordon.

Another theme was that "self-preservation is an instinct by God implanted in our nature." The Reverend John Carmichael, Presbyterian of Pennsylvania, noted that God provided plants and animals with natural defenses against their enemies. Humankind's special gift was reason, which enabled men and women to study God's word as a guide to earthly behavior. Scripture, always in harmony with "the great law of nature," taught that when rulers "lust for absolute dominion" and break covenants the people must resist in the interest of self-preservation. The Reverend Simeon Howard of Massachusetts sought in an Artillery Day sermon to demonstrate that "Self-preservation is one of the strongest, and a universal principle of the human mind."

Most preachers also invoked some form of the jeremiad [a traditional form of sermon calling for repentance]. The Anglican Duché exhorted his auditors to "Banish the Syren LUXURY. . . . Call upon honest industry, sober frugality, [and] simplicity of manners" with the same emotion that the New Light Samuel Langdon worked up against "profaneness, intemperance, unchastity, the love of pleasure, fraud, avarice, and other vices." The Charleston Baptist Oliver Hart and the Boston rationalist Charles Chauncy, with equal passion, warned the colonists to renounce sin if they would gain God's favor in the war against England. . . .

Above all, however, the familiar injunctions against passive obedience to wicked rulers supplied a common language of opposition. In a sermon to the provincial congress of Georgia the Reverend John Zubly hoped that the colonies and mother country could be reconciled, but never under the "odious doctrines [of] unlimited passive obedience and non-resistance." Rector David Griffith's sermon, *Passive Obedience Considered,* proved so acceptable to the General Convention of Virginia that it was ordered to be printed. Comparing the colonies to ancient Israel, Griffith asserted that God did not expect the Israelites in Egypt "to pay a blind obedience" to all of Pharoah's ordinances. Nor did Paul teach absolute and unlimited submission. There were times when a corrupt government made resistance not only justifiable but "a necessary duty." . . .

Once blood had actually been shed, the patriot sermon took on additional features, as the familiar lessons and allegories from Scripture—especially the Old Testament—supplied a common idiom and interpretation to events. Ministers everywhere compared America's break from Britain with the division of the Jewish tribes under the tyrant Rehoboam, or with the misunderstanding between Canaanites and Gileadites. The slavery from which the colonists were being delivered was of course like that of the Israelites under Pharoah, and as early as 1776 George Washington was cast as Moses. In sermons to militia units preachers recalled how Jonathan and his armor bearer put the mighty Philistine host to flight. And perhaps the most attractive analogy of all was that of David and Goliath.

Since the colonials could see themselves as simply responding to British aggression, especially after Lexington and Concord, the morality of a defensive war was widely emphasized as a justification for taking up arms. As a Presbyterian preacher told his congregation at Chester County, Pennsylvania, "a defensive war in a just cause [was] sinless." And meanwhile, the "appeal to heaven" for God's assistance in a righteous cause sounded from pulpits throughout the land. He might interpose with miracles, as with the drowning of Pharoah's army in the Red Sea. Or he might strike armies with panic, so that "a thousand shall put ten thousand to flight." In any case, as John Locke put it, in a conflict which no earthly judge could settle "the appeal lies only to Heaven." Trenchard and Gordon's Cato [a character based on ancient Rome who appeared in much of the Whig literature] had similarly declared that "when there is no stated Judge upon Earth, we must have Recourse to Heaven." So prevalent was the belief that God would award victory to a people fighting for justice in his name that a number of colonial regiments marched into battle bearing flags inscribed with "AN APPEAL TO HEAVEN."

And at last when it was all over, the Revolution could be recognized as a "principal Link . . . [in the] grand chain of Providence" ushering in the golden age of the church. Evidence of God's special care was everywhere, most notably in the sublime person of George Washington—"a general destined by Heaven for just such a period, country, and cause as ours!" Washington was a Moses; he was also "the Joshua of the day and admiration of the age"; he had been called by the Most High to "save his country from the chains of slavery."

Religious doctrine and rhetoric, then, contributed in a fundamental way to the coming of the American Revolution and to its final success. In an age of political moderation, when many colonials hesitated at the brink of civil war, patriotic clergymen told their congregations that failure to oppose British tyranny would be an offense in the sight of Heaven. Where political theory advised caution, religious doctrine demanded action. By turning colonial resistance into a righteous cause, and by crying the message to all ranks in all parts of the colonies, ministers did the work of secular radicalism and did it better: they resolved doubts, overcame inertia, fired the heart, and exalted the soul.

The Secular Nature of the Revolution

Jon Butler finds the role that religion played in the Revolution much smaller than does Patricia U. Bonomi. Unlike most historians who write on the subject, Butler is careful to define what he means by "religion." "Throughout this book," he writes, "religion is taken to mean belief in and resort to superhuman powers, sometimes beings, that determine the course of natural and human events." Using his definition, you might ask not only what role religion played in the Revolution but whether it can be said that the Revolution was a religious movement. Excerpted from Jon Butler, Awash in a Sea of Faith: Christianizing the American People *(Cambridge, Massachusetts, 1990), 195–206.*

At its heart, the Revolution was a profoundly secular event. . . . The Declaration of Independence provides clear-cut evidence of the secondary role that religion and Christianity played in creating the revolutionary struggle. The religious world invoked in the Declaration was a deist's world, at best; at worst, the Declaration was simply indifferent to religious concerns and issues. The god who appears in the Declaration is the god of nature rather than the God of Christian scriptural revelation, as when Jefferson wrote of "the laws of nature and nature's God." In other allusive appearances this god emerged as "the Supreme Judge of the world," to whom Americans would appeal "for the rectitude of our intentions," and as "Divine Providence," on whom they would rely for protection. Elsewhere, all was secular: taxes, troops, tyranny. Despite its length, not a single religious issue, including the dispute over the Anglican bishop, found a place in the "history of repeated injuries and usurpations" that closed the Declaration and that established the Revolution's most authoritative list of offensive British actions in America.

Yet the Declaration's remarkable silence on religious issues should not obscure the importance of religion in secondary issues. . . . The Anglican-Dissenter contest over a bishop for America escalated transatlantic political tensions for years. The controversy first appeared in the 1710s, abated until it flared in the 1750s, then flared again in 1761 when Anglicans purchased an extraordinarily large home in Cambridge, Massachusetts, which Dissenters gleefully named the "bishop's palace." After 1763 the Dissenters' argument was joined to the colonial protests against taxes and other English efforts at imperial centralization, and it climaxed in protests against the Quebec Act of 1774, through which the English government recognized the Catholic church in the conquered French territories of Canada.

Dissenters consistently linked the bishop question to the English debate on tyranny, a sensitive term in a society that had beheaded one monarch in 1649, overthrown a second in 1688, and defeated a pretender in 1745. Jonathan Mayhew not accidentally chose the 101st anniversary of Charles I's execution to excoriate the Anglicans for demanding a colonial bishop. . . . Mayhew used the word *tyranny* incessantly, sometimes four or five times on a single page. . . .

The charge of tyranny in the bishop controversy evoked a constellation of images important to the Revolution. Tyranny stemmed from conspiracies that sought to veil their participants' evil motives. The SPG [Society for the Propagation of the Gospel, an Anglican missionary society with agents in America] was thought to lead the cabal. . . . SPG ministers were agents of repression. How else to explain their half century of whining about bishops?

The Quebec Act called forth another image: secret Catholicism, associated with every attempt at tyranny in England since the 1640s. . . . Paul Revere expressed those fears in a superbly crafted engraving in 1774. . . . In it the Devil, Anglican bishops, and England's most notorious politicians, Lord North and Lord Bute, form a cabal to effect their ultimate and long secret objective—Catholicizing the American colonies.

Protestant Christianity also reinforced the Whig political convictions that lay behind early revolutionary rhetoric. Whig sentiment extended throughout the colonies, where it was descended from eighteenth-century English political culture generally rather than from more narrow sources in revivalism or New England Calvinism. Religious support for the Whigs was thus not limited to New England or to evangelical Dissenters. . . .

Political Whiggism appeared in colonial sermons in two especially important ways. First, the sermons reinforced the emphasis on virtue and morality that pervaded secular political discussion in eighteenth-century colonial and English society. . . . Listeners and clergy together, in a vast number of denominations and congregations, *assumed* that liberty proceeded from a virtuous citizenry. It was the ministers' duty to make sure that this virtue was a Christian virtue, of course. . . .

Systematic public discussion of virtue and morality came more frequently from ordained Christian clergymen than from any other single source. Especially outside New England, morality served as the most common focus of sermons, and even New England churchgoers heard more than doctrine. . . . The clerics' constant emphasis on virtue, responsibility, and, especially, morality helped make sense of revolutionary rhetoric about corruption and evil among English politicians and society. . . .

Second, as protest escalated, some ministers discussed Revolution politics specifically. This could occur in Sabbath sermons. But especially in New England it more often happened during midweek fast day and thanksgiving sermons. . . . Ministerial support for the Revolution extended beyond New England. Despite some probable exaggeration in his report that Philadelphia ministers "thunder and lighten every sabbath" with anti-British sermons, John Adams was not alone in remarking on the local clergy's political involvement. Patricia Bonomi notes Jefferson's comment that in Anglican Virginia "pulpit oratory ran 'like a shock of electricity' through the whole colony" and that "Landon Carter's minister 'did very Pathetically exhort the people in his sermons to support their Liberties . . . and in the room of God save the king he cried out God Preserve all the Just rights and Liberties of America.'"

Both ironically (in view of the Revolution's frequent appeals to liberty) and surprisingly (in view of historians' recent emphasis on evangelical Dissent), the most common denominator among pro-Revolution ministers was a state church pulpit. Middle colony Presbyterians and Virginia Baptists formed the most important exception to this pattern, and Anglican loyalism, furthermore, demonstrated that a state church pulpit did not guarantee revolutionary support. Yet tax-supported Anglican ministers also supported the Revolution in significant numbers. Though virtually all Anglican ministers in the northern and middle colonies . . . became loyalists, a third of the Anglican clergy in Virginia and Maryland, where Anglicans held tax-supported pulpits, backed the Revolution. . . . In most colonies the Revolution pitted a colonial political establishment against an expanding imperial administration, and the colonial clergy often owed more to the former than to the latter, even if the clergy involved were Anglican. . . .

Most colonial ministers, however, remained silent about politics during the upheavals of the 1760s and 1770s. It has always been known that this was true of Pennsylvania's German Reformed and Lutheran clergymen. . . . For the German Reformed Coetus [or Synod], for example, the Revolution threatened both Christianity and America. . . . In 1777 the Coetus . . . described the Revolution as a "sad war" that had uprooted "many a praiseworthy observance . . . especially in regard to the keeping of the Sabbath Day and Christian exercises in the families at home."

Clergymen in English denominations shared this fear of revolutionary upheaval. Most members of the Synod of Philadelphia refrained from public comment on the impending conflict. . . . [Further,] most Presbyterian ministers simply did not participate in revolutionary politics. . . . In a pastoral letter to its congregations in 1775, the synod acknowledged that "it is well known . . . that we have not been instrumental in inflaming the minds of the people, or urging them to acts of violence and disorder." . . . The ministers conceived of the contest as a "civil war," a phrase they used three times in their epistle. . . . In their 1775 letter the members of the Philadelphia synod ultimately both instructed the Presbyterian laity on loyalty to George III and voiced support for Whig political principles. . . .

The Presbyterian statement suggested why loyalism so frequently had a dual religious foundation and extended beyond the ranks of Church of England ministers. . . . One reason concerned the traditional emphasis on authority and obedience in colonial preaching. Loyalist clergymen could be found in every colonial denomination: most Anglican clergymen; various New England Congregationalists, . . . a Philadelphia Baptist leader, . . . and a Swiss Presbyterian in Savannah. . . . These individuals could not repudiate the sermons and catechetical lessons that they had been propounding for years. As protest turned to independence, previously abstract fears that the flight from authority and obedience would turn everything upside down became a reality. . . .

A second reason centered on religious discrimination. The political elites who guided the Revolution in so many places also had frequently mistreated religious minorities in earlier times. Scottish and Scotch-Irish Presbyterians in North and South Carolina, English Baptists in Virginia, German Lutheran and German Reformed groups in Pennsylvania, and Anglicans in New England, together with small groups such as Wesley's Methodists or a sect like the Sandemanians of Rhode Island, had all experienced religious and political discrimination. . . . Most found the patriots' anti-Parliament protests ironic and even hypocritical. . . .

The experience of William Tennent III, a Presbyterian minister in South Carolina and a son of New Jersey's charismatic William Tennent, Jr., revealed the difficulties of linking religion to the Revolution. . . . In August 1775, the South Carolina Committee of Correspondence sent Tennent and William Drayton, a Baptist layman, to the Carolina backcountry to convince former Regulators to support revolutionary agitation. Backcountry settlers remained unmoved. They told Tennent: "No man from Charleston can speak the truth, and . . . all the papers are full of lies." Tennent's techniques demonstrated his willingness to use religion to affect politics. Sometimes he preached, after which Drayton "harangued" on politics. Sometimes Tennent preached and then did the haranguing himself. On August 20 he "spoke to the people on the state of America," but two Baptist ministers opposed him, and his listeners backed away from supporting the committee. Two weeks later, better prepared and less naive, Tennent arranged a visit by a Baptist minister from Charleston, Oliver Hart, but still apparently met with only mixed success.

Questions

1. *How is it possible for historians Bonomi and Butler to disagree? How much do they disagree? Do they disagree over facts or interpretation? Which one convinces you?*
2. *How do Bonomi and Butler use some of the same material to support conflicting conclusions?*
3. *Was the Revolution a religious movement, at least for some Americans?*

American Colonists Speak for Themselves

In the eleven years between the Stamp Act and the Declaration of Independence, American colonists tried to understand the events that were alienating them from England. Most were relieved when the Stamp Act was repealed and allowed themselves to believe that there would be no more difficulty. With subsequent acts (the Townshend Duties, the Tea Act, the "Intolerable Acts," and others) many came slowly to the conclusion that separation from England was necessary. Most were very slow to blame the king: well into the 1770s, they believed instead that officials such as Lord Bute, Lord Grenville, Lord Mansfield, Lord North, and others were deceiving the king and plotting against America. They drew upon all of the ideas at their disposal—religious ideas and Whig ideology as well—to interpret the developments of their day. As you read the documents that follow, notice not only how colonists disagreed among themselves but also how slowly some of those who would support independence came to that position. Note too that some used religious ideas to make a political argument and others used the political developments of their day to win support for their own religious agenda.

A Biblical View of the Stamp Act

Americans responded to the Stamp Act on both an official and a popular level. The official response came from the Stamp Act Congress, a meeting of educated men who sent their objections to London in writing. The popular response took the form of riots and rallies by the "Sons of Liberty," a group that was less likely to include the educated elite. In the selection that follows, a speaker whose identity is no longer known addresses the Sons of Liberty near the Liberty Tree in Boston. The events of the day are interpreted in biblical terms drawing upon the symbolic verses of the Book of Revelation. Both the use of biblical prophecy and the identification of Lords Bute and Grenville were commonplace in these years. This selection is from A Discourse, Addressed to the Sons of Liberty, At a solemn Assembly, near Liberty-Tree, in Boston, February 14, 1766 (Providence, 1766), 3–6.

THE sacred books of scripture, although principally intended to direct us in our spiritual concerns, are not wanting in the best admonitions about our temporals: The inspired writers have therein foretold the great waste that would be committed in the world by monsters in the shape of men, who under a pretence of governing and protecting mankind, have enslaved them; and I think the wolves of our days are so plainly pointed out to us in the 13th chapter of the book of *Revelations*, that I crave your attention whilst I hold up the picture to you, and leave you to judge of the likeness. . . .

"AND I stood upon the sand of the sea, and saw a beast rise up out of the sea, having seven heads and ten horns, and upon his horns ten crowns." This description, my brethren, sets before our eyes the wicked Earl of *Bute*, the first contriver of all our miseries; you may see upon the map a little despicable isle in the sea, West of *Scotland*, from whence he rose, his seven heads are so many capital posts or offices, which he successively held and executed, and the crowns upon them denote that he was royally appointed to them. . . .

IN verse the 11th, it is thus written:—"And I beheld another beast coming up out of the earth; and he had two horns like a lamb, and he spake as a dragon."—Verse 12th.—"And he exerciseth all the power of the first beast before him." I dare say that there is not a man amongst you but stands ready to cry out here is *George Grenville,* the enemy of GOD and of all good men, who came to power with all the outward marks of meekness, but as soon as he was possest of it, he spake like a dragon, as he is, and said all his Majesty's good subjects of *North-America* were *rebels*; yes, my brethren, the *beast* called a people *rebels* . . . [I]f he wants to find *rebels*, let him look back upon his own family.

BUT let us examine a little further what are the exploits of this beast, and what was he to do:—Verse 16th—"And he causeth all, both small and great, rich and poor, free and bond to receive a mark in their right hand.—17th—And that no man might buy or sell, save he that had the mark." Here, my beloved brethren, he brings forth the *Stamp-Act*, that mark of slavery, the perfection and sum total of all his wickedness; he has ordained that none amongst us shall buy or sell a piece of land, except his mark be put upon the deed, and when it is delivered, the hands of both buyer and seller must infallibly become branded with the odious impression: I beseech you then to beware as good christians and lovers of your country, lest by touching any paper with this impression, you receive the mark of the *beast*, and become infamous in your country throughout all generations.—But thanks to GOD, our good King, in his gracious speech from the throne, did not call us *rebels*, and hath dismissed this monster from his service, so that we have nothing more to fear from him.

A Clergyman's Understanding of Liberty

Jonathan Mayhew (1720–1766), a Harvard-educated Congregational minister in Boston, was one of the first to preach against the Stamp Act. In his mind, the Stamp Act and the proposal for a colonial bishop were two parts of a plot—the Stamp Act would give the government control over newspapers while a colonial bishop would give it control over churches. The following excerpt reveals how his religious training and his exposure to Whig ideology combined to shape his reaction to the Stamp Act in November 1765 and to its repeal in June 1766. Taken from Jonathan Mayhew, The Snare Broken: A Thanksgiving-Discourse. . . . *Occasioned by the Repeal of the Stamp-Act (Boston, 1766), 35–37.*

Having been initiated, in youth, in the doctrines of civil liberty, as they were taught by such men as Plato, Demosthenes, Cicero and other renowned persons among the ancients; and such as Sidney and Milton, Locke and Hoadley, among the moderns; I liked them; they seemed rational. Having, earlier still learnt from the holy scriptures, that wise, brave and vertuous men were always friends to liberty; that God gave the Israelites a King [or absolute Monarch] in his anger, because they had not sense and virtue enough to like a free common-wealth, and to have himself for their King; that the Son of God came down from heaven, to make us "free indeed"; and that "where the Spirit of the Lord is, there is liberty"; this made me conclude, that freedom was a great blessing. Having, also, from my childhood up, by the kind providence of my God, and the tender care of a good parent now at rest with Him, been educated to the love of liberty, tho' not of licentiousness; which chaste and virtuous passion was still increased in me, as I advanced towards, and into, manhood; I would not, I cannot now, tho' past middle age, relinquish the fair object of my youthful affections, LIBERTY; whose charms, instead of decaying with time in my eyes, have daily captivated me more and more. I was, accordingly, penetrated with the most sensible grief, when, about the *first of November last*, that day of darkness, a day hardly to be numbered with the other days of the year, SHE seemed about to take her final departure from America, and to leave that ugly Hag *Slavery*, the deformed child of Satan, in her room. I am now filled with a proportionable degree of joy in God, on occasion of HER speedy return, with new smiles on her face, with augmented beauty and splendor.—Once more then, Hail! celestial Maid, the daughter of God, and, excepting his Son, the first-born of heaven! Welcome to these shores again; welcome to every expanding heart! Long mayest thou reside among us, the delight of the wise, good and brave; the protectress of innocence from wrongs and oppression, the patroness of learning, arts, eloquence, virtue, rational loyalty, religion! And if any miserable people on the continent or isles of Europe, after being weakened by luxury, debauchery, venality, intestine quarrels, or other vices, should, in the rude collisions, or now-uncertain revolutions of kingdoms, be driven, in their extremity, to seek a safe retreat from slavery in some far-distant climate; let them find, O let them find one in America under thy brooding, sacred wings; where *our* oppressed fathers once found it, and we now enjoy it, by the favor of Him, whose service is the most glorious freedom! Never, O never may He permit thee to forsake us, for our unworthiness to enjoy thy enlivening presence! By His high permission, attend us thro' life AND DEATH to the regions of the blessed, thy original abode, there to enjoy forever the "glorious liberty of the sons of God!"

An African American Perspective on Liberty

Phillis Wheatley (ca. 1753–1784) was an African sold into slavery in Boston. Destined to become the most famous African American poet of the eighteenth-century, Wheatley drew the attention of her master's family with her intellectual ability. She was freed by her mistress in 1774 and provided with an education in theology and literature. Samson Occum (1723–1792) was a Mohican Indian who was converted to Christianity, educated by American Christians, and ordained a Presbyterian minister. In the letter that follows, Phillis Wheatley is writing to Samson Occum. He had first written to her, criticizing Christian ministers who spoke of liberty while owning slaves. Her letter, dated 11 February 1774, was published in the Connecticut Gazette and the Universal Intelligencer *on 11 March 1774.*

Rev'd and honor'd Sir,

I HAVE this Day received your obliging kind Epistle, and am greatly satisfied with your Reasons respecting the Negroes, and think highly reasonable what you offer in Vindication of their natural Rights: Those that invade them cannot be insensible that the divine Light is chasing away the thick Darkness which broods over the Land of Africa; and the Chaos which has reign'd so long, is converting into beautiful Order, and reveals more and more clearly, the glorious Dispensation of civil and religious Liberty, which are so inseparably united, that there is little or no Enjoyment of one without the other: Otherwise, perhaps, the Israelites had been less solicitous for their Freedom from Egyptian Slavery; I don't say they would have been contented without it, by no Means, for in every human Breast, God has implanted a Principle, which we call Love of Freedom; it is impatient of Oppression, and pants for Deliverance; and by the Leave of our modern Egyptians I will assert, that the same Principle lives in us. God grant Deliverance in his own Way and Time, and get him honour upon all those whose Avarice impels them to countenance and help forward the Calamities of their fellow Creatures. This I desire not for their Hurt, but to convince them of the strange Absurdity of their Conduct whose Words and Actions are so diametrically opposite. How well the cry for Liberty, and the reverse Disposition for the exercise of oppressive Power over others agree,—I humbly think it does not require the Penetration of a Philosopher to determine.

Directions to Massachusetts Voters

Samuel Langdon (1723–1797), Congregational minister and president of Harvard College, preached the annual election sermon in Massachusetts in 1775, less than six weeks after fighting broke out at Concord and Lexington. Election Day was an occasion for clergy to address political issues. Public officials, candidates, and citizens listened to the sermon before casting their votes. The following excerpt is from Samuel Langdon, Government corrupted by Vice, and recovered by Righteousness: A Sermon Preached before the Honorable Congress of the Colony of Massachusetts-Bay . . . on 31st Day of May, 1775. Being the Anniversary fixed by Charter for the Election of Counsellors *(Watertown, Massachusetts, 1775), 6, 9–10, 15–16, 19–20, 22–24, 27–28.*

We have lived to see the time when British Liberty is just ready to expire;—when that constitution of government which has so long been the glory and strength of the English nation, is deeply undermined and ready to tumble into ruins;—when America is threatened with cruel oppression. . . .

That ever memorable day, the nineteenth of April, is the date of an unhappy war openly begun, by the Ministers of the King of Great-Britain, against his good subjects in this Colony, and implicitly against all the colonies.—But for what?—Because they have made a noble stand for their natural and constitutional rights, in opposition to the machinations of wicked men, who are betraying their Royal Master, establishing popery in the British dominions, and aiming to enslave and ruin the whole nation, that they may enrich themselves and their vile dependents with the public treasures, and the spoils of America. . . .

We must keep our eyes fixed on the supreme government of the Eternal King, as directing all events, setting up or pulling down the Kings of the earth at his pleasure, suffering the best forms of human government to degenerate and go to ruin by corruption; or restoring the decayed constitutions of kingdoms and states, by reviving public virtue and religion, and granting the favorable interpositions of his providence. . . .

By all this we may be led to consider the true cause of the present remarkable troubles which are come upon Great-Britain and these Colonies; and the only effectual remedy. . . . The general prevalence of vice has changed the whole face of things in the British government.

The excellency of the constitution has been the boast of Great-Britain, and the envy of neighbouring nations. In former times the great departments of the state . . . were filled with men of wisdom, honesty, and religion, who employed all their powers, and were ready to risque their fortunes, and their lives for the public good. . . .

But in what does the British nation now glory?—In a meer shadow of it's ancient political system?—In titles of dignity without virtue?—In vast public treasures continually lavished in corruption, till every fund is exhausted . . . ?—In the many artifices to stretch the prerogatives of the crown beyond all constitutional bounds, and make the king an absolute monarch, while the people are deluded with a meer phantom of liberty? . . .

Into what fatal policy has the nation been impelled by its public vices! To wage a cruel war with its own children in these colonies, only to gratify the lust of power, and the demands of extravagance! . . .

But, alas! have not the sins of America, and of New-England in particular, had a hand in bringing down upon us the righteous judgments of heaven? Wherefore is all this evil come upon us? Is it not because we have forsaken the Lord? . . . However unjustly and cruelly we have been treated by man, we certainly deserve, at the hand of God, all the calamities in which we are now involved. . . . Do not our follies and iniquities testify against us? Have we not, especially in our Seaports, gone much too far into the pride and luxuries of life? Is it not a fact open to common observation, that profaness, intemperance, unchastity, the love of pleasure, fraud, avarice, and other vices, are increasing among us from year to year? . . .

Let me address you in the words of the prophet—O Israel, *return unto the Lord thy God, for thou hast fallen by thine iniquity*—My brethren, let us repent and implore the divine mercy. Let us amend our ways, and our doings; reform every being which has been provoking to the most high, and thus endeavor to obtain the gracious interpositions of providence for our deliverance. . . .

Thanks be to God, that he has given us, as men, natural rights independent on all human laws whatever; and that these rights are recognized by the grandCharter of British Liberties. By the *law of nature* any body of people, destitute of order and government, may form themselves into a civil society according to their best prudence, and so provide for their common safety and advantage. When one form is found, by the majority, not to answer the grand purpose in any tolerable degree, they may by common consent put an end to it, and set up another. . . .

If the great servants of the public forget their duty, betray their trusts and sell their country, or make war against the most valuable rights and privileges of the people; reason and justice require that they should be discarded, and others appointed in their room, without any regard to formal resignations of their forfeited power. . . .

If God be for us, who can be against us? The enemy has reproached us for calling on his name, and professing our trust in him. They have made a mock of our solemn Fasts. . . . And may we not be confident that the Most High, who regards these things, will vindicate his own honor, and plead our righteous cause against such enemies to his government as well as our liberties. O, may ourCamp be free from every accursed thing! May our Land be purged from all it's sins! May we be truly a holy people . . . ! Then the Lord will be our refuge and strength, a very present help in trouble; and we shall have no reason to be afraid though thousands of enemies set themselves against us round about.

Directions to Presbyterians

The Synod of New York and Philadelphia was an official body of Presbyterian leaders in those colonies that met every year. In the weeks following the outbreak of fighting at Concord, the synod sent advice to Presbyterian churches in its jurisdiction. Citizens were to meet for Fast Day on 29 June 1775. Unlike Thanksgiving Days (or "Thanks Days") when citizens feasted and celebrated God's mercy, Fast Days were times to abstain from food and drink and contemplate God's anger. In short, the synod attributed the political crisis to God's punishment for the sins of the colonists. The following excerpt is from A Pastoral Letter from the Synod of New-York and Philadelphia, To the Congregations under their Care; *to be read from the Pulpits on Thursday June 29, 1775, being the Day of the general Fast (New York, 1775), 3–8.*

Very Dear Brethren,

The Synod of New-York and Philadelphia, being met at a time when public affairs wear so threatning an aspect, and when (unless God in his sovereign Providence speedily prevent it) all the horrors of a civil war throughout this great continent are to be apprehended, were of opinion, that they could not discharge their duty to the numerous congregations under their care, without addressing them at this important crisis. . . .

We do therefore, Brethren, beseech you in the most earnest manner, to look beyond the immediate authors either of your sufferings or fears, and to acknowledge the holiness and justice of the *Almighty* in the present visitation. . . . [T]herefore, it becomes every person, family, city and province, to humble themselves before his throne, to confess their sins, by which they have provoked his indignation, and intreat him to pour out upon all ranks a spirit of repentance and of prayer. . . . Remember and confess not only your sins in general, but those prevalent national offences which may be justly considered as the procuring causes of public judgments; particularly profaneness and contempt of God, his name, Sabbaths and sanctuary;—pride, luxury, uncleanness, and neglect of family religion and government. . . .

. . . Hostilities, long feared, have now taken place,—the sword has been drawn in one province,—and the whole continent, with hardly any exception, seem determined to defend their rights by force of arms. If, at the same time, the British Ministry shall continue to enforce their claims by violence, a lasting and bloody contest must be expected: Surely then it becomes those who have taken up arms, and profess a willingness to hazard their lives in the cause of liberty, to be prepared for death. . . .

We have long seen with concern, the circumstances which occasioned, and the gradual increase of this unhappy difference. As Ministers of the Gospel of peace, we have ardently wished that it could, and often hoped that it would have been more early accommodated. It is well known to you (otherwise it would be imprudent indeed thus publicly to profess) that we have not been instrumental in enflaming the minds of the people, or urging them to acts of violence and disorder:—Perhaps no instance can be given on so interesting a subject in which political sentiments have been so long and so [word obscured] from the pulpit, and even malice itself has not charged us with labouring from the press; but things are now come to such a state, that as we do not wish to conceal our opinions as men and citizens . . . we shall take the liberty to offer a few advices to the societies under our charge, as to their public and general conduct; and

FIRST, in carrying on this important struggle, let every opportunity be taken to express your attachment and respect to our sovereign King George, and to the revolution principles by which his august family was seated on the British throne. We recommend, indeed, not only allegiance to him from duty and principle, as the first magistrate of the empire, but esteem and reverence for the person of the Prince, who has merited well of his subjects on many accounts, and who has probably been misled into the late and present measures by those about him; neither have we any doubt, that they themselves have been in a great degree deceived by false information from interested persons residing in America. It gives us the greatest pleasure to say . . . that the present opposition to the measures of administration does not in the least arise from disaffection to the King, or a desire of separation from the parent state. . . . We exhort you, therefore, to continue in the same disposition and not to suffer oppression or injury itself easily to provoke you to any thing which may seem to betray contrary sentiments: let it ever appear, that you only desire the preservation and security of those rights which belong to you as FREE-MEN and BRITONS, and that reconciliation upon these terms is your most ardent desire.

SECONDLY, Be careful to maintain the union which at present subsists through all the colonies. . . . In particular as the Continental Congress, now sitting at Philadelphia, consists of Delegates chosen in the most free and unbiassed manner, by the body of the people, let them not only be treated with respect, and encouraged in their difficult service . . . but adhere firmly to their resolutions. . . . We would also advise for the same purpose, that a spirit of candour, charity and mutual esteem be preserved, and promoted towards those of different religious denominations. Persons of probity and principle, of every profession, should be united together as servants of the same master, and the experience of our happy concord hitherto in a state of liberty should engage all to unite in support of the common interest; for there is no example in history, in which civil liberty was destroyed, and the rights of conscience preserved entire.

THIRDLY, We do earnestly exhort and beseech the societies under our care to be strict and vigilant in their private government, and to watch over the morals of their several members. It is with the utmost pleasure we remind you, that the last Continental Congress determined to discourage luxury in living, public diversions, and gaming of all kinds, which have so fatal an influence on the morals of the people. If it is undeniable, that universal profligacy makes a nation ripe for divine judgments, and is the natural mean of bringing them to ruin, reformation of manners is of the utmost necessity in our present distress. . . .

FOURTHLY, We cannot but recommend, and urge in the warmest manner, a regard to order and the public peace; and as in many places, during the confusions that prevail, legal proceedings have become difficult, it is hoped, that all persons will conscientiously pay their just debts. . . .

FIFTHLY, We think it of importance . . . to recommend to all of every rank, but especially to those who may be called to action, a spirit of humanity and mercy. . . . It is impossible to appeal to the sword without being exposed to many scenes of cruelty and slaughter; but it is often observed, that civil wars are carried on with a rancour and spirit of revenge much greater than those between independent states. The injuries received or supposed in civil wars wound more deeply than those of foreign enemies; it is therefore the more necessary to guard against this abuse, and recommend that meekness and gentleness of spirit, which is the noblest attendant on true valour. That man will fight most bravely, who never fights till it is necessary, and who ceases to fight, as soon as the necessity is over. . . .

We conclude with our most earnest prayer, that the GOD of heaven may bless you in your temporal and spiritual concerns, and that the present unnatural dispute may be speedily terminated by an equitable and lasting settlement on constitutional principles.

A Loyalist Perspective

Charles Inglis was an Anglican employed by the Society for the Propagation of the Gospel and a Tory. His letter to the secretary of the society on 31 October 1776 reveals the loyalism of many Anglicans and the persecution that they suffered from their neighbors. The following excerpt is from John Wolfe Lydekker, The Life and Letters of Charles Inglis: His Ministry in America and Consecration as First Colonial Bishop, from 1759 to 1787 *(London, 1936), 156–60.*

REVEREND SIR,

I have the Pleasure to assure you that *all* the Society's Missionaries, without excepting one, in New Jersey, New York, Connecticut, &, so far as I can learn, in the other New England Colonies, have proved themselves faithful, loyal Subjects in these trying Times; & have to the utmost of their Power opposed the Spirit of Disaffection & Rebellion which has involved this Continent in the greatest Calamities. . . .

You have, doubtless, been long since informed . . . to what an Height our violences were risen, so early as May 1775. . . . Those violences have been gradually increasing ever since; & this, with the Delay of sending over Succours, & the King's Troops totally abandoning this Province, reduced the Friends of Government here to a most disagreeable & dangerous Situation; particularly the Clergy, who were viewed with peculiar envy and Malignity by the Disaffected. For altho Civil Liberty was the ostensible Object, the Bait that was flung out to catch the Populace at large, & engage them in the Rebellion; yet it is now past all Doubt, that an Abolition of the Church of England was one of the principal Springs of the Dissenting Leaders' Conduct. . . . I have it from good Authority that the Presbyterian Ministers, at a Synod where most of them in the Middle Colonies were collected, passed a Resolve to support the Continental Congress in all their Measures. This, & this *only* can account for the Uniformity of their Conduct. . . .

The Clergy, amidst this Scene of Tumult & Disorder, went on steadily with their Duty; in their Sermons, confirming themselves to the Doctrines of the Gospel, without touching on politics; using their Influence to allay our Heats, & cherish a Spirit of Loyalty among their People. This Conduct, however harmless, gave great offence to our flaming Patriots, who laid it down as a Maxim—"that those who were not for them, were against them." The Clergy were everywhere threatened; often reviled with the most

---

approbrious Language; sometimes treated with brutal Violence. . . . Some have been flung into Jails by Committees, for frivolous Suspicions of Plots, of which even their Persecutors afterwards acquitted them. Some who were obliged to fly their Own Province to save their Lives, have been taken Prisoners, sent back, & are threatened to be tried for their Lives because they fled from Danger. Some have been pulled out of the Reading Desk, because they prayed for the King, & that before Independency was declared. . . .

The present Rebellion is certainly one of the most causeless, unprovoked and unnatural that ever disgraced any Country—a Rebellion marked with peculiarly aggravated Circumstances of Guilt & Ingratitude. Yet amidst this general Defection, there are very many who have exhibited Instances of Fortitude & Adherence to their Duty. . . . It is but Justice to say . . . there is not one of the Clergy in the Provinces I have specified, of whom this may not be affirmed; & very few of the Laity who were respectable, or Men of Property, have joined in the Rebellion.

Thus matters continued, the Clergy proceeding regularly in the Discharge of their Duty, where the Hand of Violence did not interfere, untill the Beginning of last July, when the Congress thought proper to make an explicit Declaration of Independency. . . . This Declaration increased the Embarrassment of the Clergy. To officiate publickly, & not pray for the King & Royal Family according to the Liturgy, was against their Duty & Oath, as well as Dictates of their Consciences; & yet to use the Prayers for the King & Royal Family, would have drawn inevitable Destruction on them. The only Course which they could pursue to avoid both evils, was to suspend the public Exercise of their Function, & shut up their Churches. This accordingly was done.

Satan's Role in the Conflict

By the end of the war, most Americans were convinced that George III had been a tyrant and that the colonists themselves had been the target of a plot to destroy liberty throughout the empire. These ideas were consistent with Whig ideology. In the passage that follows, however, an anonymous pamphleteer presents the same ideas in religious language. Who-

ever this author might have been, his language suggests that he intended to reach a popular audience. The dialogue opens sometime before the Stamp Act in 1765. This selection is from A Dialogue, Between the Devil and George III, Tyrant of Britain *(Boston, 1782) 1, 14–15.*

DEVIL. GEORGE, hearken to my counsel.

George. Thy servant attends.

D. My trusty servants *Bute* and *Mansfield*, have educated thee for my service, and taught thee the way wherein thou should'st go, obey them and I will make thee a king indeed; make yourself absolute, or die in the attempt: a king dependent on the people, is no monarch; he is a mere puppy.

G. Your words I have a heart to obey; 'tis the bent of my soul, and the world shall soon know that I am a king in reality, and my people shall feel that my wrath is like the roaring of a lion.

D. I doubt not you will equal my ancient servants *Nero, Caligula, Borgia, Charles,* and others; but you must use great art lest a spirit of liberty should rise among the people and blast your great designs, as happened to my faithful servant *Charles*.

G. I will begin with my colonies; the idea of enslaving them to the power of parliament, and making them tributary to the old dominion, suits the pride and avarice of Britons: when this is done the way will be open and easy to complete the work in Britain: with places, pensions, titles and bribes, I can soon make myself as absolute as any tyrant that ever slept.

D. Go on my b:loved servant, and cut the work short; thou art the darling of my heart: I hope you will yet shed a sea of human blood sufficient for the British navy to ride in. . . .

[Discussion moves to 1781]

D. . . . George, I tell you, between me and you, this rebellion is alarming to my dominions, and threatens yours with ruin. The vast continent of America, pregnant with the richest stores of nature, inhabited with a brave and enterprising people; enthusiastic in religion and liberty; and have laid foundations to perpetuate both; penetrating and daring in all their views; inflamed by your attempts to enslave them, have written your crimes in marble, with a "cursed be he that forgets or forgives the tyrant,"—"and blessed be their memory, and only theirs who preserve *Independence.*" With whom magnanimity and virtue recommend to office (and rulers stamp the manners of the people) in whose creed I and you, are equally opposed and execrated. This people, I say, have excited and will command the admiration and imitation of mankind. In their public writings, speeches and transactions, they stamp glory on RELIGION and LIBERTY, and aim to make them both eternal:—and if they succeed, I and you are eternally excluded from their favor; and that they will succeed we have every reason to fear; for all the old world is now gazing with admiration on the new. Kings hope to derive glory from an early friendship with this rising nation; and their subjects expect to gain infinite wealth by this union. Every Dutchman has his golden dreams about the NEW WORLD; they would not have listened with half the attention to the prophet *Daniel* they did to *Adams*; and this frenzy spreads like a pestilence through the nations and fascinates the world. If America is independent, universal ruin follows; therefore, George, hold out to the last, and be as obstinate as hell.

Questions

1. *Jonathan Mayhew and Samuel Langdon were both Congregationalists from Boston. Did they share the same perspective?*
2. *The* Discourse, Addressed to the Sons of Liberty and A Dialogue Between the Devil and George III *were aimed at a more popular audience than other documents in this section. How do the ideas and the language found in these documents compare to those in the others?*
3. *How could religious ideas drive some Christians to one side and others to the opposite side in the American Revolution?*

FURTHER READING

Bernard Bailyn's classic study The Ideological Origins of the American Revolution *(Cambridge, Massachusetts, 1967), is the best starting place on the importance of ideas, including religious ideas, in the Revolution. The importance of ideas about the end of the world is developed in Ruth H. Bloch,* Visionary Republic: Millennial Themes in American Thought, 1765–1800 *(New York, 1985). Harry S. Stout,* The New England Soul: Preaching and Religious Culture in Colonial New England *(New York, 1986), develops the role of New England clergy. A basic overview of the involvement of all the major denominations is found in Mark A. Noll,* Christians in the American Revolution *(Grand Rapids, Michigan, 1977).*

The Struggle over the Constitution: Federalists vs. Anti-Federalists

Saul Cornell

INTRODUCTION

The publication of the Constitution prompted Americans from all walks of life to participate in a lively public debate over the meaning of republican government and the nature of constitutionalism. The meaning of the Constitution has been debated since it was first proposed more than two hundred years ago. While most Americans today venerate the Constitution, there was substantial opposition to the Constitution when it was first proposed.

Three issues dominated the debate over ratification: the absence of a bill of rights, the meaning of federalism, and the role of democracy in the new government. The Philadelphia Convention that proposed the Constitution did not include a basic declaration of rights. The Bill of Rights was only added during the First Congress and might never have been added had not Anti-Federalists demanded substantial amendments. Apart from the controversy over the absence of a bill of rights, Federalists and Anti-Federalists argued over the scope of power ceded to the new government. This debate raised questions about the distribution of authority between the states and the new federal government. Another controversial issue was the Anti-Federalist claim that the constitution created an aristocratic government. Federalists disputed this charge and defended the republican character of the new government.

No essay produced during this controversy has exerted a more profound impact on subsequent generations than The Federalist. *Judges and lawyers routinely consult* The Federalist *for insights into the original meaning of the Constitution. While Federalists may have won the battle over ratification, Anti-Feder-*

alist concerns have shaped the language of dissent within the American constitutional tradition. Jeffersonian and Jacksonian thought each owed a significant debt to Anti-Federalist ideas. In contemporary America, their ideas have been rediscovered by the political right and left, who have been drawn to different aspects of Anti-Federalist thought.

The Struggle Over the Constitution

The Constitution has been at the center of a number of historical controversies. Progressive historians, such as Charles Beard, viewed the Constitution as part of a conservative counterrevolution. Progressives cast American history as a struggle between the spokesmen for an agrarian democratic tradition and a more conservative merchant elite. This view was challenged by the consensus historians who dominated American history after the Second World War. For these scholars the Constitution was the logical fulfillment of the ideals of the Revolution. Rather than viewing American society as deeply divided, these scholars stressed the absence of deep economic divisions and the broad consensus on political values in American history. More recently, historians have tried to move beyond these two opposing views and analyze the debate over the Constitution in terms of how Federalists and Anti-Federalists each interpreted the legacy of the Revolution. Although both sides in the constitutional struggle agreed that only a republican form of government could protect liberty, there were important differences between how these two groups understood ideas like republicanism, liberty, and federalism.

Federalism

The Federalist *has prompted more modern comment than any other text written to defend the Constitution. Although political scientists, lawyers, and judges have analyzed the constitutional theory advanced by Publius, the essays were originally composed for publication in the New*

York press. For historians, it is important to place this set of essays within the context of the broader public debate over the Constitution conducted in the pages of newspapers and pamphlets. In this selection, Stephen Schechter considers both the philosophical argument of Publius and the rhetorical strategies he employed to sway voters in New York. Excerpted from Stephen L. Schechter, "The Federalist *on Federalism, 1787-1788,*" *in* Roots of the Republic: American Founding Documents Interpreted, *ed. Stephen L. Schechter (Madison, 1990), 293-301, 304.*

HOW AND WHY *THE FEDERALIST* WAS WRITTEN

The proposed Constitution was first printed in New York on September 21, 1787, and within a week the debate over its adoption began. A commentary by a Federalist appeared in a New York City newspaper, *The Daily Advertiser,* on September 24. It was answered three days later in the city's only blatantly Antifederalist newspaper, *The New-York Journal* in "Cato" I, the first of seven of his essays attributed by some to [New York] Governor [George] Clinton. Several days later, "Cato" was attacked in a newspaper essay by "Caesar" (once thought to be Alexander Hamilton), and the debate was well underway, nurturing two basic tools of American campaign politics—the print media and the political party.

The Federalist was an important part of the New York debate, with the first essay appearing on October 27, 1787, two days after the unanswered charges of "Cato" III were published. The decision to write the essays was made by Alexander Hamilton and fellow New Yorker John Jay. Though little is known about that decision, it is likely that Hamilton recognized the need for an authoritative series of essays in defense of the proposed Constitution to counter the early onslaught of Antifederalists like "Cato," and that *The Federalist* was intended to serve that purpose.

The essays were written by Alexander Hamilton, John Jay, and James Madison of Virginia under the pseudonym "Publius." Eighty-four essays were printed in New York City between October 27, 1787 and May 28, 1788. The essays were first published in

---

New York City newspapers. They were then widely circulated in other newspapers until January 1788 when it was announced that the M'Lean brothers would print the essays in book form. (The first of the two-volume set was published on March 22, 1788; the second, on May 28.)

The essays were addressed to the "People of the State of New York" and intended to convince New Yorkers of the necessity of ratifying the new Constitution. In particular, the essays were intended to show, in Hamilton's words:

> "The utility of the *UNION* to your political prosperity—The insufficiency of the present Confederation to preserve that Union—The necessity of a government at least equally energetic with the one proposed to the attainment of this object—The conformity of the proposed constitution to the true principles of republican government—Its analogy to your own state constitution—*and lastly,* The additional security, which its adoption will afford to the preservation of that species of government, to liberty and to property."

The essays were written on a tight schedule: at first, two were printed each week; later, the schedule was increased to four per week. This did not leave much time for careful study or coordination. As James Madison explained near the end of his life in a private memorandum, the essays "were written most of them in great haste, and without any special allotment [assignment] of the different parts of the subject to the several writers, J. M. [James Madison] being at the time a member of the then Congress [of the Confederation in New York City], and A. H. [Alexander Hamilton] being also a member, and occupied moreover in his profession at the bar [as a lawyer], which occasionally took him up to Albany."

At the time of their publication, *The Federalist* papers were widely recognized by Federalist and Antifederalist alike as one of the most serious and sophisticated defenses of the Constitution. Federalists generally regarded the essays as the best analysis of the Constitution, though some admitted that they were too "elaborate" and not "well calculated for the common people." (In other words, even friendly readers of the day found them heavy and, at times, difficult reading.)

Today, *The Federalist* is widely regarded as the authoritative statement of the intent of the framers of the Constitution. It is used by lawyers, legal scholars, and judges to interpret the meaning of particular clauses of the Constitution, and by theorists to understand the meaning of the Constitution as a whole. However, its impact on its intended audience—the people of New York—was negligible. A majority of New York voters cast their ballots for Antifederalist convention delegates, and there is no evidence that any of those Antifederalist delegates who later decided to switch their final vote for ratification were influenced by *The Federalist*.

HOW *THE FEDERALIST* BEGINS

With this background in mind, consider how *The Federalist* begins. The first paragraph of the very first essay begins:

> It has been frequently remarked, that it seems to have been reserved to the people of this country, by their conduct and example, to decide the important question, whether societies of men are really capable or not, of establishing good government from reflection and choice, or whether they are forever destined to depend, for their political constitutions, on accident and force.

Written by Hamilton, this sentence can be read in two ways; namely, as the opening statement of a campaign document and as a work of political thought.

As the opening statement of a campaign document, this sentence is a classic "gambit"—an opening move designed to occupy a favorable position (in this case, the "high ground") with a minimal amount of sacrifices. Consider how the same sentence might read in terms of today's political rhetoric:

> Once again, my fellow Americans, we have an historic opportunity to show the world that we are a thoughtful people capable of creating good government by careful planning and popular consent, not by being forced to do it or by accidentally blundering into it.

The opening sentence gains added dimension as a campaign statement when its political context is recalled. The overall context was shaped by the desire to buy time, and what better way to do that than to appeal to the "reflective" nature of the voters? The particular context is the newspapers of New York City and what was being printed that week by the opposition.

As an opening statement of political thought, the first sentence of *The Federalist No. 1* suggests that politicians (and Hamilton was one of the best) do not campaign simply to win the votes of the people, they also campaign to govern; in this instance, to inform the public (and by that I mean giving shape and form to the public mind as well as providing it with bits of information) about the better world that will be possible under the new Constitution. This involves the selection and use of words not merely as tactics in an overall strategy but also as concepts (ideas) in an overall theory.

In this sense, the opening sentence contains two basic ideas that shape America's theory of constitutionalism. Hamilton elegantly phrased those ideas but he did not invent them. In fact, they were so much a part of the eighteenth-century American mind that they were widely used by Federalists and Antifederalists alike.

The two ideas used to introduce *The Federalist* address the political question: If society is governed by laws, how can laws (and in this instance, the Constitution) be made in a way that the members of society will obey willingly? The answer to this question is, in Hamilton's words, "reflection and choice."

Reflection is the Enlightenment idea that humankind is a thinking species, capable of improving its lot by thinking before it acts. This idea was shared by both sides in the debate, and it is one of the reasons why the campaign remained a peaceful debate. It was used in *The Federalist No. 1*, but it was also used in Antifederalist "Cato" I: "Deliberate, therefore, on this new national government with coolness; analize it with criticism; and reflect on it with candour. . . . Beware of those who wish to influence your passions, and to make you dupes to their resentments and little interests . . . ." And "Cato" II wrote of the Federalist author "Caesar": "he shuts the door of true deliberation and discussion."

This is not to say that all matters of politics were objects of reason. Reprinted from a Philadelphia statement of August 29, 1787, in the *New Jersey Journal* on September 5, 1787, while the Constitutional Convention was still in session, is an interesting distinction: "The principles of liberty and the principles of government . . . are distinct things: Many understand the former which are matters of feeling, who know nothing of the latter, which are objects of reflection and reason."

Choice is the republican idea of popular consent. It occurs time and time again throughout *The Federalist* and all other commentaries on the Constitution by Federalists and Antifederalists; and it stands for the complex yet simple notion that people will obey laws of their own making (or by representatives of their own choosing), so long as they have confidence in themselves and their representatives. In the heat of debate, some Federalists accused Antifederalists of pandering to the people, while some Antifederalists accused the other side of forgetting the people. However, virtually all were advocates of popular government; and, rhetoric aside, most were advocates of popular government by some form of elected representation.

In sum, then, Federalists and Antifederalists agreed on the need for delay, the worth of cool and reasoned debate, and the goal of government by popular consent. On what did they disagree and how did federalism figure into that debate? . . .

THE FEDERALIST PLATFORM: AN EXTENDED AND COMPOUND REPUBLIC

. . . In *The Federalist No. 10,* James Madison, as "Plubius," sets out the step-by-step reasons for a large, compound republic, focusing more on the large-republic element. He resumes this theoretical discussion in *The Federalist No. 51,* focusing on the compound-republic element. In *Nos. 37* and *39,* he considers the constitutional means for securing a large, compound republic. There are other writings where the Federalist experiment is explained, but it is Madison's Tenth, like Beethoven's Fifth, which is most frequently studied and, hence, most widely known. . . .

THE MADISONIAN MODEL OUTLINED

The Federalist No. 10 and the Large Republic

1. The greatest danger facing popular government is factionalism, which occurs when a majority or minority unites around a passion or interest adverse to individual rights or the public good.
2. Madison rejects the idea of controlling factionalism by removing its causes.

   a. Controlling the people by denying their liberties would be unwise, much like throwing the baby out with the bathwater.
   b. Telling people how to think would not work because no one would listen unless they were forced to do so, and that option was rejected.
3. Madison accepts the idea of controlling factionalism by controlling its effects.
4. The effects of *minority* factions can be controlled relatively simply by the republican principle of popular consent, by which the majority would defeat the minority faction at the polls. Perhaps, however, Madison worried too little about minority factions and some of their effects.
5. The real problem facing popular governments and the "great object" of his essay is how to control the *majority* when it becomes factious.
6. There are two basic ways to control majority factions: control the motives that inspire them and the opportunities for them to organize. These are taken up in (8) and (9) below, respectively, after Madison introduces the distinction between democracies and republics.
7. Of the two forms of popular government, a republic is more likely than a democracy to control majority factions, partly because democracies are by their very nature inclined toward instability. Also, republics allow for representation and increased size of population and territory. These last two factors are considered below.
8. Republics make it possible to have elected representatives, and good ones can refine the factious spirit that might spread among the majority. Large republics are more likely than small republics to elect good representatives for two reasons:
   a. Regardless of their size, all republics need the same number of legislators in order to avoid the clubiness of too few and the confusion of too many. But in a large republic, there will be more options to fill those seats with qualified people.
   b. Since the size of the constituency is greater in the large republic, it will be less susceptible to deception by unworthy candidates. (Is it harder to fool 100,000 people than 10,000?)

   c. However, on this as on other points, one must strive for the mean. If the constituency is too large, the representative will not be sufficiently aware of local conditions. If the constituency is too small, the representative will be tied to local conditions and unable to see the larger picture or pursue the national interest. The Constitution forms a "happy combination" that refers "great and aggregate interests" to the federal Congress and "local and particular" interests to the state legislatures. (Is there one optimum ratio of representative to be represented for a national legislature, and another optimum for state legislatures? And this is a guarantor that the states are "closer" to the people?)

9. Republics make it possible to increase the size of the citizenry and territory, and larger republics make it less likely that majority factions will form.
   a. The larger the society, the greater the variety of parties and interests.
   b. The greater the diversity of interests in society, the less likely a majority will have a single passion or interest. Put differently, majorities in large societies are more likely to be coalitions of various interests than a monolithic force of one interest.
   c. The larger the number of citizens and territory, the more difficult it will be for those who could form a factious majority to discover one another and come together.

10. The Union is more likely to control the effects of faction than are the states composing it.
   a. Members of Congress are more likely to possess the enlightened views and virtuous sentiments needed to override local prejudice. (If "Cato" had a localistic "small town" bias, does Madison suffer from a cosmopolitan bias?)
   b. The greater variety of parties in the Union as a whole will prevent any one party from outnumbering the others. For example, a factious leader may be able to take over one state but not the Union; a religious sect may become a factious majority in one region, but other sects will prevent its spread; a particular fad or disruptive element or wicked group is less likely to take over the whole system than a part of it.

11. "In the extent and proper structure of the Union, therefore, we behold a Republican remedy for the diseases most incident to Republican Government." Madison fully considered the extent of the Union, but he did not go as far in addressing its "proper structure" (i.e., its compound nature); a matter which is introduced in point ten and continued in *The Federalist No. 51*. . . .

CONCLUSION

Federalism occupies a critical position in *The Federalist*, both as a campaign document and a serious work of political thought. In one master stroke, Madison preempts the federal principle, taking it away from the sole preserve of Antifederalist opposition, while at the same time redirecting it toward the goals of building a new nation and expanding the republic. In this effort, Madison provides a bridge from the way federalism had been defined to the way federalism is understood today.

Anti-Federalism

The perspective of the losing side in history is not always treated in a sympathetic manner by later generations of scholars. History does usually favor the point of view of the winners. This has certainly been true in the case of the struggle over the Constitution. A number of scholars have cast the Anti-Federalists as narrow-minded political thinkers who failed to grasp the genius of the Federalist defense of the Constitution. Still, some scholars have disputed this view and portrayed the Anti-Federalists as thoughtful dissenters, supporters of a different theory of republicanism, one that was threatened by the powerful new government created by the Constitution. In this selection, Ralph Ketcham provides a balanced account of the virtues and defects of Anti-Federalist thought. Taken from Ralph Ketcham, "Antifederalist Essays and Speeches, 1787-1788," in Roots of the Republic: American Founding Documents Interpreted, *ed. Stephen L. Schechter (Madison, 1990), 381-86.*

THE PRESENTATION OF THE PROPOSED new Constitution of the United States to the public on September 17, 1787, and its submission to the states for their approval or disapproval eleven days later by the Confederation Congress, began the "ratification debate." For all practical purposes, this debate ended on July 26, 1788, when New York became the eleventh state to ratify the Constitution, assuring that it would soon become the new form of government of the American Union. This evolving political struggle linked the usual give-and-take of politics in free societies with an intense war of words between friends and foes of the new document. Each side had able and eloquent leaders, mustered elaborate arguments, and organized within each state and across state lines to further its cause.

The ratification struggle began with a clever move by the proponents of the new Constitution. Because sentiment in the United States, hostile to the idea of a national government, preferred a confederation or federation (the words were synonymous in the eighteenth century), the proponents of the Constitution called themselves "Federalists." They appropriated this term even though the new document, strictly speaking, did not create a league of governments, as had the old Articles of Confederation. As James Madison explained in *The Federalist No. 39*, the government created by the Constitution would be a "composite," partly national in that it had power in some cases to operate directly on the people and in those cases was directly responsible to the people (most notably the taxing power and the election of the House of Representatives), partly federal in that the states acted as constituent units of the general government (most notably in the election of the Senate). By appropriating the popular word "federal" to denote the new Constitution, its backers gained an important symbolic advantage for themselves and left the Constitution's opponents with the negative designation, "Antifederalists."

Newspapers throughout the nation began to publish "federal" and "antifederal" essays, sometimes as isolated letters and sometimes as part of more systematic treatments. Furthermore, as the people of each state elected ratification conventions and as these bodies began to meet, the conventions generated speeches, majority and minority reports, and proposed amendments which in turn fed the torrent of words in the public debate. The most

---

famous pro-Constitution series of essays was *The Federalist*. Although no single antifederal publication matched "Publius" in comprehensiveness and intellectual power, there were several notable antifederal pamphlets and series of essays—among them the "Letters of Centinel" (October 1787 to April 1788), the "Letters of Cato" (September 1787 to January 1788), the "Letters from the Federal Farmer" (October 1787 to January 1788), and the "Essays of Brutus" (October 1787 to April 1788). "Centinel" was published in Philadelphia; all the rest listed above, as well as *The Federalist*, appeared first in New York.

The newspaper war took place at the same time as the series of political battles in each state comprising the struggle for ratification. Reflecting satisfaction over the Constitution's protection of state equality in the Senate, and anxiety for protection within a stronger union, conventions in three small states, Delaware, New Jersey, and Georgia, ratified early and unanimously. Connecticut, a Federalist stronghold, also ratified early and by a large margin (128-40). The vagaries of Pennsylvania politics, combined with the heavy-handedness of Federalist leaders and the zeal of James Wilson, produced an early Federalist victory there, too (46-23). When the closely divided Massachusetts convention met in January 1788, five states had already ratified and none had rejected the Constitution. After a long, spirited debate, and some clever maneuvering by the Federalists, the Massachusetts convention ratified the Constitution on February 16, 1788 (187-168).

This close vote, and the Antifederalists' strength in the critical states of Virginia and New York, created an air of uncertainty during the first six months of 1788. The easy ratifications by Maryland (63-11) and South Carolina (149-73) cheered the Federalists; only one more state ratification was needed to put the new form of government into effect. However, Antifederalists were dominant in New Hampshire; Rhode Island and North Carolina were hostile; and there was real danger that Virginia and New York would not ratify. Thus, the issue was hanging in the balance in June 1788, when three state ratifying conventions—Virginia, New Hampshire, and New York—convened.

In the most important of the ratification contests, the Virginia convention, James Madison, Governor Edmund Randolph, and other Federalists narrowly triumphed in debate and in the voting over Patrick Henry and George Mason, and their Antifederalist supporters. Virginia voted to ratify (89-79) on June 25; in the meantime, on June 21, New Hampshire had voted (57-47) to adopt the Constitution as well. With ten states having ratified, the Constitution's victory was assured. Faced with this state of affairs, the New York ratifying convention (in which Antifederalists outnumbered Federalists 46 to 19) voted to ratify after a lengthy debate (30-27). The North Carolina ratifying convention even voted against deciding whether or not to ratify (193-75); the Rhode Island legislature refused even to call a convention, and the state's voters held a referendum on the Constitution in town meetings and rejected it by a margin of ten to one, although the Federalists in the major towns of Providence and Newport boycotted the proceedings. North Carolina eventually ratified the Constitution and joined the Union in November 1789; Rhode Island followed suit in May 1790.

Though the war of words that accompanied the political battles often focused on regional rivalries and petty details, each side also set forth a larger vision of what purposes of government were embodied in the proposed Constitution and what kind of nation might develop under it. The Federalist argument is well-known, due mostly to the enduring greatness of *The Federalist* as a work of constitutional interpretation and political theory. The Antifederalist argument also deserves analysis.

Antifederalists feared what Patrick Henry termed the "consolidated government" proposed by the new Constitution. They saw in Federalist hopes for commercial growth and international prestige only the lust of ambitious men for a "splendid empire" that, in the time-honored way of empires, would oppress the people with taxes, conscription, and military campaigns. Uncertain that any government over so vast a domain as the United States could be controlled by the people, Antifederalists saw in the enlarged powers of the general government only the familiar threats to the rights and liberties of the people. The federal judiciary, for example, seemed like just another magistracy removed from the people that would enforce harsh and arbitrary laws. The broad power to lay and collect taxes, the president's role as commander in chief, Congress's authority to pass any laws "necessary and proper" to carry out its enumerated powers, and the "supreme law of the land" and treaty-making powers all seemed unbounded and at least potentially tyrannical. The Antifederalists' twin goals, therefore, were to withdraw some of the powers explicitly given to the general government and to restrain with further checks and balances the exercise of its remaining powers. Antifederalists were, in a sense, "men of little faith" as both contemporary critics and later historians (principally Cecelia Kenyon) have charged, but this was true only in the context of their abiding fear that centralized power tended to become arbitrary and impersonal.

Antifederalists also had a positive vision of what the government of the United States should be—a republican vision which they thought was far closer to the principles and goals of the American Revolution than the political and commercial ambitions of the Federalists. The Antifederalists looked to the classical ideal of the small, pastoral republic where virtuous, self-reliant citizens managed their own affairs and shunned the power and glory of empire. To them, the victory in the American Revolution meant not so much the big chance to become a wealthy world power, but rather the opportunity to achieve a genuinely republican polity, far from the greed, lust for power, and tyranny that had generally characterized human society.

To Antifederalists, the prescription for government that would preserve the virtue and happiness of the people—the preconditions for a republican polity that in turn would preserve liberty—was to retain as much as possible the vitality of local government, in which rulers and ruled could see, know, and understand one another. Thus, they prized the American Revolution's emphasis on state and local councils and committees; thus, they cherished the Articles of Confederation, whose structure rested entirely on the states, although they unitedly believed that the Articles needed to be amended to give Congress more power. In their view, the idea of self-government was tied inextricably to a quality of directness reminiscent of a town meeting or a state legislature composed of many representatives who were subject to annual elections and who would really know the people of their districts. Each such district, furthermore, would be a town or ward or region conscious of its own particular identity rather than some amorphous, arbitrary geographic entity. Only with such intimacy could the trust, good will, and deliberation essential to wise and virtuous public life be a reality. Anything else, even though resting in some fashion on the consent of the people, would not really be self-government.

The Antifederalists' intense suspicions of corruption, greed, and lust for power were directed generally at those who ruled from on high and without restraint. Corruption and tyranny would be rampant as they always had been when those who exercised power felt little connection with the people. This would be true, moreover, for elected representatives, as well as for kings and nobles and bishops, who lived in a distant capital where power, wealth, and intrigue would exert their baneful influences. The more remote and distantly powerful a government was, the more it would be reminiscent of imperial Rome or Versailles or London with all their venality, cynicism, corruption, and neglect of the people. Would some future capital of the United States be filled with courtiers, courtesans, military heroes, and superfluous officeholders as was London or Paris or St. Petersburg? Antifederalists thought so under a constitution that consolidated power in a central government remote from the people.

On the other hand, the histories and legends of the Greek and Roman republics, the maturing ideology of natural rights, and the substantial experience of local self-government in the New World seemed to offer a far more alluring prospect. If the basic decency in human nature, most evident among ordinary people at the local level amid family, church, school, and other nourishing institutions, could impinge directly and continuously on government, then perhaps it too might be kept virtuous and worthy of confidence. Then, instead of endless suspicion and guarding against the evil and corruption of government, it might be possible to trust government and use it for the public benefit. The result might even be a society where honest, hardworking people could enjoy the fruits of their labor, where institutions encouraged and rested on virtue rather than greed, where officials were servants of the people rather than oppressors, and where peace and prosperity came from vigilant self-confidence rather than from conquest and dominion. Antifederalists saw mild, grass-roots, small-scale governments in sharp contrast to the splendid edifice and overweening ambition implicit in the new Constitution and heralded by "Publius" and its other advocates. The Antifederalist ideal of government left its citizens free to live their own lives and to cultivate the virtue (public and private) vital to republicanism; the second soon entailed taxes and drafts and offices and wars damaging to human dignity and thus fatal to self-government.

The Antifederalist ideal emerged most clearly and practically in its understanding of what representation and government by consent could really mean. Instead of seeking to insulate officials from popular influence (as, for example, "Publius" had argued in

The Federalist No. 78 regarding federal judges), Antifederalists sought to ensure the public good by requiring close association. If, for example, legislators rather than federal judges appointed for life had the power to interpret the Constitution, they would do so "at their peril"; if the people disapproved the interpretation, they "could remove them." The ideal went beyond a close control of officials by the people. In a truly self-governing society, there would be such dialogue, empathy, and even intimacy that the very distinction between ruler and ruled would tend to disappear. Such a close link between the people and their officials could embody the idea of liberty as both a security of rights and a guard of the people's effective voice in public affairs. Antifederalists groped for mechanisms that would give reality to this idea: how could it be achieved, in substance as well as in form, in a large nation?

For Antifederalists, the bonds between the people and their representatives had to be trustworthy as well as close. Not only, as Melancton Smith put it, should "representatives resemble those they represent; they should be a true picture of the people"; they should possess especially the virtues most characteristic of ordinary people: temperance, morality, and restrained ambition. Smith acknowledged that "the same passions and prejudices govern all men," but it was also true that "circumstances . . . give a cast to human character." The wealthy and the powerful, sad to say, were inclined to cheat customers, disdain honest labor, raise armies, put on social airs, and oppress the people. Could they be expected to rule wisely and justly in the interests of all? Rather, it was necessary that people of the "middling sort"—average people, perhaps yeoman farmers—themselves take part in government, and perhaps even be elected to office in large enough numbers to "set the tone" in the capital. Smith observed that such people, in the daily round of their occupations, had "less temptations, [and] are inclined by habit, and by the company with whom they associate, to set bounds to their passions and appetites." He envisioned, then, a government of popular confidence and respect, vital at the local levels where the virtues of ordinary people could prevail.

Questions

1. *Interpreting the meaning of any historical document requires understanding both content and context. How do these historians approach these two problems?*
2. *What is the most important contribution of* The Federalist *to the debate over ratification?*
3. *What are the central concerns of the Anti-Federalists?*

DEBATING AND RATIFYING THE CONSTITUTION

Interpreting a document as complex as the Constitution has proven to be an exceedingly difficult task for historians, political scientists, and judges. The debate over ratification involved hundreds of delegates to state conventions and thousands of voters, as well as countless essays and letters, some of which were published in the press and others of which circulated in private. The documents below illustrate some of the sources that historians have used either to prove or refute the claim that the Constitution represented a rejection of the Revolution's principles.

Hamilton Introduces the Federalist Argument

The Federalist Papers were published pseudonymously under the pen name of Publius. By choosing to sign the essays with a name drawn from classical antiquity, the true authors of the essays, Alexander Hamilton, John Jay, and James Madison, hoped to impress readers with their commitment to the ideals of republicanism. The following is the first installment of The Federalist. *Taken from Alexander Hamilton, "The Federalist No. 1" in* The Federalist: A Commentary on the Constitution of the United States, *ed. Paul Leicester Ford (New York, 1898), 1-7.*

October 27, 1787

To the People of the State of New York:

After an unequivocal experience of the inefficiency of the subsisting federal government, you are called upon to deliberate

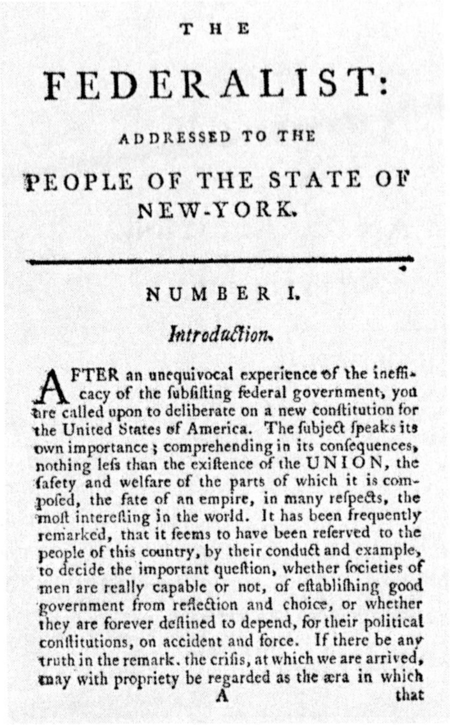

THE

FEDERALIST:

ADDRESSED TO THE

PEOPLE OF THE STATE OF NEW-YORK.

NUMBER I.

Introduction.

AFTER an unequivocal experience of the inefficacy of the ſubſiſting federal government, you are called upon to deliberate on a new conſtitution for the United States of America. The ſubject ſpeaks its own importance; comprehending in its conſequences, nothing leſs than the exiſtence of the UNION, the ſafety and welfare of the parts of which it is compoſed, the fate of an empire, in many reſpects, the moſt intereſting in the world. It has been frequently remarked, that it ſeems to have been reſerved to the people of this country, by their conduct and example, to decide the important queſtion, whether ſocieties of men are really capable or not, of eſtabliſhing good government from reflection and choice, or whether they are forever deſtined to depend, for their political conſtitutions, on accident and force. If there be any truth in the remark, the criſis, at which we are arrived, may with propriety be regarded as the æra in which

A that

A page of The Federalist *encouraging ratification of the new United States Constitution. (Courtesy of the Library of Congress.)*

on a new Constitution for the United States of America. The subject speaks its own importance; comprehending in its consequences nothing less than the existence of the UNION, the safety and welfare of the parts of which it is composed, the fate of an empire in many respects the most interesting in the world. It has been frequently remarked that it seems to have been reserved to the people of this country, by their conduct and example, to decide the important question, whether societies of men are really capable or not of establishing good government from reflection and choice, or whether they are forever destined to depend for their political constitutions on accident and force. If there be any truth in the remark, the crisis at which we are arrived may with propriety be regarded as the era in which that decision is to be made; and a wrong election of the part we shall act may, in this view, deserve to be considered as the general misfortune of mankind.

This idea will add the inducements of philanthropy to those of patriotism, to heighten the solicitude which all considerate and good men must feel for the event. Happy will it be if our choice should be directed by a judicious estimate of our true interests, unperplexed and unbiased by considerations not connected with the public good. But this is a thing more ardently to be wished than seriously to be expected. The plan offered to our deliberations affects too many particular interests, innovates upon too many local institutions, not to involve in its discussion a variety of objects foreign to its merits, and of views, passions, and prejudices little favorable to the discovery of truth.

Among the most formidable of the obstacles which the new Constitution will have to encounter may readily be distinguished the obvious interest of a certain class of men in every State to resist all changes which may hazard a diminution of the power, emolument, and consequence of the offices they hold under the State establishments; and the perverted ambition of another class of men, who will either hope to aggrandize themselves by the confusions of their country, or will flatter themselves with fairer prospects of elevation from the subdivision of the empire into several partial confederacies than from its union under one government.

It is not, however, my design to dwell upon observations of this nature. I am well aware that it would be disingenuous to resolve indiscriminately the opposition of any set of men (merely because their situations might subject them to suspicion) into interested or ambitious views. Candor will oblige us to admit that even such men may be actuated by upright intentions; and it cannot be doubted that much of the opposition which has made its appearance, or may hereafter make its appearance, will spring from sources, blameless, at least, if not respectable—the honest errors of minds led astray by preconceived jealousies and fears. So numerous indeed and so powerful are the causes which serve to give a false bias to the judgment, that we, upon many occasions, see wise and good men on the wrong as well as on the right side of questions of the first magnitude to society. This circumstance, if duly attended to, would furnish a lesson of moderation to those who are ever so much persuaded of their being in the right in any controversy. And a further reason for caution, in this respect, might be drawn from the reflection that we are not always sure that those who advocate the truth are influenced by purer principles than their antagonists. Ambition, avarice, personal animosity, party opposition, and many other motives not more laudable than these, are apt to operate as well upon those who support as those who oppose the right side of a question. Were there not even these inducements to moderation, nothing could be more ill-judged than that intolerant spirit which has, at all times, characterized political parties. For in politics, as in religion, it is equally absurd to aim at making proselytes by fire and sword. Heresies in either can rarely be cured by persecution.

And yet, however just these sentiments will be allowed to be, we have already sufficient indications that it will happen in this as in all former cases of great national discussion. A torrent of angry and malignant passions will be let loose. To judge from the conduct of the opposite parties, we shall be led to conclude that they will mutually hope to evince the justness of their opinions, and to increase the number of their converts by the loudness of their declamations and by the bitterness of their invectives. An enlightened zeal for the energy and efficiency of government will be stigmatized as the offspring of a temper fond of despotic power and hostile to the principles of liberty. An overscrupulous jealousy of danger to the rights of the people, which is more commonly the fault of the head than of the heart, will be represented as mere pretense and artifice, the stale bait for popularity at the expense of the public good. It will be forgotten, on the one hand, that jealousy is the usual concomitant of love, and that the noble enthusiasm of liberty is apt to be infected with a spirit of narrow and illiberal distrust. On the other hand, it will be equally forgotten that the vigor of government is essential to the security of liberty; that, in the contemplation of a sound and well-informed judgment, their interest can never be separated; and that a dangerous ambition more often lurks behind the specious mask of zeal for the rights of the people than under the forbidding appearance of zeal for the firmness and efficiency of government. History will teach us that the former has been found a much more certain road to the introduction of despotism than the latter, and that of those men who have overturned the liberties of republics, the greatest number have begun their career by paying an obsequious court to the people; commencing demagogues, and ending tyrants.

In the course of the preceding observations, I have had an eye, my fellow-citizens, to putting you upon your guard against all attempts, from whatever quarter, to influence your decision in a matter of the utmost moment to your welfare, by any impressions other than those which may result from the evidence of truth. You will, no doubt, at the same time have collected from the general scope of them, that they proceed from a source not unfriendly to the new Constitution. Yes, my countrymen, I own to you that, after having given it an attentive consideration, I am clearly of opinion it is your interest to adopt it. I am convinced that this is the safest course for your liberty, your dignity, and your happiness. I affect not reserves which I do not feel. I will not amuse you with an appearance of deliberation when I have decided. I frankly acknowledge to you my convictions, and I will freely lay before you the reasons on which they are founded. The consciousness of good intentions disdains ambiguity. I shall not, however, multiply professions on his head. My motives must remain in the depository of my own breast. My arguments will be open to all, and may be judged of by all. They shall at least be offered in a spirit which will not disgrace the cause of truth.

I propose, in a series of papers, to discuss the following interesting particulars:—*The utility of the UNION to your political prosperity—The insufficiency of the present Confederation to preserve that Union—The necessity of a government at least equally energetic with the one proposed, to the attainment of this object—The conformity of the proposed Constitution to the true principles of republican government—Its analogy to your own State constitution*—and lastly, *The additional security which its adoption will afford to the preservation of that species of government, to liberty, and to property.*

In the progress of this discussion I shall endeavor to give a satisfactory answer to all the objections which shall have made their appearance, that may seem to have any claim to your attention. . . .

PUBLIUS.

The Virginia Ratification Debates

The contest for ratification of the Constitution was closely fought. The selection below is from the debates in the constitutional convention of Virginia, which ratified the Constitution in June 1788 by a vote of 89 to 79. The Anti-Federalist position is aired first. Excerpted from The Debates, Resolutions, and Other Proceedings, in Convention, on the adoption of the Federal Constitution . . . *(Washington, 1828), 2:46–47, 56–58.*

Mr. HENRY.—Mr. Chairman, the public mind, as well as my own, is extremely uneasy at the proposed change of government. . . . I consider myself as the servant of the people of this commonwealth, as a centinel over their rights, liberty, and happiness. I represent their feelings, when I say, that they are exceedingly uneasy, being brought from that state of full security, which they enjoyed, to the present delusive appearance of things. A year ago, the mind of our citizens were at perfect repose. Before the meeting of the late federal convention at Philadelphia, a general peace, and an universal tranquillity prevailed in this country; but, since that period, they are exceedingly uneasy and disquieted. When I wished for an appointment to this convention, my mind was extremely agitated for the situation of public affairs. I conceive the republic to be in extreme danger. If our situation be thus uneasy, whence has arisen this fearful jeopardy? It arises from this fatal system—it arises from a proposal to change our government—a proposal that goes to the utter annihilation of the most solemn engagements of the states; a proposal of establishing nine states into a confederacy, to the eventual exclusion of four states. . . . Was our civil polity, or public justice, endangered or sapped: Was the real existence of the country threatened—or was this preceded by a mournful progression of events? This proposal of altering our federal government is of a most alarming nature: make the best of this new government—say it is composed by any thing but inspiration—you ought to be extremely cautious, watchful, jealous of your liberty; for instead of securing your rights, you may lose them forever. If a wrong step be now made, the republic may be lost forever. If this new government will not come up to the expectation of the people, and they should be disappointed—their liberty will be lost, and tyranny must and will arise. I repeat it again, and I beg gentlemen to consider, that a wrong step made now will plunge us into misery, and our republic will be lost. . . . I have the highest veneration for those gentlemen; but, sir, give me leave to demand, what right had they to say, *We, the People?* My political curiosity, exclusive of my anxious solicitude for the public welfare, leads me to ask, who authorized them to speak the language of, *We, the People,* instead of *We, the States?* States are the characteristics, and the soul of a confederation. If the states be not the agents of this compact, it must be one great consolidated national government, of the people of all the states. I have the highest respect for those gentlemen who formed the convention, and were some of them not here, I would express some testimonial of esteem for them. America had on a former occasion put the utmost confidence in them; a confidence which was well placed: and I am sure, sir, I would give up any thing to them; I would cheerfully confide in them as my representatives. But, sir, on this great occasion, I would demand the cause of their conduct. . . . The people gave them no power to use their name. That they exceeded their power is perfectly clear. . . .

[Next the Federalist view was articulated.]

Mr. PENDLETON.—Mr. Chairman, my worthy friend (Mr. HENRY) has expressed great uneasiness in his mind, and informed us, that a great many of our citizens are also extremely uneasy, at the proposal of changing our government: but that a year ago, before this fatal system was thought of, the public mind was at perfect repose. It is necessary to inquire, whether the public mind was at ease on the subject, and if it be since disturbed, what was the cause? What was the situation of this country, before the meeting of the federal convention? Our general government was totally inadequate to the purpose of its institution; our commerce decayed; our finances deranged; public and private credit destroyed: these and many other national evils, rendered necessary the meeting of that convention. If the public mind was then at ease, it did not result from a conviction of being in a happy and easy situation: it must have been an inactive unaccountable stupor. The federal convention devised the paper on your table, as a remedy to remove our political diseases. What has created the public uneasiness since? Not public reports, which are not to be depended upon; but mistaken apprehensions of danger, drawn from observations on governments which do not apply to us. When we come to inquire into the origin of most governments of the world, we shall find, that they are generally dictated by a conqueror at the point of the sword, or are the offspring of confusion, when a great popular leader taking advantage of circumstances, if not producing them, restores order at the expence of liberty, and becomes the tyrant over the people. It may well be supposed, that in forming a government of this sort, it will not be favourable to liberty: the conqueror will take care of his own emoluments, and have little concern for the interest of the people. In either case, the interest and ambition of a despot, and not the good of the people, have given the tone to the government. A government thus formed, must necessarily create a continual war between the governors and governed. Writers consider the two parties (the people and tyrants) as in a state of perpetual warfare, and sounded the alarm to the people. But what is our case? We are perfectly free from sedition and war: we are not yet in confusion: we are left to consider our real happiness and security: we want to secure these objects: we know they cannot be attained without government. Is there a single man in this committee of a contrary opinion?. . . There is no quarrel between government and liberty; the former is the shield and protector of the latter. The war is between government and licentiousness, faction, turbulence, and other violations of the rules of society, to preserve liberty. Where is the cause of alarm? We, the people, possessing all power, form a government, such as we think will secure happiness: and suppose in adopting this plan we should be mistaken in the end; where is the cause of alarm on that quarter? In the same plan we point out an easy and quiet method of reforming what may be found amiss. . . .

But an objection is made to the form: the expression, We, the people, is thought improper. Permit me to ask the gentleman, who made this objection, who but the people can delegate powers? Who but the people have a right to form government? The expression is a common one, and a favorite one with me: the representatives of the people, by their authority, is a mode wholly inessential. If the objection be, that the union ought to be not of the people, but of the state governments, then I think the choice of the former, very happy and proper.—What have the state governments to do with it? . . . It has been said that it has carried us through a dangerous war to a happy issue. Not that confederation, but common danger and the spirit of America, were the bonds of our union: union and unanimity, and not that insignificant paper, carried us through that dangerous war. "United, we stand—divided, we fall!" echoed and re-echoed through America, from congress to the drunken carpenter; was effectual, and procured the end of our wishes, though now forgot by gentlemen, if such there be, who incline to let go this strong hold, to catch at feathers; for such all substituted projects may prove.

This spirit had nearly reached the end of its power when relieved by peace. It was the spirit of America, and not the confederation, that carried us through the war: thus I prove it. The moment of peace showed the imbecility of the federal government: . . . The inefficacy of the general government warranted an idea that we had no government at all. Improvements were proposed and agreed to by twelve states, but were interrupted, because the little state of Rhode Island refused to accede to them; this was a further proof of the imbecility of that government; need I multiply instances to shew that it is wholly ineffectual for the purposes of its institution? Its whole progress since the peace proves it.

The Federalist Defense of the Constitution

James Madison provided one of the most intellectually sophisticated defenses of the Constitution. Madison's argument has since become a classic statement of American constitutional principles. The following is excerpted from James Madison, "Federalist No. 10," in The Federalist: A Commentary on the Constitution of the United States, *ed. Paul Leicester Ford (New York, 1898), 54–60, 62–63.*

November 22, 1787

To the People of the State of New York

Among the numerous advantages promised by a well-constructed Union, none deserves to be more accurately developed than its tendency to break and control the violence of faction. . . . Complaints are everywhere heard from our most considerate and virtuous citizens, equally the friends of public and private faith and of public and personal liberty, that our governments are too unstable, that the public good is disregarded in the conflicts of rival parties, and that measures are too often decided, not according to the rules of justice and the rights of the minor party, but by the superior force of an interested and overbearing majority. . . .

By a faction I understand a number of citizens, whether amounting to a majority or minority of the whole, who are united and actuated by some common impulse of passion, or of interest, adverse to the rights of other citizens, or to the permanent and aggregate interests of the community. . . .

There are again two methods of removing the causes of faction: the one, by destroying the liberty which is essential to its existence; the other, by giving to every citizen the same opinions, the same passions, and the same interests. . . .

The latent causes of faction are thus sown in the nature of man; and we see them everywhere brought into different degrees of activity, according to the different circumstances of civil society. A zeal for different opinions concerning religion, concerning government, and many other points, as well of speculation as of practice; an attachment to different leaders ambitiously contending for pre-eminence and power; or to persons of other descriptions whose fortunes have been interesting to the human passions, have, in turn, divided mankind into parties, inflamed them with mutual animosity, and rendered them much more disposed to vex and oppress each other than to co-operate for their common good. . . . But the most common and durable source of factions has been the various and unequal distribution of property. Those who hold and those who are without property have ever formed distinct interests in society. Those who are creditors, and those who are debtors, fall under a like discrimination. A landed interest, a manufacturing interest, a mercantile interest, a moneyed interest, with many lesser interests, grow up of necessity in civilized nations, and divide them into different classes actuated by different sentiments and views. The regulation of these various and interfering interests forms the principal task of modern legislation and involves the spirit of party and faction in the necessary and ordinary operations of the government. . . .

It is in vain to say that enlightened statesmen will be able to adjust these clashing interests and render them all subservient to the public good. Enlightened statesmen will not always be at the helm. . . .

The inference to which we are brought is that the *causes* of faction cannot be removed and that relief is only to be sought in the means of controlling its *effects*. . . .

By what means is this object attainable? Evidently by one of two only: Either the existence of the same passion or interest in a majority at the same time must be prevented, or the majority, having such coexistent passion or interest, must be rendered, by their number and local situation, unable to concert and carry into effect schemes of oppression. . . .

From this view of the subject it may be concluded that a pure democracy, by which I mean a society consisting of a small number of citizens, who assemble and administer the government in person, can admit of no cure for the mischiefs of faction. . . . Hence it is that such democracies have ever been spectacles of turbulence and contention; have ever been found incompatible with personal security or the rights of property; and have in general been as short in their lives as they have been violent in their deaths. . . .

A republic, by which I mean a government in which the scheme of representation takes place, opens a different prospect and promises the cure for which we are seeking. Let us examine the points in which it varies from pure democracy, and we shall comprehend both the nature of the cure and the efficacy which it must derive from the Union.

The two great points of difference between a democracy and a republic are: first, the delegation of the government in the latter, to a small number of citizens elected by the rest; secondly, the greater number of citizens and greater sphere of country over which the latter may be extended.

The effect of the first difference is, on the one hand, to refine and enlarge the public views by passing them through the medium of a chosen body of citizens, whose wisdom may best discern the true interest of their country and whose patriotism and love of justice will be least likely to sacrifice it to temporary or partial considerations. . . .

The other point of difference is the greater number of citizens and extent of territory which may be brought within the compass of republican than of democratic government; and it is this circumstance principally which renders factious combinations less to be dreaded in the former than in the latter. The smaller the society, the fewer probably will be the distinct parties and interests composing it; the fewer the distinct parties and interests, the more frequently will a majority be found of the same party; and the smaller the number of individuals composing a majority, and the smaller the compass within which they are placed, the more easily will they concert and execute their plans of oppression. Extend the sphere and you take in a greater variety of parties and interests; you make it less probable that a majority of the whole will have a common motive to invade the rights of other citizens; or if such a common motive exists, it will be more difficult for all who feel it to discover their own strength and to act in unison with each other. . . .

The influence of factious leaders may kindle a flame within their particular States but will be unable to spread a general conflagration through the other States. A religious sect may degenerate into a political faction in a part of the Confederacy; but the variety of sects dispersed over the entire face of it must secure the national councils against any danger from that source. A rage for paper money, for an abolition of debts, for an equal division of property, or for any other improper or wicked project, will be less apt to pervade the whole body of the Union than a particular member of it, in the same proportion as such a malady is more likely to taint a particular county or district than an entire State.

In the extent and proper structure of the Union, therefore, we behold a republican remedy for the diseases most incident to republican government. . . .

PUBLIUS.

The Anti-Federalist Critique of the Constitution

The Centinel essays were among the most widely reprinted Anti-Federalist attacks on the Constitution. Authored by Pennsylvania's Samuel Bryan, the essays rejected the calm disinterested tone favored by many Anti-Federalists in favor of a more polemical style. The following document is excerpted from The Documentary History of the Ratification of the Constitution, *vol. 13,* Commentaries on the Constitution: Public and Private, *ed. John P. Kaminski and Gaspare J. Saladino, (Madison, 1981), 1:332, 334–35.*

I shall now proceed to the examination of the (proposed plan of government, and I trust, shall make it appear to the meanest capacity, that it has none of the essential requisites of a free government; . . . that it is a most daring attempt to establish a despotic aristocracy among freemen, that the world has ever witnessed.) . . .

. . . [I]f the United States are to be melted down into one empire, it becomes you to consider, whether such a government, however constructed, would be eligible in so extended a territory; and whether it would be practicable, consistent with freedom? It is the opinion of the greatest writers, that a very extensive country cannot be governed on democratical principles, on any other plan, than a confederation of a number of small republics, possessing all the powers of internal government, but united in the management of their foreign and general concerns.

It would not be difficult to prove, that any thing short of despotism, could not bind so great a country under one government; and that whatever plan you might, at the first setting out, establish, it would issue in a despotism.

If one general government could be instituted and maintained on principles of freedom, it would not be so competent to attend to the various local concerns and wants, of every particular district; as well as the peculiar governments, who are nearer the scene, and possessed of superior means of information, besides, if the business of the *whole* union is to be managed by one government, there would not be time. Do we not already see, that the inhabitants in a number of larger states, who are remote from the seat of government, are loudly complaining of the inconveniencies and disadvantages they are subjected to on this account, and that, to enjoy the comforts of local government, they are separating into smaller divisions. . . .

Thus, we see, the house of representatives, are on the part of the people to balance the senate, who I suppose will be composed of the *better sort*, the *well born*, &c. The number of the representatives . . . appears to be too few, either to communicate the requisite information, of the wants, local circumstances and sentiments of so extensive an empire, or to prevent corruption and undue influence, in the exercise of such great powers.

Ratification Of The Federal Constitution 1787 - 1788

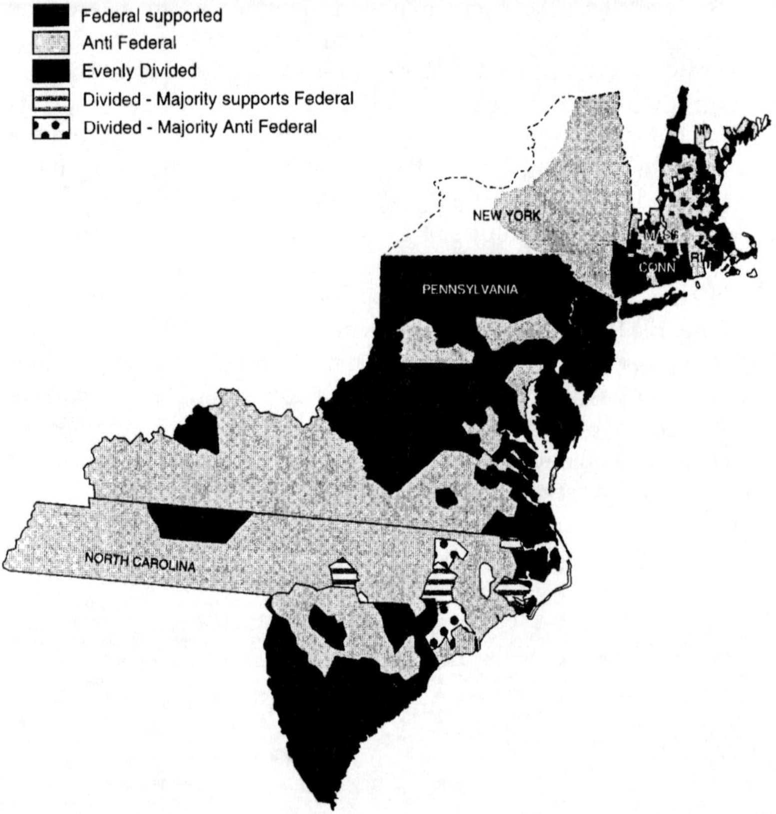

Reprinted from *The Other Founders: Antifederalism and the American Constitutional Tradition* by Saul Cornell (Chapel Hill: University of North Carolina Press, forthcoming).

Questions

1. *What are the essential points of conflict between the Anti-Federalists and the Federalists?*
2. *Does it make sense to view the Anti-Federalists as the spokesmen for democracy?*
3. *When historians interpret texts, they usually ask two questions: Who is the author? Who is the intended audience? With these questions in mind, what rhetorical strategies does Publius use in* Federalist 1 *to persuade his readers?*
4. *How does the approach of Publius compare to that of Centinel?*

FURTHER READING

Gordon S. Wood's The Creation of the American Republic, 1776–1787 *(Chapel Hill, 1969) is a study of the transformation of American political ideas in the period between the Revolution and the Constitution that puts the conflict between Federalists and Anti-Federalists in the larger context of evolving ideas about republicanism. Forrest McDonald's work explores the intellectual influences shaping the participants in the struggle over the Constitution; see* Novus Ordo Seclorum: the Intellectual Origins of the Constitution *(Lawrence, Kansas, 1985). Richard B. Morris describes the immediate political and social context of the debate over the Constitution in* The Forging of the Union, 1781–1789 *(New York, 1987). Finally, the essays in Richard Beeman's volume cover a variety of topics including: Madison's political thought, slavery, Shays's Rebellion, and the legacy of Anti-Federalism; see Richard Beeman et al.,* Beyond Confederation: Origins of the Constitution and American National Identity *(Chapel Hill, 1987).*

Jeffersonian Republicans vs. Federalists: The Struggle over the Sedition Act

Saul Cornell

Introduction

The 1790s were a period of intense partisan conflict. The notion of party politics was anathema to the Framers of the Constitution, who viewed party as a form of factionalism that was incompatible with republican virtue. Nothing better captured the antipathy to party than Washington's decision to include both Jefferson and Hamilton in his cabinet. Ultimately, Hamilton proved more adept at influencing Washington and his agenda to strengthen the new federal government and forced a realignment in politics. With the adoption of the Bill of Rights, former Anti-Federalists shifted their attentions to the dangers posed by Hamilton's program. Anti-Federalists joined forces with an important group of former Federalists who opposed Hamilton to form the Democratic-Republicans. Although many of the most important state leaders of the Democratic-Republican movement were former Anti-Federalists, the most important theorists of the opposition were the former Federalist James Madison and Thomas Jefferson. Many of the issues raised during the debate over ratification of the Constitution resurfaced a scant few years after its adoption. The conflict between the Jeffersonians and the Federalists during the 1790s cut across a broad range of issues including economics, foreign policy, law, and domestic policy.

One of the most important divisions between the Jeffersonians, who were known at the time as Democratic-Republicans, and the Federalists arose over the question of constitutional interpretation. Two key questions resurfaced time and again. What powers had the Constitution granted to the new government? How ought judges, lawmakers, and the executive interpret the text of the Constitution? For Democratic-Republicans the

Constitution was a document intended to provide a limited grant of authority. To preserve this ideal, it was vital to interpret the text of the Constitution in a strict—almost literal—manner. Federalists, by contrast, believed that within its sphere of authority the federal government had broad powers to achieve its objectives.

No issue proved more controversial during the 1790s than conflict over the Alien and Sedition Acts. This debate was not only one of the most important episodes in the struggle to protect freedom of the press, it also was a key moment in the emergence of the notion of states' rights. The material presented below deals with the constitutionality of the Sedition Act and with the political struggle between Jeffersonians and Federalists.

The Federalists and Jeffersonians: The Problem of Authority and Liberty in the New Republic

The debate between the Federalists and the Jeffersonians over the Sedition Act has been interpreted in a number of ways by modern scholars. Some historians have focused on this conflict as a political contest between two factions vying for power. While others have focused on the competing political philosophies of the two camps, the problem of constitutional interpretation was clearly central to this conflict. Analyzing the differences between Jeffersonian and Hamiltonian constitutional thought has been a key problem for scholars. For these scholars the debate over the Sedition Act is one example of the difficult task of defining the proper sphere of individual liberty within the context of republican constitutional principles.

Interpreting the Constitution

The constitutional history of the 1790s is enormously complicated and critical to the evolution of American law and politics. The different constitutional philosophies of Jefferson and Hamilton are central to understanding this history. This selection traces the major controversies that led to the emergence of these two approaches to interpreting the meaning of the Constitution. Abridged from Alfred H. Kelly, Winfred A. Harbison, and Herman Belz, The American Constitution: Its Origins and Development, 6th ed. *(New York, 1983), 129-41.*

Alexander Hamilton, the first secretary of the Treasury, formulated an economic program aimed at building up the political support needed to assure the legitimacy of the new government. In a series of reports to Congress in 1790-91 dealing with the public credit, Hamilton proposed to fund the outstanding Confederation debt at face value, assume the unpaid debts of the states contracted during the Revolutionary War, and charter a national bank to assist in handling the government's monetary and financial problems. He intended thereby to create a network of influence connecting creditors, men of property, and the commercial classes in general with the federal government. Appealing to motives of economic self-interest, which he believed could be made to serve the public good, Hamilton hoped to draw mercantile groups away from a primary attachment to the state governments and link their interest to that of the general government. The result would be a mutually beneficial relationship that would at once promote commercial growth and assure the stability and success of the new republic.

There was comparatively little opposition to the refunding of the national debt, which was guaranteed by the Constitution itself. However, certain congressmen did object to paying the old obligations off at face value, a step which they argued would redound to the advantage of the speculator class. And the states'-rights faction attacked the assumption of state debts by the federal government as a scheme to consolidate national authority at the expense of the states. The Virginia legislature adopted a resolution declaring assumption to be both dangerous to the states and repugnant to the Constitution. Representatives from states that had already paid off a large part of their debts also objected to assumption as inequitable. Hamilton nonetheless carried his proposal through Congress with the aid of a political bargain by which certain southern members voted for assumption in return for some northern support for a bill to locate the future national capital on the Potomac River.

Hamilton's proposal to charter a national bank was severely attacked in Congress on constitutional grounds. The opposition was led by Madison, who was becoming increasingly hostile to

---

Hamilton's program. Although the two men had supported strong national government in the convention and had worked together to secure ratification of the Constitution, neither their constitutional philosophies nor their economic interests were harmonious. Hamilton wished to push still further in the direction of a powerful central government, while Madison, now conscious of the economic implications of Hamilton's program and aware of the hostility which the drift toward nationalism had aroused in his own section of the country, favored a middle course between centralization and states' rights.

In the Constitutional Convention Madison had proposed that Congress be empowered to "grant charters of incorporation," but the delegates had rejected his suggestion. In view of this action, he now believed that to assume that the power of incorporation could rightfully be implied either from the power to borrow money or from the "necessary and proper" clause in Article I, Section 8, would be an unwarranted and dangerous precedent.

In February 1791, the bank bill was passed by Congress, but President Washington, who still considered himself a sort of mediator between conflicting factions, wished to be certain of its constitutionality before signing it. Among others, Jefferson was asked for his view, which in turn was submitted to Hamilton for rebuttal.

In a strong argument Jefferson advocated the doctrine of strict construction and maintained that the bank bill was unconstitutional. Taking as his premise the Tenth Amendment (which had not yet become a part of the Constitution), he contended that the incorporation of a bank was neither an enumerated power of Congress nor a part of any granted power and that implied powers were inadmissible.

He further denied that authority to establish a bank could be derived either from the "general welfare" or the "necessary and proper" clause. The constitutional clause granting Congress power to impose taxes for the "general welfare" was not of all-inclusive scope, he said, but was merely a general statement to indicate the sum of the enumerated powers of Congress. In short, the "general welfare" clause did not even convey the power to appropriate for the general welfare but merely the right to appropriate pursuant to the enumerated powers of Congress.

With reference to the clause empowering Congress to make all laws necessary and proper for carrying into execution the enumerated powers, Jefferson emphasized the word "necessary," and argued that the means employed to carry out the delegated powers must be indispensable and not merely "convenient." Consequently, the Constitution, he said, restrained Congress "to those means without which the grant of power would be nugatory."

In rebuttal Hamilton presented what was to become the classic exposition of the doctrine of the broad construction of federal powers under the Constitution. He claimed for Congress, in addition to expressly enumerated powers, resultant and implied powers. Resultant powers were those resulting from the powers that had been granted to the government, such as the right of the United States to possess sovereign jurisdiction over conquered territory. Implied powers, upon which Hamilton placed his chief reliance, were those derived from the "necessary and proper" clause. He rejected the doctrine that the Constitution restricted Congress to those means that are absolutely indispensable. According to his interpretation, "necessary often means no more than needful, requisite, incidental, useful, or conducive to. . . . The degree in which a measure is necessary, can never be a test of the legal right to adopt it; that must be a matter of opinion, and can only be a test of expediency."

Then followed Hamilton's famous test for determining the constitutionality of a proposed act of Congress: "This criterion is the *end*, to which the measure relates as a *mean*. If the *end* be clearly comprehended within any of the specified powers, and if the measure have an obvious relation to that *end*, and is not forbidden by any particular provision of the Constitution, it may safely be deemed to come within the compass of the national authority." This conception of implied powers was later to be adopted by John Marshall and incorporated in the Supreme Court's opinion in *McCulloch* v. *Maryland* on the constitutionality of the second national bank.

In his report on manufactures, Hamilton presented a powerful argument for a protective tariff for certain industries as a means of attaining a proper balance between agriculture, commerce, and manufacturing, and a prosperous and expanding economy. Since the protection of industry was not an enumerated power of Congress, the authority for such action had to rest again upon the doctrine of implied powers. Although Hamilton's recommendation to Congress was adopted in only a modified form, the opposition to the protective tariff was based more upon policy than upon alleged unconstitutionality.

Distinctly unsympathetic to the states, Hamilton used the doctrine of impled powers to advance a centralizing conception of federalism. At the Constitutional Convention Hamilton had supported a general legislative power for Congress; in interpreting the Constitution in the 1790s he fashioned virtually a plenary power out of the taxing, spending, and commerce powers of Congress. The taxing power, he held, was limited only by the restrictions contained in the Constitution that duties be uniform throughout the United States and that direct taxes be levied in proportion to population. The power to promote the general welfare through appropriations was limited only by the requirement that the objects sought be general rather than local. And the commerce power in Hamilton's view extended to all commercial activity in the United States, whether crossing state lines or confined within the borders of a single state. Although never formally disavowing the divided sovereignty of federalist theory, Hamilton came close to asserting exclusive sovereignty in the general government.

Hamilton's constitutional program secured for the federal government the support it needed to achieve legitimacy in the public mind. Confirmation of this fact came in the Whiskey Rebellion of 1794, when farmers in Pennsylvania protested and threatened to block execution of the excise tax on whisky contained in Hamilton's fiscal program. Alarmed by frontier unrest and eager to assert national authority, Congress in May 1792 enacted a law authorizing the president to call out the militia in case an insurrection occurred against federal authority or in case a state, threatened by internal disorder beyond its control, called for federal aid. Based on the idea that the employment of military power should be unequivocally subordinated to the processes of civil government, the act provided that the militia was to be employed only when "the laws of the United States shall be opposed, or the execution thereof obstructed, in any state, by combinations too powerful to be suppressed by the ordinary course of judicial proceedings, or by the powers vested in the marshals." Even then the president was required first to issue a proclamation warning the insurrectionists to disperse peaceably.

In 1794 resistance to the whisky tax in western Pennsylvania took on an organized character and threatened to result in a serious breakdown of the federal revenue laws. In August 1794, therefore, Washington issued a proclamation in accordance with the Act of 1792, commanding all insurgents to submit to federal authority within three weeks. When they failed to do so, he proceeded to call out 13,000 militiamen from Pennsylvania and nearby states to suppress the insurrection. The uprising quickly disintegrated, a few of the leading rebels being arrested and tried for treason. The episode demonstrated conclusively that the new federal government possessed ample power to enforce its authority over individuals, even recalcitrant ones.

The Rise of Political Parties

Hamilton's program depended for its success on systematic political support in the national legislature. This, in turn, provoked a rival constellation of interests and ideas that led to a major and entirely unforeseen constitutional development: the formation of political parties. Previously in the states a system of factional politics had existed in which alignments changed from one issue to the next in a fitful and episodic way. Within few years of the launching of the new government, however, something very like modern political parties—voluntary associations identified by a distinctive ideology and possessing a permanent organization that extended from the general government to the local level—became a principal force in American political life.

The requirements of organizing public opinion and directing the activity of the new continental government provided the occasion for organizing political parties. The starting point was Congress. Supporters of Hamilton's mercantilist program, most of whom had been Federalists in the ratification campaign, coordinated their votes in adopting his recommendations. Led by the Virginians James Madison and Thomas Jefferson, the latter the secretary of state in Washington's administration, critics of Hamilton's policies reacted by forming a southern-oriented and agrarian-based opposition—the Republican party. [This political party is not the same as the present Republican party.] Foreign policy questions, especially those arising out of the necessity of adopting a position on the French Revolution, presented additional issues in relation to which the nascent party groups formed distinct identities.

Sympathetic to the French republic, the party of Madison and Jefferson adhered to classical agrarian republicanism. In the political context of the 1790s the chief tenets of Republican ideology were the moral and social necessity of a virtuous and economically independent yeomanry; fear of mercantilist-designed schemes of executive influence or corruption; resistance to centralizing broad construction of federal legislative power; and support of state powers and local sovereignty. The Federalist party, in contrast, was less confident of the collective wisdom of the people and hence more elitist in its political style. Federalists promoted mercantile capitalist economic development through a broad construction of federal power, a strong and unitary executive branch, subordination of state powers to a centralizing federalism, and a foreign policy openly oriented toward British interests.

From a constitutional perspective the formation of political parties was a surprising innovation, for the framers of the Constitution had anticipated no such development. Even as political leaders conformed to the dictates of party behavior and constructed a party system in the 1790s, they persisted in the ancient belief that a permanent organized opposition was a danger to the body politic and inherently seditious. Yet ancient beliefs notwithstanding, in the expanded republic it was necessary to organize and transmit public opinion to elected officials as a guide to policy making. It was further necessary to combine, coordinate, and mobilize the welter of competing interests that characterized American society. And it was necessary also to bring together in some manner the branches of government that were disjoined under the doctrine of the separation of powers. All of these constitutional purposes were served by political parties, which accordingly may be described as having a constituent or constitutional function. In the broadest sense, then, parties were an extension and refinement of republican representation, a manifestation of popular sovereignty that transformed the idea of government by consent into a dynamic and continuing institutional process. . . .

The Sedition Act Crisis

At the end of the decade, deteriorating relations between the United States and France resulted in an undeclared naval war which provided the occasion for the new nation's first constitutional crisis. In 1798 the Federalist majority in Congress, responding to the intense excitement generated by the war, enacted the Alien and Sedition Acts. Based generally on the conventional view that equated organized political opposition with treason, these measures, of which there were four, were intended to suppress the partisan activities of the Republican opposition.

Least open to constitutional attack was a new Naturalization Act, which stipulated than an alien, to be eligible for citizenship, must prove fourteen years of residence within the United States. Far more controversial were the Alien Act, the Alien Enemies Act, and the Sedition Act. The Alien Act authorized the president to order the deportation of an alien whom he deemed dangerous to the peace and safety of the United States. The Alien Enemies Act empowered the president in case of war to deport aliens of an enemy country or to subject them to important restraints if they were permitted to remain in this country. The Sedition Act not only made it a high misdemeanor for any person to conspire to oppose any measure or to impede the operation of any law of the United States but also made it illegal for any person to write, print, or publish "any false, scandalous and malicious writing . . . against the government of the United States, or either house of the Congress . . . , or the President . . . , with intent to defame . . . , or to bring them, or either of them, into contempt or disrepute; or to excite against them, or either or any of them, the hatred of the good people of the United States."

The two Aliens Acts were aimed at French and pro-French foreigners in the United States, who were virtually unanimous in their support of the Republican party. Jefferson's followers at once attacked the laws as grossly unconstitutional. They argued, first, that the acts would deprive persons of their liberty without due process of law in violation of the Fifth Amendment and, second, that they contemplated the imposition of penalties without judicial process upon persons not convicted of any offense.

The Sedition Act posed a far more difficult constitutional problem. The sponsors of the law admittedly had intended virtually to re-enact the English common law of seditious libel as a congressional statute. The First Amendment, the Federalists contended, had merely incorporated the English common-law guarantee of "no prior restraint," which prohibited censorship before publication but which permitted very broad prosecution for seditious libel subsequent to the publication of anything unfriendly to the government. The truth of the published matter at issue did not constitute a defense, and the judge had sole power to decide whether or not it was libelous. English freedom of the press thus meant little more than a prior right to publish, or a prohibition of prior censorship. The present law softened the traditional law of seditious libel, for it permitted truth as a defense and allowed the jury to decide whether an utterance was libelous—two reforms for which the champions of free speech had long contended.

Federalists held to the existence of a federal criminal common law, received into American law from the English courts and enforceable by the federal judiciary. Under this law Federalists reasoned that it would be constitutional to institute prosecutions in the federal courts for seditious libel without benefit of any statute, and in 1797 they began two common-law prosecutions of Republican newspaper editors for seditious libel in lower federal courts. To provide a more secure political basis for dealing with the opposition, however, and because there was doubt in some circles about the existence of federal criminal common law, the Federalists enacted antisedition legislation. Their constitutional argument was that the First Amendment accepted and was compatible with the English view of freedom of speech as no prior restraint. The Sedition Act imposed no prior restraint, and thus in no way interfered with freedom of the press. The act did interfere with the licentiousness of the press, but Federalists believed that this merely maintained true liberty of the press.

The Adams administration enforced the Sedition Act with vigor, securing some fifteen indictments and ten convictions. The hope entertained by some Republicans that the federal courts might declare the law unconstitutional proved false; Federalist judges refused to allow counsel to challenge its constitutionality. Technically, most presiding judges allowed defense counsel to plead the truth of alleged libel, but in their charges to the jury refused to admit proof of libel, so this defense invariably failed. In addition, Federalist judges conducted Sedition Act trials in a partisan manner, browbeating counsel and witnesses and delivering partisan harangues to the jury.

The Virginia and Kentucky Resolutions

Republicans strenuously protested the Sedition Act. Given the risks that now attended published criticism of the government, and the refusal of the Federalist-dominated judiciary to permit the constitutionality of the measure to be tested in court, the Republicans' immediate problem was to find an appropriate forum in which to argue for repeal of the act. Their choice was the state legislatures. Accordingly, Thomas Jefferson and James Madison anonymously prepared resolutions denouncing the Sedition Act and its companion measures, which they caused to be introduced into the legislatures of Kentucky and Virginia. Framed for the practical purpose of removing what Republicans considered obnoxious legislation, the Kentucky and Virginia Resolutions also were documents of seminal importance in the development of American constitutional theory.

The Virginia legislature expressed "a warm attachment to the union of the states" and a firm resolve to support the government of the United States in all of its legitimate powers. But it viewed "the powers of the Federal Government as resulting from the compact to which the states are parties, as limited by the plain sense and intention of the instrument constituting that compact; as no further valid than they are authorized by the grants enumerated in that compact." The Kentucky legislature also subscribed to the idea of the Constitution as a compact, and both states condemned the Sedition Act as unconstitutional. Each also appealed to the other states for support in sustaining this judgment and in bringing about the repeal of the measure.

In the Kentucky and Virginia Resolutions and in related protest writings, Republicans raised four fundamental constitutional issues: the scope of federal legislative power; the settlement of constitutional disputes and the role of the states therein; the nature of the Union; and the meaning of freedom of speech and of the press and its bearing on the question of legitimate political opposition.

Republicans held the Sedition Act to be a violation of the First Amendment prohibition against congressional legislation abridging freedom of speech and of the press. But this transgression of constitutional limitations was objectionable, according to Jefferson's Kentucky Resolutions, not because it was wrong for government in general to restrict the freedom of the press, but because regulation of the press lay in the sphere of state power. "No power over the freedom of religion, speech, press being delegated to the United States by the Constitution, not prohibited by it to the states," Jefferson wrote, "all lawful powers respecting the same did of right remain, and were reserved to the states, or to the people." The states and the people thus retained "the right of judging how far the licentiousness of speech and of the press may be abridged without lessening their useful freedom." Deference to state power—or a concern for federalism—was thus the principal reason for limiting the scope of federal legislative authority.

A related consideration, pertinent to limiting not only federal legislative but also judicial power, was the Republican rejection of a federal common law of crimes. According to the Republican view, Congress could punish as crimes only those matters enumerated as such in the Constitution; seditious libel not having been so enumerated, Congress lacked the power to enact a sedition law. Repudiation of the idea of a federal common law of crimes, and by extension a general common law, was important for the implications it contained for the scope of federal legislative power. In England, a common-law country, Parliament was empowered to legislate on any subject dealt with in the common law. If the common law were regarded as federal law and liable to revision and alteration by Congress, Madison wrote in 1800,

> it then follows that the authority of Congress is coextensive with the objects of common law; that is to say, with every object of legislation; for to every such object does some branch or other of the common law extend. The authority of Congress would, therefore, be no longer under the limitations marked out by the Constitution. They would be authorized to legislate in all cases whatever.

Congress would in effect have a general legislative power, as in a unitary state, contrary to the federal requirement of divided sovereignty.

Federal judicial authority would, of course, also expand enormously if a federal common law were recognized. Jefferson warned against this danger in attacking as most "novel" and "formidable" the Federalist argument for "a system of law for the United States without the adoption of their legislature [i.e., the common law]." "If this assumption be yielded to," Jefferson predicted, "the state courts may be shut up, as there will be nothing to hinder citizens of the same state suing each other in the federal courts in every case."

A second issue in the Sedition Act crisis concerned the settlement of constitutional disputes in general, and those involving the exercise of federal powers in particular. Eventually the Supreme Court was to assume the power to resolve questions about the meaning of the Constitution, but in the early years of the republic the federal judiciary played no such role. Either the separate branches of the government presumed to exercise this power or, as in the Sedition Act episode, the states tried to determine the meaning of the Constitution and keep the federal government from transgressing constitutional limitations. Denying that the federal government had the exclusive power to judge the extent of its own powers, the legislatures of Kentucky and Virginia declared that "in case of a deliberate, palpable, and dangerous exercise of other powers not granted by the said compact, the states, who are parties thereto, have the right and are in duty bound to interpose for arresting the progress of the evil, and for maintaining within their respective limits the authorities, rights, and liberties appertaining to them." Kentucky and Virginia also expressed confidence that the other states would join in declaring the Sedition Act and the other Federalist measures unconstitutional.

Reliance on the states to decide constitutional controversies grew out of the Republican theory of the Union, the third major constitutional issue in the Sedition Act crisis. Seizing on the confederation aspect of the mixed system created by the Constitutional Convention, Jefferson and Madison declared the Union to be a compact among sovereign states, rather than the constituent act of the people of the United States considered as a single polity. In the language of the Kentucky Resolutions, the Constitution was a compact to which "each State acceded as a State, and is an integral party, its co-States forming, as to itself, the other party."

The precise meaning of the compact theory as presented in the Virginia and Kentucky Resolutions was and remains problematic even today. It may have been nothing more than a self-evident statement of political philosophy derived from the Revolution and asserting the compact theory of the state and the limited character of federal sovereignty. Probably it did not signify rejection of the divided sovereignty of federalism. Nevertheless, as John C. Calhoun and a later generation of southern political leaders showed, the language of the Kentucky and Virginia Resolutions lent itself to an interpretation denying federal sovereignty altogether. Although Madison in his last years disavowed any legitimate connection between the Virginia Resolutions and Calhoun's doctrine of state sovereignty, nullification, and secession, the conclusion is inescapable that Madison and Jefferson prepared the way for, if they did not fully anticipate, the South Carolina theory.

More pertinent perhaps than the subsequent application of Madison and Jefferson's theory of the Union are the questions of what the Republican leaders hoped to achieve in 1798 and how they expected to accomplish their goal. The Kentucky Resolves declared that the Alien and Sedition laws exceeded the constitutional power of Congress and hence were "not law" but were "altogether void and of no force." The legislature said further that the states would not tamely submit to such extension of congressional authority beyond the constitutional limits, and it added ominously that "these and successive acts of the same character, unless arrested on the threshold, may tend to drive these States into revolution and blood."

Jefferson's original draft had declared that "where powers are assumed which have not been delegated, a nullification of the act is the right remedy," and had expressed hope that the "co-States . . . will concur in declaring these [Alien and Sedition] acts void and of no force, and will each take measures of its own for providing that neither of these acts . . . shall be exercised within their respective territories." For expediency or other reasons this section was replaced by an appeal to the other states and by instructions to Kentucky's congressional representatives "to use their best endeavors to procure, at the next session of Congress, a repeal of the . . . unconstitutional and obnoxious acts."

In 1799 Kentucky issued a second set of resolves reasserting the view that if the general government was the exclusive judge of its own delegated powers, the result would be despotism. Now Jefferson stated "That the several States who formed that instrument [the Constitution] being sovereign and independent, have the unquestionable right to judge of the infraction; and, that a nullification of those sovereignties, of all unauthorized acts done under color of that instrument is the rightful remedy."

In the antebellum period "interposition" and "nullification" became terms to conjure with, and it is an intriguing question to ask what Madison and Jefferson meant in using this language in 1798. These were strong words which conceivably implied the use of force. At a time when the Revolution was vividly etched in recent memory, this eventuality would not have been farfetched or illegitimate. Yet it is likely that Madison and Jefferson had something else in mind—a coordinated and peaceful state response, employing the convention method of political action in preference to state legislative decision. Their purpose, it should be recalled, was to get the Sedition Act and the other Federalist measures repealed.

Madison and Jefferson's success in protesting the Sedition Act depended on the cooperation of the other states. On this score the results were not encouraging. The other southern states made no official response, sentiment being fairly evenly divided in their legislatures, and the northern states, controlled by Federalists, endorsed the Alien and Sedition measures. The northern states also held that the federal courts, not the state legislatures, were the proper tribunal for settling constitutional disputes. The Sedition Act was thus not repealed, but expired according to its original terms at the end of the Adams administration in March 1801.

Behind the controversy over state interposition and the settlement of constitutional disputes lay the fact that there was no general agreement on the precise nature of the Union. Everybody agreed that the powers of the government were divided between the states and the central government. It was also evident that the Constitution had made no explicit provision for the settlement of disputes over power between the two units of government. Article VI, which provides for the supremacy of the Constitution and federal laws, might be balanced against the Tenth Amendment, which provides for the reservation of undelegated powers to the states, without producing a conclusive answer. The government established under the Constitution was essentially a compromise between a confederation and a unitary state. In limited and varying degrees the political leaders realized that in the long run such a compromise might prove unworkable and that the federal system might evolve either into modified confederation or into a strongly centralized national government. The Republicans were essentially right in claiming that if a branch of the federal government had the final power to judge of the extent of federal authority, the states would ultimately and inevitably be reduced to a subordinate position. On the other hand, the Federalists were correct in asserting that the recognition of the right of each state to act as final judge in case of vital disputes would lead to utter confusion and probably to "an interruption of the peace of the states by civil discord." No decision on this all-important issue was reached in 1799, and in one form or another the question was to crop up almost continuously through the years until it was finally settled on the battlefield.

The Sedition Act gave rise to a fourth constitutional issue: the meaning of freedom of speech and of the press and the relevance of these First Amendment freedoms to the legitimacy of an organized political opposition. From the Republican standpoint the reforms that the Federalists had put into the Sedition Act were inconsequential: the very idea that freedom of the press existed so long as there was no prior restraint of publication suddenly appeared inadequate. Punishment after publication, Republicans argued, was every bit as inhibiting as prior censorship. Accordingly, they repudiated the whole idea of seditious libel and drew a modern libertarian distinction between critical, even inflammatory words, which they believed should be permitted, and overt actions injurious to the state, which they believed government could properly prevent. Republicans furthermore rejected the notion that political opinions could be subjected to tests of truth and falsehood, as the existing law on seditious libel assumed. On the contrary, it now began to appear that political opinions were subjective and relative, and thus not capable of evaluation according to objective criteria. Moreover, Republicans turned their new libertarian view of the First Amendment to the legitimation of party activity. In a republican constitutional order, they reasoned, a free press was an essential means of shaping the public opinion needed to control and direct government. An organized political opposition was but a refinement of this process of forming and expressing the public opinion on which republican government rested.

The Republican argument for a modern view of freedom of the press and a legitimate opposition was by no means conclusive or decisive. For one thing, despite the existence of the rule that defined freedom of the press as no prior restraint, in the American colonies there had been relatively little punishment after publication and hence much that we would recognize as freedom of the press in a modern sense. Second, when the Republicans came to power after 1800 they violated the standards of free speech and a free press which they had invoked against the Federalists in 1798. On several occasions they prosecuted Federalist editors in the state courts for seditious libel against state governments. Nor did the Republican justification of an organized political opposition compel an abandonment of earlier views denying the legitimacy of party. Nevertheless, despite the persistence of rhetoric suggesting otherwise, political opposition in the United States was not subsequently to be treated as subversive. Nor had it been so regarded in actual practice. The Sedition Act, although understandable under the circumstances, was an aberration.

Although constitutional theory lagged behind events, in a practical sense political parties were recognized as legitimate in the election of 1800. With Jefferson's election as president, power was transferred peacefully from the party that had written and implemented the Constitution to the organized opposition, whose protests of government policy only a few months earlier had been branded seditious. The "Revolution of 1800" ended the period of constitutional formation and inaugurated an era of Republican constitutionalism.

The Debate on the Alien and Sedition Acts

The Alien and Sedition Acts prompted the most intense partisan conflict of the 1790s. In this selection, historian James Sharp explores the different perspective of Federalists and Jeffersonians over the necessity of enacting this controversial legislation. The argument between Federalists and Jeffersonians extended beyond the question of the constitutionality of the legislation. In the view of the participants in this conflict, the outcome of this debate would determine the political destiny of America. Excerpted from James Roger Sharp, American Politics in the Early Republic: The New Nation in Crisis *(New Haven, 1993), 176-80.*

[T]he Federalists moved to consolidate their strength and destroy their political opposition in June and July of 1798 by proposing and passing the Alien and Sedition Laws. As the Federalist minister to Great Britain, Rufus King, was told by a correspondent, the "Spirit of the People is roused" and "ripe for the Support of the most decisive Measures of the Government." And this "spirit of patriotism" could be used, Hamilton suggested, to crush the Republicans so that "there will shortly be *national unanimity.*" And if the Republican "leaders of Faction" continued their opposition to the government, he said, the public would revile them much like "the *Tories* of our Revolution."

The three repressive anti-alien acts, including the Act Concerning Aliens, the Naturalization Act, and the Alien Enemies Act, reflected the increasing Federalist concern about the growing number of immigrants coming into the United States. Not only did what were considered dangerous political ideas circulate among these new residents, but also the vast majority of them seemed to support the Republican opposition. The legislation, then, established a registration and surveillance system for foreign nationals in the United States and gave the president extensive powers over them, including the power to deport any whom he considered dangerous to the country's peace and security. These measures, which Jefferson deemed as "worthy of the 8th or 9th century," had "so alarmed the French who are among us," he said, "that they are going off," and a "ship, chartered by themselves for this purpose, will sail within about a fortnight for France, with as many as she can carry."

The Sedition Law, however, was even more ominous and threatening to the Republicans because of its potential to stifle internal dissent. It provided for the punishment of any persons who "unlawfully combine or conspire together, with intent to oppose any measure or measures of the government of the United States . . . or to impede the operation of any law of the United States, or to intimidate . . . any person holding a place or office in or under the government of the United States." The law further prohibited "any false, scandalous and malicious writing or writings against the government . . . or either house of the Congress of the United States; or the President . . . with intent to defame . . . or to bring them . . . into contempt or disrepute; or to excite against them . . . the hatred of the good people of the United States." Infractions could be punished by fines of up to $5,000 and imprisonment for up to five years.

Hamilton had urged that his fellow Federalists use caution in shaping the Alien and Sedition Acts, having been concerned that his colleagues might push too far and cause a reaction that could have considerable political liabilities. "Let us not be cruel or violent," he had warned Timothy Pickering. Also upon reading an earlier and more radical version of the Sedition Act, Hamilton had exhorted his successor, Oliver Wolcott, that the act might "endanger civil War." "Let us not establish a tyranny," he had written, for "energy is a very different thing from violence," and "if we make no false steps we shall be essentially united; but if we push things to an extreme we shall give to faction *body* and solidarity."

The debate within Congress over the measures was acrimonious and accusatory. Federalist Robert Goodloe Harper of South Carolina, one of the most outspoken and zealous supporters of the laws, noted that the same persons who had been against the military measures were now opposing the proposed Alien laws and charged that they did so from the fear that the laws would put "a hook into the nose of persons who are leagued with the enemies of this country." The "zeal shown in this House, and in other places, against this bill," he charged, was evidence of "the deadly hatred of certain people toward . . . [the United States]." Furthermore, Harper saw the efforts of the Republican opposition as treasonable in that the goal was "to completely stop the wheels of Government, and to lay it prostrate at the feet of its external and internal foes."

Although a number of Federalists outdid themselves in conjuring up sinister images of seditious conspiracies, a giant of a man, "Long John" Allen, a six-foot-five-inch, 230-pound Federalist representative from Connecticut, was probably the most passionately and creatively vituperative and paranoid. Accusing Republican newspapers as well as congressmen of treasonable plotting against the government, Allen defended the Sedition Law as essential to the country's well-being. If there ever "was a nation which required a law of this kind," he said, it was the United States. He challenged his colleagues to look at certain newspapers and "ask themselves whether an unwarrantable and dangerous combination does not exist to overturn and ruin the Government by publishing the most shameless falsehoods against the Representatives of the people." These falsehoods and seditious statements, Allen said, included claims that Federalist representatives were "hostile to free Governments and genuine liberty, and of course to the welfare of this country" and should "therefore . . . be displaced" by the people "rais[ing] an *insurrection* against the Government." Allen's apparent equating of Republican efforts to defeat the Federalists at the polls with "an *insurrection* against the Government" reflected a view of the opposition shared by most Federalists.

The Republicans, of course, opposed the Federalist-backed measures. For them there were disquieting parallels between their own government and that of Great Britain in that both governments seemed willing to use almost any means, no matter how arbitrary, to solidify and retain power. For example, in the same year the William Pitt government, fearing a French invasion, suspended habeas corpus and moved against radical clubs in Britain. And indeed, some of the Federalists' arguments during the debate over the Alien and Sedition Laws admitted an admiration for the stringent policies governing internal security in England. Harper maintained that both countries faced similar situations in that their external enemy relied upon "an internal support," which he referred to as being made up of "domestic traitors."

Albert Gallatin was one of the major Republican spokesmen against the Sedition Act. He charged that advocates of the bill had failed to show evidence of any criminal conspiracies or seditious intent. "This bill and its supporters suppose in fact," he concluded, "that whoever dislikes the measures of Administration and of a temporary majority in congress, and shall, either by speaking or writing, express his disapprobation and his want of confidence in men now in power, is seditious, is an enemy, not of Administration, but of the Constitution, and is liable to punishment." Thus, the Sedition bill was no more than a blatant power grab by the Federalists, who hoped to use it to "perpetuate their authority and preserve their present places."

Gallatin's distinction between opposition to the administration and opposition to the Constitution was one that most Americans of both proto-parties of the late eighteenth and early nineteenth centuries were not able to make. The political crisis, coupled with the lack of a tradition of a "loyal opposition," had created a climate of opinion inhospitable to political dissent. Congressman "Long John" Allen, for example, had been so outraged by Gallatin's remarks that he accused the Pennsylvanian of promoting "that spirit which, by preaching up the rights of man, had produced the Western insurrection [Whiskey Rebellion]."

The debate was not confined to Congress. President Adams responded to a large number of petitions from citizens around the country with a series of addresses, some quite inflammatory in their depiction of the dangers posed by the country's external as well as internal foes. He told the citizens in and around Baltimore that while republics were often divided in opinion, these divisions were normally harmless "except when foreign nations interfere, and by their arts and agents excite and foment them into parties and factions." This kind of insidious interference, he said, however, "must be resisted and exterminated" or it would result "in our total destruction as a republican government and independent power."

The Republicans thought that Adams's vehement addresses, which Madison said contained some of "the most abominable and degrading [language] that could fall from the lips of the first magistrate of an independent people," and the scathing attacks being made upon the opposition within Congress and in the Federalist newspapers were just a prelude to war with France, which was being called for by many Federalists. James Lloyd, for instance, author of the Senate version of the Sedition Bill, looked upon a declaration of war as vital to the success of the Federalist program. "I fear that Congress will close the Session" without a declaration of war, he wrote Washington, "which I look upon as necessary to enable us to lay our hands on traitors."

Other Federalists, however, were less enthusiastic. Although Theodore Sedgwick thought that "a wise policy required a declaration of war," he explained to Rufus King, several Federalists were unwilling to go along, fearing that "it would tend to discredit them among their constituents" and that the "opposition would endeavor to create, in the popular estimation, a new denomination of parties–those of peace and war."

The Republicans had expected the declaration of war to coincide with the anniversary of independence, but they later reported to Jefferson that a Federalist caucus had not been able to agree on the timing. The Federalists *were* able, however, to pass the Sedition Act through the Senate on July 4, and a colorful account of the proceedings was given to Jefferson. "The drums, Trumpets and other martial music which surrounded us, drown'd the voices of those who spoke on the question," Jefferson was told, and the "military parades so attracted the attention of the majority that much the greater part of them stood with their bodies out of the windows and could not be kept to order." Finally in the uproar and confusion the bill was passed.

The martial spirit was widespread elsewhere and not just on the Fourth of July. "Our city resembles a camp rather than a commercial port," one of Rufus King's correspondents wrote from New York. "Volunteer companies of horse and infantry are raising; and meetings of the old officers of the army and navy—and of the citizens, in the different wards have been had to concert measures for the defence of our port."

Questions

1. *Discuss the difference between Jeffersonian and Hamiltonian views of the Constitution.*
2. *How did each side view the constitutionality of the Sedition Act?*
3. *Did the Jeffersonian opposition to the Sedition Act reflect their commitment to states' rights or individual rights?*

The Debate over the Sedition Act

Federalist fears about the threat of sedition were intensified by the rising tension between the United States and France. The Jeffersonians were closely identified with the French cause, and Federalists took every opportunity to denounce their opponents as champions of French atheism and anarchism. Suspicion of French influence among the Jeffersonians led the Federalists to pass a strict federal sedition law. The debate between Federalists and Jeffersonians on the legality of the Sedition Act reveals a number of important philosophical differences between these two groups. The conflict over this issue provides an excellent illustration of the profound divisions that arose within a decade of the ratification of the U.S. Constitution.

Sir William Blackstone Defines Seditious Libel

The English jurist, Sir William Blackstone, compiled the most influential study of the English common law. American judges and lawyers in the revolutionary era consulted Blackstone as a standard reference work. In the period after the Revolution a number of radical thinkers attacked aspects of Blackstone's jurisprudence because of its anti-republican character. In particular, a number of legal reformers believed that his view of seditious libel was inappropriate for a republican government in which the people, not the monarch, were sovereign. Abridged from Sir William Blackstone, Commentaries on the Laws of England *(London, 1765–69), Book 4 (1769), Chapter 11, 150–53. Punctuation has been altered to clarify meaning.*

Of a nature very similar to challenges are *libels, libelli famosi,* which, taken in their largest and most extensive sense, signify any writings, pictures, or the like, of an immoral or illegal tendency; but, in the sense under which we are now to consider them, are malicious defamations of any person, and especially a magistrate, made public by either printing, writing, signs, or pictures, in order to provoke him to wrath or expose him to public hatred, contempt, and ridicule. The direct tendency of these libels is the breach of the public peace, by stirring up the objects of them to revenge, and perhaps to bloodshed. The communication of a libel to any one person is a publication in the eye of the law; and therefore the sending of an abusive letter to a man is as much a libel as if it were openly printed, for it equally tends to a breach of the peace. For the same reason it is immaterial, with respect to the essence of a libel, whether the matter of it be true or false, since the provocation, and not the falsity, is the thing to be punished criminally; though, doubtless, the falsehood of it may aggravate its guilt, and enhance its punishment. . . .

In this, and the other instances which we have lately considered, where blasphemous, immoral, treasonable, schismatical, seditious, or scandalous libels are punished by the English law, some with a greater, others with a less degree of severity, the *liberty of the press,* properly understood, is by no means infringed or violated. The liberty of the press is indeed essential to the nature of a free state; but this consists in laying no *previous* restraints upon publications, and not in freedom from censure for criminal matter when published. Every freeman has an undoubted right to lay what sentiments he pleases before the public; to forbid this, is to destroy the freedom of the press; but if he publishes what is improper, mischievous, or illegal, he must take the consequence of his own temerity. To subject the press to the restrictive power of a licenser, as was formerly done, both before and since the revolution [meaning the English revolution of 1642–1660], is to subject all freedom of sentiment to the prejudices of one man, and make him the arbitrary and infallible judge of all controverted points in learning, religion, and government. But to punish (as the law does at present) any dangerous or offensive writings, which, when published, shall on a fair and impartial trial be adjudged of a pernicious tendency, is necessary for the preservation of peace and good order, of government and religion, the only solid foundations of civil liberty. Thus the will of individuals is still left free; the abuse only of that free will is the object of legal punishment. Neither is any restraint hereby laid upon freedom of thought or enquiry: liberty of private sentiment is still left; the disseminating or making public, of bad sentiments, destructive of the ends of society, is the crime which society corrects. A man (says a fine writer on this subject) may be allowed to keep poisons in his closet, but not publicly vend them as cordials. . . . So true will it be found, that to censure the licentiousness, is to maintain the liberty of the press.

Jeffersonian Republican Congressman Albert Gallatin Attacks the Sedition Act

Gallatin was a leading spokesman for the Jeffersonian Republican forces in Congress. His speech captures a number of the essential philosophical and constitutional beliefs of the Jeffersonians. His argument seeks to dismantle the Federalist case in favor of the Sedition Act. Excerpted from Annals of Congress, *5th Cong., 2d sess. (July 5 and 10, 1798), 2:2107, 2109, 2159–60, 2162.*

Does the situation of the country, at this time, require that any law of this kind should pass? Do there exist such new and alarming symptoms of sedition, as render it necessary to adopt, in addition to the existing laws, any extraordinary measure for the purpose of suppressing unlawful combinations, and of restricting the freedom of speech and of the press? For such were the objects of the bill, whatever modifications it might hereafter receive. . . .

Was the gentleman afraid, or rather was Administration afraid, that in this instance error could not be successfully opposed by truth? The American Government had heretofore subsisted, it had acquired strength, it had grown on the affection of the people, it had been fully supported without the assistance of laws similar to the bill now on the table. It had been able to repel opposition by the single weapon of argument. And at present, when out of ten presses in the country nine were employed on the side of Administration, such is their want of confidence in the purity of their own views and motives, that they even fear the unequal contest, and require the help of force in order to suppress the limited circulation of the opinions of those who did not approve all their measures. One of the paragraphs says, that it will soon become a question whether there will be more liberty at Philadelphia or Constantinople. . . .

. . . It was in order to remove these fears [that the Constitution could be interpreted to permit the government to suppress free speech], that the amendment, which declares that Congress shall pass no law abridging the freedom of speech or the liberty of the press, was proposed and adopted—an amendment which was intended as an express exception to any supposed general power of *passing laws,* &c., vested in Congress by the other clause. The sense, in which he and his friends understood this amendment, was that Congress could not pass any law to punish any real or supposed abuse of the press. The construction given to it by the supporters of the bill was, that it did not prevent them to punish what they called the licentiousness of the press, but merely forbade their laying any previous restraints upon it. It appeared to him preposterous to say, that to punish a certain act was not an abridgement of the liberty of doing that act. It appeared to him that it was an insulting evasion of the Constitution for gentlemen to say, "We claim no power to abridge the liberty of the press; *that,* you shall enjoy unrestrained. You may write and publish what you please, but if you publish anything against us, we will punish you for it. So long as we do not prevent, but only punish your writings, it is no abridgment of your liberty of writing and printing." Congress were by that amendment prohibited from passing any law abridging, &c.; they were, therefore, prohibited from adding any restraint, either by previous restrictions, or by subsequent punishment, or by any alteration of the proper jurisdiction, or of the mode of trial, which did not exist before; in short, they were under an obligation of leaving that subject where they found it—of passing no law, either directly or indirectly, affecting that liberty. . . .

. . . Whilst, therefore, they [the Federalists] support the bill in its present shape, do they not avow that the true object of the law is to enable one party to oppress the other; that they mean to have the power to punish printers who may publish against them, whilst their opponents will remain alone, and without redress, exposed to the abuse of Ministerial prints? Is it not their object to frighten and suppress all presses which they consider as contrary to their views; to prevent a free circulation of opinion; to suffer the people at large to hear only partial accounts, and but one side of the question; to delude and deceive them by partial information, and, through those means, to perpetuate themselves in power?

The Federalists Defend the Sedition Act

Harrison Gray Otis was a leading Federalist politician from Massachusetts. His defense of the constitutionality of the Sedition Act demonstrates the continuing importance of Blackstone to American legal thought. This account of Otis's speech before Congress is taken from Annals of Congress, *5th Cong., 2d sess. (July 10, 1798), 2:2145–48.*

Mr. OTIS said the professions of attachment to the Constitution, made by the gentleman from Virginia [Republican John Nicholas, a critic of the sedition bill], are certainly honorable to him; and he could not believe that an attachment so deeply engrafted as he states his to be would be shaken by this bill. The gentleman had caught an alarm on the first suggestion of a sedition bill, which had not yet subsided; and though the present bill is perfectly harmless, and contains no provision which is not practised upon under the laws of the several States in which gentlemen had been educated, and from which they had drawn most of their ideas of jurisprudence, yet the gentleman continues to be dissatisfied with it.

. . . In the first place, had the Constitution given Congress cognizance over the offences described in this bill prior to the adoption of the amendments to the Constitution? and, if Congress had that cognizance before that time, have those amendments taken it away? With respect to the first question, it must be allowed that every independent Government has a right to preserve and defend itself against injuries and outrages which endanger its existence; for, unless it has this power, it is unworthy the name of a free Government, and must either fall or be subordinate to some other protection. Now some of the offences delineated in the bill are of this description. Unlawful combinations to oppose the measures of Government, to intimidate its officers, and to excite insurrections, are acts which tend directly to the destruction of the

Constitution, and there could be no doubt that the guardians of that Constitution are bound to provide against them. And if gentlemen would agree that these were acts of a criminal nature, it follows that all means calculated to produce these effects, whether by speaking, writing, or printing, were also criminal. . . .

It was . . . most evident to his mind, that the Constitution of the United States, prior to the amendments that have been added to it, secured to the National Government the cognizance of all the crimes enumerated in the bill, and it only remained to be considered whether those amendments divested it of this power. . . . "Congress shall make no law abridging the freedom of speech and of the press." The terms "freedom of speech and of the press," he supposed, were a phraseology perfectly familiar in the jurisprudence of every State, and of a certain and technical meaning. It was a mode of expression which we had borrowed from the only country in which it had been tolerated. . . . In support of this doctrine, he quoted *Blackstone's Commentaries*, under the head of libels, . . . in several of the State constitutions, the liberty of speech and of the press were guarded by the most express and unequivocal language, the Legislatures and Judicial departments of those States had adopted the definitions of the English law, and provided for the punishment of defamatory and seditious libels.

The Sedition Act

The Constitution details treason as the levying of war against the United States or the giving of aid and comfort to the enemy in time of war. Even though America had not declared war on France, the original version of the Sedition Act defined adherence to the French cause as treason, carrying a penalty of death. The final version of the act, less severe, passed by a slim three-vote majority in the House. The text of the Sedition Act is taken from Public Statutes at Large of the United States of America. . . *(Boston, 1848), 1:596–97.*

SECTION 1. *Be it enacted by the Senate and House of Representatives of the United States of America, in Congress assembled,* That if any persons shall unlawfully combine or conspire together, with intent to oppose any measure or measures of the government of the

United States, which are or shall be directed by proper authority, or to impede the operation of any law of the United States, or to intimidate or prevent any person holding a place or office in or under the government of the United States, from undertaking, performing or executing his trust or duty; and if any person or persons, with intent as aforesaid, shall counsel, advise or attempt to procure any insurrection, riot, unlawful assembly, or combination, whether such conspiracy, threatening, counsel, advice, or attempt shall have the proposed effect or not, he or they shall be deemed guilty of a high misdemeanor, and on conviction, before any court of the United States having jurisdiction thereof, shall be punished by a fine not exceeding five thousand dollars, and by imprisonment during a term not less than six months nor exceeding five years; and further, at the discretion of the court may be holden to find sureties for his good behaviour in such sum, and for such time, as the said court may direct.

SEC. 2. *And be it further enacted*, That if any person shall write, print, utter or publish, or shall cause or procure to be written, printed, uttered or published, or shall knowingly and willingly assist or aid in writing, printing, uttering or publishing any false, scandalous and malicious writing or writings against the government of the United States, or either house of the Congress of the United States, or the President of the United States, with intent to defame the said government, or either house of the said Congress, or the said President, or to bring them, or either of them, into contempt or disrepute; or to excite against them, or either or any of them, the hatred of the good people of the United States, or to stir up sedition within the United States, or to excite any unlawful combinations therein, for opposing or resisting any law of the United States, or any act of the President of the United States, done in pursuance of any such law, or of the powers in him vested by the constitution of the United States, or to resist, oppose, or defeat any such law or act, or to aid, encourage or abet any hostile designs of any foreign nation against the United States, their people or government, then such person, being thereof convicted before any court of the United States having jurisdiction thereof, shall be punished by a fine not exceeding two thousand dollars, and by imprisonment not exceeding two years.

SEC. 3. *And be it further enacted and declared*, That if any person shall be prosecuted under this act, for the writing or publishing any libel aforesaid, it shall be lawful for the defendant, upon the trial of the cause, to give in evidence in his defence, the truth of the matter contained in the publication charged as a libel. And the jury who shall try the cause, shall have a right to determine the law and the fact, under the direction of the court, as in other cases.

Sec. 4. *And be it further enacted,* That this act shall continue and be in force until the third day of March, one thousand eight hundred and one, and no longer: *Provided,* that the expiration of the act shall not prevent or defeat a prosecution and punishment of any offence against the law, during the time it shall be in force.

APPROVED, July 14, 1798.

Thomas Cooper Is Tried for Sedition

Cooper, an ardent supporter of the Jeffersonian movement, published a volume entitled Political Essays *(1799) and was the editor of a newspaper in Pennsylvania. The judge in the case, Samuel Chase of Maryland, had been a leading Anti-Federalist during the struggle over the Constitution. Frightened by the radicalism of the French Revolution, Chase became a staunch Federalist during the 1790s. Abridged from "Trial of Thomas Cooper, for a Seditious Libel. In the Circuit Court of the United States for the Pennsylvania District. Philadelphia, 1800" in* State Trials of the United States . . ., ed. Francis Wharton *(Philadelphia, 1849), 659, 663–65, 670–71, 677, 679.*

The libellous matter complained of was as follows:—

"Nor do I see any impropriety in making this request of Mr. Adams. At that time he had just entered into office; he was hardly in the infancy of political mistake; even those who doubted his capacity thought well of his intentions. Nor were we yet saddled with the expense of a permanent navy, or threatened, under his auspices, with the existence of a standing army. Our credit was not yet reduced so low as to borrow money at eight per cent. in time of peace, while the unnecessary violence of official expressions might justly have provoked a war. Mr. Adams had not yet projected his embassies to Prussia, Russia and the Sublime Porte, nor had he yet interfered, as President of the United States, to influence the decisions of a court of justice—a stretch of authority which the monarch of Great Britain would have shrunk from—an interference without precedent, against law and against mercy. This melancholy case of Jonathan Robbins, a native citizen of America, forcibly impressed by the British, and delivered up, with the advice of Mr. Adams, to the mock trial of a British court-martial, had not yet astonished the republican citizens of this free country; a case too little known, but of which the people ought to be fully apprised, before the election, and they shall be."...

Mr. COOPER then addressed the jury as follows:...

But I hope, in the course of this trial, I shall be enabled to prove to your satisfaction, that I have published nothing which truth will not justify. That the assertions for which I am indicted are free from malicious imputation, and that my motives have been honest and fair....

You, and all who hear me, well know that this country is divided, and almost equally divided, into two grand parties; usually termed, whether properly or improperly, *Federalists* and *Anti-Federalists*: and that the governing powers of the country are ranked in public opinion under the former denomination—of these divisions, the one wishes to increase, the other to diminish, the powers of the executive; the one thinks that the people (the democracy of the country) has too much, the other too little, influence on the measures of government: the one is friendly, the other hostile, to a standing army and a permanent navy: the one thinks them necessary to repel invasions and aggressions from without, and commotions within; the other, that a well-organized militia is a sufficient safeguard for all that an army could protect, and that a navy is more dangerous and expensive than any benefit derived from it can compensate; the one thinks the liberties of our country endangered by the licentiousness, the other, by the restrictions of the press. Such are some among the leading features of these notorious divisions of political party. It is evident, Gentlemen of the Jury, that each will view with a jealous eye the positions of the other, and that there cannot but be a bias among the partisans of the one side, against the principles and doctrines inculcated by the other....

But in the present state of affairs, the press is open to those who will praise, while the threats of the law hang over those who blame the conduct of the men in power. Indiscriminate approbation of the measures of the executive is not only unattacked, but fostered, and received with the utmost avidity; while those who venture to express a sentiment of opposition must do it in fear and trembling, and run the hazard of being dragged like myself before the frowning tribunal, erected by the Sedition Law. Be it so; but surely this anxiety to protect public character must arise from fear of attack.—That conduct which will not bear investigation will naturally shun it; and whether my opinions are right or wrong, as they are stated in the charge, I cannot help thinking they would have been better confuted by evidence and argument than by indictment. Fines and imprisonment will produce conviction neither in the mind of the sufferer nor of the public.

Nor do I see how the people can exercise on rational grounds their elective franchise, if perfect freedom of discussion of public characters be not allowed. Electors are bound in conscience to reflect and decide who best deserves their suffrages; but how can they do it, if these prosecutions in *terrorem* close all the avenues of information, and throw a veil over the grossest misconduct of our periodical rulers? . . .

Judge CHASE then charged the jury as follows:—Gentlemen of the jury—When men are found rash enough to commit an offence such as the traverser is charged with, it becomes the duty of the government to take care that they should not pass with impunity. It is my duty to state to you the law on which this indictment is preferred, and the substance of the accusation and defence.

Thomas Cooper, the traverser, stands charged with having published a false, scandalous and malicious libel against the President of the United States, in his official character as President. There is no civilized country that I know of, that does not punish such offences; and it is necessary to the peace and welfare of this country, that these offences should meet with their proper punishment, since ours is a government founded on the opinions and confidence of the people. . . .

All governments which I have ever read or heard of punish libels against themselves. If a man attempts to destroy the confidence of the people in their officers, their supreme magistrate, and their legislature, he effectually saps the foundation of the government. A republican government can only be destroyed in two ways; the introduction of luxury, or the licentiousness of the press. This latter is the more slow, but most sure and certain, means of bringing about the destruction of the government. The legislature of this country, knowing this maxim, has thought proper to pass a law to check this licentiousness of the press: by a clause in that law it is enacted—(Judge C. here read the second section of the Sedition Law.) . . .

After the jury had returned with a verdict of Guilty . . . Mr. Cooper attended, and the court sentenced him to pay a fine of four hundred dollars; to be imprisoned for six months, and, at the end of that period, to find surety for his good behaviour, himself in a thousand, and two sureties in five hundred dollars each.

A Jeffersonian Jurist Rejects Blackstonian Principles

St. George Tucker set out to adapt Blackstone's Commentaries *to the realities of American law and society. His discussion of the differences between English common law and American constitutionalism exerted an enormous influence on Jeffersonian jurisprudence. Selected from St. George Tucker,* Blackstone's Commentaries: With Notes of Reference to the Constitution and Laws, of the Federal Government of the United States; and the Commonwealth of Virginia *(Philadelphia, 1803), appendix to vol. 1, part 2, 15–16, 20, 29–30.*

The consequences of this act [the Sedition Act], as might have been foreseen, were a general astonishment, and dissatisfaction, among all those who considered the government of the United States, as a limited system of government; in it's nature altogether federal, and essentially different from all others which might lay claim to unlimited powers; or even to national, instead of federal authority. The constitutionality of the act was accordingly very generally denied, or questioned by them. They alleged, that it is to the freedom of the press, and of speech, that the American nation is indebted for it's liberty, it's happiness, it's enlightened state, nay more, for it's existence. That in these states the people are the only sovereign: that the government established by themselves, is for their benefit; that those who administer the government, whether it be that of the state, or of the federal union, are the agents and servants of the people, not their rulers or tyrants. That these agents must be, and are, from the nature and principles of our governments, responsible to the people, for their conduct. That to enforce this responsibility, it is indispensibly necessary that the people should inquire into the conduct of their agents;

that in this inquiry, they must, or ought to scrutinize their motives, sift their intentions, and penetrate their designs; and that it was therefore, an unimpeachable right in them to censure as well as to applaud; to condemn or to acquit; and to reject, or to employ them again, as the most severe scrutiny might advise. That as no man can be forced into the service of the people against his own will and consent; so if any man employed by them in any office, should find the tenure of it too severe, because responsibility is inseparably annexed to it, he might retire: if he can not bear scrutiny, he might resign: if his motives, or designs, will not bear sifting; or if censure be too galling to his feelings, he might avoid it in the shades of domestic privacy. . . .

. . . [I]n the United States the case is altogether different [than it is in Great Britain]. The people, not the government, possess the absolute sovereignty. The legislature, no less than the executive, is under limitations of power. Encroachments are regarded as possible from the one, as well as from the other. Hence in the United States, the great and essential rights of the people, are secured against legislative, as well as against executive ambition. They are secured, not by laws paramount to prerogative; but by constitutions paramount to laws. This security of the freedom of the press requires, that it should be exempt, not only from previous restraint by the executive, as in Great-Britain; but from legislative restraint also; and this exemption, to be effectual, must be an exemption, not only from the previous inspection of licencers, but from the subsequent penalty of laws. . . . A further difference between the two governments was also insisted on. In Great-Britain, it is a maxim, that the king, an hereditary, not a responsible magistrate, can do no wrong; and that the legislature, which in two thirds of it's composition, is also hereditary, not responsible, can do what it pleases. In the United States, the executive magistrates are not held to be infallible, nor the legislatures to be omnipotent; and both being elective, are both responsible.

. . . Whoever makes use of the press as the vehicle of his sentiments on any subject, ought to do it in such language as to shew he has a deference for the sentiments of others; that while he asserts the right of expressing and vindicating his own judgment, he acknowledges the obligation to submit to the judgment of those whose authority he cannot legally, or constitutionally dispute. In his statement of facts he is bound to adhere strictly to the truth; for any deviation from the truth is both an imposition upon the public, and an injury to the individual whom it may respect. In his restrictures on the conduct of men, in public stations, he is bound to do justice to their characters, and not to criminate them without substantial reason. The right of character is a sacred and invaluable right, and is not forfeited by accepting a public employment. Whoever knowingly departs from any of these maxims is guilty of a crime against the community, as well as against the person injured; and though both the letter and the spirit of our federal constitution wisely prohibit the congress of the United States from making any law, by which the freedom of speech, or of the press, may be exposed to restraint or persecution under the authority of the federal government, yet for injuries done the reputation of any person, as *an individual,* the state-courts are always open, and may afford ample, and competent redress as the records of the courts of this commonwealth abundantly testify.

Jefferson Defends His Vision of Liberty and Republicanism

In his first Inaugural Address (1801), Jefferson sought to heal the nation's political wounds and articulate the essential principles of America's political creed. Excerpted from A Compilation of the Messages and Papers of the Presidents, *comp. James D. Richardson (Washington, 1910), 1:310–12.*

During the contest of opinion through which we have passed the animation of discussions and of exertions has sometimes worn an aspect which might impose on strangers unused to think freely and to speak and to write what they think; but this being now decided by the voice of the nation, announced according to the rules of the Constitution, all will, of course, arrange themselves under the will of the law, and unite in common efforts for the common good. All, too, will bear in mind this sacred principle, that though the will of the majority is in all cases to prevail, that will to be rightful must be reasonable; that the minority possess their equal rights, which equal law must protect, and to violate would be oppression. Let us, then, fellow-citizens, unite with one heart and one mind. Let us restore to social intercourse that harmony and affection without which liberty and even life itself are but dreary things. And let us reflect that, having banished from our land that religious intolerance under which mankind so long bled and suffered, we have yet gained little if we countenance a political intolerance as despotic, as wicked, and capable of as bitter and bloody persecutions. During the throes and convulsions of the ancient world, during the agonizing spasms of infuriated man, seeking through blood and slaughter his long-lost liberty, it was not wonderful that the agitation of the billows should reach even this distant and peaceful shore; that this should be more felt and feared by some and less by others, and should divide opinions as to measures of safety. But every difference of opinion is not a difference of principle. We have called by different names brethren of the same principle. We are all Republicans, we are all Federalists. If there be any among us who would wish to dissolve this Union or to change its republican form, let them stand undisturbed as monuments of the safety with which error of opinion may be tolerated where reason is left free to combat it. I know, indeed, that some honest men fear that a republican government can not be strong, that this Government is not strong enough; but would the honest patriot, in the full tide of successful experiment, abandon a government which has so far kept us free and firm on the theoretic and visionary fear that this Government, the world's best hope, may by possibility want energy to preserve itself? I trust not. I believe this, on the contrary, the strongest Government on earth. I believe it the only one where every man, at the call of the law, would fly to the standard of the law, and would meet invasions of the public order as his own personal concern. Sometimes it is said that man can not be trusted with government of himself. Can he, then, be trusted with the government of others? Or have we found angels in the forms of kings to govern him? Let history answer this question.

Let us, then, with courage and confidence pursue our own Federal and Republican principles, our attachment to union and representative government. . . .

. . . Equal and exact justice to all men, of whatever state or persuasion, religious or political; peace, commerce, and honest friendship with all nations, entangling alliances with none; the support of the State governments in all their rights, as the most competent administrations for our domestic concerns and the surest bulwarks against antirepublican tendencies; the preservation of the General Government in its whole constitutional vigor, as the sheet anchor of our peace at home and safety abroad; a jealous care of the right of election by the people—a mild and safe corrective of abuses which are lopped by the sword of revolution where peaceable remedies are unprovided; absolute acquiescence in the decisions of the majority, the vital principle of republics, from which is no appeal but to force, the vital principle and immediate parent of despotism; a well-disciplined militia, our best reliance in peace and for the first moments of war, till regulars may relieve them; the supremacy of the civil over the military authority; economy in the public expense, that labor may be lightly burthened; the honest payment of our debts and sacred preservation of the public faith; encouragement of agriculture, and of commerce as its handmaid; the diffusion of information and arraignment of all abuses at the bar of the public reason; freedom of religion; freedom of the press, and freedom of person under the protection of the habeas corpus, and trial by juries impartially selected. These principles form the bright constellation which has gone before us and guided our steps through an age of revolution and reformation. The wisdom of our sages and blood of our heroes have been devoted to their attainment. They should be the creed of our political faith, the text of civic instruction, the touchstone by which to try the services of those we trust; and should we wander from them in moments of error or of alarm, let us hasten to retrace our steps and to regain the road which alone leads to peace, liberty, and safety.

Questions

1. *What exactly was the doctrine of seditious libel and how did it function in American and English legal theory? In Jeffersonian legal theory? In Federalist legal theory?*
2. *Were the Federalists justified in passing the sedition law in legal terms? In political terms?*
3. *Is the controversy over the Sedition Act best thought of as a controversy over civil liberties or over federalism?*

Further Reading

Richard Buel explores the ideological tensions between Jeffersonians and Federalists in Securing the Revolution: Ideology in American Politics, 1789–1815 *(Ithaca, 1972). Leonard Levy's* Emergence of a Free Press *(New York, 1985) demonstrates the importance of Blackstonian ideals before the outbreak of the sedition crisis. Norman Rosenberg's* Protecting the Best Men: An Interpretive History of the Law of Libel *(Chapel Hill, 1986) examines the way seditious libel functioned within the context of the debate over republican constitutional ideas. Stanley Elkins's and Eric McKitrick's detailed narrative history,* The Age of Federalism *(New York, 1993), provides a panoramic overview of the political issues of the 1790s.*

Lewis and Clark: The Opening of the American West

C. Edward Skeen

INTRODUCTION

No exploration has excited the American imagination more than the 1804-1806 expedition of Meriwether Lewis and William Clark and their Corps of Discovery up the Missouri, across the Rockies, and down the Columbia River to the Pacific Ocean. Enduring incredible hardships, their trek yet remains one of the greatest adventures in human history. They returned with descriptions of huge herds of buffalo and of contact with Native Americans who had never encountered white men. They also made the first map of the trans-Mississippi West, and they provided much new scientific data on the flora and fauna of this region. Perhaps most importantly, they helped to establish the American claim to the Oregon territory.

The story of the Lewis and Clark expedition is a tale of high adventure and the lead characters, Lewis and Clark, are well known. It is also a story about Sacagawea, the Native American woman who acted as a guide on the trip, and about York, William Clark's slave, who accompanied the Corps of Discovery. It is a tale of two cultures: of Euro-American explorers encountering a Native American population and the implications of this contact.

In many ways, Lewis and Clark were advance agents for the opening of the west for American trade and eventually settlement. President Thomas Jefferson's instructions to Lewis not only focused on finding a passage to the Pacific but also, significantly, on the possibilities of establishing trade with the Indians in the far West and by implication gaining an advantage over other nations seeking to open trade in this region.

Modern Perspectives of the Lewis and Clark Expedition

In the accounts that follow, modern-day historians assess the Lewis and Clark expedition and attempt to place the characters involved in the exploration in perspective. Historians of the nineteenth and early twentieth centuries often reflected in their writings nationalistic and cultural biases. The myth-making about Sacagawea, for example, as Donna J. Kessler explains, served a useful purpose to the historians of that time to show Native American acceptance of American rule and superiority. Conversely, York, an African American, as Robert B. Betts relates, was relegated to obscurity, reflecting the cultural and racial bias of the authors. Finally, James P. Ronda explains that the interaction between the explorers and the Native Americans was far more complex than earlier historians had suspected, and that the other participants needed to be included in the story of the expedition. Through these newer perspectives, a far more realistic and accurate portrayal of the exploration may be gained.

The Lewis and Clark Expedition Assessed

William H. Goetzmann won the Pulitzer Prize in History in 1967 for his encyclopedic survey of the exploration of the American West. He set the stage for this study by assessing the expedition of Lewis and Clark. Excerpted from William H. Goetzmann, Exploration & Empire: The Explorer and the Scientist in the Winning of the American West *(New York, 1966), 3-8.*

The exploration of the American West was never an isolated event. It belongs to world rather than to national history, and never more so than in the opening decades of the nineteenth century. When Captain Meriwether Lewis and Lieutenant William Clark of the United States Army crossed the North American continent from the Mississippi River to the Pacific Ocean between May 14, 1804, and September 26, 1806, they brought to a close nearly three centuries of searching, on the part of European and colonial powers, for a Northwest Passage to India. A new country, the United States, had entered the ancient struggle for control of the trade routes to the Orient, but in so doing, thanks to the work of the Great Captains, it had altered the focus of international rivalry, at least for a time, from the far-off Orient to the Western interior of the North American continent itself. Lewis and Clark had discovered no easy route to Cathay. But theirs had been the final stroke that swept away the eighteenth-century geographers' view that one needed only to cross a single height of land—a ridge of the "Stony Mountains," in Jefferson's terms—before one could look upon the broad Pacific with Cathay on its Western shore. Instead their expedition demonstrated to the world at large the great width of western North America and its potential riches in furs, minerals, fishes, and untold other natural resources. Thus they succeeded in making the West itself an object of desire—a virgin wilderness that formed a thousand-mile vacuum between the great powers of the world and the United States, and into which, by whatever laws of imperialistic physics prevailed, they must inevitably rush. It was a vacuum that acted, as one historian has pointed out, like a greatly expanded European political frontier with intense pressures on either side. As such, the explorer became more than a mere curiosity-seeker. When he led his nation and his culture into the Western "vacuum" so richly endowed by nature, the buckskin explorer became a vital factor in international diplomacy. For much of the nineteenth century it was the explorer out in the wilderness as much as the diplomats in London and Paris and Washington who took the lead in establishing,

---

through his increased geographical knowledge and his control of the Indians, the practical limits of each nation's frontier on the edges of the vast terrestrial sea that lay between them.

It was not by accident that Lewis and Clark so changed the focus of international rivalry for the West. Rather it was a function of their unique role as explorers with a broad sense of national purpose. They were not fur traders, for example, nor even strictly speaking men of commerce. Instead both men were soldiers with extensive experience in frontier regions, chosen for their general intelligence and knowledge of wilderness skills, and programmed by an elaborate set of instructions from Thomas Jefferson, who saw their mission in the very broadest terms. In his appeal to Congress for funds, Jefferson described the expedition as a commercial one because it thus fell within the limits of his Constitutional powers. Yet privately Jefferson also saw it as a "literary" undertaking, which in the parlance of the day meant that it was to collect information covering the whole range of natural history from geology to Indian vocabularies. As explorers, Lewis and Clark might almost be considered a logical extension of the American Philosophical Society, which existed to promote the general advancement of science and "the useful arts."

The repeated attention given to the details of their overland trip has tended to obscure what is perhaps the most important fact about the Lewis and Clark expedition, and that is the degree to which it was "programmed," or planned in advance, down to the smallest detail by Jefferson and his scientific associates in Philadelphia. . . . After years of collecting information about the West, and several abortive attempts to launch an expedition, Jefferson, who also had some backwoods experience as a surveyor in his native Virginia, had a very clear idea of the kinds of information the explorers should collect. This was first and foremost geographical information of the wide-ranging, nonspecialized kind that characterized the returns of such an eminent scientific man as Alexander von Humboldt. If Jefferson's famous *Notes on Virginia* can be said to constitute a perfect model of the rational eighteenth-century mind organizing the many facts of physical and human nature into a broadly conceived and generally useful pattern, then in equal measure the same can be said for the instructions given to Lewis and Clark.

They were called upon first of all to explore the Missouri and Columbia rivers to locate "the most direct and practicable water communication across this continent for the purposes of commerce." But they were also to "fix" geographical positions by astronomical observations so that a map of the region could be made. Moreover, they were to study the Indian inhabitants very carefully, including their numbers, their relations with other tribes, "their language, dress and monuments," their economic and military pursuits, their food, clothing, and houses, their diseases and remedies, and their laws and customs. In addition Lewis and Clark were to study the "soil and face of the country," particularly its vegetable production, its animals, its fossils, the existing minerals, including metals, limestone, coal, salts, mineral waters, and saltpeter. They were also to take note of volcanic action and to keep statistics on the weather. In short, though commerce in furs was to be a prime objective, the explorers were to inquire into almost every phenomenon that might prove useful to settlers from the United States. The very strength of Jefferson's instructions was in their broadness and lack of limitations. It was this general approach that called for the study of any and all useful phenomena that set the pattern for much of the early American exploration in the Far West and gave it a tremendous advantage over the more specialized efforts by competing nations. It keynoted what was to be a more flexible and economically mobile American approach to the West. When American explorers, following Lewis and Clark, went out into the West, they characteristically found many more uses for the land than did their counterparts under different flags.

That this was no accident can further be illustrated by a brief glance at the kind of training received by Meriwether Lewis, the nominal head of the expedition. During the summer of 1803 Lewis was in Philadelphia studying natural history . . . [with several well-known scientific experts]. These men also furnished him with advice in the techniques of collecting, and gave him detailed lists of questions to ask the Indians and other people whom he might meet. Part of his time, too, was spent mastering the sextant, the theodolite, and other instruments that were to be used for the careful calculation of longitude and latitude so necessary for the compilation of an accurate map of the unknown region. He also had opportunity to study maps, such as those of John Mitchell and Guillaume De Lisle, in Jefferson's library; and later, in St. Louis, he studied the Spanish maps of Antoine Soulard and the Missouri River charts of John Evans and James Mackay, as well as their journals. In a few short months his head was crammed with the rudimentary outlines of virtually every branch of natural and physical science, and before the expedition got under way, Clark, too, began to master some of these skills. Clark's field notes show, for example, that the bluff frontier soldier had mastered the arts of geography well enough to be able to calculate with some approximate degree of accuracy the probable distance from Camp DuBois to the Pacific Ocean. Thus, despite their apparent use of erroneous maps of the day that indicated an easy progress over a single mountain ridge from the Missouri to the Columbia, Lewis and Clark, before they started, were able to use the longitude calculations of . . . others to determine the magnitude of the trek that lay before them. Had they never made the trip at all, they would at least have added this datum to the existing body of geographical knowledge.

It was as carefully trained agents of a civilized and flexible culture, then, that Lewis and Clark set out into the wilderness and injected the United States into the struggle for a national empire. Their journey took them up the Missouri to Fort Mandan, in present-day North Dakota, where they spent the winter of 1804-05. . . . Then they followed the Missouri along its great bend and down to the Three Forks, where they headed up the Jefferson River and crossed over into Montana's Bitterroot Valley via Lemhi Pass, in one of the most critical stretches of the entire trip. From the Bitterroot they made their way northward to the Clearwater and thence to the Columbia. Then they followed the main Columbia to the Pacific, which they reached on November 7, 1805. In one of the most dramatic moments in the history of exploration, William Clark stood one winter day in a slashing rain and carved on a tall yellow pine overlooking the Pacific: "William Clark December 3rd 1805. By Land from the U. States in 1804 and 1805."

It was in imitation of Alexander McKenzie's announcement of his earlier arrival at the shores of the Pacific far to the north on the Bella Coola River, and a conscious challenge to all other nations who wished to lay claim to the Columbia country. Not only had they collected the required data, filled the notebooks and journals demanded by Jefferson, but they also had served as diplomatic agents of the United States in establishing a claim to the Columbia.

After wintering at Fort Clatsop, the first American settlement west of the Continental Divide, they returned over a new route, with Lewis leading one party overland from Lo-Lo Pass via the

Sun River to the Great Falls of the Missouri, and Clark swinging southward to explore the Yellowstone River. They were reunited at the junction of the Missouri and the Yellowstone and gradually descended the Missouri to St. Louis, where they arrived on September 26, 1806, to the cheers of a small crowd assembled on the bank of the river. The story of their trip, which has been told many times, needs no recapitulation in detail. Its significance for the later history of American exploration lies in the flexible point of view which they brought to the West and which was to set the pattern for the many expeditions to follow. They had sketched in the broad outline of the continent, and they had brought back collections and data enough to suggest the immense value of the interior to all kinds of American enterprise. In so doing, they altered forever the focus and nature of the imperial struggle for North America.

But despite the fact that Lewis and Clark had made known such essentials as the width of the continent, the existence of numerous ranges of high mountains, the location and description of the major rivers of the Northwest and the rich resources of the whole region, what was eventually to become the American West was still largely a geographical mystery in the immediate years after their return. Not until 1814, with the publication of their report . . . , was there even a satisfactory cartographic representation of the whole region south and west of the Missouri River. Instead, for a long time the West remained an immense unknown, whose limits were gradually being defined by the explorers sent out into it by the governments and fur-trading companies along its margins.

They Also Traveled with Lewis and Clark: Sacagawea

One of the enduring stories of the Lewis and Clark expedition is that of Sacagawea, who accompanied the exploring party across to the Pacific and back. Donna J. Kessler has studied the image of Sacagawea in Euro-American legend and the uses that have been made of that legend. The following passage is taken from Donna J. Kessler, The Making of

Sacagawea: A Euro-American Legend *(Tuscaloosa, 1996), 9, 15, 17, 29-30.*

Sacagawea, a woman whose life and activities intersected with the most significant continental expedition in the history of the United States, has become the subject of a Euro-American legend. Because of the number of statues, paintings, novels, films, musical compositions, and histories that have featured her story, as well as an abundance of landmarks named in her honor, scholars from a variety of disciplines declare that she has been the most celebrated of all "American" heroines. . . .

The Lewis and Clark Expedition of 1804-1806 explicitly illustrated, in philosophy as well as in action, the nation's foundation myths. Also known as the Corps of Discovery, the exploration signified civilization's rightful penetration into a savage wilderness. As historian Bernard DeVoto argues in *The Course of Empire*, the expedition was no mere fact-finding mission. Thomas Jefferson, who had long planned the journey, outlined its manifold purposes: discovering the North West Passage, surveying uncharted areas, asserting American authority over the huge expanse of the Louisiana Purchase, and strengthening U.S. claims to the Columbia.

DeVoto further claims that aspirations to expand America to the edge of the continent constituted only part of the expedition's purpose. Another objective was to institute trade with indigenous tribes and nations while simultaneously asserting American sovereignty over them. Functioning as ambassadors of American's "Great Father," Lewis and Clark viewed themselves as offering the benefits of an "advanced" culture to native peoples. The spirit and actuality of exploration not only represented American notions of the land but also illustrated long-standing actions and beliefs concerning aboriginal populations. Associated with dominant ideologies of continental expansion and assimilation or removal of its native inhabitants, the trek embodied American frontier myths.

Acknowledging the mythic import of the expedition, many critics have designated the endeavor as "America's national epic."

Helen West argues, for instance, that the expedition continues to capture the imaginations of generations because it has symbolized uniquely American perceptions of strength, courage, and justice. Demonstrating the saga's grasp on an American populace in each decade since the return of the Corps, amateur and professional researchers have generated thousands of pages of data, drawings, maps, statues, paintings, and photographs featuring the Lewis and Clark Expedition. . . .

A participant in the most consequential continental expedition in the nation's history, Sacagawea has become an important adjunct of frontier traditions. Because hundreds of texts have connected her to this endeavor and declared her its sometime "savior," she has illustrated and validated critical facets of myths of manifest destiny. Very often featured as the sole native joining the Corps of Discovery, Sacagawea has come to signify "Indian" compliance with the mission to carve a sacred space out of the wilderness. As a result, creators have "made" her into an American cultural heroine. Texts embracing her story have initiated and propagated the Sacagawea legend, which has addressed the needs and interests of the dominant culture. Most of these works have simultaneously sustained socially constructed notions about the land, and many have reinforced stereotypes of America's indigenous peoples. . . .

Suppression of alternate interpretations inevitably occurs when culturally condoned understandings become fortified and enriched. Such has been the case with the legendary Sacagawea, at least until recently. Since Euro-America has assumed ownership of the Sacagawea narrative, almost no text embracing her story has pondered a number of compelling questions. Could credible alternate motivations, for example, have spurred her actions? Might Sacagawea have hurt others by helping the explorers to reach the Pacific? Would some readers interpret her behaviors as other than helpful? Rather than address these issues, most Euro-American writers and artists have applied "positive" words and meanings to Sacagawea. They have sustained the viability of the Indian princess stereotype as they have silenced other representations.

They Also Traveled With Lewis and Clark: York

Another traveler with Lewis and Clark was York, William Clark's body servant. York accompanied Clark across the continent, and while he was a slave, he was much more than that. He became an integral part of the Corps of Discovery. While Sacagawea has become an American heroine, little is known about York. Few Americans even know that an African American was a part of the Lewis and Clark expedition. Robert B. Betts examines this anomaly in this passage from his work, In Search of York: The Slave Who Went to the Pacific with Lewis and Clark *(Boulder, 1985) 147-49, 55-60.*

From documents written while or soon after York lived, we know he was the son of two slaves called Rose and "old York"; grew to be an unusually large and powerful man who was "black as a bear"; was inherited by William Clark from his father in 1799; went to the Pacific with his master and Meriwether Lewis on their exploration of the western two-thirds of North America in 1804-1806; was viewed with awe as "big medicine" by Indians who had never seen a black man; proved to be instrumental in keeping the Shoshonis from departing with the horses needed for the expedition to cross the Rockies; returned to civilization and continued to perform his duties as a body servant until at least the time of Clark's marriage in 1808; had a falling out with Clark prior to 1811 and was hired to a man in Louisville who treated him shabbily; in all probability lost his wife when her master moved to Natchez; was eventually freed and given a wagon and six horses, only to learn that freedom brought neither prosperity nor happiness; and died somewhere far from the relatives and friends he had been close to most of his life.

From what has been written and said about York by those who knew him, he had his full share of human foibles and admirable traits. When freed and on his own, he is reported to have been so lazy he could not get up in the morning, so careless with

---

Excerpts from *In Search of York: The Slave Who Went to the Pacific with Lewis and Clark*, by Robert B. Betts, 1985, Colorado Associated University Press, reprinted by permission of the publisher.

his horses that two of them died, and such a total failure in business and domestic service that he decided to give up his freedom and return to his former master. He also at one point did something which must have been shocking in Clark's eyes, for it was an all but unheard-of act for a master to reduce his body servant to the lowly state of a hired slave. On the other side of the coin, York was a kind man, as is testified to by the care he gave the dying Sergeant Floyd. He was a man of sufficient intelligence and polish to be a body servant, a position at the very top of the slave hierarchy. He was a man whose loyalty led him to search for Clark at risk to himself during the violent storm at the Great Falls. He was a man with a sense of humor, as well as a talent for drawing a long bow. And he was a man whose courage his comrades who kept journals on the expedition never once questioned.

It is ironic that although not a single derogatory remark was made about York in any of the journals of the Lewis and Clark Expedition, most of what has been written about him since has been tainted with prejudice. Time and again, he has been depicted as a jolly, irresponsible "darkie" whose only contribution to the enterprise was to make his companions laugh. In this regard, York is a classic example of the way American history was for so long written from an almost exclusively white point of view, with blacks more often than not presented as stereotypes of the ridiculous kind found in minstrel shows. But the real York, the York who continues to elude us, was no simple stereotype. As a living, breathing man, he was as complex and full of contradicitons as any other. As a man who endured the degradation and despair of slavery, he had thoughts and feelings which today cannot even be imagined. And as a man who was among the first to go beyond the sunset to the end of the continent, he knew the rare satisfaction of having done what no one had ever done before. For him to continue to be thought of as a racial stereotype would be, to put it mildly, a sad perversion of both history and common decency.

From the time he was a slave boy until he died in Tennessee (or just possibly among the Crows), York's life touched the heights and the depths of the world in which he lived. He served and was intimately associated with two men whose names rank high among all explorers; he knew one of the giants of the American Revolution, George Rogers Clark; he was for many months the daily companion of Sacagawea, one of this country's most honored women; and in all likelihood he met the man who dreamed of and designed the expedition, Thomas Jefferson. He saw with his own eyes whole new horizons of prairies, plains, and gigantic snow-capped mountains, and he shared the exultation expressed for all by his master when the expedition's objective was at last reached: "*Ocian in view*! O! the joy." At the same time, he knew what it was like to be the personal property of another man, to have a market value placed upon his body, to be helpless to prevent his wife from being taken from him, and to be despised because of his blackness even after he was legally free. In many different ways, the best and the worst York's world had to offer was reflected in his life. . . .

While it is regrettable that most people have never heard of York, it is deplorable that the relatively few who have read something about him have in all likelihood been led to believe he was a buffoon. This is because in much of what has been written about Lewis and Clark he has been treated as a racial stereotype, a ludicrous figure not to be taken seriously and certainly one not to be thought of as having contributed to the exploration in any significant way. To illustrate how effectively prejudice has denied him the recognition he deserves, it is almost certain that if an opera is ever written about the expedition, Sacagawea will be the prima donna and he will only carry a spear. At least this is the way they have been cast to date, with Sacagawea receiving "what in the United States counts as canonization if not deification" for her role in the enterprise, whereas York has been relegated to the background. This is by no means to detract from the Indian girl, who was helpful in a number of ways, but rather to point out how the myth-makers have either ignored or distorted the words of the original sources in order to glorify one while more often than not making the other the butt of biased humor. . . .

Putting aside for the moment the many misrepresentations of York . . . the York of the Lewis and Clark journals stands on his own. A close reading of those basic documents reveals that he did indeed play a meaningful role, if for no other reason than that he carried his share of the daily duties and labors required to advance the expedition along its course. This by itself was no small contribution and should have earned him the same degree of recognition given his companions, the rank and file who collectively have been honored for leading the way into the American West. But York's contributions do not end there. By his very presence he was of value to Lewis and Clark in their dealings with a number of Indian tribes, and, at the critical moment when Lewis met the Shoshonis, he was a factor—perhaps even the decisive factor—in making it possible for them to obtain horses and continue on.

The journals strongly suggest that York's blackness served the expedition as a passport to western tribes who were so curious to see such a strange creature, and so impressed after they had, they greeted the white visitors more cordially than they might otherwise have done. While it goes without saying that the white man's domination of the Indians was primarily due to his advanced weapons, he often reminded them of his superiority by displaying mysterious scientific instruments or by performing tricks with such simple gadgets as mirrors and magnets. These the astonished Indians called "big medicine," meaning something they could not comprehend and therefore viewed with awe as sacred, and part of this awe was in turn transferred to those who controlled the magic. Of all the wonders Lewis and Clark paraded before tribes who had never seen a black man, none was more wonderful than York, as is testified to by Pierre Antoine Tabeau, a Missouri River trader who was with the Arikaras when the expedition arrived. Providing one of the rare physical descriptions of York written by anyone who saw him in the flesh, Tabeau observed: "The quadrant, phosphorous, and the magnet were regarded at the Captains' as medicine; that is to say, as supernatural and powerful. The most marvelous was, though, a large, fine man, black as a bear, who spoke and acted as one." (The reference to York speaking and acting like a bear has to do with him telling the Arikaras he had been wild until caught and tamed by Clark.)

Time and again, the color of York's skin impressed the Indians, and at one point may even have intimidated them. A Nez Perce legend has it that when the hungry and weakened expedition came out of the Bitterroots, most of the tribe wanted to kill the white intruders, but were frightened of the black man who was with them. One version of the story describes the tribe's reaction in these words: "He had shining eyes that rolled around in his head. 'If we kill these others,' they said, 'the black man will surely kill us.' So they let the strangers come on." Whether or not this legend has been enlarged and embroidered over the years (as is often the case with legends), it is true a number of tribes were awed by York's singularity, and it is also true he was the main attraction in Lewis and Clark's traveling magic show. While descending the Columbia, Clark gave Sacagawea's presence credit for having signaled the potentially hostile natives along the way that the expedition's intentions were peaceful, "as no woman ever accompanies a war party of Indians in this quarter." Perhaps he and others since should have given York a little credit for also having smoothed the path. . . .

Solely on the basis of what is written in the journals, there is reason to believe that York conducted himself in such a manner as to gain the esteem of his comrades as time went on. To recap some of the things he did which must have impressed them favorably, he was kind to Sergeant Floyd in his last hours; he regularly brought in welcome meat and fowl; he participated in the important reconnaissance of the Marias River; he continued to search for Clark and the Charbonneaus during the height of the fierce storm at the Great Falls; he went ahead with Clark and just two others to find the Shoshonis when it was not known whether they would be friendly or hostile; and his success in trading with the Nez Perces for badly needed food for the return crossing of the Bitterroots was applauded by Lewis himself. Moreover, because one of the journalists would have said so if York had conducted himself otherwise, it can be taken for granted he did everything that was asked of him, did not shrink from the hardships and the dangers, and served Lewis and Clark as faithfully as any of the other men. Perhaps most meaningful of all, when the location of winter quarters was being decided at the Pacific, his captains and his comrades waived all accepted practices and allowed him, a slave, to vote. Surely, this is not the profile of a man who, as so many writers would have us believe, was little more than a buffoon.

Lewis and Clark Among the Indians

In the nearly two and a half years of almost constant contact between the Corps of Discovery and the native Americans, there were moments of apprehension during encounters with various tribes. There were also periods where the good-will of the Indians was essential to the survival of the small band of Americans. James P. Ronda has pointed out that exploration was a shared experience and that Indian cooperation was crucial to the eventual success of the expedition. Excerpted from James P. Ronda, Lewis and Clark Among the Indians *(Lincoln, 1984), 252-55.*

Exploration was a cooperative endeavor requiring substantial information and support from the Indians. The Indians shaped the exploratory effort by their very presence on the land. They were people to be reckoned with, whether as potential sources of aid or as possible enemies. No latter-day Coronado or Champlain could ignore them. The anticipated behavior of the Indians was a decisive factor in the choice of equipment, personnel, routes, camp rules, and even ultimate destination. Whatever the official objectives, explorers carefully considered their presence.

But we need to measure more than explorer's reactions to a passive population. Indians were active participants in exploration, as the first comers to the land and, later, as guides for Euro-Americans. To a vast enterprise they lent their intelligence, skill, and nerve. Certainly the Lewis and Clark expedition benefited greatly from the Indians' knowledge and support. Maps, route information, food, horses, open-handed friendship—all gave the Corps of Discovery the edge that spelled the difference between success and failure. The presence of Sacagawea on the expedition's roster is only the barest hint of what Indian support meant to Lewis's "darling project." That roster should also include names like Sheheke, Cameahwait, Old Toby, Tetoharsky, Twisted Hair, and Flint Necklace. There needs to be a place for those unnamed Shoshoni women who carried expedition baggage over Lemhi Pass as well as for countless Indians who traded food and affection. As guides, packers, interpreters, and cartographers, native Americans were essential to Lewis and Clark's achievement.

Lewis and Clark left St. Louis filled with apprehension about encounters with hostile Indians. But what emerged over nearly two and a half years of western travel was an atmosphere of friendship and mutual trust between men and women who shared a common frontier life. Indians and explorers stood together in the rituals of hunting, holidays, and horse racing. Sex, sports, and music were simple pleasures that united strangers.

Lewis admitted as much when he wrote, "So long have our men been accustomed to a friendly intercourse with the natives, that we find it difficult to impress on their minds the necessity of always being on guard with rispect to them." The assertion that the Corps of Discovery acted like "a conquering army" of hungry imperialists does not square with either the Lewis and Clark record or the larger history of North American exploration. . . .

The typical patterns of friendship and sharing that generally characterized Indian-expedition relations were not the result of any special nobility of character on either side of the cultural divide. Native hospitality was both genuine and useful as tribal people sought trade or attempted to manipulate the expedition for personal ends. For their party, Lewis and Clark recognized the necessity of Indian cooperation. There were undeniable moments of swagger, bluster, and arrogance, but more often than not good sense and patience won the day. . . . For most of the journey there was mutual respect born of expediency. That respect and friendship was genuine nonetheless. Lewis and Clark left behind among many Indians a legacy of nonviolent contact. Those who came later enjoyed that legacy and too often betrayed it.

If expedition-Indian personal relations were amiable, success did not come so easily when Lewis and Clark ventured into diplomatic waters. . . . Lewis and Clark believed that official diplomacy was a simple matter of rearranging Indian patterns to suit the needs of the new nation. Proclaiming American sovereignty, establishing trade connections, and constituting delegations to visit Jefferson all seemed goals within easy reach. Who could deny the rationality of intertribal peace or a united front against common enemies? But when the captains sought to implement those policies, they met the often unyielding realities of village and band politics. Lewis and Clark's ill-considered attempt to forge a villager alliance against the Teton Sioux illustrates the depth of their ignorance. The explorers comprehended neither river economics nor plains politics. In a world where "peace" meant "truce" and where warriors fought one day and traded the next, Lewis and Clark were simply unable and sometimes unwilling to face the facts of native life.

Lewis and Clark's Indian diplomacy failed in part because the explorers were blind to those western facts of life. But the failure of the villager alliance and the promises of intertribal peace extracted at so many councils came from something more fundamental than naive optimism. What seemed failure for the captains was often success for the chiefs. It was more than inept policy and cultural arrogance that kept federal goals just out of reach. When Lewis and Clark came into the West and Pacific Northwest, native political sovereignty and autonomy were still potent realities. Men like Le Borgne, Cameahwait, and Broken Arm enjoyed genuine power. They and their counselors could make decisions without bowing to the dictates of faraway white fathers. Despite Lewis and Clark's rhetoric, western Indians were not "our red children." Rather, they were mature adults with a substantial measure of freedom to choose those parts of the American program that best suited their own needs. Diplomacy during the journey was ceremony and talk among equals, even if Lewis and Clark did not always recognize that fact. If the captains failed to persuade the Indians to become children of a distant father, it was because the Indians still had the power to accept American guns while rejecting less useful gifts.

Bernard DeVoto once wrote that the records of the Lewis and Clark expedition amounted to "the first detailed account of whatever length, of the western tribes." The ethnographic legacy has proven to be one of Lewis and Clark's most durable contributions, although its value was not plain at the time of the expedition. Guided by Jefferson's precise instructions and their own curiosity, expedition ethnographers amassed a virtual library of information about the Indians. Journal entries, vocabularies, drawings, maps, artifacts, population estimates—all hold priceless knowledge about Indian ways from the great river to the western sea. When Nicholas Biddle first examined that ethnographic data, he felt some reason to apologize for its inadequacies. "Those who first visit the ground," wrote the Philadelphian, "can only be expected to furnish sketches, rude and imperfect." But Biddle's evaluation missed the mark. The expedition gathered far more than "rude and imperfect" records. In their writing, drawing, and collecting they managed to capture an essential part of American life on the edge of profound change.

In 1821 an obscure North West Company mariner named Peter Corney wrote, "By the journey of Captains Lewis and Clark across the Rocky mountains to the Pacific Ocean, the whole of that western region is now laid open." It was more than rivers and mountains that were laid open to view. Lewis and Clark were part of an expansionist movement that steadily brought traders, bureaucrats, ranchers, and farmers into Mandan, Shoshoni, Nez Perce, and Chinookan homelands.

Questions

1. *How would you describe the purpose of the Lewis and Clark expedition? What were their major achievements?*
2. *What explains the making of the legend of Sacagawea? How has this myth-making served the purposes of American writers?*
3. *Donna J. Kessler suggests that alternative interpretations of Sacagawea have been, until recently, suppressed. Explain what she means, and describe what alternative interpretations there might be.*
4. *York's role in the Lewis and Clark expedition, unlike that of Sacagawea, has been relegated to obscurity. Why did historians reduce York to a stereotype? What evidence did Robert B. Betts present to show that York was an important and integral part of the Corps of Discovery? How did the Indians react to York?*
5. *James P. Ronda suggests that while Lewis and Clark's Indian diplomacy failed, their relations with the Indians were successful in many other ways. Explain the reasons for the failure of their diplomacy, and evaluate what they did achieve.*

The Lewis and Clark Expedition

As William H. Goetzmann explained in the first section, the Lewis and Clark expedition was more than a simple exploration of the American West. It involved the national aspirations of the United States, as well as the interests of European nations, who also hoped to exploit the natural resources of the western part of the North American continent. The Louisiana Purchase, concluded in 1803, brought under the American flag a large portion of the region from the Mississippi to the Rocky Mountains, including the Missouri River and its tributaries. The Lewis and Clark expedition helped to lay the basis for the American claim to the Oregon Country. Beyond claiming more land for the United States, the exploration also clearly served commercial purposes. Based largely on the groundwork laid by Lewis and Clark among the western Indians, the American Fur Company, established by John Jacob Astor, opened operations in the far West as early as 1808. It was also, as Jefferson termed it, a "literary" undertaking, to satisfy the curiosity of Jefferson and other scientists about this largely unknown region. Lewis and Clark, in many ways, satisfied this thirst for knowledge about the natural history, the geography and geology, and the inhabitants of the West.

Jefferson's Role in Beginning the Expedition

Although Jefferson never visited the West himself, his interest in that region and his intuitive recognition that the future destiny of his country lay in claiming and exploring the vast unknown region beyond the Mississippi River to the Pacific led him to promote the Lewis and Clark expedition. His role in gaining congressional approval for the Lewis and Clark trek and his aspirations for the exploration are explained in the following excerpt from his message to Congress on 18 January 1803. Taken from Donald Jackson, ed., Letters of the Lewis and Clark Expedition: With Related Documents, 1783-1854 *(Urbana, 1962), 11-13. (The original spelling has been maintained, but punctuation conventions have been modernized in the following selections.)*

Jefferson's Message to Congress [18 January 1803]

The Indian tribes residing within the limits of the U.S. have for a considerable time been growing more & more uneasy at the constant diminution of the territory they occupy, altho' effected by their own voluntary sales: and the policy has long been gaining strength with them of refusing absolutely all further sale on any conditions, insomuch that, at this time, it hazards their friendship, and excites dangerous jealousies & perturbations in their minds to make any overture for the purchase of the smallest portions of their land. A very few tribes only are not yet obstinately in these dispositions. In order peaceably to counteract this policy of theirs, and to provide an extension of territory which the rapid increase of our numbers will call for, two measures are deemed expedient. First, to encourage them to abandon hunting, to apply to the raising [of] stock, to agriculture and domestic manufacture, and thereby prove to themselves that less land & labour will maintain them in this, better than in their former mode of living. The extensive forests necessary in the hunting life, will then become useless, & they will see advantage in exchanging them for the means of improving their farms, & of increasing their domestic comforts. Secondly to multiply trading houses among them, & place within their reach those things which will contribute more to their domestic comfort than the possession of extensive, but uncultivated wilds. Experience & reflection will develope to them the wisdom of exchanging what they can spare & we want, for what we can spare and they want. In leading them thus to agriculture, to manufactures & civilization, in bringing together their & our settlements, & in preparing them ultimately to participate in the benefits of our government, I trust and believe we are acting for their greatest good. At these trading houses we have pursued the principles of the act of Congress, which directs that the commerce shall be carried on liberally, & requires only that the capital stock shall not be diminished. We consequently undersell private traders, foreign & domestic, drive them from the competition, & thus, with the good will of the Indians, rid ourselves of a description of men who are constantly endeavoring to excite in the Indian mind suspicions, fears & irritations towards us. A letter now inclosed shows the effect of our competition on the operations of the traders, while the Indians, percieving the advantage of purchasing from us, are solliciting generally our establishment of trading houses among them. . . .

While the extension of the public commerce among the Indian tribes may deprive of that source of profit such of our citizens as are engaged in it, it might be worthy the attention of Congress, in their care of individual as well as of the general interest to point in another direction the enterprize of these citizens, as profitably for themselves, and more usefully for the public. The river Missouri, & the Indians inhabiting it, are not as well known as is rendered desireable by their connection with the Missisipi, & consequently with us. It is however understood that the country on that river is inhabited by numerous tribes, who furnish great supplies of furs & peltry to the trade of another nation carried on in a high latitude, through an infinite number of portages and lakes, shut up by ice through a long season. The commerce on that line could bear no competition with that of the Missouri, traversing a moderate climate, offering according to the best accounts a continued navigation from it's source, and, possibly with a single portage, from the Western ocean, and finding to the Atlantic a choice of channels through the Illinois or Wabash, the Lakes and Hudson, through the Ohio and Susquehanna or Potomac or James rivers, and through the Tennessee and Savannah rivers. An intelligent officer with ten or twelve chosen men, fit for the enterprize and willing to undertake it, taken from our posts, where they may be spared without inconvenience, might explore the whole line, even to the Western ocean, have conferences with the natives on the subject of commercial intercourse, get admission among them for our traders as others are admitted, agree on convenient deposits for an interchange of articles, and return with the information acquired in the course of two summers. Their arms & accoutrements, some instruments of observation, & light & cheap presents for the Indians would be all the apparatus they could carry, and with an expectation of a soldier's portion of land on their return would constitute the whole expense. Their pay would be going on, whether here or there. While other civilized nations have encountered great expense to enlarge the boundaries of knowledge, by undertaking voyages of discovery, & for other literary purposes, in various parts and directions, our nation seems to owe to the same object, as well as to its own interest, to explore this, the only line of easy communication across the continent, and so directly traversing our own part of it. The interests of commerce place the principal object within the constitutional powers and care of Congress, and that it should incidentally advance the geographical knowledge of our own continent can not but be an additional gratification. The nation claiming the territory, regarding this as a literary pursuit which it is in the habit of permitting within it's dominions would not be disposed to view it with jealousy, even if the expiring state of it's interest there did not render it a matter of indifference. The appropriation of two thousand five hundred dollars 'for the purpose of extending the external commerce of the U.S.,' while understood and considered by the Executive as giving the legislative sanction, would cover the undertaking from notice, and prevent the obstructions which interested individuals might otherwise previously prepare in it's way.

Lewis Reports on the Prospects of the Expedition

The Corps of Discovery began their trek up the Missouri on 14 May 1804, and they spent their first winter at Fort Mandan (in present-day North Dakota). From this vantage point, Lewis assessed the state of the expedition in letters to his mother, Lucy Marks, and to President Jefferson. Clearly, he was enthusiastic and pleased not only with the country he was passing through but also with the success of the exploration up to that point in time. Excerpted from Donald Jackson, ed., Letters of the Lewis and Clark Expedition: With Related Documents, 1783-1854 *(Urbana, 1962), 222, 225, 231-34.*

Lewis to Lucy Marks, 31 March 1805

I arrived at this place on the 27th of October last with the party under my command, destined to the Pacific Ocean, by way of the Missouri and Columbia rivers. The near approach of winter, the low state of the water, and the known scarcity of timber which exists on the Missouri for many hundred Miles above the Mandans, together with many other considerations equally important, determined my friend and companion Capt. Clark and myself, to fortify ourselves and remain for the winter in the neighbourhood of the Mandans . . . who are the most friendly and well disposed savages we have yet met with. . . .

This immence river so far as we have yet ascended, waters one of the fairest portions of the globe, nor do I believe that there is in the universe a similar extent of country, equally fertile, well watered, and intersected by such a number of navigable streams. . . .

[T]he ice in the Missouri has now nearly dissapea[red.] I shal set out on my voyage in the course of a few [days.] I can foresee no material obstruction to our progress, and [I] feel the most perfect confidence that we shall reach [the Pa]cific Ocean this sum[mer.] For myself individually I [enjoy] better health than I [have] since I commenced my [voyage. The] party are now in [good] health and excellent sperits, [are at]tatched to the enterp[rise and] anxious to proceed; not a whisper of discontent or murmur is to be heared among them, but all act in unison, and with the most perfect harmony. With such men, I feel every confidence necessary to insure success. The party with Capt. Clark and myself, consists of thirty one white persons, one negroe man, and two Indians. . . .

Lewis to Jefferson, 7 April 1805

Herewith inclosed you will receive an invoice of certain articles, which I have forwarded to you from this place. Among other articles, you will observe by reference to the invoice, 67. specimens of earths, salts and minerals; and 60 specimens of plants; these are accompanyed by their rispective labels expressing the days on which obtained, places where found, and also their virtues and properties when known. By means of these labels, reference may be made to the Chart of the Missouri forwarded to the Secretary at War, on which, the encampment of each day has been carefully marked; thus the places at which these specimens have been obtained may be easily pointed out, or again found, should any of them prove valuable to the community on further investegation. These have been forwarded with a view of their being presented to the Philosophical society of Philadelphia, in order that they may under their direction be examined or analyzed. After examining these specimens yourself, I would thank you to have a copy of their labels made out, and retained untill my return. The other articles are intended particularly for yourself, to be retained, or disposed off as you may think proper.

The Trek Across the Continent

The journey to the Pacific Ocean and back was by no means as easy as Lewis apparently assumed. Along the way they encountered great dangers and incredible hardships. Nevertheless, they persevered. The journals of Lewis and Clark relate the great adventure. A few highlights of their experience are excerpted from Bernard DeVoto, The Journals of Lewis and Clark *(Boston, 1953), 75, 108-9, 118, 171.*

[Clark], 1 January 1805

The Day was ushered in by the Descharge of two Cannon, we Suffered 16 men with their Musick to visit the 1st Village for the purpose of Danceing, by as they Said the perticular request of the Chiefs of that Village. About 11 oClock I with an inturpeter & two men walked up to the Village, (my views were to alay Some little Miss understanding which had taken place thro jelloucy and mortification as to our treatment towards them.) I found them much pleased at the Danceing of our men. I ordered my black Servent to Dance which amused the Croud Verry much, and Somewhat astonished them, that So large a man should be active &c. . . .

[Lewis], 14 May 1805

. . . In the evening, the men in two of the rear canoes discovered a large brown bear lying in the open grounds about 300 paces from the river, and six of them went out to attack him, all good hunters;

they took the advantage of a small eminence which concealed them and got within 40 paces of him, unperceived. Two of them reserved their fires as had been previously conscerted, the four others fired nearly at the same time and put each his bullet through him, two of the balls passed through the bulk of both lobes of his lungs. In an instant this monster ran at them with open mouth, the two who had reserved their fir[e]s discharged their pieces at him as he came towards them, boath of them struck him, one only slightly and the other fortunately broke his shoulder. This however only retarded his motion for a moment. The men unable to reload their guns took to flight, the bear pursued and had very nearly overtaken them before they reached the river; two of the party betook themselves to a canoe and the others seperated an[d] concealed themselves among the willows, reloaded their pieces, each discharged his piece at him as they had an opportunity. They struck him several times again but the guns served only to direct the bear to them. In this manner he pursued two of them seperately so close that they were obliged to throw aside their guns and pouches and throw themselves into the river altho' the bank was nearly twenty feet perpendicular. So enraged was this anamal that he plunged into the river only a few feet behind the second man he had compelled [to] take refuge in the water, when one of those who still remained on shore shot him through the head and finally killed him. They then took him ashore and butch[er]ed him when they found eight balls had passed through him in different directions. The bear being old the flesh was indifferent, they therefore only took the skin and fleece, the latter made us several gallons of oil. . . .

[Lewis], 26 May 1805

. . . I beheld the Rocky Mountains for the first time. . . . [W]hile I viewed these mountains I felt a secret pleasure in finding myself so near the head of the heretofore conceived boundless Missouri; but when I reflected on the difficulties which this snowey barrier would most probably throw in my way to the Pacific, and the sufferings and hardships of myself and party in thim, it in some measure counterballanced the joy I had felt in the first moments in which I gazed on them; but as I have always held it a crime to anticipate evils I will believe it a good comfortable road untill I am compelled to believe differently. . . .

[Lewis], 28 July 1805, at the three forks of the Missouri

. . . Our present camp is precisely on the spot . . . [where] the Minnetarees . . . killed 4 men 4 women a number of boys, and mad[e] prisoners of all the females and four boys. *Sah-cah-gar-we-ah* o[u]r Indian woman was one of the female prisoners taken at that time; tho' I cannot discover that she shews any immotion of sorrow in recollecting this event, or of joy in being restored to her native country; if she has enough to eat and a few trinkets to wear I believe she would be perfectly content anywhere.

Sacagawea Reunites with Her Brother

By an incredible coincidence, Sacagawea was not only reunited with her people, she also found her brother. This excerpt is from the Nicholas Biddle edition of the Lewis and Clark journals and is found in Bernard DeVoto, ed. The Journals of Lewis and Clark *(Boston, 1953), 203.*

While Sacagawea was renewing among the women the friendships of former days, Captain Clarke went on, and was received by Captain Lewis and the chief, who after the first embraces and salutations were over, conducted him to a sort of circular tent or shade of willows. Here he was seated on a white robe; and the chief immediately tied in his hair six small shells resembling pearls, an ornament highly valued by these people, who procure them in the course of trade from the sea-coast. The moccasins of the whole party were then taken off, and after much ceremony the smoking began. After this the conference was to be opened, and glad of an opportunity of being able to converse more intelligibly, Sacagawea was sent for; she came into the tent, sat down, and was beginning to interpret, when in the person of Cameahwait she recognised her brother: She instantly jummped up, and ran and embraced him, throwing over him her blanket and weeping profusely: The chief was himself moved, though not in the same degree. After some conversation between them she resumed her seat, and attempted to interpret for us, but her new situation seemed to overpower her, and she was frequently interrupted by her tears.

Further Experiences on the Journey

Along the way, Lewis and Clark encountered Indians who had never seen white men. One encounter revealed an unanticipated consequence in having Sacagawea with the party. The Corps of Discovery faced many hardships and survived on meager rations. One delicacy they relied on frequently was the flesh of dogs. The following excerpts are from Bernard DeVoto, The Journals of Lewis and Clark *(Boston, 1953), 256-57, 298.*

[Clark], 19 October 1805

I observed a great number of Lodges on the opposit Side at some distance below, and Several Indians on the opposit bank passing up to where Capt. Lewis was with the Canoes. Others I saw on a knob nearly opposit to me at which place they delayed but a Short time, before they returned to their Lodges as fast as they could run.

I was fearfull that those people might not be informed of us. I deturmined to take the little canoe which was with me and proceed with the three men in it to the Lodges. On my aproach not one person was to be seen except three men off in the plains, and they sheared off as I saw approached near the Shore. I landed in front of five Lodges which was at no great distance from each other, Saw no person the enterance or Dores of the Lodges wer Shut with the Same materials of which they were built a Mat. I approached one with a pipe in my hand entered a lodge which was the nearest to me found 32 persons men, women and a few children Setting permiscuisly in the Lodge, in the greatest agutation, Some crying and ringing there hands, others hanging their heads. I gave my hand to them all and made Signs of my friendly dispo[si]tion and offered the men my pipe to Smok and distributed a fiew Small articles which I had in my pockets. This measure passified those distressed people verry much. I then sent one man into each lodge and entered a Second myself the inhabitants of which I found more fritened than those of the first lodge. I destributed Sundrey Small articles amongst them, and Smoked with the men. I then Set my self on a rock and made signs to the men to come out and Smoke with me not one come out untill the canoes arrived with the 2 Chiefs, one of whom spoke aloud, and as was their custom to all we had passed. the Indians came out & Set by me and smoked. They said we came from the clouds &c. &c. and were not men &c. &c. this time Capt. Lewis came down with the canoes in which the Indian[s were]. as Soon as they Saw the Squar wife of the interperter they pointed to her and informed those who continued yet in the Same position I first found them. they imediately all came out and appeared to assume new life, the sight of This Indian woman, wife to one of our interprs. confirmed those people of our friendly intentions, as no woman ever accompanies a war party of Indians in this quarter. . . .

[Clark], 3 January 1806

At 11 A.M. we were visited by our near neighbour Chief . . . and six Clatsops. they brought for Sale Some roots berries and 3 Dogs also a Small quantity of fresh blubber. this blubber they informed us they had obtained from their neighbours the *Cal la mox* who inhabit the coast to the S.E. near one of their Villages a Whale had recently perished. this blubber the Indians eat and esteem it excellent food. our party from necescity have been obliged to Subsist some length of time on dogs have now become extreamly fond of their flesh; it is worthey of remark that while we lived principally on the flesh of this animal we wer much more helthy strong and more fleshey then we have been Sence we left the Buffalow Country. as for my own part I have not become reconsiled to the taste of this animal as yet.

[*Lewis's notation of the same date says: "I have become so perfectly reconciled to the dog that I think it an agreeable food and would prefer it vastly to lean Venison or Elk."*]

Lewis Reports a Successful Conclusion of the Expedition

Immediately upon arriving in St. Louis, Lewis sent a letter to Jefferson reporting their safe arrival and summarizing the exploration. In doing so, Lewis laid out some of the benefits of his trek across the continent. Excerpted from Donald D. Jackson, ed., Letters of the Lewis and Clark Expedition: With Related Documents, 1783-1854 *(Urbana, 1962), 319-25.*

Lewis to Jefferson, 23 September 1806

It is with pleasure that I anounce to you the safe arrival of myself and party at 12 OClk. today at this place with our papers and baggage. In obedience to your orders we have penitrated the Continent of North America to the Pacific Ocean, and sufficiently explored the interior of the country to affirm with confidence that we have discovered the most practicable rout which doese exist across the continent by means of the navigable branches of the Missouri and Columbia Rivers. . . .

We view this passage across the Continent as affording immence advantages to the fur trade, but fear that the advantages which it offers as a communication for the productions of the Eeast indies to the United States and thence to Europe will never be found equal on an extensive scale to that by way of the Cape of Good hope; still we believe that many articles not bulky brittle nor of a very perishable nature may be conveyed to the United States by this rout with more facility and at less expence than by that at present practiced. . . .

In the infancy of the trade across the continent, or during the period that the trading establishments shall be confined to the Missouri and it's branches, the men employed in this trade will be compelled to convey the furs collected in that quarter as low on the Columbia as tide water, in which case they could not return to the falls of the Missouri untill about the 1st of October, which would be so late in the season that there would be considerable danger of the river being obstructed by ice before they could reach this place and consequently that the comodites brought from the

East indies would be detained untill the following spring; but this difficulty will at once vanish when establishments are also made on the Columbia, and a sufficient number of men employed at them to convey annually the productions of the East Indies to the upper establishment on the Kooskooske, and there exchange them with the men of the Missouri for their furs, in the begining of July. By this means the furs not only of the Missouri but those also of the Columbia may be shiped to the East indies by the season before mentioned, and the comodities of the East indies arrive at St. Louis or the mouth of the Ohio by the last of September in each year. . . .

With rispect to the exertions and services rendered by that esteemable man Capt. William Clark in the course of the late voyage I cannot say too much; if sir any credit be due for the success of that arduous enterprize in which we have been mutually engaged, he is equally with myself entitled to your consideration and that of our common country. . . .

Questions

1. *How did Jefferson justify the Lewis and Clark expedition to Congress? To what extent was trade with the Indians a means of government control over the Indians? How did Jefferson rationalize the extension of trade into the Missouri River region?*
2. *How did Lewis characterize his exploration to his mother? How did he foresee their prospects for the remainder of the expedition?*
3. *In what ways does Lewis's letter to Jefferson from Fort Mandan reveal the scientific purposes of the expedition? What accounts for his optimism about the prospects for the success of his mission?*
4. *What do the journals of Lewis and Clark reveal about the caliber of men who led the expedition? What characteristics are displayed that made this trek so successful?*
5. *Why do you suppose Lewis devoted much of his report after his return to the commercial prospects arising from his discoveries? Since his expedition had shown there was no easy passage to the Pacific Ocean, what commercial development did he foresee?*

FURTHER READING

The literature on the Lewis and Clark expedition is vast. The most complete edition of their original journals is Gary Moulton, ed., The Journals of the Lewis and Clark Expedition *11 vols. (Lincoln, 1983-87). A recent, highly acclaimed biography, which also covers the expedition in great detail, is Stephen E. Ambrose,* Undaunted Courage: Meriwether Lewis, Thomas Jefferson, and the Opening of the American West *(New York, 1996). James P. Ronda's* Lewis and Clark among the Indians *(Lincoln, 1984), is excellent. There are several very good works that examine the Lewis and Clark expedition in the broader context of western exploration. These include: Bernard De Voto,* The Course of Empire *(Boston, 1952); William H. Goetzmann,* Exploration and Empire: The Explorer and the Scientist in the Winning of the American West *(New York, 1966); and Donald Jackson,* Thomas Jefferson & the Stony Mountains: Exploring the West from Monticello *(Urbana, 1981).*

Growing Up in Nineteenth-Century America

Randolph A. Roth

Introduction

Young people in early and mid-nineteenth-century America were typically the sons and daughters of parents who owned small shops or farms. Such parents supported local schools and churches. They spent a great deal of time and money educating their children and teaching them the rudiments of faith in hopes they would prosper financially and live in harmony with their neighbors. In times of trouble, these families turned to relatives and churches for help. If children worked hard, stayed in school, and followed God's commandments, and if death or crippling illness did not strike their parents, children usually followed in their parents' footsteps and carried on their way of life.

After 1815, as population pressure and economic change diminished opportunities for self-employment, more young men sought their fortunes in the cities and on the frontier, and more young women supported themselves by working in textile mills or by manufacturing shoes and clothes for local merchants. Young people married later and took longer to set up their own households and businesses. But growing up remained, for all that, a more leisurely process than it is today. Young people seldom felt, as middle and upper-class students in high schools and colleges do today, that "this year" would make or break them.

A substantial minority of young people, however, grew up in poverty. There was no "safety net" in the nineteenth century for families in economic trouble. There was no unemployment insurance, no social security insurance to replace the wages of a deceased or disabled parent, and no means of tracking down deadbeat parents and garnishing their wages. Nor did the law do much to protect children. There were no laws against child labor or corpo-

ral punishment. There were no compulsory school attendance laws in the North prior to the 1850s, and none in the South until the twentieth century. Many poor children worked full-time outside the home by the age of ten or eleven. Working children were vulnerable, their fates dependent upon chance and the whims of strangers.

Rebellious Youths

Young people who would grow up to become hardworking, God-fearing members of the upper or middle classes still fought with their parents and teachers from time to time. As historians Randolph A. Roth and Helen Lefkowitz Horowitz show, the American Revolution gave young people in the countryside and on college campuses new ideas about their own power and prompted them to turn the "means of socialization"—education, religion, and civic rituals—against adults. They put their own interpretations on the Bible and other books and used patriotic holidays and disciplinary proceedings to assert their independence and defy authority. Parents and teachers adjusted, recognizing that their power over their young people had diminished.

Wayward Youths: Raising Adolescents in Vermont

The following selection looks at the experience of rural Vermont during the early nineteenth century. From Randolph A. Roth, The Democratic Dilemma: Religion, Reform, and the Social Order in the Connecticut River Valley of Vermont, 1791–1850 (Cambridge, 1987), 46–52, 54.

The Calvinists of southern New England, had had difficulties for decades with young members and prospective or potential

---

members of their churches. As always, the problem was the youthful penchant for mischief and for experimentation with alcohol, tobacco, gambling, and sex. Young people also had difficulties transforming their youthful religious zeal into mature piety. Adult Calvinists, north and south, tried to deal with these problems straightforwardly, doubling their efforts to supervise, discipline, and convert the young. Despite exhortations to righteousness, however, they could not bring even penitent youths to give up their irreverent attitudes toward certain sins. Nor could they sustain or moderate the intense outbursts of moral fervor and religious conviction that occurred at intervals throughout the period among young people. This was especially true if these outbursts got out of hand, and the young converted before reaching moral maturity or—what was worse—turned their perfervid enthusiasm against adult church members, condemning them for inconsistent doctrines and lack of piety. These problems were not in themselves new, but adult Calvinists seemed to be at a loss as to how to deal with them.

Henry Stevens, a farmer and innkeeper from Barnet, demonstrated how reputable, churchgoing young people could impede the Calvinist cause by at once delighting in and repenting the wrongfulness of their escapades. Stevens began a diary in 1811 at age twenty. He expressed regret about not going to meeting more often and lamented that he lived in a place "inhabited by many young people and Devilish proud." As he began to confess his misdeeds, however, Stevens often forgot to be remorseful. His accounts of his "boyish courtships" turned into "some fine stories about some Lyman [New Hampshire] ladies," the girls across the Connecticut River with whom Henry and his friends most often dallied (the Barnet boys preferred to risk their reputations a safe distance from home). Later in the diary, a regretful account of youthful "scrapes" was interrupted by the entry of July 4, 1812, passing judgment on a day that saw Stevens and several young friends drink grog all morning, offering seventeen patriotic toasts to their country "in less than an hour," and march to the town's Liberty Pole to offer seventeen more "in presence of a Large company. Done well."

How could reputable youths like Stevens, dedicated to their churches, simultaneously lament and delight in their misdeeds? That question confounded Calvinists throughout the valley. They knew that human nature allowed contrary impulses to reside together in weak souls. What they did not want to acknowledge was that young people lived by two standards and felt the continual pull of two lives and two sets of values.

Young woman reading a book. Reading was an important form of recreation (and means of edification) by the early nineteenth century. (Courtesy of PhotoDisc, Inc.)

Like all but the most otherworldly of their friends and relatives, young people dwelt in at least two overlapping but distinct spheres of social life, one within their churches and one outside in the community at large. Both spheres offered the young people of the valley opportunities to meet with neighbors, to test their attractions on the opposite sex, to court, and to forge and express loyalty to their neighborhoods, communities, and nation. Whereas one centered on the church, however, on displaying moral and spiritual maturity, on striving for unity, on observing Christian rituals and Christian holidays—in other words, on realizing the Calvinist communal ideal—the other sphere centered on the tavern, on displaying physical strength and beauty, on working with neighbors at raisings and bees [barn raisings and sewing bees], and on militia training and the Fourth of July.

For men in particular, social life outside the churches revolved around the many taverns of the valley. There people could congregate casually, gossip, exchange business information, play cards or quoits [a ring-toss game], while away inclement weather, celebrate personal triumphs, and mull over failures. Of course, churches offered some of these attractions, and were the only places where most women could find them outside their own homes. But the churches were not as numerous as taverns. In 1815, the nine towns studied here had thirty-two licensed inns and taverns and only twenty-six churches. Nor could churches keep the hours, offer the comforts, gather the range of neighbors, or provide the atmosphere of easy camaraderie that taverns could. Most devout Calvinists, not to speak of those who were not regular churchgoers, probably spent more time in taverns than in churches.

The sphere of social life outside the churches attracted more inhabitants, including women, to festive gatherings around the taverns. Sporting events were especially popular, even though they sanctioned ostensibly immoral behavior. A wild title match for the wrestling championship of St. Johnsbury, held by lantern light on a Saturday night, carried on so late that the referee set back his watch as midnight approached, so that no one who stayed for the conclusion would "violate" the Sabbath. Horse racing on St. Johnsbury's main street was also popular; especially memorable to residents of that town was "the superior equestrienneship of Sally Tute . . . who leaping on a barebacked horse called for a glass of stimulant and challenged any man of the crowd to overtake her." These contests drew admiring throngs eager to cheer their neighborhood champions onward, and to pay homage to the physical strength, horsemanship, courage, and tenacity so admired on the farming frontier.

Most frequent of all social events in the valley were the various raisings and bees held to make light work of arduous physical tasks. The major events, however, were the patriotic holidays, the militia training days, and the Fourth of July. Those days were the high points of the year in the towns of the valley, provided that tragedy did not strike in a firearms accident, as it too often did. Such accidents were common because drunkenness was widespread on these occasions. Not only was it the custom for captains to "treat" their men from early morning on to sustain their strength and enthusiasm, but drunkenness allowed the men to level all distinctions among themselves and to celebrate their liberty in intoxicated abandon. Like patriotic songs and martial fervor, alcohol drew townspeople together. But the celebrations served other purposes as well, particularly for the younger participants. Young men took the opportunity to show they could outdrink, outdrill, and outsloganize any patriot in the valley and took pride in having "done well" before friends, neighbors, and most especially, the young women in the crowd.

This sphere of valley life, and that which centered on the church, were inhabited by much the same people. Most church members, including non-Calvinists, participated in the social life outside their churches, and most people were included to some degree in the circle of a church. The spheres were not necessarily inimical to each other. Calvinists young and old felt it possible to be pious and at the same time patriotic, good-natured, and neighborly to those outside their churches. Still, the spheres were distinct, and potential for antagonism was great. In the church's circle, patriotism and good fellowship were not to be sought (and were indeed censured) as ends in themselves. Conversely, in the community sphere, where patriotism and good fellowship were valued as ends in themselves, rectitude and piety were admirable, but there was a point where quibbling over the morality of a national policy or a neighbor's actions became bad manners.

These spheres posed a perpetual problem for the adult Calvinists in the valley, whose mission "to be in but not of the world" required them to participate in the social life outside their churches without becoming creatures of that life. The burden of that problem rested most heavily, however, on the young people of the valley who were of an age to be attracted by the worldly sphere and who were all too ready to place camaraderie ahead of their duty to God. The young also had to face temptation without having mastered the subtle code that told adult Calvinists when they had partaken enough of revelry, when they had shown enough charity toward human frailty, when they should chastise, when they should let matters pass.

Thus it was not strange that young people like Henry Stevens were doomed to repeat what in more sober moods they knew to be sins. As a tavern owner and a promising Presbyterian, Henry Stevens epitomized the dilemma, for he lived in two worlds, amidst piety and promiscuity, and knew the attractions of both.

Drinking and carousing among young people were not the only problems that confronted the Calvinists. Fervent Calvinist evangelicals also faced problems that had their source solely in the religious sphere—in particular, too-early conversions. It was natural for evangelical parents to tell their children at an early age how Christ had died for their sins and how only conversion—the evangelical experience of being "born again," in which God fills the sinner's soul with saving grace—could bring peace and salvation. They meant to shake children into seriousness and to encourage them to think and pray about their own souls. Such conversations produced the desired effect with surprising frequency. Children would try immediately to improve their behavior and would sit down with their friends and play preacher to them—a common enough pastime before the games of cowboys and Indians or cops and robbers came into being. But at times young children were terrified. They hid during thunder and lightning storms for fear of dying before receiving God's grace. Some even made mild attempts at mortification of the flesh. As Joel Winch, a young Hartland boy, recalled in his memoirs (written at the age of twenty-one), he thought "much about dying" after such a conservation with his father, and would "git alone and cry."

Few parents knew what to make of children who were so desperately concerned about their souls. Joel Winch's parents, being dedicated New Lights and full church members, had no wish to discourage their twelve-year-old son from seeking God, but they had hoped he would be a little older before he found Him. Joel did not yet know, they thought, what real sin or real religion was about. His mother tried to reclaim her son and, as Joel wrote later, "being a quick woman twitted me of my pretending to be good." She was none too gentle in her teasing, however, and Joel was crushed. "O how it sunk me down," he wrote. For three years he lived with the knowledge of his own sinfulness. When at last the Lord "broke into" Joel's soul at age fifteen, "the Congregationalist professores would take no notis of that which the Lord had don for me." It was not at that time customary for the church to accept young people as full members.

Joel did gain admittance to the church while still a teenager, as did a number of other young people, even though "it made some talk" among church members. Their elders feared that no matter how fervent the religious commitment the young professed, it was at bottom unreliable. At the age of fourteen, fifteen, or sixteen, young people, particularly those from farm, artisan, and laboring families, were entering the most difficult years of their lives. It was then that they would begin working, often for long periods away from home—the girls as domestics, the boys as farmhands or apprentices. Their wages would go toward augmenting the family income, building dowries, or, in the case of males, towards saving for a farm or a shop. Once they reached the age of twenty-one, young people were responsible for themselves and could "journey" where they wished to find suitable employment. Until then, however, their parents controlled their destinies.

It was the prevailing notion among Calvinists and non-Calvinists alike that responsible relatives, neighbors, and fellow church members handled young people better than did parents, because they did not face rebellion against specifically parental authority and because they were not reluctant to administer strict discipline out of the "false" love that sometimes prevented parents from correcting their children. Putting children out was not always a solution to disciplinary problems, however. There is little evidence that masters and mistresses actually had any less trouble than parents in governing young people. Then, too, even if parents were careful in their selection of an employer, the moral and spiritual lives of their children were sometimes neglected. Masters and mistresses might prove more lukewarm toward the church than parents expected and allow their wards to stay home on the Sabbath or to strike up friendships with freethinkers. Under these circumstances young converts would quickly become backsliders.

The greatest problem for those who converted at a young age, however, was the temptation to cast off godliness for a while and return to carefree, reckless ways. A few truly rebelled against religion, indulging in drunkenness or fornication; others sought release in flirtation, playing pranks, or vandalism. Upon his return from journeying in the fall of 1800, Joel Winch fought with his parents and fell headlong into sin. He stayed out nights, leaving his parents to fear that he had compromised several young women in the neighborhood. In fact he and his friends were trying to start a witchcraft scare. They opened people's doors, made "all manner of noises," threw carts down wells, and put hogs in cow pens and cows in hog pens. The seriousness of what he was doing did not strike Joel until he tried to seduce a young Baptist girl at a party and was repulsed. Her righteous rejection of him made him realize that he had become an ally of the Devil. In his own defense, he protested that he was not as bad as some of his friends. He did not dance, swear, or play cards, for he knew he "could not have the name of being religious" if he did so.

Joel's behavior was typical of many young converts who backslid. They behaved frivolously or wickedly, but were careful not to do anything that would injure their churches. Their sins were committed in secret and were usually minor, having to do with wasting time, gossiping, daydreaming about parties and courting, or fishing when there was work to be done (one young man confessed to catching 1,117 fish in two years). They suffered remorse periodically and rededicated themselves to Christ for weeks or even months, only to lapse again. Unable to live in two worlds at once, they traversed the cycles of sin and salvation.

Even when young people turned to Christ for good, they often confounded their friends, relatives, and congregations with rigorous searches for doctrinal truth and purity. They could do so privately, or they could do so openly and aggressively. Unwilling to confront the leaders of her church, or perhaps merely loath to make trouble, Lois Leverett of Windsor decided secretly that predestination and infant damnation were unscriptural foolishness. There were a great many young people in the valley who went so far as to leave their churches over some difference in scriptural interpretation. Twenty-year-old Elias Smith of South Woodstock, distressed at not finding the Baptist doctrines he learned as a child supported by the Bible, demanded that open discussion of complex theological questions be allowed in his church. When his request was denied, he quit to found a church that would allow honest disagreements among sincere Christians.

Backsliding and overzealousness presented enduring problems for Calvinists and their communal ideals. In part, of course, the problem was that young people were just that—young and immature. They had none of the attachments of adulthood that provided a firm basis for social, moral, and spiritual maturity: a spouse, a household, a shop or farm, respectable friends, and a commitment to the community and its values. It took time to aquire such connections and commitments. The young people of the valley remained half in and half out of the adult world at least until their mid-twenties or early thirties.

Adult church members in the valley deliberately chose to let the young mature in their own good time. In a radical departure from the ways of their fathers, they decided not to subject the young to anything more than gentle moral suasion. . . . Members of one church actually sided against their minister in favor of several young converts who had "returned to their sports, carousing, and dancing," maintaining "that abstinence from mirthful recreation could not be expected of those who were in the heat and vigor of youth." A new balance of power had been struck between the Calvinists and their young and potential members.

There were now religious and political movements in the valley that were hostile to the Calvinists and their idea of a covenanted community, and adults recognized that they could drive the young into those movements if they pressed them too hard or if they failed to take them seriously. . . . In addition . . . , the attitudes of young people seemed to have undergone a change. Relative to southern New England, workers were in great demand in the valley and opportunities for marriage and for independent proprietorship were plentiful. The young considered their futures secure. Therefore they may have been truly less careful of their reputations than before. It is also possible that the Revolution compounded the Calvinists' problems by leading young people to confuse their right to hold their own religious and political opinions with their ability to arrive at opinions that were as valid as those of their elders. Young people had on occasion challenged the beliefs of authorities in southern New England before the Revolution, but on a less widespread basis.

Campus Life

Helen Lefkowitz Horowitz examines the experiences of college students in the post-revolutionary era. Excerpted from Helen Lefkowitz Horowitz, Campus Life: Undergraduate Cultures from the End of the Eighteenth Century to the Present *(New York, 1987), 23–31.*

College life was born in revolt. Not just the insubordination inherent in youth, but a wave of violent, collective uprisings in the late eighteenth and early nineteenth centuries against the combined authority of college professors and presidents. In every case forcibly suppressed, the conflict went underground. Losing the preliminary battles, college men won the war. Collegians withdrew from open confrontation to turn to covert forms of expression. In the interstices of the nineteenth-century college, college men forged a peer consciousness sharply at odds with that of the faculty. They created college life.

I do not mean to suggest that the collective life of students was a creation of the new Republic. Undergraduate culture has a long and rich history. . . . Records of youthful hedonism and collegiate customs in North America go back to Harvard's beginnings. Its poverty, simplicity, piety, and small scale may have initially inhibited adolescent enthusiasm, but Harvard in the heart of Puritan New England caught its students playing cards, drinking, and stealing the turkeys of their Cambridge neighbors. As early as 1667 the Overseers complained that upperclassmen were sending freshmen out on private errands, that the English practice of "fagging" [an experience similar to modern fraternity hazing] had reached Massachusetts. High spirits continued to plague college authorities. By the eighteenth century the faculty recorded a new kind of misdemeanor: students put live snakes in their tutor's room and drank his wine. Such pranks suggested disrespect as well as distance.

Eighteenth-century American collegians enjoyed a vigorous, creative fellowship in the literary societies of their own devising. Beginning in 1750 at William and Mary and at Yale, these student societies supplemented the formal course of study. Open to all,

Military academies, both public and private, offered many young men an opportunity to receive a college education. (Courtesy of Naval Historical Center.)

the societies organized debates, criticized written compositions, established libraries, and gave to students meeting places and public events. . . .

Although student culture has existed as long as the university, that particular American form we call college life—still with us today—was forged in the faculty-student warfare of the post-revolutionary years.

The revolts were extensive. Students rioted at the long-established colonial colleges and at the newer denominational ones. Some disturbances lasted only a few hours. Others placed the colleges in a state of siege for weeks. The North Carolina legislature suspended its university's endowment after the violent riot of 1799. None of the New England colleges was immune from revolt in the years between 1820 and 1860. A few colleges went into permanent decline, losing students, faculty, and patronage.

The continuing conflicts at Princeton give some sense of the temper of both sides. In 1800 students disturbed morning prayers by scraping, insulting the speaker by rubbing their boots against the rough floor. President Samuel Stanhope Smith called in three seniors and, when they admitted their wicked deed, dismissed them from the college. When their fellow students learned of this harsh penalty, they set off a riot. They shot pistols, crashed brickbats [brick fragments used as missiles] against walls and doors, and rolled barrels filled with stones along the hallways of Nassau Hall, the principal college building. One of the expelled seniors did not leave the area and returned to the college two weeks later. He beat up the tutor whom he suspected of reporting on him. This set off a second riot that Smith quelled only by threatening to close the college.

Seven years later the suspension of three students again angered their classmates. This time undergraduate leaders acted responsibly and drew up a letter of remonstrance that questioned the justice of the dismissals and requested that the three be allowed to return. President Smith found this conscious, collective act more threatening than spontaneous violence: Princeton students had illegally combined against proper authorities. At evening prayers, he, his faculty, and a trustee presented their case against the letter and began to call the roll. Each student at the calling of his name had to disavow the letter and remove his signature from it. Refusal meant suspension. A student leader led the way out of the room, followed by 125 Princetonians. Riot followed. Angry students seized Nassau Hall, smashed windows, and armed themselves with banisters against villagers who had assembled at the request of the president. The revolt ended when Smith closed the college for an early recess. . . .

. . . At the University of North Carolina students horsewhipped the president, stoned two professors, and threatened the other members of the faculty with personal injury. Yale students in the 1820s bombed a residence hall. In a later Yale conflict, a student killed a tutor who tried to break up a melee.

What was at issue? . . . Like participants in the early student riots in the 1960s, students at each college had a particular grievance. At Union College they wanted a professor dismissed. At Dickinson College they demanded the right to take all classes simultaneously, making graduation possible with a single year of study. Princeton undergraduates, restive under monastic rule, insisted that the college not suspend their fellows for minor breaches of public order. When their demands were ignored, students rioted.

Despite these varied demands, at bottom collegians fought over power. College students of the early Republic inherited a system in which they were completely dependent upon their faculty not only for their system of education but also for their living arrangements. The prescribed student role was to pay, pray, study, and accept. If they found their instructor vindictive or their food rotten, they had no legitimate recourse other than withdrawal. That may have suited young scholars of 1740, but it no longer fit those of 1805. What had happened?

Undoubtedly the Revolution had worked its way. During the years of conflict, college men had been remarkably untouched by revolutionary fervor. A generation later, however, the patriots' sons entering college were less willing to exhibit those marks of deference faculty had traditionally expected. Nineteenth-century collegians simply had been trained to less hierarchical manners. A frequent, illuminating demand was the right to call each other Mister or Sir.

In addition, these young men came to college for reasons less clear than those of earlier scholars. Far fewer were headed for the ministry. College was for them the literary society where they gathered in comfortable quarters to write on and debate issues of philosophy and politics. At Princeton, influential members of these societies led the revolts. At all the colleges wealthier students broke the rules and turned out for the fight. They could afford to. They did not depend upon college for a position in the world. . . .

. . . Genteel sons who went off to college took their extroverted ways with them along with their servants. They brought to college a love of pleasure, an attention to manners, a restless ambition, and an easy conscience.

Early-nineteenth-century colleges, however, were institutions created and sustained by those of a different spirit. Presidents and professors trained as ministers in eighteenth-century colleges could comprehend neither the changes of their era nor many of their students. To shift from absolute monarch to consultative ruler threatened the known order. As men of evangelical temperament, they assumed they could break the will of the young and errant. Instead of compromise they insisted on their traditional prerogatives. Although the heads of all colleges shared similar assumptions, the conflicts these evoked were particularly acute in the Southern institutions where planters' sons confronted rules invented in New England and largely maintained by New England-trained clergy. "Young Georgians at Athens, young North Carolinians at Chapel Hill, young South Carolinians at Columbia, young Mississippians at Oxford—all objected to such a system," suggestive to them of the subordination of slavery.

The refusal of college faculty to hear and act on complaints or reconsider disciplinary judgments often provoked the original outburst. Gregarious, moderate young men presumed that they were reasonable adults. If they met with respect, they were apt to accept the world that they found; if denied respect, they might join in opposing what they regarded as unjust authority. The orthodoxy and intransigence of college heads convinced students of a moderate temperament that the authority over them was unreasonable, and they joined their more spirited brothers in rioting in protest.

As colleges moved to suppress disturbances, they found support outside in a public that feared civil disorder. College heads seemingly triumphed after every riot. At the end of each conflict the seditious apologized and sought mercy, withdrew, or were suspended. Colleges were determined to put students in their place.

Technically they did. Presidents supported by faculty reasserted their right to determine who taught what, and how. They wrote the rules. They admitted students and could expel them. But the apparent victory hid the reality. Suppressed though it was, the mutinous spirit survived. It ceased to confront authority directly but turned to covert forms that grew in strength during the nineteenth century.

The student culture that emerged from the revolts differed profoundly from its eighteenth-century predecessor. The literary society that held a dominant place from its mid-eighteenth-century founding until the 1820s offered a means for self-improvement, the "junto" [a group of persons joined for a common purpose] of the leisured college man. Did the required course of study ignore the basic education desired by collegians aspiring to become men of culture? Then build outside its bounds a fellowship to address contemporary philosophy and politics. Did recitation allow no real cultivation of manners and style? Then use the society to improve writing and public speaking. Did the college not provide the necessary books to study the great questions of the day? Then organize a library within the society.

What is striking about the eighteenth-century society is its seriousness of purpose. . . . The literary society offered an excellent education for public life. Though its course of study remained outside the formal curriculum, the two were complementary, not antagonistic. Professors neither organized nor led these associations, but they were welcome on their premises to use the library or to attend the debates. Generally each campus had two rival societies, each of which engaged with its competitor in a lively contest for newcomers' loyalty. The two included in their ranks all undergraduates who sought membership.

The revolts ended such a judicious, amicable system. Combatants emerged from the conflicts with a sense of deep injury and anger. Many students saw themselves at war with their faculty and with fellow students. They turned away from the literary society to create in the college fraternity an institutional expression of both their grievances and their divisions. . . . By 1840 fraternities had spread to most New England colleges and would take solid root in the Midwest before 1850. . . .

The fraternity appealed because it captured and preserved the spirit of the revolts. Unlike the eighteenth-century literary society, the fraternity consisted of a small, select band pledged to secrecy. Although rhetoric paid tribute to serious, high-minded purpose, the real concern of each fraternity was to create within the larger college a small group of compatible fellows for friendship, mutual protection, and good times.

On most campuses the conflicts had disclosed a sharp division among students. Only a small minority of young men attended college in the early Republic, perhaps 2 percent. Two groups deemed college as appropriate: the wealthy who chose it to "finish" their young and the poor who hoped to become ministers. Very few in the middle class brought their aspirations to college until later in the nineteenth century, when higher education emerged as the principal route to the professions. In this bifurcated world, the wealthier students tended to fight authority, the poorer complied. The future ministers came to college for the formal training it offered. Raised in evangelical households, introspective sons expected to work hard, be governed by their professors, and strive intensely for self-improvement.

Affluent, secular classmates looked askance at these good students. They labeled a studious classmate a "dig," a "fag," a "grub," or a "blue." . . . The language of college life lacked any positive term for hardworking classmates or for study. The line collegians drew between those who took their studies seriously and those who tried to ingratiate themselves with their professors was a thin one. A "blue" studied hard; a "blue-light" spied on other students for the faculty. . . .

. . . The demography of early-nineteenth-century New England swelled the numbers of such serious students in Northern schools. Younger sons sought an alternative to the family farm that could support only an elder brother. With little time for socializing and no money, the pauper scholars did not join in the hell-bent amusements of their peers. Reared in evangelical homes, in college they encountered professors whose expectations fit their own internal standards. As fraternities formed, some of them stayed aloof; others formed counter-groups committed to teetotalism or to non-secrecy. Economic and psychic disparities among students dissolved the basis for collegiate community. The fraternity system underscored these differences and gave them form.

In the South, although conflicts between faculty and students remained explosive, the more homogeneous body of affluent undergraduates had less need for exclusive organizations. . . . [L]iterary societies remained vital until after the Civil War, and communal celebrations such as commencements attracted wide attention. Only in 1866—on a campus that included for the first time state-supported veterans and future teachers and ministers on scholarship—did the first Greek-letter fraternity at the University of Georgia take hold, with effects as disruptive of the old societies and celebrations as elsewhere.

Questions

1. *How did adolescents defy or frustrate adults after the Revolution? What gave them the incentive? the means?*
2. *Discuss the attitudes of adolescents and adults toward violence and nonviolence; obedience and independence; principle and tolerance; and piety and humor. Did parents or college professors ask young people to behave in contradictory ways? Did the American Revolution similarly push them in opposing directions?*

WORKING CHILDREN

The memoirs of Harriet Robinson and Charlie Siringo are stories of working children who triumphed over adversity. They were written, like most American autobiographies, as success stories. These memoirs tell us much about the lives of working children and the adult decisions they faced.

Harriet Hanson Robinson (1825–1911)

Harriet Hanson Robinson was born in 1825 in a working-class neighborhood in Boston, Massachusetts. Her father, a carpenter, died when she was only six. Her mother opened a small dry goods store to support the family, but it failed. She then took her four children to Lowell, Massachusetts, where she ran a boarding house for a large textile firm. She sent Harriet to work in the mills at age ten, but remained committed to her education. Harriet attended school part-time until her mother could save enough money for her to attend high school.

She worked when high school was not in session and wrote for the Lowell Offering, *a company-sponsored literary journal published by mill workers. Harriet renounced her early involvement in strikes and labor unions, and praised the mill owners for the opportunities they had given her family.*

Harriet married William S. Robinson, a journalist, in 1848, and worked with him in the antislavery movement throughout the Civil War. Afterwards, she joined the National Woman Suffrage Association. She fought for women's rights until her death in 1911. The following excerpt is from Harriet H. Robinson, Loom and Spindle, or Life Among the Early Mill Girls *(New York, 1898), 25–29, 18–21, 30–31, 35–38,83–86.*

Our home was in Boston, in Leverett Court. . . . We lived under the shadow of the old jail . . . and we children used to hear conversation, not meant for small ears, between the prisoners and the persons in the court who came there to see them.

. . . The tide came in at the foot of Leverett Court, and we could look across the water and see the sailing vessels coming and going. There the down-east wood-coasters landed their freight; many a time I have gone "chipping" [searching for wood chips that could serve as fuel] there, and once a generous young skipper offered me a stick of wood, which I did not dare to take.

In 1831, under the shadow of a great sorrow, which had made her four children fatherless,—the oldest but seven years of age,—my mother was left to struggle alone; and, although she tried hard to earn bread enough to fill our hungry mouths, she could not do it, even with the help of kind friends. And so it happened that one of her more wealthy neighbors, who had looked with longing eyes on the one little daughter of the family, offered to adopt me. But my mother, who had had a hard experience in her youth in living amongst strangers, said, "No; while I have one meal of victuals a day, I will not part with my children." . . .

My father was a carpenter, and some of his fellow-workmen helped my mother to open a little shop, where she sold small stores, candy, kindling-wood, and so on, but there was no great income from this, and we soon became poorer than ever. Dear me! I can see the small shop now, with its jars of striped candy, its loaves of bread, the room at the back where we all lived, and my oldest brother (now a "D.D." [Doctor of Divinity]) sawing the kindling-wood which we sold to the neighbors.

That was a hard, cold winter; and for warmth's sake my mother and her four children all slept in one bed, two at the foot and three at the head,—but her richer neighbor could not get the little daughter; and, contrary to all the modern notions about hygiene, we were a healthful and a robust brood. We all, except the baby, went to school every day, and Saturday afternoons I went to a charity school to learn to sew. My mother had never complained of her poverty in our hearing, and I had accepted the conditions of my life with a child's trust, knowing nothing of the relative difference between poverty and riches. And so I went to the sewing-school, like any other little girl who was taking lessons in sewing and not as a "charity child;" until a certain day when something was said by one of the teachers, about me, as a "poor little girl,". . . . When I went home I told my mother that the teacher said I was *poor*, and she replied in her sententious manner, "You need not go there again."

Shortly after this my mother's widowed sister, Mrs. Angeline Cudworth, who kept a factory boarding-house in Lowell, advised her to come to that city. She secured a house for her, and my mother, with her little brood and her few household belongings, started for the new factory town. . . .

. . . [Thus], in the first block of tenements then built, I began my life among factory people. My mother kept forty boarders, most of them men, mill-hands, and she did all her housework, with what help her children could give her between schools; for we all, even the baby three years old, were kept at school. My part in the housework was to wash the dishes, and I was obliged to stand on a cricket [a low wooden stool] in order to reach the sink! . . .

Free co-educational schools were established in Lowell as early as 1830-1832, and a rule was made by the several corporations that every child under fourteen should attend them three months in the year.

Master Hills taught the North Grammar School, after it occupied its present site. I remember him in 1835; and I . . . wonder if, in some other sphere, he remembers whipping a little girl to overcome her persistent denials of an accusation made against her, thereby forcing her to tell a lie. She was accused by one of her schoolmates of taking a one cent multiplication table from her desk, and tearing it in two. For this slight offence, he, a strong man, unheeding her denials of the charge, with a heavy strap, struck with his whole strength on the tender palm of the little hand of a child of scarcely ten years. He punished her till she could not see, for pain and terror, and then she gave in, *whipped into a lie,* and said she did it.

The punishment over she staggered to her seat, thinking that at last it was all over. But the end was not yet, for she had to learn by this early experience that one is but the beginning of a sum, and that she must tell many lies and keep on telling them, in order to maintain her position. Her little schoolmates said, "Why did you not say sooner that you did it, and save yourself all that whipping?" She could not tell them the truth, for they would not believe her. Her dear mother said, "If you wanted another multiplication table, why did you not ask me for one?" . . . [S]he went on throwing out lie after lie (a heavy ballast), to save herself and to maintain her standing as a liar, till she was heartily sick of the whole matter, and wished that she had stuck to the truth, even if the master had killed her. . . .

Master Jacob Graves followed Mr. Hills, and he was the first teacher that I remember who used moral suasion, and instilled into our minds what honor among children meant. He taught us to be truthful for truth's sake, his rule was mild and pleasant, he never punished with the rod, and his kind, remonstrating voice was more powerful than any whipping. . . .

I had been to school constantly until I was about ten years of age, when my mother, feeling obliged to have help in her work besides what I could give, and also needing the money which I could earn, allowed me, at my urgent request (for I wanted to earn *money* like the other little girls), to go to work in the mill. I worked first in the spinning-room as a "doffer." The doffers were the very youngest girls, whose work was to doff, or take off, the full bobbins, and replace them with the empty ones.

I can see myself now, racing down the alley, between the spinning-frames, carrying in front of me a bobbin-box bigger than I was. These mites had to be very swift in their movements, so as not to keep the spinning-frames stopped long, and they worked only about fifteen minutes in every hour. The rest of the time was their own, and when the overseer was kind they were allowed to read, knit, or even to go outside the mill-yard to play. . . .

We were paid two dollars a week; and how proud I was when my turn came to stand up on the bobbin-box, and write my name in the paymaster's book, and how indignant I was when he asked me if I could "write." "Of course I can," said I, and he smiled as he looked down on me. . . .

Holidays came when repairs to the great mill wheel were going on, or some late spring freshet caused the shutting down of the mill; these were well improved. With what freedom we enjoyed those happy times! My summer playhouse was the woodshed, which my mother always had well filled; how orderly and with what precision the logs were sawed and piled with the smooth ends outwards! . . . [H]ere, in my castle of sawed wood, was my vacation retreat, where, with my only and beloved wooden doll, I lunched on slices of apple cut in shape so as to represent what I called "German half-moon cakes." I piled up my bits of crockery with sticks of cinnamon to represent candy, and many other semblances of things, drawn from my mother's housekeeping stores. . . .

Sometimes we rambled by the "race-way" or mill-race, which carried the water into the flume of the mill, along whose inclining sides grew wild roses, and the "rock-loving columbine;" and we used to listen to see if we could hear the blue-bells ring. . . .

The North Grammar school building stood at the base of a hilly ridge of rocks, down which we coasted in winter, and where in summer, after school-hours, we had a little cave, where we sometimes hid, and played that we were robbers; and together we rehearsed the dramatic scenes in "Alonzo and Melissa," "The Children of the Abbey," or the "Three Spaniards." . . .

Our home amusements were very original. We had no toys, except a few homemade articles or devices of our own. I had but a single doll, a wooden-jointed thing, with red cheeks and staring black eyes. Playing-cards were tabooed, but my elder brother (the incipient D.D.), who had somehow learned the game of high-low-jack, set about making a pack. The cards were cut out of thick yellow pasteboard, the spots and figures were made in ink, and, to disguise their real character, the names of the suits were changed. Instead of hearts, diamonds, spades, and clubs, they were called charity, love, benevolence, and faith. The pasteboard was so thick that all together the cards made a pile at least two or three feet high, and they had to be shuffled in sections! He taught my second brother and me the game of high-low-jack; and, with delightful secrecy, as often as we could steal away, we played in the attic, keeping the cards hidden, between whiles, in an old hair trunk. In playing the game we got along very well with the names of the face-cards,—the "queen of charity," the "king of love," and so on; but the "ten-spot of faith," and particularly the "two-spot of benevolence" (we had never heard of the "deuce") was too much for our sense of humor, and almost spoiled the "rigor of the game." . . .

One of the first strikes of cotton-factory operatives that ever took place in this country was that in Lowell, in October, 1836. When it was announced that the wages were to be cut down, great indignation was felt, and it was decided to strike, *en masse*. . . .

My own recollection of this first strike (or "turn out" as it was called) is very vivid. I worked in a lower room, where I had heard the proposed strike fully, if not vehemently, discussed; I had been an ardent listener to what was said against this attempt at "oppression" on the part of the corporation, and naturally I took sides with the strikers. When the day came on which the girls were to turn out, those in the upper rooms started first, and so many of them left that our mill was at once shut down. Then, when the girls in my room stood irresolute, uncertain what to do, asking each other, "Would you?" or "Shall we turn out?" and not one of them having the courage to lead off, I, who began to think they would not go out, after all their talk, became impatient, and started on ahead, saying, with childish bravado, "I don't care what you do, *I* am going to turn out, whether any one else does or not;" and I marched out, and was followed by the others. [She was then eleven years and eight months old.]

As I looked back at the long line that followed me, I was more proud than I have ever been since at any success I may have achieved, and more proud than I shall ever be again until my own beloved State gives to its women citizens the right of suffrage.

The agent of the corporation where I then worked took some small revenges on the supposed ringleaders; on the principle of sending the weaker to the wall, my mother was turned away from her boarding-house, that functionary saying, "Mrs. Hanson, you could not prevent the older girls from turning out, but your daughter is a child, and *her* you could control."

It is hardly necessary to say that so far as results were concerned this strike did no good. The dissatisfaction of the operatives subsided, or burned itself out, and though the authorities did not accede to their demands, the majority returned to their work, and the corporation went on cutting down the wages.

Charles Siringo (1855–1928)

Charlie Siringo was born in 1855 in Texas. His parents owned a small ranch on the peninsula that separates Matagorda Bay from the Gulf of Mexico. His father died in 1862, leaving Charlie and his mother and sister to fend for themselves as Union and Confederate forces fought for control of the peninsula. At the end of the war, Charlie's mother married a man who claimed to own a large farm in Michigan. But there was no farm, and Charlie's stepfather soon deserted the family. Charlie's mother and sister sought work in St. Louis. They put Charlie to work on a farm in Lebanon, Illinois. He was thirteen years old.

Charlie did not hear from his mother for months. Finally he struck out for St. Louis to look for her. He could find no trace of her. For the next three years, he survived on his own in the Mississippi Valley. When he was sixteen, Charlie made his way back to Texas, where friends helped him learn the whereabouts of his mother and sister. By then he was independent, a full-fledged cowboy.

Siringo rode the range in Texas and New Mexico for the next thirteen years. He married and spent a few years as a storekeeper. In later years, he worked as a detective in the West, tracking down rustlers and train robbers for cattlemen's associations, railroads, and territorial governments. The following excerpt is from Chas. A. Siringo, A Texas Cow Boy or, Fifteen Years on the Hurricane Deck of a Spanish Pony. *(Chicago, 1885), 43–53, 55–64.*

I . . . pulled out for the bustling city [St. Louis], where I was soon lost in the large crowd which thronged the levee. I left my satchel in a saloon and struck out to find Mr. Socks, hoping he could give me some information as to mother and sister's whereabouts, but I was sadly disappointed, he had left that part of the city in which he lived when I knew him. I put in the rest of the day gazing through the show windows, especially of the bakeries, at the fat pies, cakes, etc., for I was getting very hungry, my last meal being dinner the day before.

About dark I strolled up to a second-hand book store and asked how much a bible, nearly new, would bring? . . . I hated the idea of parting with the book for it had been presented to me by my late employer's mother Mrs. Moore, a nice old lady who had taken a liking to me. But you know how it is when a fellow is hungry, or would have known had you been in my shoes.

I got twenty-five cents for the bible and immediately invested fifteen cents of it in a mince pie.

That night I stowed myself away in an empty dry goods box. I did not sleep well, and when I did sleep it was to dream of snakes and other venomous reptiles.

I put in the whole of the next day hunting work, but failed to find it. I had bought a five cent ginger-cake for my dinner and now I got a five cent pie for my supper; this broke me flat and I had nothing else that I could sell; so I put up for the night in a pile of bailed hay, which was stacked up behind a store.

The next morning I struck out again hunting work, but this time on an empty stomach. . . . Finally about three o'clock my courage and what few sparks of hopes that still remained, wilted. . . .

I was sitting on the edge of the sidewalk, with my face buried in both hands, crying, when someone touched me on the shoulder. I was scared at first for I thought it was a "peeler" [a hustler or a police officer]; but my fears vanished when I looked up into the gleaming countenance of a small, red complexioned man, who said in a pleasant tone:—"Is there anything I can do for you my little man?"

His kindness proved too much for me, I burst out crying and it was quite awhile before I could tell him my trouble. . . . He took me to his boarding place, a fancy restaurant, right across the street; he said he was just fixing to go to bed when he spied me across the street, acting as though in trouble.

When he found out that I hadn't had a square meal for three days he remarked that it was a d—d shame and then told the night clerk . . . to have me a good supper fixed up and to give me a good room. He then bid me good night and started to bed, telling me to remain there until I found work, if it was a month, that he would arrange everything with the proprietor in the morning before he went to work. I thanked him with tears in my eyes, for his kindness.

I was so tired and sleepy that I never woke up until nearly noon next day. After eating breakfast, I struck out to hunt a job, but failed as usual.

Three days after, while out hunting work, I stopped an old man and asked him if he knew where I could find a job? He smiled and said: "My boy this is the fourth time you have asked me that same question in the last three days. You must like my looks, for I have noticed you pass scores of men without stopping them. . . . Follow me and I will find you work before I stop."

The first place we went into was the Planters' House . . . and he asked the clerk if they needed a bell boy. "No," was the short answer he received.

He then asked where he could find the proprietor. "Up in his room, No.—on first floor," was the answer.

We found the "boss" busily writing. My new friend plead my case like a dutch uncle and told him if I didn't prove to be just what he recommended me to be—a wide-awake, get-up-and-get, honest boy, that he would pay all damages, etc

That seemed to settle it, for I was told to go down to the office and wait for orders.

I was too happy to live. I thanked the kind old gentleman from the bottom of my heart and offered to pay him for his trouble as soon as I earned some money. He told me I could pay him for his trouble by being a good boy. . . .

I was put on the forenoon watch which went on duty at eight in the morning and came off at one in the afternoon. There were five of us on at a time.

We would always make from twenty-five cents to five dollars a day while on duty, for we hardly ever went to wait on a person but what they would give us something in the shape of money. Gamblers generally gave us the most; sometimes a lot of them would get together in a room to play cards and send down to the bar after their drinks and may be send a ten or twenty dollar bill and tell the bell boy to keep the change. With this money we used to have some gay old times taking in the city after coming off guard.

The next fall, nearly one year after landing at the "Planters," I had a fight with one of the bell boys, Jimmie Byron. He called me a liar and I jumped aboard of him. When it was over with, the clerk, Mr. Cunningham, called me up to the counter and slapped me without saying a word.

I went right straight to my room, packed up my "gripsack" and went to the proprietor for a settlement.

He was surprised and wanted to know what in the world had gotten into me.

I told him the whole thing, just as it happened. He tried to get me to stay but I was still mad and wouldn't listen to him. I had made up my mind to buy a pistol, come back and get square with Mr. Cunningham for slapping me.

I left the house with eighteen dollars in my pocket; jumped aboard of a street car and rode down to the levee. I left my valise at a saloon and then started back to find a gun store. I finally found one and gave ten dollars for a fancy little ivory handled five-shooter.

I then started for the "Planters" still as mad as an old setting hen. I had not gone far when I came across a large crowd gathered around one of those knife rackets, where you pay a quarter for five rings and try to "ring" a knife.

I watched the thing awhile and finally invested a quarter. I got a little "Jim Crow" barlow [knife] the first throw. That made it interesting, so I bought another quarters worth, and another until five dollars was gone. This did not satisfy me, so I kept on until I didn't have a nickel left.

But wasn't I mad when I realized what I had done! I forgot all about my other troubles and felt like breaking my own head instead of Cunningham's.

I went to the levee and found out that the "Bart Able" would start for New Orleans in a few minutes, so I ran to get my satchel, not far off, determined on boarding the steamer and remaining there until kicked off. Anything to get nearer the land of my birth, I thought, even if I had to break the rules of a gentleman in doing so.

When the Purser came around collecting fares, I laid my case before him with tears in my eyes; I told him I was willing to work—and hard, too, to pay my fare. He finally, after studying awhile, said, "Well go ahead, I'll find something for you to do." . . .

. . . [W]e stopped at a landing to take on some freight, mostly grain. We pulled up by the side of an old disabled steamer which was being used for a wharf-boat and went to work loading. The job given to me was sewing sacks when ever one was found out of order.

There were two sets of men loading, one in the stern and the other in the bow, and I was supposed to do the sewing at both ends. When they came across a holey sack, if I happened to be at the other end they would holloa for me and I would go running through the narrow passage way, leading from one end to the other.

I was in the stern when the sound of my name came from the other end; I grabbed my ball of twine and struck out in a dog trot through the passage the sides of which were formed of grain piled to the ceiling. When about half way through I thought I heard my name called from the end I had just left; I stopped to listen and while waiting, being tired, I went to lean over against the wall of sacked grain, but instead of a wall there was an old vacated hatchway and over into that I went. There being no flooring in the boat, there was nothing but the naked timbers for my weary bones to alight upon.

The next day about noon I came to my senses. I found myself all alone in a nice little room on a soft bed. I tried to get up but it was useless; my back felt as if it was broken. . . . [I]n stepped a doctor, who explained the whole matter. He said the captain . . . fished me out almost lifeless. I was in the captain's private room and having the best of care. The back of my head was swollen out of shape, it having struck on one of the cross timbers, while my back landed across another. The doctor said I owed my life to the captain for finding me. . . .

. . . [A]fter arriving in New Orleans the "Bart Able" pulled back, for Saint Louis, leaving me there flat broke and among strangers. . . . I could not hire out even if I had applied and got a job, for my back was still stiff, so much so that I couldn't stoop down without terrible pain.

That night I laid down under an old tarpaulin which was spread over a lot of sugar.

After getting up and shaking the dust off next morning, I went down the river about a mile where scores of small boats were being unloaded.

Among them were several boat loads of oranges, bananas, etc., which were being unloaded. In carrying the bananas on shore the over ripe ones would drop off. On those I made my breakfast, but I wished a thousand times before night that I had not eaten them, for Oh Lord, how my head did ache!

That night I went to sleep on a pile of cotton bales—that is I tried to sleep, but my headache was terrible, I could get but little repose. . . .

Finally a well dressed old man about fifty years of age, with an umbrella over his head, came out of Couens' office, a small building a short distance from where I sat, and walking up to me said, in a gruff voice, "young man what are you sitting out here in the sun for, so upright and stiff, as if nailed to that old stove?"

I told him I was compelled to sit upright on account of a lame back. In fact I laid my case before him in full. He then said in a much more pleasant voice: "My boy I'm going to make you an offer, and you can take it or let it alone—just as you like. I will give you four dollars a month to help my wife around the house and at the end of four months will give you a free pass to Texas. You see I am agent for Couens' Red River line of boats and, therefore, can get a pass cheap."

I accepted his offer at once and thanked him with all my heart for his kindness. . . . Walking up a pair of nicely finished steps at No. 18 Derbigny street, he rang a bell. A negro servant whom he called "Ann," answered the call. Everything sparkled within, for the house was furnished in grand style. The old gentleman introduced me to his wife as a little Texas hoosier that had strayed off from home and was about to starve.

After supper "Miss Mary," as the servants called Mrs. Myers and as I afterwards called her showed me to the bath house and told me to give myself an extraordinary good scrubbing. . . .

The next day Miss Mary took me to a clothing house and fitted me out in fine style. I admired all but the narrow brimmed hat and peaked toed gaiters. I wanted a broad brimmed hat and star top boots, but she said I would look too much like a hoosier with them on.

That evening I got a black eye. After Mr. Myers came home from his work about four o'clock, we all went out on the front steps to breathe the fresh air. There being a crowd of boys playing at the corner I asked Mr. and Mrs. Myers if I could go over and watch them awhile. Both consented, but told me not to stay long as they didn't want me to get into the habit of mixing with the street loafers.

On arriving there all eyes were turned towards me. One fellow yelled out, "Hello dandy, when did you arrive!" and another one remarked, "He is a stiff cuss—aint he?"

I concluded there was nothing to be seen and turned back; just as I turned around a yellow negro boy slipped up behind me and pulled my hair. The white boys had put him up to it, no doubt.

I jumped aboard of him quicker than a flash and forgot all about my sore back. It was nip and tuck for awhile—we both being about the same size, but I finally got him down and blooded his nose in good shape. As I went to get up he kicked me over one eye with his heavy boot. Hence the black eye, which was swollen up in a few minutes to an enormous size.

I expected to get a scolding from Mr. and Mrs. Myers, but they both gloried in my spunk for taking my own part. They had witnessed the whole thing. . . .

Mr. and Mrs. Myers had no children and after I had been with them about a month, they proposed to adopt me, or at least they made me promise to stay with them until I was twenty-one years of age.

They were to send me to school until I was seventeen and then start me in business. They also promised to give me everything they had at their death.

So they prepared me for school right away. . . . I had not been going to this school long when I had trouble with the lady teacher, Miss Finnely. It happened thus: A boy sitting behind me, struck me on the neck with a slate pencil, and when I turned around and accused him of it he whispered, "you lie." I gave him a lick on the nose that made him bawl like a calf.

Of course the teacher heard it and called us up to take our medicine.

She made the other boy hold out his hand first and after giving him five raps told him to take his seat.

It was then my time, and I stuck out my hand like a little man. She gave me five licks and was raising the rule to strike again when I jerked my hand away, at the same time telling her that it wasn't fair to punish me the most when the other boy caused the fuss. She insisted on giving me a little more so finally I held out my hand and received five more licks and still she was not satisfied; but I was and went to my seat. She told me two or three times to come back but I would not do it, so she sent a boy upstairs after Mr. Dyer, the gentleman who taught the large boys.

I had seen Mr. Dyer try his hand on boys, at several different times, therefore didn't intend to let him get hold of me if I could help it. She saw me looking towards the door, so she came over and stood between me and it.

I heard Mr. Dyer coming down the stairs; that was enough; I flew for the door. I remember running against something soft and knocking it over and suppose it must have been Miss Finnely. When I got to the street I pulled straight for home.

About a week afterwards Mr. Myers sent me to pay school, where I was taught German, French and English. My teacher was an old gentleman who only took a few select scholars.

Everything went on fine until the following spring, in May or June, when I got into a fuss with one of the scholars and skipped the country.

The way it happened: One day when school let out for dinner we all, after emptying our dinner baskets, struck out for the "green" to play "foot and a half."

There was one boy in the crowd by the name of Stemcamp who was always trying to pick a fuss with me. He was twice as large as I was, therefore I tried to avoid him, but this time he called me a liar and I made for him.

During the scuffle which followed, I got out my little pearl handled knife, one "Miss Mary" had given me just a few days before and was determined to use it the first opportunity.

I was down on all fours and he astride of my back putting it to me in the face, underhanded. The only place I could get at with the knife was his legs, so I stuck it in up to the handle, on the inside of one leg, just below the groin and ripped down.

He jumped ten feet in the air and roared out "Holy Moses!"

As soon as I regained my feet he took to his heels, but I soon overtook him and got another dig at his back. I thought sure I had done him up for good this time but found out afterwards that I had done no harm, with the exception of ripping his clothes down the back.

The next day at that time I was on my way to Saint Louis. I had stowed myself away on board of the "Mollie Able" among the cotton bales.

Questions

1. *How did Harriet Robinson and Charlie Siringo cope with the problems they faced as working children? Who did they look to for support and guidance? Would you say that they raised themselves?*
2. *Did adversity make Robinson or Siringo better citizens? more courageous? compassionate? honest? perceptive?*
3. *Did Robinson and Siringo have similar attitudes toward violence and authority? Do you see dissimilarities that might be related to gender or regional culture?*
4. *How did their lives differ from those of children from prosperous homes? Would their lives have been different had they grown up in the late twentieth century?*

FURTHER READING

Joseph F. Kett, Rites of Passage: Adolescence in America, 1790 to the Present *(New York, 1977), offers an excellent overview of the lives of young people. On schools, see Stanley Schultz,* The Culture Factory: Boston Public Schools, 1789–1860 *(New York, 1973); on textile mills, Thomas Dublin,* Women at Work: The Transformation of Work and Community in Lowell, Massachusetts, 1826–1860 *(New York, 1979); and on rural life, John Mack Faragher,* Sugar Creek: Life on the Illinois Prairie *(New Haven, 1986) and Joan E. Cashin,* A Family Venture: Men and Women on the Southern Frontier *(New York, 1991).*

Nat Turner and Slave Resistance

Merton L. Dillon

Introduction

Africans, who were forcefully brought to North America, did not willingly accept enslavement. They used every opportunity to prove to their "owners" that, even though the law considered them slaves, they still were human beings with wills of their own and that there were limits beyond which they would not allow themselves to be pushed. Most slaveowners accepted these limits as the price they had to pay for getting an acceptable amount of work from their labor force and for maintaining order on the plantation. Most slaves, in turn, learned that there also were limits to the degree of resistance that their owners—or the state—would tolerate. Outright defiance of authority or overt rebellion risked such severe punishment that only the bravest or most aggrieved dared undertake them. Thus life on every plantation was marked by tension between the slaves, who were trying to gain advantage in order to create a tolerable life for themselves, and the owners and overseers, who were trying to maintain strict control in order to run a profitable plantation. On rare occasions, this uneasy accommodation broke down, and violence, even revolt, was the result.

Slaves in the West Indies and in South America, like slaves in ancient Greece and Rome, carried out extensive uprisings. In contrast, only three such outbreaks occurred in North America: the Stono revolt in South Carolina (1739), the revolt in Louisiana (1811), and Nat Turner's revolt in Virginia (1831). Of these, Nat Turner's was the costliest in human life, for both races, and the most momentous in its impact on official policy and public opinion. It was also the most difficult for the white population to understand, first, because its leader apparently had been subjected to no unusually cruel treatment and, second, because the revolt was characterized by a messianic quality foreign to the experience of many, if not most, white people at the time.

Placing Nat Turner's Revolt in Context

In order to understand a slave revolt such as that led by Nat Turner in 1831, we need to examine the specific events that occurred and to place those events in a larger historical context. The following selections are intended to help you do that.

Nat Turner's Revolt, August 1831

This essay explains the events and influences that led Nat Turner, an otherwise obscure slave, to plan his revolt. Little is known about Turner's life except for the information that he himself disclosed to Thomas Gray in an interview conducted in his prison cell shortly before he was hanged. All accounts, including this one, of the background of the revolt are based on that source. Modern readers will ask themselves, as contemporaries did, whether mistreatment alone accounted for Nat Turner's actions or whether other influences were at work in the revolt. If, as some suspected, his actions resulted from unavoidable aspects of slavery, then others might be expected to follow the same destructive course. Abridged from R. Jackson Wilson et al., The Pursuit of Liberty: A History of the American People *(Glenview, Illinois, 1996), 3d ed., 1:424–439.*

The voice of the spirit had told him the sign would appear in the sky. Now, as Nat Turner looked at the sun on the morning of Saturday, August 13, 1831, he knew this was the signal he had been waiting for. It was a strange phenomenon, one that many people on the east coast of the United States were noticing that day, even though it did not mean to them what it meant to Nat Turner as he worked in the fields of Southampton County, Virginia. First, the sun grew dim in the cloudless sky. Then it began to change colors—turning green, then blue, finally almost white. By the afternoon the sun was looking almost like a silvery mirror. Then, as Nat stared in fascination, on the solar surface appeared a single black spot.

Nat Turner thought he knew exactly what it all meant. The sun had become a mirror of what was about to happen on the earth. Just as a black spot had passed across the sun, so black men would rise up and move across the earth. This was the signal Nat had been waiting for—the signal the spirit had promised him. He knew the time for delay had passed. The massacre must begin. The white people of Southampton County must be killed or put to flight.

Nine days later, fifty-five whites lay slaughtered—forty-two of them women and children. Most were hacked to death with axes. Many had been decapitated. Then vengeful whites struck back. The luckier blacks were captured alive and held for trial; others were simply killed outright by enraged and terrified white men. It was by far the bloodiest uprising in the long history of American slavery. Nat Turner himself managed to evade capture for more than two months, far longer than any of his fellow conspirators. He was finally taken in late October, duly tried and convicted, and publicly hanged on November 11, 1831. . . .

Nat was about thirty years old at the time of the massacre. Even in his earliest years, though, he had felt himself to be no ordinary slave but someone who was marked for greatness—or, as he put it, "called to superior righteousness." Nat had taught himself how to read—his parents were both illiterate—and he seemed to "remember" things that had happened before he was born. Around the farm on which his parents worked, his abilities soon became a "source of wonder." More than once Nat had overheard his mother and father tell each other that he was "intended for some great purpose.". . .

Nat Turner grew up with great expectations and . . . with a determination to make something of himself. He played with the

---

Nat Turner's capture; he had managed to evade authorities for over two months.

white children around the farm. His mind was restless. He read every book that came his way. He performed experiments with everyday materials, devising things like paper and gunpowder. When he reached his teens, he decided to adopt a life of "austerity": never to touch alcohol or tobacco, and "studiously" to avoid any kind of carousing with his fellow slaves. Through this program of self-improvement and self-discipline, Nat Turner tried to show others something of his great promise and to prepare himself for the rewards it would bring.

What happened was a bitter disappointment. He hoped to be emancipated at the death of his master. But when Benjamin Turner died, ten-year-old Nat was simply handed on to Turner's son Samuel, who was just setting himself up on a nearby farm of his own. . . . For the first time it occurred to him . . . that he might have to spend his entire life as a field hand. When Nat reached his twenty-first birthday, his future had become clear: "I had arrived to man's estate," he recalled, "and was a slave." The prospect was unbearable.

In his frustration, Nat ran away from his owner. For an entire month he hid in the woods. But for some reason he changed his mind. At the end of the month he voluntarily returned, to resume the drudgery of field work.

But still he held his ambition. It was about this time that Nat discovered his hopes might be fulfilled through religion. His mind fastened on one verse he had read in the Bible: "Seek ye the kingdom of heaven, and all things shall be added to you." The words seemed to promise that if Nat would only concentrate his energy on spiritual matters—the kingdom of heaven—everything else would follow. In order to win the world, he must look to heaven. But what did that involve?

One day, while working alone behind the plow in one of his owner's fields, Nat heard a voice intoning the biblical passage he had been pondering. He was sure the voice was the spirit of God, speaking directly to him as He had spoken ages before to the biblical prophets. From that time on, the divine spirit addressed him regularly. And this confirmed Nat's belief that he was "ordained to some great purpose."

But there were worldly disappointments. About 1822, Nat's young master, Samuel Turner, died, and Nat was sold . . . to a neighboring farmer named Thomas Moore. What made this event even more unsettling was the fact that Nat had recently married a slave woman on Samuel Turner's farm, and the couple was now forced to live apart. All in all, it was a vivid display of Nat's inability to control the ordinary course of his life. But he had decided to focus his attention elsewhere. He fasted, he prayed, and he avoided contact with his fellow slaves. And through it all the spirit continued to talk to him, to reassure him that "something was about to happen that would terminate in fulfilling the great promise that had been made to me."

For the time being, though, Nat did not know just how his "great promise" would be fulfilled, and he awaited further revelations. First, the spirit gave him secret understandings of the natural world around him: "knowledge of the elements, the revolution of the planets, the operation of the tides, and changes of the seasons." In essence, Nat was resuming his old program of self-improvement in the only way still open to him—through mystic revelation instead of white men's books. . . .

One day in 1825, Nat had his first vision of racial violence:

> I saw white spirits and black spirits engaged in battle, and the sun was darkened—the thunder rolled in the heavens, and blood flowed in streams. And I heard a voice saying, "Such is your luck, such you are called to see, and let it come rough or smooth, you must surely bear it."

Was race war, then, the "great purpose" for which Nat was chosen? It was a shocking prospect. Nat decided not to tell this terrible vision to his fellow slaves, and for several years he even withdrew from associating with them in order to ponder it, and to understand more fully what he was expected to bear.

Nat looked everywhere for signs—in the sky, in the woods, even in the crops he worked for his master. And slowly, with the aid of his spirit voice, he came to discover strange connections—between heaven and earth, between religious salvation and slave rebellion, between Jesus Christ and Nat Turner.

He learned that what people called the Milky Way was really "the lights of the Savior's hands, stretched forth from east to west, as they were extended on the cross on Calvary for the redemption of sinners." One day, at work in the corn field, Nat found "drops of blood on the corn, as though it were dew from Heaven." And the spirit explained to him that the Milky Way and the blood on the corn were both symbols of Christ's sacrifice:

> The blood of Christ had been shed on this earth, and had ascended to heaven for the salvation of sinners, and was now returning to earth again in the form of dew.

Searching the night sky once again, Nat saw that the stars were arranged to form pictures of men in different poses. Then, walking in the woods, he discovered certain leaves that contained the very same pictures, along with mysterious hieroglyphic markings—all marked in blood. Once more the spirit explained the meaning—the ominous meaning—of this strange discovery:

> As the leaves on the trees bore the impression of the figures I had seen in the heavens, it was plain to me that the Savior was about to lay down the yoke he had borne for the sins of men—and the Day of Judgment was at hand.

The signs were beginning to become clear. Nat was finally putting together the diverse elements in his life: religion, self-improvement, the promise of greatness, and the bitter, incomprehensible frustration. But what did it all mean for Nat himself? What was his personal role in the tremendous mystery he was coming to unravel? Finally, the answer to that question began to emerge. On May 12, 1828—he would always recall the exact date—Nat heard "a loud noise in the heavens." Then, in fateful language, the spirit spoke again:

> The serpent was loosened [let loose], and Christ had laid down the yoke he had borne for the sins of man, and *I should take it on, and fight against the serpent—for the time was fast approaching when the first should be last, and the last should be first.*

Finally, it was all fitting into place: the patterns in the leaves and the stars, the blood on the corn, the vision of race war, and the abiding question of Nat's own great purpose in life. Christ had not simply laid down his burden of suffering, he had passed it on, to Nat Turner himself. By taking up the cross, Nat would fulfill both Christ's purpose and his own burning ambition.

The "serpent" in Nat's vision was of course the white man, and by doing battle against him, Nat would "redeem" his own black race in both a religious sense and a political one—freeing them simultaneously from the bonds of both sin and slavery. The final result would not be race war but a more just reordering of society—"the first should be last, and the last should be first." Nat himself might die in the struggle, but his death, like Christ's, would only seal his triumph. . . .

The Day of Judgment was nearly at hand. All that now remained was to discover the details. And even these the spirit promised to reveal. . . . The promised signs took almost three years to appear. . . . Finally, in February 1831, there was an eclipse of the sun. Nat determined this to be the promised sign—the sign that removed "the seal from my lips." He now revealed his intentions to four trusted black friends who had fallen under the influence of his personality. The four men soon agreed to participate in his great work. The time had come "to slay my enemies with their own weapons," to plan strategy, to convert a private religious vision into a political and military operation. . . .

Through the spring months of 1831, the five men engaged in long debates and formulated any number of plans. But they could come to no agreement. "The time passed," Nat later recalled, "without our coming to any determination how to commence." Nat himself was so disturbed by this turn of events that he fell ill.

. . . The conspirators were "still forming new schemes and rejecting them." It was at this confused and discouraged point, on August 13, that Nat was finally jolted into action by a sign too clear to be ignored: This was, of course, the day the sun grew dim and changed colors, and the black spot appeared on its surface. Now Nat knew that the Day of Judgment could be delayed no longer.

Eight days later, on Sunday, August 21, Nat's four associates gathered at a secluded pond in the neighborhood: Hark, Nelson, Sam, and Henry. Hark (his full name was Hercules) brought a pig he had filched from his master. Henry brought some brandy. There were also present two new conspirators, slaves who had not previously been part of the group. Both were well known to the original four. The pig was killed and cooked.

Nat himself did not join this last meal until the middle of the afternoon. The seven men ate and drank (though Nat himself, true to his temperance principles, refused to touch the brandy). After the food was finished, the group continued to sit around the pond and debate their plans—for even at this late hour they had not formulated any clear strategy. There was, however, general agreement that the group could delay no longer—that very night they had to rise up and "kill all the white people." . . .

Nat was determined above all to maintain secrecy. Until the moment of the actual onslaught, only seven men knew what was going to happen. And these seven were closely related to each other by ties of friendship or kinship. . . . Among such a tight-knit group, the risk of betrayal was minimal.

But by ensuring secrecy, Nat was forced to . . . give up the possibility of systematic recruitment and effective organization. He would have to recruit his forces in spontaneous fashion as the group moved on from one farm to another. Their numbers would increase as they went along, he argued. The places Nat planned to attack were all familiar to him. He had lived his entire life in the neighborhood, and his party of insurrectionists was well known to many of the slaves in the region. When these slaves saw their owners actually lying dead, and felt themselves masterless, they would surely join the liberating army. And since the slaves in Southampton County outnumbered the whites, the county would belong to *them.*

So Nat argued, as he and his six friends sat by the pond, watching afternoon turn to dusk, and dusk slip into darkness.

Finally, then, it was agreed: That very night they would begin. They would head to the house of Joseph Travis, the master of Nat and Hark. There they would stop and "kill all the white people." Then they would collect weapons and horses, recruit other male Travis slaves—slaves now without a master—to join them, and march on to other farms and plantations. There the scene would be repeated, and their army of recruits would swell to overwhelming proportions. At first, they would spare no white person in their path, whether man, woman, or child—that much was necessary in order to "strike terror and alarm" through the countryside and cause the remaining white people of the county to flee for their lives. Within a day, if all went well, the black army could march unopposed and triumphant into the county seat—a town whose biblical name, Jerusalem, could not have escaped Nat's notice.

The killings had to be brutal, to intensify the general terror. The heads of some victims were to be severed, and the bodies of others dismembered. But Nat also insisted on clear limits: There was to be no torture, no rape, and (except for necessary supplies) no looting. There was no room for indulging in simple revenge or personal gratification. Furthermore, the slaughter would not continue indefinitely. Nat later told a white questioner that "indiscriminate massacre was not their intention after they obtained a foothold. Women and children would afterward be spared, and men too who ceased to resist."

An Historian Explains the Scarcity of Slave Revolts

The small number of slave revolts in North America as compared with the numerous large-scale uprisings that plagued other slave societies has long intrigued historians. The following selection identifies some of the factors that account for this striking disparity. Which of them best explains the failure of Nat Turner's revolt? Abridged from John B. Boles, Black Southerners, 1619–1869 *(Lexington, Kentucky, 1983), 172–76.*

Many factors mitigated against successful armed insurrection by slaves in the Old South. Unlike the situation in Latin America, in the Old South as a whole whites far outnumbered slaves, and of course totally controlled the police power of the states. . . . [N]onslaveholding whites almost unanimously supported slavery as a method of controlling blacks even if slave ownership was not their personal goal. . . . In certain regions like the sea islands of South Carolina and Georgia and the sugar districts of Louisiana, blacks were in a significant majority, yet even there the distance between individual plantations and the maze of unbridged estuaries, rivers, bayous, sloughs, and swamps made communication and travel between plantations difficult. The geography of the Old South conspired with demography to complicate still further slave attempts at rebellion and escape. Slaves in Brazil and in the Guiana region of northeastern South America, for example, had the huge, unexplored jungle fastness of the Amazon River basin in which to escape; similarly, plantations were located on the perimeters of the West Indian islands, whose interiors offered sure havens for runaways. In both regions slaves escaped to the interior and in maroon settlements often managed to survive for years, occasionally fighting white authorities to a

This wood engraving shows escaping slaves. Although attempts were made, the geography of the Old South made successful slave escapes nearly impossible.

standstill and achieving treaty recognition of their status (often in exchange for returning newly escaped slaves).

This kind of escape from slavery was never possible for the overwhelming majority of bondsmen in the Old South. Except for those few who lived near the Dismal Swamp on the eastern Virginia-North Carolina boundary, and some in Florida and Georgia near the Okefenokee Swamp and the trackless Everglades, there was no safe hinterland where maroons could survive. Moreover, cold winters, particularly in the Upper South, made the prospect of hiding out in the woods uninviting. In the early decades of plantation development, the Indians in the backcountry quickly learned they would be rewarded for capturing and returning slave runaways. The Indians were replaced in later decades by yeoman farmers who either returned the runaways for the reward or kept them. For most slaves the freedom territory north of the Mason-Dixon line or the Ohio River was simply too far away, and while several thousand bondsmen in the last half-century of slavery did escape by way of the Underground Railroad, most of them came from the border states of Maryland and Kentucky.

In Latin America and the Caribbean Islands, where hundreds of slaves lived on huge plantations, the owners were absent, and the working conditions were far more harsh than those typical in the South, desperate slaves, often plagued with famine as well as overwork, occasionally struck out against their brutal oppression and escaped to preexisting maroon communities. The working conditions on the tropical sugar plantations drove slaves to rebellion, and the example of successful escape offered by the maroon settlements in the backcountry emboldened otherwise hesitant bondsmen to act. There was, in other words, a heritage of insurrection in the Caribbean and Latin America that offered slaves not only incentive to rebel but the expectation of success. No such vital spark of hope was possible in the Old South. The few insurrections were small, localized, and quickly and brutally suppressed, with many innocent slaves usually punished and the general restrictions against all slaves made temporarily more harsh. . . .

During the era of the cotton kingdom most slaves were American born, the sex ratio was practically equal (more so than the white ratio), and slaves typically lived in family groupings. As a result the slave family became the single most important bond holding members together[;] . . . naming practices and kinship systems evolved to cement relationships made fragile by the possibility of sale or removal. This demographic development also prevented slave insurrection.

While a population composed mostly of unattached young males can be very explosive (especially when faced with harsh conditions and the possibility of escape), a population where males and females are equally present, family relationships have been formed and there are small children to love and care for, is far more conservative. The possibility of an entire family escaping was practically nil, and parents were loath to forsake their children to save themselves. Likewise few men would leave their loved ones for an escape attempt with little chance of success. If family attachments lessened runaway efforts, so much more did the ties of family affection reduce the possibilities of insurrection. Few male slaves would risk almost sure death when to do so would leave their families fatherless. Moreover, the knowledge that family members and innocent bystanders would be pitilessly punished and their rights severely circumscribed in the aftermath of a rebellion attempt must have restrained many discontented slaves.

In the Old South, where family structures, leisure time, and fairly good living conditions prevented most slaves from being driven into utter desperation, slaves usually found less risky avenues of countering the dehumanization of chattel bondage. Because hunger and abject hopelessness were less common in the Old South, slaves calculated their options more carefully, waiting—sometimes all their lives—for good chances for successful rebellion. Thousands did not find the right moment to strike until the Civil War and the presence of Union troops profoundly changed the balance. Then no one was more shocked than complacent planters when droves of their seemingly most devoted, most responsible slaves "deserted" and chose freedom.

The realities of power and geography in the Old South also minimized the kind of slave rebellion that often occurred in the other New World plantation societies. In the antebellum South, slaves were very seldom driven to mindless, suicidal acts of outrage and rebellion. Fully aware of their situation, they learned, socialized, and passed on to their children a wide range of behavior—voice intonations, facial expressions, feigned illness, purposeful laziness and slowness of motion, dumb-like-a-fox incomprehension—that combined equal portions of insubordination and minor rebellion to produce a constant undercurrent of resistance to psychological bondage. Although never completely giving in to authority, most slaves were able, at least in the eyes of their master, to acquiesce in their state of servitude and thus survive with their essential humanity intact. In the most fundamental sense, racial slavery as it existed in the Old South was premised on the assumption by whites that blacks were inferior, either a subhuman or a permanently childlike race. Planters' everyday experience, of course, gave the lie to this assumption, and therein may have been the cause of the guilt that some historians believe troubled many whites, particularly those who constructed elaborate proslavery defenses. Had slaves in general accepted this racial subordination and aspired to be only what the white man prescribed, then blacks would have been total slaves, and all resistance—except occasional outbursts of violence—would have disappeared. But the rich panoply of Afro-American culture, their tales, music, art, and religion protected bondsmen from complete capitulation. Out of the inner reserves of their humanity slaves in measured ways resisted servitude and defended the limited rights that had become, through mutual accommodation, accepted by whites. The black community evolved a culture from which proceeded all forms of slave resistance other than rebellion.

Questions

1. *What effect do you think the presence of a hostile and potentially dangerous element in southern society had on southern life and culture?*
2. *Were resistance and revolt inevitable in a slaveholding society? Was there any way to avoid them?*
3. *Did the danger that slaves posed to the security of white southern society have any effect on the North, or was it solely a southern concern?*
4. *What do such events as Nat Turner's revolt tell us about the institution of slavery itself? Can you think of any way a successful slave revolt could have been organized in spite of obstacles?*
5. *Does Nat Turner appear to be a fanatic or a shrewd planner and leader? Could he have been both?*

Slave Revolt and Slave Violence: Their Causes and Consequence

Resistance to slavery, common throughout its existence, took various forms, each of them annoying and costly to the owners. Feigning illness, breaking or losing tools, slow or shoddy work, insolence, running away—these were only a few of the many unspectacular ways slaves exerted their independence and countered their owners' power.

Every slaveowner and every plantation experienced such resistance to some degree at one time or another. It apparently was inseparable from the institution itself. Rarer than any of these mundane forms of resistance, but more to be feared, was slave violence directed against whites. Most incidents of assault and murder resulted from identifiable grievances experienced by individual slaves; the motive appeared limited to personal revenge and retribution. In rare instances, however, slaves joined together in overt action calculated to damage, or even destroy, the institution of slavery itself and to free themselves from it. On those occasions when slaves organized revolts, they used violence to achieve a political rather than a personal end. North American slaves made only a few such attempts, and their success was nil, especially when compared with the more frequent, extensive, and long lasting revolts undertaken by slaves in the West Indies and in South America. The Stono Revolt in South Carolina (1739), the revolt in Louisiana (1811), and Nat Turner's revolt in Virginia (1831) practically exhaust the list. Each was limited in scope and readily put down. Nevertheless, each of them had important consequences for the slave community and for white southerners as well as for the future of slavery itself and of opposition to it. Of the three North American revolts, the one led by Nat Turner (sometimes called the Southampton revolt) is by far the best known and the most extensively documented. That revolt, like its predecessors, led to vicious reprisals against black people and to intensified efforts by slaveholders to make slavery more secure. In the North it contributed to the growth of an antislavery movement.

A Virginia State Official Explains Nat Turner's Revolt

John Floyd, governor of Virginia, pondering the causes of Turner's revolt, concluded that it resulted from influences other than those inherent in slavery itself. Here Floyd tells James Hamilton, Jr., the governor of South Carolina, his explanation of the revolt and the plan he will propose to prevent its repetition. Excerpted from The Southampton Slave Revolt of 1831, *ed. Henry Irving Tragle (Amherst, 1971), 275–76.*

Richmond
November 19, 1831

Sir:

I received your letter yesterday and with great pleasure will give you my impressions freely—

I will notice this affair in my annual message, but here only give a very careless history of it, as it appeared to the public—

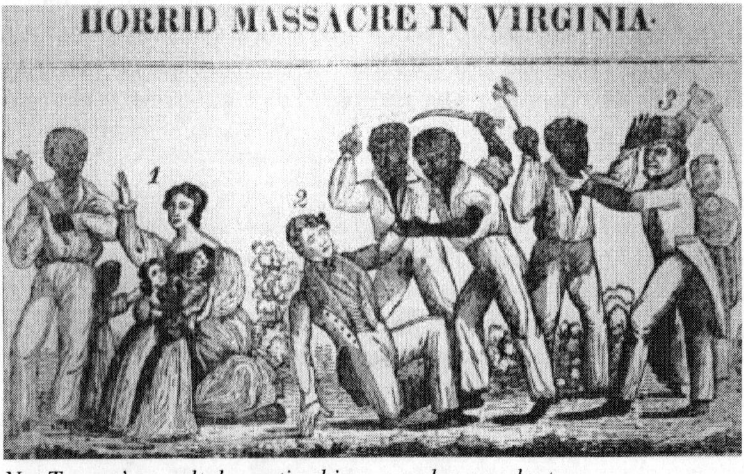

Nat Turner's revolt dramatized in a popular woodcut.

I am fully persuaded, the spirit of insubordination which has, and still manifests itself in Virginia, had its origin among, and eminated . . . from, the Yankee population, upon their *first* arrival amongst us, but mostly especially the Yankee pedlers and traders.

The course has been by no means a direct one—they began first, by making them religious—their conversations were of that character—telling the blacks God was no respecter of persons—the black man was as good as the white—that all men were born free and equal—that they cannot serve two masters—that the white people rebelled against England to obtain freedom, so have the blacks a right to do.

In the mean time, I am sure without any purpose of this kind, the preachers, principally Northern—were very assidious in operating upon our population, day and night, they were at work—and religion became, and is, the fashion of the time—finally our females and of the most respectable were persuaded that it was piety to teach negroes to read and write, to the end that they might read the Scriptures—many of them became tutoress in Sunday schools and, pious distributors of tracts, from the New York Tract Society.

At this point, more active operations commenced—our magistrates and laws became more inactive—large assemblages of negroes were suffered to take place for religious purposes—Then commenced the efforts of the black preachers, often from the pulpits these pamphlets and papers were read—followed by the incendiary publications of Walker, Garrison and Knapp of Boston, these too with songs and hymns of a similar character were circulated, read and commented upon—We resting in apathetic security until the Southampton affair.

From all that has come to my knowledge during and since this affair—I am fully convinced that every black preacher in the whole country east of the Blue Ridge was in [on] the secret, that the plans as published by those Northern presses were adopted and acted upon by them—that their congregations, as they were called knew nothing of this intended rebellion, except a few leading and intelligent men, who may have been head men in the

---

Church—*the mass* were prepared by making them aspire to an equal station by such conversations as I have related as the first step.

I am informed that they had settled the form of government to be that of white people, whom they intended to cut off to a man—with the difference that the preachers were to be their Governors, Generals and Judges. I feel fully justified to myself, in believing the Northern incendiaries, tracts, Sunday Schools, religion and reading and writing has accomplished this end.

I shall in my annual message recommend that laws be passed—To confine the Slaves to the estates of their masters—prohibit negroes from preaching—absolutely to drive from this State all free negroes—and to substitute the surplus revenue in our Treasury annually for slaves, to work for a time upon our Rail Roads etc etc and these sent out of the country, preparatory, or rather as the first step to emancipation—This last point will of course be tenderly and cautiously managed and will be urged or delayed as your State and Georgia may be disposed to co-operate.

In relation to the extent of this insurrection I think it greater than will ever appear. . . .

I am Sir,
with consideration and respect
your obt Sevnt
[obedient servant,]
s/John Floyd/

Religion as a Bulwark of Slavery

As Governor Floyd suggests, slaveowners generally did not object to their slaves being exposed to religious teachings. In fact, some viewed such instruction as one of their responsibilities, but, like Governor Floyd, they believed that in the "wrong" hands (as in Turner's), religion could be a subversive or revolutionary force. The following excerpt was written in 1842 by Lunsford Lane, a North Carolina slave. This memoir illustrates the use of religion for conservative ends. Excerpted from Five Slave Narratives: A Compendium *(New York, 1968), 20–21, with some minor grammatical corrections.*

I had never been permitted to learn to read; but I used to attend church, and there I received instruction which I trust was of some benefit to me. . . .

I often heard select portions of the scriptures read. And on the Sabbath there was one sermon preached expressly for the colored people which it was generally my privilege to hear. I became quite familiar with the texts, "Servants be obedient to your masters."—"Not with eye service as men pleasers."—"He that knoweth his master's will and doeth it not, shall be beaten with many stripes," and others of this class: for they formed the basis of most of these public instructions to us. The first commandment impressed upon our minds was to obey our masters, and the second was like unto it, namely, to do as much work when they or the overseers were not watching us as when they were. But connected with these instructions there was more or less that was truly excellent; though mixed up with much that would sound strangely in the ears of freedom. There was one very kind hearted Episcopal minister whom I often used to hear; he was very popular with the colored people. But after he had preached a sermon to us in which he argued from the Bible that it was the will of heaven from all eternity we should be slaves, and our masters be our owners, most of us left him; for like some of the faint hearted disciples in early times we said,—"This is a hard saying, who can bear it?"

Popular Reaction to Nat Turner's Revolt

Following revolts, retribution against African Americans, slave or free, guilty or innocent, was severe and indiscriminate and may help to account for the rarity of such revolts. The following newspaper report describes the aftermath of Nat Turner's revolt and the part that armed forces played in halting the reprisals. From the Constitutional Whig, *Richmond, Virginia, 3 September 1831, reprinted in* The Southampton Slave Revolt of 1831, *ed. Henry Irving Tragle (Boston, 1971), 69–70.*

It is with pain we speak of another feature of the Southampton Rebellion; for we have been most unwilling to have our sympathies for the sufferers diminished or affected by their misconduct. We allude to the slaughter of many blacks, without trial, and under circumstances of great barbarity. How many have thus been put into death (generally by decapitation or shooting) reports vary; probably however some five and twenty and from that to 40; possibly a yet larger number. To the great honor of General Eppes, he used every precaution in his power, and we hope and believe with success, to put a stop to the disgraceful procedure.—We met with one individual of intelligence, who stated that he himself had killed between 10 and 15. He justified himself on the grounds of the barbarities committed on the whites; and that he thought himself right is certain from the fact that he narrowly escaped losing his own life in an attempt to save a negro woman whom he thought innocent but who was shot by the multitude in despite of his exertions. We (the Richmond Troop) witnessed with surprise the sanguinary temper of the population who evinced a strong disposition to inflict immediate death on every prisoner. Not having witnessed the horrors committed by the blacks, or seen the unburried and disfigured remains of their wives and children, we were unprepared to understand their feelings, and could not at first admit of their extenuation, which a closer observation of the atrocities of the insurgents suggested. Now, however, we feel individually compelled to offer an apology for the people of Southampton, while we deeply deplore that human nature urged them to such extremities. Let the fact not be doubted by those whom it most concerns, that another such insurrection will be the signal for the extirmination of the whole black population in the quarter of the state where it occurs. . . .

The presence of the troops from Norfolk and Richmond alone prevented retaliation from being carried much farther.

Popular Reaction to a Rumored Revolt in Louisiana

Solomon Northup, a slave in Louisiana during the 1840s, describes an abortive attempt by slaves to organize a mass escape to Mexico and the retaliation that followed. Note the apparent absence of a religious im-

pulse for the revolt and the similarities with the aftermath of Nat Turner's revolt. Note, too, that the violence against slaves came to an end in a similar way. Abridged from Solomon Northup, Twelve Years a Slave: Narrative of Solomon Northup . . . *(Auburn, 1853), 246–49.*

The year before my arrival in the country there was a concerted movement among a number of slaves on Bayou Boeuf, that terminated tragically indeed. It was, I presume, a matter of newspaper notoriety at the time, but all the knowledge I have of it, has been derived from the relation of those living at that period in the immediate vicinity of the excitement. It has become a subject of general and unfailing interest in every slave-hut on the bayou, and will doubtless go down to succeeding generations as their chief tradition. Lew Cheney, with whom I became acquainted—a shrewd, cunning negro, more intelligent than the generality of his race, but unscrupulous and full of treachery—conceived the project of organizing a company sufficiently strong to fight their way against all opposition, to the neighboring territory of Mexico.

A remote spot, far within the depths of the swamp back of Hawkins' plantation, was selected as the rallying point. Lew flitted from one plantation to another, in the dead of night, preaching a crusade to Mexico, and, like Peter the Hermit, creating a furor of excitement wherever he appeared. At length a large number of runaways were assembled; stolen mules, and corn gathered from the fields, and bacon filched from smoke-houses, had been conveyed into the woods. The expedition was about ready to proceed, when their hiding place was discovered. Lew Cheney, becoming convinced of the ultimate failure of his project, in order to curry favor with his master, and avoid the consequences which he foresaw would follow, deliberately determined to sacrifice all his companions. Departing secretly from the encampment, he proclaimed among the planters the number collected in the swamp, and, instead of stating truly the object they had in view, asserted their intention was to emerge from their seclusion the first favorable opportunity, and murder every white person along the bayou.

Such an announcement, exaggerated as it passed from mouth to mouth, filled the whole country with terror. The fugitives were surrounded and taken prisoners, carried in chains to Alexandria, and hung by the populace. Not only those, but many who were suspected, though entirely innocent, were taken from the field and from the cabin, and without the shadow of process or form of trial, hurried to the scaffold. The planters on Bayou Boeuf finally rebelled against such reckless destruction of property, but it was not until a regiment of soldiers had arrived from some fort on the Texan frontier, demolished the gallows, and opened the doors of the Alexandria prison, that the indiscriminate slaughter was stayed. Lew Cheney escaped, and was even rewarded for his treachery. He is still living, but his name is despised and execrated by all his race throughout the parishes of Rapides and Avoyelles.

Such an idea as insurrection, however, is not new among the enslaved population of Bayou Boeuf. More than once I have joined in serious consultation, when the subject has been discussed, and there have been times when a word from me would have placed hundreds of my fellow-bondsmen in an attitude of defiance. Without arms or ammunition, or even with them, I saw such a step would result in certain defeat, disaster and death, and always raised my voice against it.

During the Mexican war I well remember the extravagant hopes that were excited. The news of victory filled the great house with rejoicing, but produced only sorrow and disappointment in the cabin. In my opinion—and I have had opportunity to know something of the feeling of which I speak—there are not fifty slaves on the shores of Bayou Boeuf, but would hail with unmeasured delight the approach of an invading army.

A Northern Editor Reacts to Nat Turner's Revolt

Slave unrest obviously was primarily a southern problem, but Nat Turner's revolt led even northerners who were not abolitionists to worry about its probable effects on the nation at large. Here, a northern newspaper editor speculates on possible solutions to the "problem" of slave revolts. From the Ohio State Journal and Columbus Gazette, *October 20, 1831, 3.*

Since the suppression of the late Negro insurrection in Southampton county, Va. it appears that similar outrages have been attempted by the slaves and free colored people in different parts of North and South Carolina, Louisiana, Delaware, and the Eastern Shore of Maryland; and although the designs of the poor wretches concerned therein have been for the most part discovered and frustrated before much actual mischief had been done, yet the frequency of their late attempts has occasioned no little alarm in those parts of the union which have most to fear from a servile war. Whether these almost simultaneous movements in sections of the country so remote from each other be the result of accident, or of something like a preconcerted plan for a general insurrection among the slaves about this time does not fully appear. The latter supposition, however, is not altogether improbable; and although every man possessed of common sense will at once see that an attempt of this kind, however well matured, must ultimately result in the total extermination of at least all those engaged in it, if not of the entire colored population, yet, it is evident that it would inevitably occasion the loss of many valuable lives, and be productive of a vast amount of misery, before it could be suppressed.

A southern paper, speaking of these movements, and of the probability of their frequent recurrence so long as slavery shall be tolerated among us, suggests, whether it would not be right and expedient, after the National Debt shall have been paid, to apply the surplus revenue to the general emancipation of the slaves, and their removal beyond our territorial limits; and without intending to express an opinion, either as to the expediency or the feasibility of such a measure, we must say that it appears to us to be worthy of serious consideration. We believe that the people of these United States ought no longer to shut their eyes to the dreadful evils of slavery, and the consequences which, sooner or later, must inevitably result from it; and that the time has fully arrived when some plan should be devised for the removal of this curse from among us. We shall probably recur to the subject in a future number.

An Abolitionist Reacts to Nat Turner's Revolt

For many years before 1831, opponents of slavery had warned that slaves in the South would someday follow the example of the slaves in Saint-

Domingue who successfully rebelled in the 1790s. In this selection, William Lloyd Garrison, the best known of the abolitionists, interprets Nat Turner's revolt as a fulfillment of that prophecy, calling for immediate emancipation as the only means to prevent a catastrophic race war for liberation. Abridged from William Lloyd Garrison, "The Insurrection," Liberator, *Boston, September 3, 1831, 143.*

What we have so long predicted,—at the peril of being stigmatized as an alarmist and declaimer,—has commenced its fulfilment. The first step of the earthquake, which is ultimately to shake down the fabric of oppression, leaving not one stone upon another, has been made. The first drops of blood, which are but the prelude to a deluge from the gathering clouds, have fallen. The first flash of the lightning, which is to smite and consume, has been felt. The first wailings of a bereavement, which is to clothe the earth in sackcloth, have broken upon our ears. . . .

True, the rebellion is quelled. Those of the slaves who were not killed in combat, have been secured, and the prison is crowded with victims destined for the gallows!

'Yet laugh not in your carnival of crime
Too proudly, ye oppressors!'

You have seen, it is to be feared, but the beginning of sorrows. All the blood which has been shed will be required at your hands. At your hands alone? No—but at the hands of the people of New-England and of all the free states. The crime of oppression is national. The south is only the agent in this guilty traffic. But, remember! the same causes are at work which must inevitably produce the same effects; and when the contest shall have again begun, it must be again a war of extermination. In the present instance, no quarters have been asked or given.

[Garrison now attempts to voice the slaveholders' justification for revenge against Nat Turner's band:]

But we have killed and routed them [the slaves] now. . . We have the power to kill *all*—let us, therefore, continue to apply the whip and forge new fetters! . . . They were black—brutes, pretending to be men—legions of curses upon their memories! They were black—God made them to serve us! . . .

[Garrison, as an abolitionist, now addresses the slaveholders:]

Ye accuse the pacific friends of emancipation of instigating the slaves to revolt. Take back the charge as a foul slander. The slaves need no incentives at our hands. They will find them in their stripes—in their emaciated bodies—in their ceaseless toil—in their ignorant minds—in every field, in every valley, on every hill-top and mountain, wherever you and your fathers have fought for liberty—in your speeches, your conversations, your celebrations, your pamphlets, your newspapers—voices in the air, sounds from across the ocean, invitations to resistance above, below, around them! What more do they need? Surrounded by such influences, and smarting under their newly made wounds, is it wonderful that they should rise to contend—as other 'heroes' have contended—for their lost rights? It is *not* wonderful.

In all that we have written, is there aught to justify the excesses of the slaves? No. Nevertheless, they deserve no more censure than the Greeks in destroying the Turks, or the Poles in exterminating the Russians, or our fathers in slaughtering the British. Dreadful, indeed, is the standard erected by worldly patriotism!

For ourselves, we are horror-struck at the late tidings. We have exerted our utmost efforts to avert the calamity. We have warned our countrymen of the danger of persisting in their unrighteous conduct. We have preached to the slaves the pacific precepts of Jesus Christ. We have appealed to christians, philanthropists and patriots, for their assistance to accomplish the great work of national redemption through the agency of moral power—of public opinion—of individual duty. How have we been received? We have been threatened, proscribed, vilified and imprisoned—a laughing-stock and a reproach. Do we falter, in view of these things? Let time answer. If we have been hitherto urgent, and bold, and denunciatory in our efforts,—hereafter we shall grow vehement and active with the increase of danger. We shall cry, in trumpet tones, night and day,—Wo to this guilty land, unless she speedily repent of her evil doings! The blood of millions of her sons cries aloud for redress! IMMEDIATE EMANCIPATION can alone save her from the vengeance of Heaven, and cancel the debt of ages!

Slave Violence Directed against Individual Owners

Instances of slaves murdering their masters were frequent enough to cause concern even though slaveowners usually insisted that their own slaves could be trusted. Here, Mary Chesnut of South Carolina recounts the fate of two white women, one her acquaintance, the other her relative, who met their deaths at the hands of aggrieved slaves. Note that in each instance, the cause of the murders, as Mrs. Chesnut understands it, was not too much, but too little, discipline. How might the slaves' explanation for the murders differ from that given by Mrs. Chesnut? Excerpted from Mary Chesnut's Civil War, *ed. C. Vann Woodward (New Haven, 1981), 209–12.*

And now comes back on us that bloody story that haunts me night and day, Mrs. Witherspoon's murder.

The man William, who was the master spirit of the gang, once ran away and was brought back from somewhere west. And then his master and himself had a reconciliation, and the master henceforth made a pet of him.

The night preceding the murder, John Witherspoon went over to his mother's to tell her of some of William and Rhody's misdeeds. While their mistress was away from home, they had given a ball fifteen miles away from Society Hill. To that place they had taken their mistress's china, silver, house linen, &c&c. After his conversation with his mother, as he rode out of the gate, he shook his whip at William and said, "Tomorrow I mean to come here and give every one of you a thrashing."

That night Mrs. Witherspoon was talking it all over with her grandson, a half-grown boy who lived with her—slept, indeed, in a room opening into hers.

"I do not intend John to punish these negroes. It is too late to begin discipline now. It is all nonsense. I have indulged them past bearing, they all say. I ought to have tried to control them. It is all my fault. That's the end of it."

Mrs. Edwards, who was a sister of Mrs. Witherspoon, was found dead in her bed. It is thought this suggested their plan of action to the negroes. What more likely than she should die as her sister had done.

They were all in great trouble when John went off. William said, "Listen to me, and there will be no punishment here tomorrow." They made their plan, and then all of them *went to sleep,* William remaining awake to stir up the others at the proper hour.

What first attracted the attention of the family was the appearance of black and blue spots about the face and neck of the body of their mother. Then someone in moving the candle from the table at her bedside found blood upon their fingers. . . .

. . . [T]hey began to scent mischief and foul play in earnest, and they sent for the detective. Before he came they searched all houses and found bloody rags.

The detective dropped in from the skies quite unexpectedly. He saw that one of the young understrappers of the gang looked frightened and uncomfortable. This one he fastened upon and got up quite an intimacy with him. Finally he told this boy that he knew all about it. William had confessed privately to him to save himself and hang the others. But as the detective had taken a fancy to this boy, if he would confess everything, he would take him as state's evidence instead of William. The young man was utterly confounded at first but fell in the trap laid for him and told every particular from beginning to end.

Then they were all put in jail, the youth who had confessed among them, as he did not wish them to know of his *treachery* to them.

This was his story. "After John went away that night, Rhody and William made a great fuss—were furious at Mars John threatening them after all these years—to talk to them that away."

William said: "Mars John more than apt to do what he say he will do. You-all follow what I say and he'll have something else to think of beside stealing and breaking glass and china and tablecloths. If ole Marster was alive now, what would he say? Talk of whipping us at this time of day, &c&c."

Rhody kept the key of the house to let herself in every morning. So they arranged to go in at twelve. And then William watched, and they slept the sleep of the righteous.

Before that, however, they had a "rale fine supper and a heap of laughing at the way dey's all look tomorrow."

They smothered her with a counterpane [quilt] from a bed in the entry. He had no trouble the first time because they found her asleep and "done it all 'fore she waked." But after Rhody took her keys and went into the trunk and got a clean nightgown—for they had spoiled the one she had on—and fixed everything, candle, medicine, and all—she came to! Then she begged them hard for life. She asked them what she had ever done that they should want to kill her? She promised them before God never to tell on them. Nobody should ever know. But Rhody stopped her mouth by the counterpane. William held her head and hands down. And the other two sat on her legs. Rhody had a thrifty mind and wished to save the sheets and nightgown. She did not destroy them—they were found behind her mantelpiece. There the money was also, all in a hole made among the bricks behind the wooden mantelpiece.

A grandson of Rhody's slept in her house. Him she locked up in his room. She did not want him to know anything of this fearful night.

That innocent old lady and her gray hairs moved them not a jot.

Fancy how we feel. I am sure I will never sleep again without this nightmare of horror haunting me.

Mrs. Chesnut [Mary Chesnut's mother-in-law], who is their good angel, is and has always been afraid of negroes. In her youth the St. Domingo stories were indelibly printed on her mind.

She shows her dread now by treating everyone as if they were a black Prince Albert or Queen Victoria.

We were beginning to forget Mrs. Cunningham, the only other woman we ever heard of murdered by her negroes.

Poor Cousin Betsey was goodness itself. After years of freedom and indulgence and tender kindness, it was an awful mistake to threaten them like children. It was only threats. Everybody knew she would never do anything.

How about Mrs. Cunningham? He [Mr. Cunningham] was an old bachelor, and the negroes had it all their own way till he married. And then they hated her. They took her from her room, just over one in which her son-in-law and her daughter slept. They smothered her, dressed her, and carried her out—all without the slightest noise—and hung her by the neck to an apple tree, as if she had committed suicide. Waked nobody in the house by all this. If they want to kill us, they can do it when they please—they are noiseless as panthers.

They were discovered—first, because dressing her in the dark, her tippet [nightcap] was put on hind part before. And she was supposed to have walked out and hung herself in a pair of brand-new shoes whose soles evidently had never touched the ground.

We ought to be grateful that any one of us is alive. But nobody is afraid of their own negroes. These are horrid brutes—savages, monsters—but I find everyone like myself, ready to trust their own yard. I would go down on the plantation tomorrow and stay there, if there were no white person in twenty miles. My Molly and half a dozen others that *I know*—and all the rest I believe—would keep me as safe as I should be in the Tower of London.

Questions

1. *How do you account for the indiscriminate fury directed against African Americans in the wake of Nat Turner's revolt and the abortive revolt in Louisiana? Why do you think the armed forces quelled that fury instead of supporting it?*
2. *Both Governor John Floyd and William Lloyd Garrison agreed that outside influences were partly responsible for slave unrest, but their understanding of those influences varied greatly. Explain.*
3. *Religion is sometimes assumed to be a conservative force. Yet, it appears to have been a prime influence in the Nat Turner revolt. How do you account for this discrepancy? Can you think of other situations in which religion has been employed in support of radical causes?*

Further Reading

Nearly all the surviving sources for studying Nat Turner's revolt can be found in The Southampton Slave Revolt of 1831: A Compilation of Source Material Including the Full Text of the Confessions of Nat Turner, *ed. Henry Irving Tragle (Boston, 1971). For two good accounts of the revolt based on the documents in Tragle's book, see Stephen B. Oates,* The Fires of Jubilee: Nat Turner's Fierce Rebellion *(New York, 1975); and Herbert Aptheker,* Nat Turner's Slave Rebellion *(New York, 1966). Herbert Aptheker,* American Negro Slave Revolts *(New York, 1943), provides extensive information about various forms of African American resistance to slavery. For a discussion of the relation of slave discontent to American political and diplomatic history and to American wars see Merton L. Dillon,* Slavery Attacked: Southern Slaves and Their Allies, 1619–1865 *(Baton Rouge, 1990).*

Abolitionism

Merton L. Dillon

INTRODUCTION

Opposition to slavery in North America was as old as the institution itself. Africans—after being transported forcibly from their homes—resisted their enslavement from the day they reached American shores. At an early date, a few sympathetic whites joined them in condemning bondage. A religiously inspired movement aimed at abolishing slavery began in the middle of the eighteenth century when Quakers made opposition to slavery a condition of membership in their sect. Soon after, during the revolutionary period, a new concern for Natural Rights helped end slavery in the northern states. Some southerners also freed their slaves at that time, but antislavery sentiment in the South never became general enough to lead any southern state to abolish the institution.

Most early opponents of slavery assumed that it would be ended gradually by state legislative action, and that abolition would be accompanied by colonization—the removal of at least some of the freed men and women from the United States. But around 1830 a younger, more determined, more spirited group of abolitionists rejected each of these assumptions. Their demand for the immediate end of slavery and the abandonment of all plans for the expatriation of African Americans ushered in a new, exceedingly contentious phase of the antislavery movement. African Americans heartily endorsed the new "immediatist" program and joined in promoting it. They focused on the plight of their race in the northern states more consistently than did most of their white colleagues and were more intent than were most whites on working against such evidences of prejudice as segregated schools and discriminatory laws. Nonetheless, from beginning to end, the antislavery movement was a partnership, albeit an unequal one, of white and African American abolitionists.

Abolitionists condemned slavery as a cruel and sinful institution that ought to be ended at once. They argued, first, that it violated the principles set forth in the Declaration of Independence upon which the nation was founded, and, second, that it conflicted with such fundamental biblical teachings as the Golden Rule.

The majority of Americans at the time, patriotic and religious though they may have been, did not find these arguments persuasive. Abolitionists always comprised only a minority in the northern populution and typically were both scorned and feared as dangerous fanatics. Their campaign to end slavery aroused fierce opposition throughout the north as well as the south. Abolitionist lecturers were regularly mobbed, their printing presses were wrecked, and one abolitionist editor, Elijah P. Lovejoy, was murdered.

A later generation may find such resistance to a call for freedom, justice, and equality hard to understand because the abolitionists' program and their point of view now form part of the American consensus: They are taken for granted. But we should remember that this achievement came only at the cost of a horrendous civil war and, a century later, the painful social and political upheaval incident to the civil rights struggles of the1960s.

Aspects of the Movement for Abolition

If abolitionists imagined that their program would be welcomed and easily achieve success, they quickly learned otherwise. Hostility met their every effort. Mobs assailed antislavery lecturers in the north; legislatures in the south offered rewards to anyone who would deliver them for trial. What explains such intense resistance? Since the majority apparently found the abolitionists' program utterly unacceptable, how and why was slavery ended? The following readings suggest answers to these perplexing questions.

The African American Contribution

The central role played by African Americans in the antislavery movement is not always acknowledged. In this selection, historian C. Peter Ripley describes their influence in developing the Abolitionist agenda. Taken from Witness for Freedom: African American Voices on Race, Slavery, and Emancipation *(Chapel Hill, 1993), 1-2, 4, 6.*

On a brisk December morning in 1833, sixty-two reformers from eleven northern states gathered in Philadelphia to transform the American antislavery movement. Ignoring threats of violence, they opened their proceedings at Adelphi Hall to a skeptical

---

public and an unfriendly press. The founding convention of the American Anti-Slavery Society (AASS) brought together Quakers, Protestant clergymen, and distinguished reformers, including three blacks: Robert Purvis, a handsome, urbane young Philadelphian who, despite his light complexion, proudly identified himself as an African American; James G. Barbadoes, a Boston clothier and barber; and James McCrummill, a barber and dentist, who provided accommodations for the tempestuous young editor of the Boston *Liberator*, William Lloyd Garrison. After the first day-long session, Garrison retired to McCrummill's comfortable Philadelphia home a few blocks away on Third Street. With an oil lamp burning through the night, he worked intently on a draft of the society's Declaration of Sentiments. The delegates debated the draft during the following sessions, and on 6 December, the final day of the convention, they came forward to sign the document, just as the Founding Fathers had signed the Declaration of Independence in Philadelphia fifty-seven years before.

The AASS Declaration of Sentiments represented an interracial consensus on goals and methods of the antislavery movement. It called for an immediate end to slavery without compensation for slave owners and rejected violence and the use of force, trusting instead in "the overthrow of prejudice by the power of love—and the abolition of slavery by the spirit of repentance." The declaration repudiated the colonization movement's plan to remove all free blacks to Africa as "delusive, cruel and dangerous."

By addressing the issues of prejudice, slavery, and colonization, the Declaration of Sentiments gave voice to the primary concerns of African Americans. Freeing the two million slaves and ending the racism that contaminated American society were long-sought goals, but colonization had been the most pressing concern of free blacks throughout the decade preceding the Philadelphia convocation.

The colonization movement was a mix of diverse interests that came together to settle free blacks and newly emancipated slaves in Africa. Most colonizationists believed that free blacks endangered American society. They accepted the popular myth that blacks lacked the moral character and ability to become useful citizens. Even whites who considered slavery evil reasoned that sending blacks to a colony in Africa would ease white anxieties and thereby encourage manumissions, and at the same time provide free blacks with a refuge from American oppression. Most white abolitionists and antislavery organizations at the time supported colonization. These gradual abolitionists theorized that emancipation would be achieved, gradually and peacefully, through the courts, individual manumissions, and the political system. Removing freed blacks would hasten that process, they believed. Some southern slaveholders shared these sentiments, but most supported colonization for very different reasons. They feared that the presence of emancipated slaves would threaten slavery and hoped to purge the nation of free blacks before they "whisper[ed] liberty in the ears of the oppressed."

The movement emerged after the American Colonization Society (ACS)—the leading proponent of free black repatriation to the African continent—was established in 1816. . . .

Free blacks—particularly in the northern states—rejected colonization as a threat to their future on the American continent. "Here we were born, and here we will die," promised a defiant New York City group. Philadelphia blacks took the lead, holding four mass meetings between 1817 and 1819 to condemn colonization. Their angry protests set the tone for the struggle that followed. . . .

An organized black abolitionist movement grew out of the battle against colonization. Anticolonization efforts showed what careful organization and continued protest could accomplish. During the mid-1820s, leaders in the struggle against the ACS in Boston, New Haven, Philadelphia, Baltimore, and other free black communities banded together in local abolitionist groups to advance broad and ambitious reform goals, including emancipation and equality.

Newly organized and growing in confidence, African Americans set out to discredit colonization among white abolitionists and to convince them that an immediate end to slavery was the only true antislavery course. African American protests against colonization and calls for immediate emancipation came at an opportune moment. During the 1820s, the American antislavery movement was transformed by a complex set of intellectual, social, and economic forces. By 1830, black abolitionism joined with these forces to prepare the ground for the rise of immediate abolition.

The conversion of William Lloyd Garrison proved to be enormously important in the shift of the American antislavery movement to the black abolitionist viewpoint. Garrison, who would become America's best-known and most influential white abolitionist, began his career committed to colonization and the gradual demise of slavery, but as he worked with blacks in Baltimore and Philadelphia during the 1820s, he abandoned colonization, embraced racial equality, and advocated immediate emancipation.

Grateful for their new ally, African Americans did all they could for the energetic and irascible Garrison. Without their support, his *Liberator* would not have survived its crucial early years; blacks underwrote the printing costs for the first issue in 1830. . . .

Together with Garrison and a small but earnest band of white reformers, black abolitionists redirected the American antislavery movement. Encouraged by Garrison's example, and informed about colonization by blacks, a growing number of white abolitionists adopted immediatist beliefs, rejecting what Garrison now called the "pernicious doctrine of *gradual* emancipation." They demanded a quick end to slavery, supported racial equality, and repudiated colonization. Blacks and whites came together in 1833 to organize the American Anti-Slavery Society and within three years established five hundred auxiliaries across the North.

The Failure of the Abolitionists

The following essay discusses the abolitionists' program and tactics and argues that they did not achieve their original goals. Abridged from Merton L. Dillon, "The Failure of the American Abolitionists," Journal of Southern History *25 (May 1959): 160, 163-76.*

The success of any historical movement, it would seem, ought to be judged by its own terms and values; the extent of its accomplishments ought to be measured against its professed aims and methods. Viewed in such fashion, the antislavery movement must be ranked not as a triumph but as one of the major failures of our history. This is not to depreciate either the sincerity and nobility of the abolitionists or their ultimate effect upon the course of events. It is to say, however, that they failed to carry out their announced mission. The abolitionists—from the gentle Benjamin Lundy to the fanatical John Brown—had much to do with establishing emotional commitments in both North and South. By their remorseless agitation they sharpened sectional antagonisms; by their insistence upon viewing all issues in terms of principle, they transmuted sectional controversies into titanic moral struggles, thus rendering compromise unlikely if not impossible. Southerners, reacting to their verbal attacks, defended slavery and "Southern Rights" more stubbornly. Northerners, accepting at least part of the abolitionist indictment of slavery and slaveholders, thereby became more willing to fight an intersectional war. That the abolitionists in such fashion helped to bring about the Civil War and thus to end slavery few can doubt. But this is by no means the same thing as saying that they succeeded in accomplishing their program. . . .

Surveying the nation in 1830, the reformers saw (as reformers have always been able to see) vast numbers of people ignoring the ordinary imperatives of morality. This seemed to be true in whichever quarter they looked but in no place quite so flagrantly as the South. There, they concluded, a proud and powerful section of the country flourished in wickedness, quite beyond the pale of New England's moral influence. The Southern practice of slavery provided salient evidence of this fact, the abolitionists believed. For they had pronounced slavery a sin—it was not merely bad policy, it was not merely evil (theologians would understand the distinction), it was a positive sin. The abolitionists, in their role as the dedicated instruments of God, set themselves to destroy this palpable violation of God's law. . . .

. . . No calamity that might have befallen America could have taken the abolitionists by surprise. They thoroughly expected God momentarily to wreak His awful vengeance upon both the North and the South for their persistence in maintaining slavery, the nation's most conspicuous sin. "Look at the manner in which our sister state, Louisiana, is treating her slaves!" commanded the indignant antislavery editor Elijah P. Lovejoy. "Why, as surely as there is a thunderbolt in Heaven and strength in God's right arm to launch it, so surely will it strike the authors of such cruel oppression." If the holocaust of the Civil War proved such

Abolitionists in fashionable attire listen to a gesturing orator during an anti-slavery meeting on a town common in 1856. (Courtesy of The Library of Congress.)

predictions at least circumstantially correct, it also measured the extent of abolitionist failure, for judgment—whether from God or not—came in the form of war, and abolitionist efforts had been powerless to end slavery and thus to avert war.

The abolitionists' apocalyptic view was by no means a casual or an incidental thing; indeed it came to be generally accepted. The pervasiveness of their interpretation of the Civil War as Divine retribution may be gauged in the vivid conceits of Julia Ward Howe's "Battle Hymn of the Republic," in which God is pictured amidst the carnage of war "trampling out the vintage where the grapes of wrath are stored." The idea appears with equal clarity in the solemn sentences of the penultimate paragraph of Abraham Lincoln's second inaugural address, which are informed by echoes of Lovejoy's prophecy written thirty years before. . . .

Thus with motives grand and obligations solemn, the abolitionists inaugurated their crusade to banish slavery from the land. . . . By speeches and publications they would attempt to persuade all Americans—but especially slaveholders—that slavery was a heinous sin calling for immediate repentance. Since slaveholders, however misdirected, were assumed to be reasonable creatures whose better natures when properly enlightened could be trusted to govern them, the abolitionists hoped they would repent and free their slaves as soon as the incontrovertible fact of their sin had been laid before them.

The abolitionists soon realized, however, that the process of enlightenment was not likely, by itself, to end slavery. A formidable obstacle, they concluded, blocked the success of their program. This was the conviction held by most people, North and South, of the Negro's anthropological inferiority. That belief, more than anything else, caused even many Northerners who otherwise accepted the abolitionists' view of slavery to hesitate to espouse their program for ending it. . . . Unless racial prejudice might in some way be destroyed, the antislavery crusade could hardly succeed, for adherence to the idea of the Negro's inferiority, the abolitionists discovered, tended to produce not ardent crusaders but half-hearted antislavery "men who would abolish slavery only in the abstract, and somewhere about the middle of the future."

Most Americans in the early nineteenth century considered the presence of large numbers of free Negroes within the community so dangerous to society as to be intolerable. How, then, could prudent men contemplate freeing the slaves, it was often asked, unless some way were found to transport the freedmen out of the country? And that had proved to be a physical impossibility. The American Colonization Society, the major national organization concerned with slavery before 1833, had long worked to send free Negroes to Africa, but it had accomplished little. Few of the objects of its philanthropy desired to leave their homes in order to move to Africa, nor did the society ever have available enough ships or money to transport in significant numbers even that minority of Negroes willing to emigrate. The abolitionists, unlike the colonizationists, denied both the necessity and the morality of attempting expatriation. The slaves, abolitionists insisted, must be freed at once and the freedmen allowed to remain in the United States. The abolitionists made no concessions whatever to the prevailing racial prejudice, which had served as one of the main bulwarks of the American Colonization Society, nor did they become discouraged when they found that prejudice was nearly universal. While readily granting the fact that racial prejudice existed, the abolitionists denied its inevitability. As radical reformers they refused to recognize any view or any institution as unmalleable under the blows of heaven-inspired emotion and logic. "They contended," as Henry B. Stanton, an official of the American Anti-Slavery Society, explained, "that this prejudice was visible; that being a sin it could be repented of, being a folly it could be cured." . . .

The abolitionists' two goals—(1) to spread the doctrine of the sin of slavery and (2) to eradicate the nearly universal prejudice—once accomplished would, they supposed, work a moral revolution in the country. They viewed the two goals as inseparable. Indeed, so intertwined were they in abolitionist thought that it is quite impossible to imagine their acceptance of the one without the other. If anything, they believed the ending of prejudice must precede, not follow, the abolition of slavery. As soon as the Negro is "felt to be in *fact* and in *right* our own countryman, the benevolence of the country will be emancipated from its bondage," predicted an early abolitionist. "It will flow out to meet the colored man . . . it will proclaim his rights—and the fetters of the slave will fall asunder." In such a spirit of optimism the reformers began their work, assuming that with the Negro recognized as an equal and slaveholders convinced of their sin, the slaves would be freed. The entire nation would accept this event, the abolitionists supposed, and the freedmen would be welcomed by their fellow countrymen. Thus the caste system would end, justice and harmony prevail, and God's will be done on earth. . . .

The abolitionists directed their program of moral suasion with equal vigor toward both the North and the South, and it was rejected with almost equal vehemence by the people of both sections. The abolitionists perhaps asked too much—and it was no doubt simple-minded to ask it at all—when they pleaded with Southerners to relinquish their valuable slave property. In any event, after 1830 Southerners managed largely to stifle abolitionist efforts to persuade them of their sin. Southern states passed laws imposing severe punishment on those who circulated antislavery literature or uttered antislavery sentiments. Abolitionists who ventured into the South were threatened with punishment so extreme that few dared enter the area, and most of those native Southerners who opposed slavery either kept their views to themselves or fled to the North. . . .

Meanwhile the abolitionists attempted to carry out their program to end racial prejudice in areas and among groups more easily accessible to them. In the Northern states, especially in the cities bordering the Ohio and Mississippi Rivers, lived thousands of free Negroes—most of them social outcasts, economically depressed, and suffering the pressures of legal and extra-legal discrimination. They were living proof, some thought, of the fact of racial inferiority and the dangers inherent in emancipation. The abolitionists, on the other hand, saw in the miseries of the free people of color an opportunity and a challenge. If they could improve the condition of these people, Northern skeptics and perhaps Southerners, too, would be compelled to discard their racial prejudices and admit the feasibility and safety of emancipation. Very early, therefore, the abolitionists began humanitarian work with this group. . . .

Efforts of this kind produced a strong, hostile reaction in both North and South. When Theodore Dwight Weld and his fellow students at Lane Seminary in 1834 undertook to aid the colored people of Cincinnati, school authorities objected, apparently because they saw implications of racial equality in the close interracial relationships which Weld's projects involved. The consequent disciplinary measures imposed by the Lane trustees led some forty students to withdraw from the seminary. Two years later an anti-abolitionist mob in Cincinnati turned their wrath against the Negro section of the city, wrecking and burning as they went. Prudence Crandall's attempts to enroll Negro students in her school at Canterbury, Connecticut, caused so much popular opposition that she abandoned the project. In Jacksonville, Illinois, in 1844, a proposal to allow colored children from the local Sunday schools to participate in the Fourth of July celebration nearly rent the city's churches. . . .

Implicit in much of the opposition to educating free Negroes was the suspicion that racial equality would lead inevitably to racial amalgamation. The widespread fear of Negro social equality provided a powerful incentive to riot against abolitionists throughout the North and became a major factor in Northern opposition to them. Years of antislavery activity failed measurably to eliminate racial prejudice, especially in the states of the Old Northwest. "By nature, education, and association, it is believed that the [N]egro is inferior to the white man, physically, morally, and intellectually," asserted a legislative committee in Illinois after more than a decade of abolitionist agitation in that state; "whether this be true to the fullest extent, matters not, when we take into consideration the fact that such is the opinion of the vast majority of our citizens . . . ."

The abolitionists could not change Southern convictions of the Negro's anthropological inferiority, and they had been little more successful in the North. While it is true that in some limited areas, especially in New England, the abolitionists won local victories in altering views toward Negroes, these victories only dented and did not break the wall of prejudice, and the Civil War began with the bulwark essentially intact. The Union Army, which was to be the effective instrument in the destruction of slavery, contained many soldiers who exhibited extreme racial prejudice, and the three earliest settled states of the Northwest Territory—Ohio, Indiana, and Illinois—maintained legal discriminations against free people of color until the eve of the Civil War, and in some instances long after it.

The antislavery crusade gained numerous recruits in the North in the later 1830's. It may even be true, as some have thought, that as many as 200,000 Northerners belonged to antislavery societies at the height of the movement. But it is surely a mistake to suppose that this figure represents the number of Northerners who were anxious to free the slaves *and* grant them equality. The large accessions to antislavery society membership after 1835 did not, in fact, result solely from a disposition to aid and elevate the Negro. As Catherine Beecher observed at the time, a great many men either declared or implied that in joining the abolitionists "they were influenced, not by their arguments . . . but because the violence of opposers had identified that cause with the question of freedom of speech, freedom of the press, and civil liberty." . . . Each important mob incident brought accessions to the antislavery cause from among those . . . who believed that popular opposition to the abolitionists imperiled civil liberties. Many antislavery recruits, especially those in the West, entered the movement in order to preserve their own rights; they did not necessarily feel any considerable interest in Negro rights. . . . They were indeed eager to end slavery at once; yet they gave little attention to the corollary of emancipation—equal rights for the freedmen. The original abolitionists, therefore, soon found themselves and their aims submerged by the very success of their movement.

. . . Encountering failure at every turn, many of the antislavery leaders changed their methods in the late 1830's, frankly adopting political action, with its implied threat of coercion, as the only means offering a possibility of success for their campaign to end slavery. A shift in that direction had long been underway. James G. Birney, a leader in the political antislavery movement, had concluded as early as 1835, "that repentance is far off, if at all to be expected . . . ." Benjamin Lundy had early declared his belief that slavery could be ended only at the ballot box and by the national government. . . . As the issue became increasingly involved with politics, those who insisted on using only the old methods to achieve the old goals gradually found themselves thrust farther into the background. . . . Opposition to slavery and to the South continued as vigorously as ever in the 1840's, but it was henceforth to be expressed primarily in direct action, with decreasing emphasis upon moral suasion.

This was a momentous change. . . . [T]he change constituted a tacit admission by the antislavery group of the failure of the abolitionist program as a moral reform. . . . Other appeals, more practical and perhaps more selfish, were recognized to possess greater effectiveness than pleas for conformity to the moral law. Moreover, by failing to maintain its original position, the antislavery movement abandoned all hope of achieving its original goals of ending racial prejudice and persuading slaveholders to abandon their sin. For although force might end slavery, no coercion could possibly end prejudice, and repentance gained by force would not be repentance at all. Since public opinion toward Negroes had not been significantly changed, it became nearly certain that even if the slaves were freed, the freedmen would still be condemned to a long period of depressed status.

Most important at that time, however, was the fact that the refusal of the nation to accept the abolitionists' original program increased the chances for war. Slavery would not be ended voluntarily; yet abolitionists had succeeded in persuading Northerners that the South and its institutions were evil. Even if few Northerners believed in or wanted Negro equality, a great many of them had become convinced that slavery must somehow end. By succeeding to that extent, the antislavery crusade had moved the nation closer to war. . . .

. . . Although slavery was ended by the Civil War, racial prejudice was not; for abolition had come through the use of military power, without general willingness to relinquish the idea of racial inequality.

Abolitionism as Revolution

Abolitionism is customarily listed as one of the many reform movements that pervaded antebellum America. Historian Herbert Aptheker argues that abolitionists should be thought of as revolutionaries, not reformers. Abridged from Herbert Aptheker, Abolitionism: A Revolutionary Movement *(Boston, 1989), xi-xiii.*

In the first six decades of the nineteenth century, the malignancy of slavery affected every facet of life in the United States. Constant ferment marked its existence; countervailing forces were finally sufficiently potent to overcome it, but only after a fierce war had taken hundreds of thousands of lives and the survival of the Republic had been in doubt.

Leading the momentous struggle against slavery, informing it, inspiring it, was the Abolitionist movement—the second successful revolutionary movement in the history of the United States.

The bulk of the vast literature on Abolitionism treats it as simply one of numerous reform movements of the pre-Civil War era; in this sense the literature ignores the question of its revolutionary character. . . .

The fact is that many, perhaps most, of the Abolitionists were revolutionists in their own minds, and the movement as a whole was a revolutionary one in every respect. . . .

The term *revolutionary movement* is used in this work in its precise sense. That is, the Abolitionists sought the uncompensated emancipation, at once, of the slaves. This meant the confiscation of billions of dollars worth of private property, the ownership of which constituted the power of, and defined the nature of, the slave-owning class, which predominated in the South and nationally, in the latter case until the mid-1850s. It was the ruling class. In its ownership of the slaves, the best land, the animals and tools to make that land productive, and the crops thereby realized, the slaveholding class possessed wealth far in excess of any other property-owning class prior to the Civil War. Fundamentally because of this economic dominance, slaveholders controlled both political parties—usually favoring one, but dominating the other, too. It also controlled thereby the executive, legislative, and judicial arms of the federal government and so dominated its domestic and foreign policy. This economic and political predominance assured the slaveholding class effective control, too, over the ideological structure of the society. The slaveholding influence was decisive in publishing—books, periodicals, and newspapers; in education—texts, faculties, and administrators; and in religion—preferred texts and personnel.

The Abolitionists led a movement whose basic aim was the termination of the base of this power, the slaveholding system. It meant the overthrow of the propertied ruling class in the only way such a class can be overthrown—by the elimination of the property upon which its power rests. . . .

Given its fundamental aim, one would expect this second revolution to be more truly democratic than was the first American Revolution, with its less profound property challenge and its less ambitious transformation of society. Indeed it was more democratic: it was a black-white movement much more fully than its predecessor; it was a male-female movement much more fully than its predecessor; it was more fully conscious of its challenge to property rights. Moreover, that challenge was a fundamental characteristic of the second revolution, whereas it was only at the fringes of the first. . . .

Although a salient feature of the Abolitionist movement was its black-white character, it is important to emphasize the overwhelming consequence of its black component. Slavery was the unique experience of black people in the United States. . . . They alone endured it, survived it, and combated it. They were the first and most lasting Abolitionists. Their conspiracies and insurrections, individual struggles, systematic flights, maroon [runaway slave] communities, efforts to buy freedom, cultural solidity, creation of antislavery organizations and publications—all preceded the black-white united efforts. They developed a convention movement, with delegates from many states meeting annually from 1830 to the Civil War and collectively deciding on priorities and strategies for their people. They rejected colonizationism. Without the initiative of the Afro-American people, without their illumination of the nature of slavery, without their persistent struggle to be free, there would have been no national Abolitionist movement.

Questions

1. *How would you explain the fact that, until recently, few accounts of the antislavery movement gave much attention to the contribution of African Americans?*
2. *How would you explain the fact that most histories of the antislavery movement characterize it as an effort at reform and neglect to take its revolutionary aspects into account? Do you think that these radical aspects are overemphasized?*
3. *What was the relation between slavery and racial prejudice? Do you think abolitionists were wise in placing so much emphasis on eliminating prejudice? What was the relation between prejudice and plans for African American colonization?*
4. *Some of the essays suggest that abolitionists failed to eliminate prejudice and failed to convince Northerners that slavery was morally wrong and should be ended. In light of this, why was there a Civil War? Put another way, what was the relation between the abolitionists and the Civil War?*

ABOLITIONISM: ACTION AND RESPONSE

Abolitionists tried to publicize their program through lectures, newspapers, and pamphlets. Opposition to this effort by a resistant and sometimes enraged public (one abolitionist was mobbed two hundred times) inevitably raised the issue of civil rights for white Americans as well as for blacks and brought in to the open this important question: Should public opinion be allowed to stifle the rights of free speech, free assembly, and free press simply because a majority finds certain ideas or expressions objectionable or judges them dangerous? Abolitionist activism and rhetoric highlighted the debate on the proper limits of free speech, including the extent to which a community is obliged to tolerate speech that it deems offensive.

In order to consider these issues with respect to the abolitionists, it is necessary to examine their program, their rhetoric, and their mode of agitation, as well as the opposition to them.

The American Anti-Slavery Society Declares its Sentiments

At its founding in 1833, the American Anti-Slavery Society adopted this Declaration of Sentiments. In his characteristically impassioned rhetoric, William Lloyd Garrison condemned slavery and set forth the new organization's principles and proposed activities. Excerpted from William Lloyd Garrison, Selections from the Writings and Speeches of William Lloyd Garrison *(Boston, 1852), 66-71.*

More than fifty-seven years have elapsed, since a band of patriots convened in this place, to devise measures for the deliverance of this country from a foreign yoke. The corner-stone upon which they founded the Temple of Freedom was broadly this—'that all men are created equal; that they are endowed by their Creator with certain inalienable rights; that among these are life, LIBERTY, and the pursuit of happiness.' At the sound of their trumpet-call, three millions of people rose up as from the sleep of death, and rushed to the strife of blood; deeming it more glorious to die instantly as freemen, than desirable to live one hour as slaves. They were few in number—poor in resources; but the honest conviction that Truth, Justice and Right were on their side, made them invincible.

We have met together for the achievement of an enterprise, without which that of our fathers is incomplete; and which, for its magnitude, solemnity, and probable results upon the destiny of the world, as far transcends theirs as moral truth does physical force. . . .

Their principles led them to wage war against their oppressors, and to spill human blood like water, in order to be free. Ours forbid the doing of evil that good may come, and lead us to reject, and to entreat the oppressed to reject, the use of all carnal weapons for deliverance from bondage; relying solely upon those which are spiritual, and mighty through God to the pulling down of strong holds.

Their measures were physical resistance—the marshalling in arms—the hostile array—the mortal encounter. Ours shall be such only as the opposition of moral purity to moral corruption—the destruction of error by the potency of truth—the overthrow of prejudice by the power of love—and the abolition of slavery by the spirit of repentance.

Their grievances, great as they were, were trifling in comparison with the wrongs and sufferings of those for whom we plead. Our fathers were never slaves—never bought and sold like cattle—never shut out from the light of knowledge and religion—never subjected to the lash of brutal taskmasters.

But those, for whose emancipation we are striving—constituting at the present time at least one-sixth part of our countrymen—are recognized by law, and treated by their fellow-beings, as marketable commodities, as goods and chattels, as brute beasts; are plundered daily of the fruits of their toil without redress;

really enjoy no constitutional nor legal protection from licentious and murderous outrages upon their persons; and are ruthlessly torn asunder—the tender babe from the arms of its frantic mother—the heart-broken wife from her weeping husband—at the caprice or pleasure of irresponsible tyrants. For the crime of having a dark complexion, they suffer the pangs of hunger, the infliction of stripes, the ignominy of brutal servitude. They are kept in heathenish darkness by laws expressly enacted to make their instruction a criminal offence.

These are the prominent circumstances in the condition of more than two millions of our people, the proof of which may be found in thousands of indisputable facts, and in the laws of the slaveholding States.

Hence we maintain—that, in view of the civil and religious privileges of this nation, the guilt of its oppression is unequalled by any other on the face of the earth; and, therefore, that it is bound to repent instantly, to undo the heavy burdens, and to let the oppressed go free.

We further maintain—that no man has a right to enslave or imbrute his brother—to hold or acknowledge him, for one moment, as a piece of merchandize—to keep back his hire by fraud—or to brutalize his mind, by denying him the means of intellectual, social and moral improvement.

The right to enjoy liberty is inalienable. To invade it is to usurp the prerogative of Jehovah. Every man has a right to his own body—to the products of his own labor—to the protection of law—and to the common advantages of society. It is piracy to buy or steal a native African, and subject him to servitude. Surely, the sin is as great to enslave an American as an African.

Therefore we believe and affirm—that there is no difference, in principle, between the African slave trade and American slavery:

That every American citizen, who detains a human being in involuntary bondage as his property, is, according to Scripture, (Ex. xxi. 16,) a man-stealer:

That the slaves ought instantly to be set free, and brought under the protection of law:

That if they had lived from the time of Pharaoh down to the present period, and had been entailed through successive generations, their right to be free could never have been alienated, but their claims would have constantly risen in solemnity:

That all those laws which are now in force, admitting the right of slavery, are therefore, before God, utterly null and void . . .

We further believe and affirm—that all persons of color, who possess the qualifications which are demanded of others, ought to be admitted forthwith to the enjoyment of the same privileges, and the exercise of the same prerogatives, as others; and that the paths of preferment, of wealth, and of intelligence, should be opened as widely to them as to persons of a white complexion.

We maintain that no compensation should be given to the planters emancipating their slaves:

Because it would be a surrender of the great fundamental principle, that man cannot hold property in man:

Because slavery is a crime, and therefore is not an article to be sold:

Because the holders of slaves are not the just proprietors of what they claim; freeing the slave is not depriving them of property, but restoring it to its rightful owner; it is not wronging the master, but righting the slave—restoring him to himself:

Because immediate and general emancipation would only destroy nominal, not real property; it would not amputate a limb or break a bone of the slaves, but by infusing motives into their breasts, would make them doubly valuable to the masters as free laborers; and

Because, if compensation is to be given at all, it should be given to the outraged and guiltless slaves, and not to those who have plundered and abused them.

We regard as delusive, cruel and dangerous, any scheme of expatriation which pretends to aid, either directly or indirectly, in the emancipation of the slaves or to be a substitute for the immediate and total abolition of slavery.

We fully and unanimously recognise the sovereignty of each State, to legislate exclusively on the subject of the slavery which is tolerated within its limits; we concede that Congress, under the present national compact, has no right to interfere with any of the slave States, in relation to this momentous subject:

But we maintain that Congress has a right, and is solemnly bound, to suppress the domestic slave trade between the several States, and to abolish slavery in those portions of our territory which the Constitution has placed under its exclusive jurisdiction. . . .

These are our views and principles—these our designs and measures. With entire confidence in the overruling justice of God, we plant ourselves upon the Declaration of our Independence and the truths of Divine Revelation, as upon the Everlasting Rock.

We shall organize Anti-Slavery Societies, if possible, in every city, town and village in our land.

We shall send forth agents to lift up the voice of remonstrance, of warning, of entreaty, and of rebuke.

We shall circulate, unsparingly and extensively, anti-slavery tracts and periodicals.

We shall enlist the pulpit and the press in the cause of the suffering and the dumb.

We shall aim at a purification of the churches from all participation in the guilt of slavery.

We shall encourage the labor of freemen [free African Americans] rather than that of slaves, by giving a preference to their productions: and

We shall spare no exertions nor means to bring the whole nation to speedy repentance.

Our trust for victory is solely in God. We may be personally defeated, but our principles never! Truth, Justice, Reason, Humanity, must and will gloriously triumph. Already a host is coming up to the help of the Lord against the mighty, and the prospect before us is full of encouragement.

The Influence of Slavery

In the following excerpt, Garrison claims that slaveholders virtually controlled national policy and politics and exerted a governing influence on ideas and institutions even in the North. According to this analysis, ending slavery would do much more than restore freedom to the slaves. It also would destroy the base of the slaveholders' power and thus bring revolutionary change to power relationships throughout the country. With this insight, Garrison accounted for the intense opposition that abolitionists encountered. Abridged from William Lloyd Garrison, Selections from the Writings and Speeches of William Lloyd Garrison *(Boston, 1852), 137-39.*

For more than two centuries, slavery has polluted the American soil. It has grown with the growth, and strengthened with the strength of the republic. Its victims have multiplied, from a single cargo of stolen Africans, to three millions of native-born inhabitants. In our colonial state, it was deemed compatible with loyalty to the mother country. In our revolutionary struggle for independence, it exchanged the sceptre of monarchy for the star-spangled banner of republicanism, under the folds of which it has found ample encouragement and protection. From the days of the Puritans down to the present time, it has been sanctified by the religion, and upheld by the patriotism of the nation. From the adoption of the American Constitution, it has declared war and made peace, instituted and destroyed national banks and tariffs, controlled the army and navy, prescribed the policy of the government, ruled in both houses of Congress, occupied the Presidential chair, governed the political parties, distributed offices of trust and emolument among its worshippers, fettered Northern industry and enterprise, and trampled liberty of speech and of conscience in the dust.

It has exercised absolute mastery over the American Church. In her skirts is found 'the blood of the souls of the poor innocents.' With the Bible in their hands, her priesthood have attempted to prove that slavery came down from God out of heaven. . . .

If slavery be thus entwined around the civil, social, and pecuniary interests of the republic—if the religious sects and political parties are banded together for its safety from internal revolt and external opposition—if the people, awed by its power and corrupted by its influence, are basely bending their knees at its foot-

The masthead of the abolitionist Liberator *newspaper from 1833 features an illustration of a slave auction alongside the name of editor William Lloyd Garrison. (Courtesy of The Library of Congress.)*

stool—is it wonderful that Church and State are shaken to their foundations by the rallying cry of Liberty? . . .

Slavery must be overthrown. No matter how numerous the difficulties, how formidable the obstacles, how strong the foes to be vanquished—slavery must cease to pollute the land. . . . No matter, though, to effect it, every party should be torn by dissensions, every sect dashed into fragments, the national compact dissolved, the land filled with the horrors of a civil and a servile war—still, slavery must be buried in the grave of infamy, beyond the possibility of a resurrection.

If the State cannot survive the anti-slavery agitation, then let the State perish. If the Church must be cast down . . . to be free, then let the Church fall. . . . If the American Union cannot be maintained . . . then let the American Union be consumed by a living thunderbolt, and no tear be shed over its ashes.

A Call for Women to Become Abolitionists

Women helped organize the American Anti-Slavery Society, held fundraising antislavery bazaars, circulated antislavery petitions, and otherwise promoted the abolitionist cause. This essay is one of the earliest appeals to women. It also shows that women's participation in the movement was sometimes opposed even by women themselves. This excerpt is a response to a woman who objected to other women publicly advocating emancipation. Taken from Elizabeth Margaret Chandler, The Poetical Works of Elizabeth Margaret Chandler *(Philadelphia, 1836), 21-23.*

We have been so long accustomed to consider the duty of the female sex, with regard to slavery, as entirely plain, that we had almost imagined it must be equally so to any unprejudiced thinker upon the subject. Not that we expected to find no difference of feeling, or contrariety of sentiment; apathy and prejudices we were prepared for; but we certainly had not thought that the interference of woman in behalf of suffering humanity, could be seriously objected to, as improper, and at variance with right principles. Yet this we are sorry to find is the light in which it is regarded by one of our own sex—a lady, whose talents and char-

DECLARATION OF THE ANTI-SLAVERY CONVENTION.

The declaration of the American Anti-Slavery Society from its founding convention in Philadelphia, Pennsylvania in 1833. (Courtesy of The Library of Congress.)

acter we respect very highly, and whose approbation of the course we are pursuing, we should be proud to have obtained. But as this is withheld, and it is probable she may not be singular in her opinions, we have taken the liberty of quoting some of her sentiments, and appending to them a statement of our own ideas on the same subject.

"Should you inquire why I do not devote myself more sedulously to promote the cause of emancipation?—I would tell you, that I think it is a work which requires the energies of *men*."

And so it does; but it requires also the *influence of woman*. She was given to man 'to be a helpmeet [helpmate] for him;' and it is therefore her duty, whenever she can do so, to lend him her aid in every great work of philanthropy. In *this* her cooperation may be of essential service, without leading her one step beyond her own proper sphere. . . .

"It is a subject so connected with those of government, of law and politics, that I should fear the direct or even apparent interference of my own sex, would be a departure from that propriety of character which nature, as well as society, imposes on woman."

It is true that it is a question of government and politics, but it also rests upon the broader basis of humanity and justice; and it is on *this* ground only, that we advocate the interference of women. We have not the least desire to see our own sex transformed into a race of politicians; but we do not think that in this case such consequences are in the least to be apprehended. To plead for the miserable, to endeavour to alleviate the bitterness of their destiny, and to soften the stern bosoms of their oppressors into gentleness and mercy, can never be unfeminine or unbefitting the delicacy of woman! She does not advocate Emancipation because slavery is at variance with the political interests of the state, but because it is an outrage against *humanity* and *morality* and *religion;* because it is *criminal,* and because her own supineness makes her a *sharer in the crime;* and because a great number of *her own sex* are among its victims. It is therefore, that she should steadily and conscientiously rank among the number of its opponents, and refuse to be benefited by its advantages. She does not by this become a partizan of any system of policy—she seeks only to shield from outrage all that is most holy in her religion! She does not seek to direct, or share with men, the government of the state; but she entreats them to lift the iron foot of despotism from the neck of her sisterhood; and this we consider not only quite within the sphere of her privileges, but also of her positive duties.

A Northern Woman Condemns Prejudice

This passage was one of the most powerful early critiques of slavery and the prejudice that supported it. The author is nearly as critical of the racial prejudice exhibited by Northerners as she is of slavery itself. Excerpted from Lydia Maria Child, An Appeal in Favor of that Class of Americans Called Africans *(Boston, 1833), 208-9, 211, 232.*

While we bestow our earnest disapprobation on the system of slavery, let us not flatter ourselves that we are in reality any better than our brethren of the South. Thanks to our soil and climate, and the early exertions of the Quakers, the *form* of slavery does not exist among us; but the very *spirit* of the hateful and mischievous thing is here in all its strength. The manner in which we use what power we have, gives us ample reason to be grateful that the nature of our institutions does not intrust us with more. Our prejudices against colored people is [are] even more inveterate than it is at the South. The planter is often attached to his negroes, and lavishes caresses and kind words upon them, as he would on a favorite hound; but our cold-hearted, ignoble prejudice admits of no exception—no intermission.

The Southerners have long continued habit, apparent interest and dreaded danger, to palliate the wrong they do; but we stand without excuse. They tell us that Northern ships and Northern capital have been engaged in this wicked business; and the reproach is true. Several fortunes in this city [Boston] have been made by the sale of negro blood. If these criminal transactions are still carried on, they are done in silence and secrecy, because public opinion has made them disgraceful. But if the free States wished to cherish the system of slavery forever, they could not take a more direct course than they now do. Those who are kind and liberal on all other subjects, unite with the selfish and the proud in their unrelenting efforts to keep the colored population in the lowest state of degradation; and the influence they unconsciously exert over children early infuses into their innocent minds the same strong feelings of contempt.

The intelligent and well informed have the least share of this prejudice; and when their minds can be brought to reflect upon it, I have generally observed that they soon cease to have any at all. But such a general apathy prevails and the subject is so seldom brought into view, that few are really aware how oppressively the influence of society is made to bear upon this injured class of the community. . . .

. . . [A]n unjust law exists in this Commonwealth [Massachusetts], by which marriages between persons of different color is [are] pronounced illegal. I am perfectly aware of the gross ridicule to which I may subject myself by alluding to this particular; but I have lived too long, and observed too much, to be disturbed by the world's mockery. In the first place, the government ought not to be invested with power to control the affections, any more than the consciences of citizens. A man has at least as good a right to choose his wife, as he has to choose his religion. His taste may not suit his neighbors; but so long as his deportment is correct, they have no right to interfere with his concerns. . . .

There is among the colored people an increasing desire for information, and a laudable ambition to be respectable in manners and appearance. Are we not foolish as well as sinful, in trying to repress a tendency so salutary to themselves, and so beneficial to the community? Several individuals of this class are very desirous to have persons of their own color qualified to teach something more than mere reading and writing. But in the public schools, colored children are subject to many discouragements and difficulties; and into the private schools they cannot gain admission. A very sensible and well-informed colored woman in a neighboring town, whose family have been brought up in a manner that excited universal remark and approbation, has been extremely desirous to obtain for her eldest daughter the advantages of a private school; but she has been resolutely repulsed, on account of her complexion. . . .

By publishing this book I have put my mite into the treasury [expressed my thoughts]. The expectation of displeasing all classes has not been unaccompanied with pain. But it has been strongly impressed upon my mind that it was a duty to fulfil this task; and earthly considerations should never stifle the voice of conscience.

An Abolitionist Lecturer's Instructions

In 1834 the American Anti-Slavery Society commissioned Theodore Dwight Weld to serve as an abolitionist agent in Ohio. These are his instructions. Abridged from Letters of Theodore Dwight Weld, Angelina Grimké Weld and Sarah Grimké, *1822-1844, vol. 1, ed. Gilbert H. Barnes and Dwight L. Dumond (New York, 1934), 125-27.*

Dear Sir—You have been appointed an Agent of the American Anti-Slavery Society; and will receive the following instructions from the Executive Committee. . . .

The general principles of the Society are set forth in the Declaration, signed by the members of the Convention which formed it at Philadelphia, Dec. 7, 1833. Our object is, the overthrow of American slavery, the most atrocious and oppressive system of bondage that has ever existed in any country. We expect to accomplish this, mainly by showing to the public its true character and legitimate fruits, its contrariety to the first principles of religion, morals, and humanity, and its special inconsistency with our pretensions, as a free, humane, and enlightened people. In this way, by the force of truth, we expect to correct the common errors that prevail respecting slavery, and to produce a just public sentiment, which shall appeal both to the conscience and love of character, of our slave-holding fellow-citizens, and convince them that both their duty and their welfare require the immediate abolition of slavery.

You will inculcate every where, the great fundamental principle of IMMEDIATE ABOLITION, as the duty of all masters, on the ground that slavery is both unjust and unprofitable. Insist principally on the SIN OF SLAVERY, because our main hope is in the consciences of men, and it requires little logic to prove that it is always safe to do right. To question this, is to impeach the superintending Providence of God.

We reprobate the idea of compensation to slave holders, because it implies the right of slavery. It is also unnecessary, because the abolition of slavery will be an advantage, as free labor is found to be more profitable than the labor of slaves. We also reprobate all plans of expatriation, by whatever specious pretences covered, as a remedy for slavery, for they all proceed from prejudice against color; and we hold that the duty of the whites in regard to this cruel prejudice is not to indulge it, but to repent and overcome it.

The people of color ought at once to be emancipated and recognized as citizens, and their rights secured as such, equal in all respects to others, according to the cardinal principle laid down in the American Declaration of Independence. . . .

Do not allow yourself to be drawn away from the main object, to exhibit a detailed PLAN of abolition; for men's consciences will be greatly relieved from the feeling of present duty, by any objections or difficulties which they can find or fancy in your plan. Let the *principle* be decided on, of immediate abolition, and the plans will easily present themselves. What ought to be done can be done. . . .

You will make yourself familiar with FACTS, for they chiefly influence reflecting minds. Be careful to use only facts that are well authenticated, and always state them with the precision of a witness under oath. You cannot do our cause a greater injury than by overstating facts. . . .

In traversing your field, you will generally find it wise to visit first several prominent places in it, particularly those where it is known our cause has friends. In going to a place, you will naturally call upon those who are friendly to our objects, and take advice from them. Also call on ministers of the gospel and other leading characters, and labor specially to enlighten them and secure their favor and influence. Ministers are the hinges of community, and ought to be moved, if possible. If they can be gained, much is gained. . . .

Form Auxiliary Societies, both male and female, in every place where it is practicable. Even if such societies are very small at the outset, they may do much good as centres of light, and means of future access to the people. Encourage them to raise funds and apply them in purchasing and circulating anti-slavery publications gratuitously. . . .

You are not to take up collections in your public meetings, as the practice often prevents persons from attending, whom it might be desirable to reach.

The Attorney General of Illinois Defends a Mob

In Alton, Illinois, in 1837 a mob destroyed Elijah P. Lovejoy's printing press while a group of armed men attempted to defend it. During the confrontation, Lovejoy was shot and killed. Some mob members were brought to trial and defended by Usher Linder, the state's attorney general. This portion of Linder's remarks to the jury is abridged from William S. Lincoln, Alton Trials: of Winthrop S. Gilman, Who Was Indicted . . . For the Crime of Riot . . . *(New York, 1838), 72-77.*

I ask you to travel along with me as I relate to you the facts in this case. Last August [1837], the first press was destroyed: the "boys" broke it to pieces and threw it into the river. Another was brought here, and after repeated failures to establish a press by which they [abolitionists] could disseminate their fiendish doctrines, another course was adopted. A convention [to form a state antislavery society] was called at Upper Alton. Alton was chosen as the scene of their operations. Alton was to be made the theatre of their preachings—and all their presses, and all their preachings, and all their conventions were to be held in the poor, devoted city of Alton. . . . [T]hese people thought they were going to have it all their own way. But it happened that these Western boys knew a thing or two: knew a trick worth two of that; and so they got together and out-voted them, and the convention blew up in smoke. It was a farce. Not satisfied with this; not satisfied with the blowing up of this farce; not satisfied with the result of this convention, headed by interlopers from other states, headed by an alien to our laws and our country, they issued their handbills, they made proclamation in the streets, of their intention to preach their doctrines in the Church. They posted up placards, notifying the world that Dr. [Edward] Beecher would preach upon this damning doctrine of abolition. . . . [Linder then criticizes the abolitionists' decision to protect themselves with arms.]

. . . So that you see, gentlemen, when all other sources fail . . . the doctrines of abolition are to be forced down our throats. . . . And was not all this calculated to disturb the peace? was not this calculated to excite terror? to stir up the feelings? to rouse the passions, and to provoke an attack? . . .

But the press came at last: the press which was intended to preach insurrection, and to disseminate the doctrines which must tend to disorganization and disunion. With what delight they caught the first glimpse of their new-born child; with what joy they hugged it to their hearts! . . .

. . . Suppose this press had not been guarded; suppose that, taking advantage of the absence of those who had assembled for its protection, the mob had destroyed it. Had these people [the abolitionists] no remedy? Is there no law which would have given them redress? They talk of being friends to good order; lovers of law!! Have they not taken the law into their own hands, and violated the laws of man and of God in depriving man of life? And for what? For a press! a printing press! A press brought here to teach rebellion and insurrection to the slave; to excite servile war; to preach murder in the name of religion; to strike dismay to the hearts of the people, and spread desolation over the face of this land. Society esteems good order more than such a press: sets higher value upon the lives of its citizens than upon a thousand such presses. I might depict to you the African, his passions excited by the doctrines intended to have been propagated by that press. As well might you find yourself in the fangs of a wild beast. I might portray to you the scenes which would exist in our neighbor states from the influence of that press: the father aroused to see the last gasp of his dying child, as it lays in its cradle, weltering in its blood; and the husband awakened from his last sleep by the shrieks of his wife as she is brained to the earth. I might paint to you a picture which would cause a demon to start back with affright, and still fall short of the awful reality which would be caused by the promulgation of the doctrines which this press was intended to disseminate.

[The jury found the defendants not guilty.]

Questions

1. *What might account for the anti-abolitionist sentiment of rural and small-town people in northern Ohio, who owned no slaves and who did not live among African Americans? The remarks of Usher Linder provide an explicit explanation for opposition in Alton, Illinois. What is it? Did it have any validity?*
2. *In what ways may abolitionism have especially appealed to women? Why did some oppose their participation?*
3. *Describe the tactics adopted by the abolitionists. Why did they select these? Might different tactics have been more effective?*
4. *Why did abolitionists focus so much of their attention on ministers and church members? Would present-day advocates of fundamental change adopt the same mode of operation? Why or why not?*

FURTHER READING

James Brewer Stewart, *Holy Warriors: The Abolitionists and American Slavery* (New York, 1976), is a concise account of abolitionism. Benjamin Quarles, *Black Abolitionists* (New York, 1969), traces the antislavery activities of African Americans. Merton L. Dillon, *Slavery Attacked: Southern Slaves and Their Allies, 1619-1865* (Baton Rouge, 1990), shows how African Americans, both slave and free, influenced abolitionism. Biographies especially pertinent to these readings are James Brewer Stewart, *William Lloyd Garrison and the Challenge of Emancipation* (Arlington Heights, 1992); Merton L. Dillon, *Elijah P. Lovejoy, Abolitionist Editor* (Urbana, 1961); and Robert H. Abzug, *Passionate Liberator: Theodore Dwight Weld and the Dilemma of Reform* (New York, 1980).

Why Confederate Soldiers Fought

Earl J. Hess

INTRODUCTION

In 1861, more than a million Southern men began fighting the bloodiest war in American history. Over the course of the following four years, they would be involved in more than 10,000 battles, fights, and skirmishes, winning many but losing the most important ones. They suffered incredible hardships owing to improper clothing, food, transportation facilities, medical care, and ordnance supplies. Although often times led by brilliant generals who gave them victory after victory, they also were burdened frequently with incompetent commanders who could offer them only one dismal defeat after another. In successive campaigns, the invading Northern army occupied increasingly more territory until there were only a few spots on the map that could be called the Confederacy. Throughout all this, most Confederate soldiers remained loyal to the cause until the loss of their home state, or the gnawing hunger, or the increasing hopelessness of the war effort overwhelmed their spirits. Then they deserted to the enemy or quietly slipped home. The hard core of dedicated Southerners fought to the bitter end.

The Confederate soldier embarked on a war that was far longer, bloodier, and much more complex than he could have imagined in 1861. During four years of terrible strife his society saw its basic foundations shaken and changed forever, the physical infrastructure and a large percentage of its people destroyed, and four million newly freed slaves in their midst. Yet they and succeeding generations found something compelling in that tragedy. Our society has elevated the "Lost Cause" to the status of a national legend, as relevant in its own way to the country at large as it is to the Southern section of the United States. We tend to recall the romanticism of the Old South and its peculiar lifestyle, defined by slavery, and we often try hard to make sense of the conflict. But our modern views of the Civil War do not necessarily coincide with the perspectives of the men who fought it.

Keep in mind, when thinking about this topic, that the motivation to join the army and fight the Civil War was a complex phenomenon. Each Southern soldier had his own set of reasons for fighting, many of them personal and related only to his own life. But many soldiers fought for similar reasons. These reasons are the most signficant because they connected each soldier with his comrades and created a bond of mutual support among them. These larger reasons that were common to all soldiers added something higher to their war effort and enabled many men to make sense of the conflict.

Historians have long ignored the motivations that impelled men to fight, assuming that the actions and writings of political and military leaders were more important in understanding the past. But during the last few years more and more scholars have been studying the personal papers of ordinary soldiers to understand how the common man dealt with the challenges of warfare. We cannot scientifically survey combatants as the U.S. Army did in World War II and Korea; public opinion polls and intensive interviews were not conducted by Civil War contemporaries and we cannot duplicate that kind of research with the surviving personal accounts the Confederate soldier. Thus, historians who want to enter the world of "Johnny Reb" and understand why the Confederate soldier fought the Civil War have to be content with reading the rich storehouse of letters, diaries, and memoirs, most of them unpublished and housed in dozens of archives and historical societies across the Southern states. There is no better foundation for military studies of that conflict.

What drove the average Southerner to war? Remember that slavery played a major role in bringing on the sectional conflict, yet about three fourths of white Southerners belonged to families that owned no slaves. What motivated the non-slaveowning Southerner to go to war? Was protection of their homeland against an invading Northern army a factor in their motivation?

Were constitutional issues relating to the right of secession and the protection of personal property a major issue? Were states rights really as important as many people think? Did the Confederate soldier truly believe that the Confederacy had a chance to be independent? Did he believe it was really a separate nation and that the United States government had grown corrupt along with the Northern people?

These questions relate to the way Confederate soldiers interpreted the causes of the war. It is important to take what Civil War contemporaries wrote and said seriously, for they believed the issues of the war were serious enough to justify risking their lives. Yet, as citizens of modern America, we also have a responsibility to evaluate those reasons to see if they make sense. Do you think the Confederate war effort was a "just war?" What would have been the result for our society, Southern and national, if the Confederacy had won the war and its independence? Does it seem as if the Confederate soldier considered the interests of African Americans in his evaluation of the war and its issues? What really was at stake in this most tragic of all American conflicts? Think about the results of Reconstruction, when an attempt to give citizenship rights to African Americans failed twelve years after Lee's surrender. The resulting period of racial segregation and denial of black rights, which was supported by most Confederate veterans, ushered in a long era of suffering for the ex-slaves. To what extent, then, did the Confederate soldier win or lose the war?

"We Are Fighting For Existence"

Southerners were keenly aware of their Revolutionary heritage, in fact, the story of the Founding Fathers of the United States was the key national legend in America. It defined and overshadowed all American politics since 1776. Southerners were aware that their section had played a role equal to that of New England in establishing the United States.

But the South's prominent role in national affairs seemed to be threatened by Northern abolitionism, industrialization, and a growing competition for the right to exploit the western territories. The Northern concept of Free Labor and the Southern heritage of Slave Labor increasingly came to define national politics in the decade of the 1850s. What Abraham Lincoln would call the inevitable conflict between these two conflicting ideals of work, which epitomized the cultural values of each section, seemed to be a major threat to the South.

All That We Hold Dear

Historian Randall C. Jimerson takes a wide yet focused view of the motivation behind the Confederate war of independence. He looks intently at several major issues Confederates believed were at stake in the sectional conflict, and defines their meaning to the average Southerner, men and women alike. Slavery and its protection was the starting point as the South was growing increasingly fearful of its status as a minority section in a rapidly growing America, a minority section, moreover, with a "peculiar institution" that was not welcomed or understood by the rest of the country. The right of self-government, the fear of losing liberty in a political sense, and a fierce determination to protect their homeland all grew out of this fear of losing status as a focal point of national power.

The following excerpt is from Randall C. Jimerson, The Private Civil War: Popular Thought During the Sectional Conflict *(Baton Rouge: 1988), 8-26.*

When Abraham Lincoln was elected president in November, 1860, Elizabeth Grimball was visiting her aunt in Philadelphia, far away from the excitement that prevailed at her home in Charleston, South Carolina. Her father, John Berkley Grimball, feared Lincoln's victory as a dangerous omen. A prominent rice planter and member of Charleston's select society, Grimball soon became an ardent advocate of secession, which he justified as a defense of southern rights. "The prospect before us in regard to our Slave property, if we continue in the Union, is nothing less than utter ruin," he wrote in his private diary. "The people have therefore with unexampled unanimity resolved to secede and to dare any consequence that may follow the act." Elizabeth could not understand such alarms. She had observed virtually no hostility toward the South during her stay in Philadelphia and could see no justification for the secession fever that raged in South Carolina.

Acting as family spokesman, Elizabeth's brothers wrote several letters trying to convince her that southern rights were indeed threatened and that secession was the only remedy. . . . William declared that South Carolina property holders had united "in the belief that now a stand must be made for African slavery or it is forever lost." He told Elizabeth that her father and brothers carried loaded pistols to protect the family from "dishonor and death." He then enumerated the wrongs suffered by the South: "Is it nothing to *yell* about that we are prevented from carrying our property into the common territory of the United States. Is it nothing to yell for that the government is to be in the hands of men pledged to carry on the 'irrepressible conflict' against us. Is it nothing that they send incendiaries to stir up the slaves to poison & murder us? Is it nothing that our brothers at the North robb us of our property and beat us when we reclaim it?" Surely such abuses justified secession. . . .

Elizabeth was not persuaded by her brother's arguments. She replied that the Republicans would have little power to carry out their hostile purposes because the Democratic majority in both houses of Congress could easily thwart the president's actions. Her brother Lewis responded on November 27, arguing that "every one at the North, who does not own slaves, is opposed to the Institution. They are all enemies of Slavery and hope for its extinction." . . .

Finally, in another letter Elizabeth's brother Berkley Grimball also hailed South Carolina's secession. "I hope it will end in establishing a Southern Confederacy who will have among themselves slavery a bond of union stronger than any which holds the north together," he wrote. The southern cause, as outlined by the Grimball men, demanded total commitment from every southern patriot. Defense of slavery and their rights would bring unity.

The arguments advanced by the Grimballs in justification of secession encompassed the southern interpretation of the war's meaning. Few southerners attributed the conflict to a single cause. They fought not for one clearly defined purpose but for a combination of interrelated motives, which formed a logical chain of reasoning. From specific incidents of injury they foresaw potential consequences fatal to their way of life, and they built their ideological defense on fundamental American principles. The southern interpretation of the war derived from one basic premise: that a hostile northern majority opposed slavery. Southerners anticipated an attack on slavery that would eventually result in destruction of their property rights, emancipation, and disruption of race relations. With an antagonistic northern majority wielding such power, all of southerners' cherished constitutional rights would be endangered. Liberty itself would be overthrown, as the majority forced the helpless minority to submit to its will. The result would be to jeopardize all that southerners most dearly treasured—honor, family, home, religion, and their entire social order. As the cornerstone of their civilizations, slavery must be protected at all costs.

Except among a small group of planters, slavery was not frequently discussed as a reason for fighting. Yet it was the danger to slavery that first prompted appeals to constitutional rights and liberty. Whether deliberately or inadvertently, secessionists quickly advanced from the narrow defense of property interests to appeals to principle. They assumed a defensive posture by portraying the danger to existing institutions as a threat to law, social order, family, and true religion. It was on this ground that most southerners could unite in protecting their identity and pride. Abstractions, moreover, have an emotional force greater than that called forth by specific cases of injury. The Civil War became a total war involving the entire population precisely because both sides fought for ideological principles. Compromise and surrender were unthinkable when so much was at stake.

Overt northern actions could not justify the emotional intensity displayed by secessionists such as Lewis Grimball at the end of 1860. Only a small number of radical abolitionists advocated emancipation, and President-elect Lincoln had publicly disavowed any intention of interfering with slavery. Specific incidents of injury were few; only John Brown's raid and scattered violations of the fugitive slave law indicated any northern intent to meddle with southern institutions. Nevertheless, once a Republican majority gained power in the North the sectional balance was disrupted. White southerners feared that they would become a perpetual minority within the Union. From this perspective, it seemed probable that the South would soon stand helpless before an overwhelming northern majority. The Republican party did want to restrict the expansion of slavery, thereby limiting the spread of southern influence, disrupting the sectional balance in politics, and striking at southern pride in the beneficial effects of slavery. The South would be powerless to stop such developments. From this premise, southerners deduced a succession of anticipated dangers, finally reaching the conclusion that their entire way of life was threatened. Although relatively few recognized the logic behind this ideological defense of the Confederate cause, most southerners felt the compelling emotional force of these arguments.

Lincoln's election confirmed southerners' fears that a malignant sectional majority dominated public opinion in the North. . . .

Southern radicals depicted all northerners as fanatical "Black Republicans" determined to subjugate the South. . . .

Lincoln's election had destroyed the slaveowners' confidence that their interests would be protected by the federal government and that the Republicans represented only a small radical faction in the North. "I always knew that all the North lacked to work our ruin was *Power*," David Schenck warned. Now that the Republicans controlled the government, southerners feared that northern fanaticism would lead to tyranny. A delegate to North Carolina's secession convention, Schenck rejoiced when his state seceded, hailing the event as a liberation from "the bondage and unjust oppression of our degenerate brethren in the North." Similarly, Edmund Patterson, an Ohio native who moved to Alabama in 1859 and enlisted in the 9th Alabama Regiment in May, 1861, wrote at the end of that year that the war had commenced because "the Southern people [were] unable longer to bear the tyranny of the North, or rather of Northern fanaticism," just as their ancestors had revolted against British tyranny.

Slaveowners perceived a clear threat to their slave property. For many this was the central issue, from which all others fears derived. "We of the South see nothing now in the Union but danger to our sacred rights," declared Susan Cornwall Shewmake, a graduate of Wesleyan College and wife of a Georgia slaveowner, in January, 1861. "The Black Republicans rejoice that they are to be the instruments of final emancipation for that is undoubtedly their aim in spite of their declarations that they will not interfere with slavery in the states where it now exists." . . . Their fear, based on potential dangers rather than the current situation, was nevertheless reasonable. Even Abraham Lincoln based his apparently moderate determination to resist the expansion of slavery on a belief that such containment would guarantee its ultimate extinction.

As the cornerstone of southern society, slavery seemed essential for the survival of southern civilization. Not only was slave labor necessary for the economy, but the institution was essential to maintain control of the large black population and to reserve the structure of the social order. Mississippi lawyer William L. Nugent, who owned no slaves himself, declared that without slave labor the country would be "a barren waste and desolate plain" not worth fighting for. "We can only live and exist by this species of labor," he wrote, "and hence I am willing to continue to fight to the last." David Schenck, a North Carolina lawyer who owned nine slaves, asserted that the "fundamental principle" of the Republican party was "war on our property" and that its object was the "Equality of the negro and white man." He therefore gave the "cause of Revolution" his hearty approval: "Free negro equality or resistance is the issue." Few white southerners would hesitate in choosing between such alternatives.

Threats to slavery and southern race control would jeopardize all other constitutional rights. For most white southerners, protecting their rights transcended loyalty to the Union that had established and nourished those principles. The decision often caused anguish and pain, even for ardent defenders of southern rights. . . .

The right of self-government was foremost among the constitutional rights for which southerners contended. In justification of their cause they invoked America's revolutionary heritage and the ghosts of the founding fathers, those "immortal, patriotic sires" who had declared their independence from British tyranny. Ella Clanton Thomas, a graduate of Wesleyan College and wife of a wealthy Georgia planter, stated the issue clearly: "We are only asking for self government and freedom to decide our own destinys. We claim nothing of the North but—*to be let alone*—and *they*, a people like ourselves whose republican independence was won by a rebellion, whose liberty was achieved by a secession—to think that they should attempt to coerce us—the idea is preposterous.". . .

If the North denied their right of self-government, southerners feared the loss of their American liberties. Susan Cornwall Shewmake distrusted Republican intentions. "They fight for dominion," she wrote. "We fight for our liberty and our constitutional rights." Echoing Patrick Henry, a North Carolina woman declared in June, 1861, that the South was engaged in "busy preparation for *liberty* or death." The sins of the North were legion and must be resisted: "Infatuation, total blindness has spread over the whole North—the Bible and the Constitution trampled under foot—God forgotten—the 'Father of his Country' forgotten—the memory of patriot fathers insulted—the 'star[s] and stripes' glorious emblems of the free, forever *forever* disgraced." The Confederacy, she believed, would now become the great bastion of the liberty for the world. "May our Southern Constellation take [the] high place from which America has fallen, and shine the brighter, to the oppressed of all nations, to guide them on to liberty," she proclaimed.

Liberty was central to the war's meaning for many Southern patriots. To a people whose social order faced assault by an external foe, liberty meant being free to direct their own affairs without interference. Shortly before the first battle of Manassas, Ella Thomas of Georgia warned of northern efforts to curtail the South's liberty. "Our country is invaded—are homes are in danger," she exclaimed. "We are deprived or they are attempting to deprive us of that glorious liberty for which our Fathers fought and bled and shall we tamely submit to this? Never!" Confederate soldiers were soon fighting and dying in the cause of liberty. "How we should prize our liberties if ever gained—when they are bought at such a price!" Kentucky soldier Edward Guerrant wrote early in 1862, "Every day witnesses the sacrifice of tens and hundreds of bloody victims laid upon the bloody altar of Freedom's Cause."...

Southerners fought for liberty because the only alternative they knew was slavery. White southerners saw every day the effects of slavery and hence gained special appreciation for the benefits of liberty. Using language common to revolutionary movements, but particularly meaningful for a slave society, they repeatedly vowed that defeat would mean slavery, which they would undertake any sacrifice to avoid....

Such was their expectation of treatment at the hands of the North. In May, 1861, a Virginia volunteer warned that southerners must defend their liberty or accept servitude to the Yankees. "Now, in the condition in which our country is now plunged, it is the *duty* of every man, woman & child who can understand the difference between Liberty and Vassalism, to do all in their power no matter what that may be . . . and assist in driving back the foe," he urged his cousin. . . .

Warning that northern actions endangered southern liberty, Susan Cornwall Shewmake denounced the Republicans as "a horde of ambitious tyrants and their tools," determined to force the South into submission. The attempt to coerce the southern states to remain in the Union presented an intolerable threat to southerners' liberty. "Do they think that we are as degenerate as our slaves, to be whipped into obedience at the command of our self styled masters?" she demanded. "Has freedom made them the slaves of their own passions?" Her choice of imagery is significant. White southerners had intimate daily experience with slavery and coercion. Now they feared that they were to become victims rather than masters, to lose the rights and liberties they had cherished as the exclusive prerogatives of free white Americans. Yet in another sense they accused their would-be masters of being slaves—to their own passions. "Folly and fanaticism blind the eyes of those who are at the head of affairs," Shewmake charged. "A domineering spirit influences them to desire to have their way or break asunder every tie that has hitherto bound us together. We *will not be ruled* by them."

The prospect of subjugation sustained Confederate soldiers in their dedication to the southern cause. At the beginning of the 1863 spring campaign, a Tennessee soldier wrote from Virginia that he anticipated hard fighting and hoped that this would be the war's last campaign. Yet even if the war did not end soon, he told his father, "I have one glorious consolation: that as long as a yankee can stand the war for my subjugation, I can stand it for my honor and liberty." One year later, Samuel Lockhart, a North Carolina farmer and private who later died in battle, mourned the growing lists of "noble officers" and "gallant" privates who had met their deaths. Nevertheless, he justified such sacrifices as "part of the heavy price we must pay for deliverance from servile subjugation and ruin." Georgia lieutenant William R. Redding stated in 1864 that he was willing to endure still more hardships and sacrifices to protect his liberty from northern despotism. "I do not regret the hardships if I can gain my Independence," he told his wife. "I consider it a duty that I owe to my children to battle for their liberty as well as my own, for where is the Nation who has ever submitted to the yoke of despotism that have ever regained their liberty."

This belief that the loss of liberty was irrevocable made white southerners adamant in defending their freedom. They had good cause, in their knowledge of their own system of Negro slavery, to perceive clear, rigid distinctions between freedom and slavery. A slave had little chance to become free. Unlike the slave systems in Latin America, in the South slavery meant not only a total lack of freedom but also, in most cases, its permanent loss. Just as their own slaves had little hope of gaining freedom, so southerners feared that they could never regain their cherished liberties once they bowed to northern rule. Absolute and permanent slavery was an unbearable prospect for people dedicated to liberty, and white southerners reacted violently when their freedom seemed jeopardized.

The irony of slaveholders claiming to be the champions of liberty was not apparent to most white southerners. So completely had they excluded blacks from consideration as members of society that they scarcely entertained the possibility that civil rights or liberty could apply to this subservient race. There were, of course, exceptions. Religious humanitarianism led to occasional efforts to ameliorate slavery's harshness, including a wartime campaign for legal reform. Some slaveowners, chiefly women, expressed a measure of guilt. Yet virtually none questioned the necessity of white domination. The vast majority of white southerners entertained no feelings of guilt over slaveholding. Nor did they perceive any conflict between the ideal of liberty and the reality of slavery. Slavery was the foundation of southern society, and the planters proclaimed that the superiority and beauty of the gracious edifice sprang from the divinely ordained institution that supported it.

Far from expressing guilt over slavery, most Confederate patriots boasted that God would lead them to victory over the corrupt and aggressively hostile North. Religious arguments had long been advanced to justify slavery and the social order it supported, and slaveholders easily transferred this belief in divine favor to the Confederate cause. . . .

Belief in a just God who punished sinners but redeemed the faithful led many southerners to attribute defeats to their people's moral failings. They implored their countrymen to turn to God for salvation. "Our people is so wicked that the good being is determined to punish them for it," wrote Virginia lieutenant Ben Andrews during the gloomy days of December, 1864. "When ever we become humble and feel our dependence on him then I believe our cause will brighten and the sunny bright days of peace will return." When such hopes were finally crushed at Appomattax, some of the Confederate faithful found their religious convictions severely tested. Most, however, refused to doubt either God or the justice of their cause.

Faith in the righteousness of their crusade found strength in contrast to the wickedness of the Yankee war of conquest. The North's determination to coerce the Rebel states into submission converted many southern Unionists to the Confederate cause. Lincoln's call for seventy-five thousand volunteers following the attack on Fort Sumter was the decisive act prompting the secession of the Upper South states—Virginia, Tennessee, and North Carolina. "I see nothing left us but to secede lawful or not," concluded the Reverend Richard Wills of North Carolina. "I do not wish to fight . . . but if fight we must let it not be in favor of the North against the South.

Faced with a choice between loyalty to the Union or to the South, most southerners joined the Confederate cause. John Houston Bills, a Tennessee slaveowner and Unionist, predicted that not a single man from the slave states would respond to Lincoln's call for volunteers. "*Now* the south will be a unit," he predicted, "however wrong the leaders may have acted, no one will see the south Coerced into submission to such a Motley Abolition Crew as is headed by Lincoln." Bills blamed "bad politicians north & south" for dividing the Union but charged that the North's refusal to compromise had brought on the war. "I go with my section come what will," he vowed, "but give up the government as I would an old friend; in sorrow." For those who had treasured their identity as citizens of the United States, secession was often a painful action taken with deep regret. . . .

Few white southerners could remain loyal to the Union after their "sacred soil" was invaded. One of the most prominent Unionist spokesmen in Shepherdstown was the Reverend Charles Wesley Andrews, rector of the Protestant Episcopal church. A former advocate of freeing the slaves and colonizing them in Africa, Andrews in May, 1861, voted against secession, which he called "a monstrous delusion & a monstrous wrong." Secession was not only "wrong in principle," but it would be "ruinous" to the South and result in widespread destruction and death. Yet his son Matthew, a young lawyer in Moorefield, canvassed for votes in favor of secession and sought his parents' consent to enlist. "I cannot reconcile Union with my obligations to Virginia," he told his mother after the state had seceded. He stated that he had been "a Union man up to the last and opposed to secession," but that rather than submit to the North, he would "sacrifice life property and Everything else that was dear to me in the world.". . .

Even nonslaveowners, who had little vested interest in slavery and no concern for legalistic arguments over the fugitive slave law, felt the importance of protecting home and family from an invading army. Here was a danger so immediate, so palpable, that few could doubt its magnitude. North Carolina private Jonathan F. Coghill explained to his mother and sister the importance he attached to the war: "I love you all for I know that you love me and I love my country too it has called me fourth to proteck you and I will do my best for you and my country and I pray that god may proteck me and defend me wharever I go." Listing his reasons for fighting, a barely literate Georgia private covered the major points of the southern rationale for the war: "i am fiten for a go[o]d cos I fite for my rits and for my fredom and for my poor brother and sisters and espe[cial]ly for my seethart."

Every Confederate soldier believed that in some way he fought to protect his own home and family. Even when suffering seemed to engulf the South, this belief remained the strongest support for soldiers' morale.

Confederate soldiers were willing to sacrifice their lives in defending their homes. This masculine duty to protect the family has always been one of the most powerful motivations for warriors, and it has been evoked repeatedly by political and military leaders seeking to arouse the fighting spirit of their people. Even when invasion is not a distinct threat, the enemy is often depicted as vicious and eager to despoil homes and murder women and children. Embattled southerners saw an immediate, tangible danger. "I shall fight like I was standing at the threshold of my door fighting against robbers and savages for the defense of my wife & family," Texas lieutenant Theophilus Perry vowed at the beginning of the 1864 campaign in Louisiana. . . .

Invasion posed for southerners an all-inclusive danger. Not only might their property be stolen, their rights trampled, and their liberty extinguished, but even their homes and their very lives were now directly threatened. Defeat would be total. Following the battle of Manassas in July, 1861, Charles C. Jones, Jr., scion of a prominent Georgia plantation family, summed up the Confederate cause: "A freeman's heart can beat in no nobler behalf, and no more sacred obligations can rest upon any people than those now devolved upon us to protect our homes, our loves, our lives, our property, our religion, and our liberties, from the inhuman and infidel hordes who threaten us with invasion, dishonor, and subjugation.". . .

Faced with the destruction of their unique civilization, southerners risked all in its defense. Even nonslaveowners recognized the need to protect their homes and their identity as white southerners. "Conquer or die" became the Confederate slogan. As early as January, 1862, Charles C. Jones, Jr., predicted that "we must in meeting the invasions suffer much, and many a brave man surrender his life in the defense of all we hold pure in honor, true in principle, honest in religion, dear in life, and sacred in death." The prospect of defeat made compromise or submission unthinkable. Jones pledged absolute loyalty to the cause, whatever sacrifice was required. "There can be no retreat," he proclaimed. "The ultimatum with every true lover of his country who is able to bare his breast in support of the principles for which we are contending must be *victory or death.*" Defeat would mean absolute and permanent subjugation. Just as there was no middle ground between liberty and slavery, so southerners saw no intermediate condition between victory and desolation. There could be no room for negotiation or compromise. One ideological system of the other must triumph.

As the war entered its fourth year, William Calder, a young junior officer serving in the North Carolina coastal defenses, measured his comrades' morale by the mounting sacrifices they were called on to bear. "During the past week our spirits have been uniformly raised and depressed as the thermometer of war news was more or less favorable to our cause," he explained. The war's progress gave little encouragement, as diminishing resources and military reversals portended defeat. Yet there was one conviction that sustained what patriotism his weary comrades could muster. "Victory now is life to us," he proclaimed. "Defeat is worse than death." Reinforced by this foreboding belief, many Confederate soldiers continued to fight desperately for their cause until the last guns were silenced and all hope destroyed.

Civil War Soldiers

Historian Reid Mitchell dwells on the factors that motivated the Southern soldier to continue to fight even after he had initially joined the army and realized how terrible war could be. He suggests that the experience of fighting began to change the soldier from the naive recruit who thought the war would be over in three months into a hardened veteran with few illusions left about armed conflict. The war created a whole new set of circumstances, perils, sufferings, and dashed hopes for the soldier. Yet he found new ideas and goals to inspire his continued loyalty to the Confederacy until the bitter end. Chief among them were his commitment to his comrades, his faith in a divine purpose, his desire to seek revenge for the destruction of his homeland, and his fear of losing racial superiority in a defeated South.

The following selection is from Reid Mitchell, Civil War Soldiers *(New York, 1988), 172-77, 179-80.*

The Confederate soldier became a folk hero because of his bravery and endurance, and this heroic myth had a basis in fact. Many Confederate soldiers had been volunteers; volunteers are more likely to stand the hardships of war. Furthermore, the very hardships themselves and the mixture of pride and resentment they produced set soldiers apart from the civilian population. This feeling, combined with the shared dangers of battle and hardships of the march, helped produce the Confederate soldier's *esprit de corps*. His suffering proved his patriotism and thus raised his self-esteem.

From volunteerism and the shared misery of combat and campaigning came another aspect of Confederate loyalty. With the exception of Jefferson Davis, the Confederate authorities who inspired the most devotion both during the Civil War and after were the army officers—and even Davis's popularity seems to have been more a product of his postwar imprisonment than it was of his service as the Confederate head of state. The military experience created loyalty in the soldier to those who suffered by his side, whether officers or common soldiers, and a corresponding distance from those civilians who stayed at home. . . .

During the war desertion did not simply mean desertion from some abstract entity called the Confederate States of America; it meant abandoning the men with whom one had fought. It meant becoming one of the stay-at-homes. . . . And after the war the veteran's loyalty often stayed with the men who had served with him in the Confederate army.

Confederate loyalty was also based upon a distinctive world view. Nineteenth-century Americans were committed to politics in a way almost incomprehensible to twentieth-century Americans; they had not yet been taught cynicism. Nonetheless, the Confederate soldier's understanding of the political world—and of the world at large—was based on Christianity, and on a Christianity almost entirely conceived of as personal morality. Evangelical Protestantism, which produced the religious ethos of both the North and South, placed individual salvation as the most

---

important single goal of the religious life. Salvation was manifested through a conversion experience and through a subsequent godly life. The emphasis was on personal morality, not on larger social institutions. Sin, which would earn God's displeasure, was a personal matter.

This emphasis on personal morality set many Confederates to searching their own souls in the dark years of the war, rather than examining their institutions with a critical eye. A wave of revivals swept the Confederate armies during the winter of 1863-1864. Pious Confederates—like pious Yankees—could interpret the war as God's punishment for a guilty nation, and hope that repentance would bring peace. The hand of God could be seen in Confederate defeats. . . .

Another reason for the continued loyalty of the soldier to the cause was that of racial solidarity. Nervous politicians in the North had argued that the Emancipation Proclamation would help unite the white South: they were right. In particular, Confederate soldiers hated black troops and murdered black prisoners. While much had been made of the "revolutionary" proposals to arm Confederate blacks that were entertained and reluctantly acted upon the final days of the war, it is not at all clear that the average Confederate soldier would have ever accepted these desperate measures. They certainly did not accept blacks as legitimate foes. . . .

The massacres at Fort Pillow and the Crater are well-known examples of the Confederate soldiers' virulent hatred of black troops, but their steady hatred was revealed in unspectacular day-to-day hostilities as well. In the lines around Petersburg, where black troops were used, a Pennsylvania regiment found it advisable, when replacing a black regiment on a picket, to call over to the Confederates "that the 2nd Pa was back again." A soldier in that regiment explained to his mother that when white troops were on picket, an informal truce was maintained, but when black troops were on picket, the Confederates opposite kept up a constant fire. . . .

The final reason for Confederate loyalty is the simplest. During the war the primary alternative to Confederate rule was Yankee rule. Whatever the sectional rancor before 1861, fighting a war does not engender love for one's opponents. Even if the sufferings of the white men and women might be traced ultimately to those who led them into secession, they were frequently inflicted by the soldiers of the North.

Fighting in a familiar yet foreign country helped define the Union war experience; resisting an invader distinguished the Confederate experience. When they burned or pillaged the Southern countryside, Union soldiers gave Confederates more reason to hate them. The psychological strain that invasion and occupation placed upon the Union soldier matched the rage and despair that enemy occupation and defeat placed upon the Confederate. . . .

Yankee treatment of Southern civilians generated the most Confederate resentment. Soldiers complained of Northern soldiers cursing gray-haired old men, threatening women and children, and "running off" unwilling slaves. Killing civilians aroused the greatest hatred of all. In Guntersville, Alabama, Union shelling killed the mother of a Confederate captain, "a helpless old woman who could not escape out of the range of their shells as fast as the others." Men who knew of this death could not easily forgive the North.

No matter how bad Yankee murder was, Confederate soldiers feared something worse. Appeals to Southern men sometimes made it clear that the ultimate Yankee threat was rape. In 1862, when soldiers were asked to reenlist for the duration of the war, one company was asked, "Can it be that you are *men* and yet with the enemy besmeared with the blood of your brothers knocking at your very doors, you will leave these defenseless women to be violated before the eyes of aged Fathers, unable to protect them?" . . .

The Confederate experience left behind a legacy of bitterness, a legacy of defeat. This bitterness might fuel resentment toward the Southern upper class. More often, however, it expressed itself in hatred of blacks and of Yankees. As the Civil War became the defining Southern memory, Southern whites developed a myth of Confederate unity and nobility of purpose that transcended the reality of their experience. In the sanctioned memory of the war, the Confederate soldier achieved an odd kind of victory. Defeat itself became glorious.

It did not seem so in 1865. For some soldiers, Confederate defeat had been almost unthinkable; it was not an algebraic solution, logically obtained by contrasting Northern and Southern resources; it was a mystery to be explained only by God's will. If the South had been defeated, the Southern people were at fault—

a conclusion that some accepted in 1865 but that would be denied in later years. In view of the social crisis the Confederacy underwent, it was not too farfetched to blame defeat on the people's lack of will. A Confederate surgeon summed up much of this attitude immediately after the war. He had retained his optimism as late as March 1865, but was forced to admit in June, "The war is over, and we are a Subjugated people, perfectly right, just as it should be, we are too damned worthless and corrupt to be in any other condition."

Questions

1. *Notice the rhetoric, the words, Southerners used in the many quotes Jimerson presents for the reader. How would you describe the kind of language used by Confederates to justify secession and their war for independence? How was this language used to define the South as right and the North as wrong? What kind of picture of Northern society and the Republican Party is painted by this rhetoric?*
2. *Think about how the issue of slavery suffused nearly every argument presented by Southerners. Is it possible to believe that secession could have happened and the Civil War have occurred if slavery had never been present in America? Was the Civil War inevitable because the North and South were so different, or just because the South was a slave society and the North was not?*
3. *Imagine the fears Southerners felt as they grew increasingly aware of their minority status in fast-growing America. Does this mean that, if the primary issue of the war had not been slavery, that some other major issue would have taken its place to become the lightning rod for Southern fears of being overwhelmed by a modernizing North?*
4. *Which of the several factors supporting continued Confederate morale during the course of the war, as discussed by Mitchell, seem to be the most important?*
5. *Did the result of the war tend to justify the initial fears of the South when it decided to secede from the Union, or did it tend to disprove the validity of those fears?*

The Soldiers Speak for Themselves

The five selections that follow represent the range of concerns Confederate soldiers had about the issues of the war. They present the views or life stories of men from the Deep South and the Upper South, from well-to-do families and from obscure origins, and they represent a range of service from the famed Army of Northern Virginia under Robert E. Lee to the backwater regions of the frontier. There also is a range of ethnic background among the authors of these readings.

Yet all the readings, taken as a whole, encompass the varied reasons Confederate soldiers went to war. Keep in mind that most of these readings are taken from post-war memoirs. There are thousands of letters written by Confederate soldiers during the war years, but some of the most interesting and thoughtful comments on why the Confederate soldier fought the war are contained in accounts penned after the conflict ended. Then, the soldier had more time to reflect on what he had done. While the rhetoric might be less heated or vicious, if you compare these readings with the quotes in Jimerson's study, they are consistent in detailing the same issues that one can read in the letters written during the war.

Fighting for the Confederacy

The first reading comes from the pen of General Edward Porter Alexander, who wrote a lengthy and detailed memoir after the war. Alexander had served in the U.S. army before the war and knew well many of the men who became generals in both the Union and Confederate armies. Alexander was from Georgia, and his account illustrates the difficulties suffered by Southern officers who were torn between loyalty to their state and devotion to their comrades in the regular army. James B. McPherson, who helped Alexander to come to terms with his resignation, became a major Union commander who was killed at the Battle of Atlanta. Alexander went on to become a major commander of artillery in Lee's army and bore a heavy responsibility for trying to soften up the Union lines for Pickett's Charge at Gettysburg. This selection is taken from Gary W. Gallagher, ed., Fighting For the Confederacy: The Personal Recollections of General Edward Porter Alexander *(Chapel Hill, 1989), 23-27.*

On the 20th of April we steamed in through the "Golden Gate" to San Francisco harbor, & as we entered we passed the steamer for Panama due to leave on that day going out (there were always 3 steamers a month—10th, 20th, & 30th). We had hoped to be in time to get on this steamer, but now knew we would have to be 10 days in San Francisco.

But as we touched the wharf a special messenger came aboard with special orders for me, sent by the "Pony Express" (which at that day filled the gap between the lines east & west of the Rocky Mts.), and which upset all of my calculations. I was relieved from duty with the detachment of sappers & was ordered to report to Lieut. Jas. B. McPherson for duty upon Alcatraz Island in San Francisco harbor—in the construction of fortifications. When we landed & went up to Gilmer's another copy of the order awaited me there & Gen. Albert Sidney Johnston had still a third for me. So it was evidently intended that I should not return east with the co.

I was very sorry for this, because it precipitated my resignation & compelled me to pay my own expenses on the journey, but I did not feel any doubt about what I had to do under the circumstances. Georgia had seceded. All the seceded states had united & organized a Confederacy, & the Confederacy was raising an army. The only place for me was in that army.

So in the course of a day or two I had a talk with McPherson, telling him that I felt bound to resign & go home, & asking that he would receive & forward my resignation & give me leave of absence that I might sail on [the] same steamer taking it & not be required to wait in California to receive its acceptance, which would detain me about two months.

McPherson's reply was remarkable for its foresight & appreciation of the real situation & its plain common sense, & the real kindness & affection which prompted it appealed to me very deeply. . . . It seems to me that I can very nearly give his talk to me in his own words, my impression of it all is so vivid. He said:

> Aleck if you must go I will do all I can to facilitate your going. But don't go. These orders, sent by pony express to stop you here, are meant to say to you that if you wish to keep out of the war which is coming you can do so. You will not be required to go into the field against your own people, but will be kept out on this coast on fortification duty. Gen. Totten likes you & wants to keep you in the coprs & that is what this order means.
>
> Now this is not going to be any 90 days or six months affair as some of the politicians are predicting. Both sides are in deadly earnest, & it is long & desperate & fought out to the bitter end.
>
> If you go as an educated soldier you are sure to be put in the front rank & where the fighting will be hardest. God only knows what may happen to you individually, but for your *cause* there can be but one possible result. It must be lost.
>
> The population of the seceding states is only eight million while the North has twenty million. Of your 8 million over 3 million are slaves & may prove a dangerous element. You have no army, no navy, no treasury, no organisation & practically none of the manufacturers—the machine shops, coal & iron mines & such things—

which are necessary for the support of armies & carrying on war on a large scale.

You are but scattered agricultural communities & will be isolated from the world by blockades.

It is not possible for your cause to succeed in the end & the individual risks you must run meanwhile are very great.

On the other hand, if you stay out here you will soon be left the ranking & perhaps the only engineer officer on the Pacific Coast; for every one of us older officers are sure to be very soon called in for active service. You will get promotion, for the chances of battle are sure to make many vacancies in our ranks.

You will have charge of all the government reservations. That on Lime Point has about ten thousand acres all growing up in wild oats. Buy a flock of sheep & hire a Mexican to herd them & in four years you will be a rich man.

The City of San Francisco too is filling in water lots, & the Engineer Corps is consulted & you will be able to make good investments. In short, remaining here you have every opportunity for professional reputation, for promotion & for wealth. Going home you have every personal risk to run & in a cause foredoomed to failure.

Nothing could exceed the kindness & real affection with which McPherson urged these views on me. He was one of the most attractive & universally popular men whom I ever met. There was a gentleness & refinement about him which was almost feminine. He was one of those whom a man might love almost like a woman. Physically to he was a rarely fine specimen. The equestrian statue of him in Washington City is a wonderful success & conveys an excellent idea of him in face, figure, & carriage. I never miss an opportunity to pass it.

Of all the people I knew & talked with over the coming war his judgement & foresight was the clearest. It even seems as if there was a premonition of his own fate in his urging the promotion which the casualties of battle would surely bring. Poor fellow, he was killed before Atlanta July___, 1864. He had been Grant's right hand man at Vicksburg & Sherman's in his Georgia campaign. And he had been noted among Confederates everywhere for his kind & considerate treatment of the non combatants with whom he came in contact. No finer specimen of soldier or gentleman ever lived—or died.

His earnest talk impressed me deeply & made me realize that a crisis in my life was at hand. But I felt utterly helpless to avert it or even to debate the question what I should do. I could not doubt or controvert one of McPherson's statements or arguments; I could only answer this: "Mac, My people are going to war, & war for their *liberty*. If I don't come & bear my part they will believe me a coward—and I will feel that I am occupying the position of one. I must go & stand my chances."

Mac appreciated the situation & said, "I suppose in your situation I should feel as you do." And he gave me the leave of absence I wanted & was as kind and affectionate to me as a brother to the last moment when he bade me goodbye on the steamer.

Perhaps this is as good a place as any to say a little say about the war & its results &c.

I told McPherson we were going to fight for our "liberty." That was the view the whole South took of it. It was not for slavery but the *sovereignty of the states*, which is practically the right to resume self government or to secede.

I think it is even now admitted by all candid & unprejudiced Northern writers that when the states formed the Union by the adoption of the Constitution they reserved their sovereignty in that instrument itself. And it is beyond dispute that some of the states in their acts adopting the Constitution even more expressly stated that they reserved sovereignty—Massachusetts I think is one of these. But in such a partnership any right expressly reserved by one is equally the right of all, even if the constitutional reservation were of doubtful interpretation.

We had the right therefore to secede whenever we saw fit, & it was truly for our liberty that we fought. Slavery brought up the discussion of the right in Congress & in the press, but the South would never have united as it did in secession & in war had it not been generally denied at the North & particularly by the Republican party.

Well that was the issue of the war; & as we were defeated that right was surrendered & a limit was put upon state sovereignty. And the South is now entirely satisfied with that result. And the reason of it is very simple. State sovereignty was doubtless a wise political institution for the condition of this vast country in the last century. But the railroad, the steamboat & the telegraph began to transform things early in this century & have gradually made what may almost be called a new planet of it. Facility of communication & trade & commerce have entirely altered all the conditions of life.

As in ancient geological eras whenever the climate of a country changed, the fauna & flora of the country changed to conform to the altered conditions. Similarly our political institutions have had to change to conform to altered geographical, social, & commercial relations. Briefly we had the right to fight, but our fight was against what might be called a Darwinian development—or an adaptation to changed & changing conditions—so we need not greatly regret defeat.

I think it too a very fortunate result of the war that our Southern armies, though defeated in the end, scored so many brilliant victories in its course & gave the world so many fine examples of soldiers whom all nations & ages will honor for courage, loyalty, honor & the highest Christian principle. For at the beginning there was on each side a great deal of depreciation of the personal qualities of the other.

It would have been most unfortunate for the South, as the losing party in the game, not to have at least fully vindicated her courage & manly qualities, & the high type of the men her civilization produced. But, thank God! she did *that*, & left as a heritage to her sons of future generations, & not only to them but to the whole country, a record of which any nation may be proud. For each side may take equal pride in Lee who surrendered & in Grant who rose to the occasion by giving such honorable & generous terms, as I will tell in due course.

Have I ever regretted resigning when McPherson begged me not to? No, never. I have sometimes perhaps regretted the quiet, easy & prosperous life without a care for the future which my old position in the Engineer Corps would have brought me (I would now be the chief & able to retire in two years with a large salary for life), but I would not give up my recollections & experiences of life & action for anything that could possibly be given me.

But would I do it again now? That is a harder question. When I was young I was willing to take risks & I would take them not only for myself but for those dependent upon me as well. I did not then as fully realize, as I now do, how inexorable are the *conse-*

quences of mistakes—that sins may be repented of, &, we hope, forgiven, but mistakes laugh at repentance & go on piling up the consequences.

So that if I had now to take for my wife & children the tremendous chances of overwhelming disaster which I took in 1861, there would at least be much more deliberation about my choice than there was then. There is a popular story of an old Confederate whose philosophy commends itself to my maturer years & the experiences with which they have been fraught. It is said that the old soldier in question during a halt in a forced march sat on a stump & mentally passed in review his ragged clothes, his empty haversack, his worn out shoes & his sore & sockless feet, & then audibly remarked, "D—n me if ever I love another *country*!"

Fortunately for me, & even more fortunately for those dependent upon me, a kind Providence watched over me & brought me safely through the risks of battle, & not only that but the no less fearful risks of all the financial storms & stresses of the subsequent years so that at least we have never yet wanted for the necessities of life.

But of the other Southern officers who resigned from the U.S. Army as I did to take service with our native states, scarcely one I think in a hundred has been so fortunate & the fates of a great number have been sad tragedies.

So I wrote my resignation of my beautiful position in the Engineer Corps, & my sweet Miss Teen cried when I did it; although she knew it had to be done, & she had never said a word to discourage it. And McPherson gave me a written leave of absence to go east & await the acceptance of my resignation at home. And I may say here that my resignation was duly accepted to take effect May 1st, the date stated in it, & the notification of it was sent me by mail & duly received—the very last mail from Washn. City that I knew of. At that time too the resignations of many Southern officers were being rejected & the officers being discharged, for "resigning in the face of the enemy" or other disreputable reasons. So I considered the acceptance of mine as strong evidence of good will & regrets from the headquarters of the corps.

Lawyer to Lieutenant

The following selection was written in 1903 by another artilleryman, William Thomas Poague of Virginia. He came from a middle-class slave owning family near Lexington, Virginia and graduated from Washington College in 1857. Located in Lexington, next to the Virginia Military Institute, the college later became known as Washington and Lee University because Robert E. Lee served as its president after the war. Poague studied law after graduation and moved to St. Joseph, Missouri, but found the area and the profession not to his liking. After moving back to Lexington and joining the army, Poague gained fame as a battery and battalion commander of artillery in Lee's army. The selection is from Monroe E. Cockrell, ed., Gunner With Stonewall: Reminiscences of William Thomas Poague *(Jackson, Tenn., 1957), 2-5.*

[W]hen Lincoln called on all the non-seceding states—Virginia among the number—for troops to force back into the Union the states that had seceded, there was at once a complete change of sentiment. Our people did not stop half way and try to maintain a neutral position, but Virginia with a unanimity almost entire, east of the Alleghany mountains, took her stand in front of her Southern sisters to resist the invader of her soil. In Lexington where the lines between the Unionist and the Secessionists were so broadly marked, where party feeling ran high and where serious clashes were with difficulty prevented, all differences forever disappeared as soon as the news of Lincoln's call for troops reached the town. The same change took place at once all over Rockbridge and throughout the state.

Two volunteer companies, the Rockbridge Rifles and Rockbridge Dragoons—organized in November, 1859, soon after John Brown's attempt to incite the negroes to insurrection—were at once called into service, and proceeded to Harper's Ferry. My brother James, a medical student at the University of Virginia, left his books and went with his company, the "Dragoons." I wanted to join his company, but was prevailed on by my partner,

Colonel Massie, to remain and look after our business, who said that he . . . felt it to be his duty to go into military service at once. He believed there would be but little fighting if any; that at the last moment a satisfactory adjustment would be found; and that his absence would be of short duration. Many of our leading men fell into the same error. The average politicians and newspapers on both sides misjudged the signs of the times and made the same mistake, believing that the great mass of the people would rise up at the critical moment and compel a peaceable settlement of our differences and thus avert the threatening clash.

The biographies of Mr. Lincoln are wide of the mark in saying that the masses of the Southern people were forced into the war by the secession leaders. It was the act of Mr. Lincoln and his party that precipitated the conflict which many think was inevitable. Had he not made war upon the South, Virginia would not have left the Union. He and his advisers managed affairs so as to compel South Carolina to fire the first gun. The North was the aggressor. The South resisted her invaders. History will vindicate her course.

After our two volunteer companies and the corps of cadets under "Old Jack" left, our people set about forming other companies, and by April 21, 1861, in three days time, the Rockbridge Artillery of seventy men was organized. . . .

We thus had the very best material for a battery—men who knew how to manage and take care of the horses and educated, high spirited men for the guns. Farmers, mechanics, merchants, laborers, lawyers, university students and theological students, made up the bulk of the company.

Native Americans and the War

Roughly 5,000 Native Americans served in the Confederate army, but precious few of them left behind personal accounts of their experiences. In this rare selection, George Washington Grayson helps to fill that gaping hole. Grayson was born in the Creek Nation in what is modern day Oklahoma, the old Indian Territory, where the Five Civilized Tribes were forcibly removed by the Federal government in the 1830s. His father was half white and his mother was three-quarters white, and thus Grayson was born into the mixed blood minority of the nation. This faction tended to be more progressive and was more willing to acculturate within white culture. It also strongly sided with the Confederacy when the Civil War broke out. Grayson studied at mission schools in the Indian Territory and later attended Arkansas College at Fayetteville, which later became the University of Arkansas. He finally joined the army at age twenty, after much hesitation, and served as the chief of the Creek Nation long after the war ended. The selection is from W. David Baird, ed., A Creek Warrior for the Confederacy: The Autobiography of Chief G.W. Grayson *(Norman, 1988), 58-61.*

By the time [my father had died the] war between the North and South which had been so long threatened had broken out and gun-play was on. Quite all of the able bodied men capable of bearing arms throughout the country were enthusiastically enlisting in some one of the many military organizations that were being formed, and going from their homes into military encampments. Although completely captivated by the glowing reports of the excitement, the novelty and other enchantments of the life of the soldier in camps and on duty, I ignored my boyish inclinations and declined to join the army. . . . [I could] not see how Mother and the children could possibly support themselves without my assistance who was the oldest of the flock, and now quite useful as a bread earner. Besides, the enlistments of men in this country were not for service beyond the Mississippi river at or near the seat of war, but were to be devoted to such military service as was necessary in the Indian Territory. And as the enemy was no where threatening the peace or safety of our territory, there seemed little need for us all to rush pell mell to arms as the people were doing.

I therefore held back for quite a while longer helping to look after the welfare of Mother and the children. [At the same time] those who at first enlisted with so much spirit and éclat began to show signs of tiring of the life of a soldier in camp and to declare that if they must bear that which they now discovered was a hardship, others now in their comfortable homes must get out too, enlist and bear their share of the hardships of war. In some quarters it was said—"Here is Wash Grayson who is a well educated young man, capable of making a useful soldier in the army as a commissioned officer or otherwise, and yet he declines to join the army. He should be made to take his place in one of the companies and do duty as others are doing." This kind of talk, besides occasional inuendos derogatory to my personal courage in case of a conflict of arms, determined me to enter the field and show my critics, if occasion offered, the stuff I was made of, even if it cost my life to make the exhibition.

Just when or where I enlisted has escaped my memory, but it was perhaps after the war had been in progress for nearly or quite a year. D. H. Cooper who was an ex-U.S. Indian Agent for the Choctaws, was the General in command of the Indian brigade composed of the soldiers of the Creeks, Cherokees, Choctaws, Chickasaws and Seminoles. [Cooper] had followed the retreating Creeks, who under Hu-pui-helth Ya-ho-la [Opothleyaholo] were hastening to join the Federals in the state of Kansas and had one or perhaps two engagements with them without any important results. [There being no] . . . other of the enemy . . . in menacing distance of us, there was really not much to call into martial activity our spirit of patriotism. . . .

My pride of manhood had been ruffled by the criticisms I had heard of and the hints given out that I was slow to enlist probably because of fear of the danger incident to hostile engagement with the enemy. It was my fixed determination to prove to my detractors that I sought not the ease and immunities supposedly belonging to the position of a commissioned officer. . . . [Instead I] was willing to take my place in the ranks with the rest of the boys subject to all the duties and hardships incident to the life a private soldier. No one I think understood my motives for declining to stand for an office when all that was required of me was to express my consent, but I was actuated as I clearly remember by the impulses and considerations as above stated.

How long I served as a private soldier in Co. K, 2d Creek regiment I do not know, but the need of my services, especially in view of my supposed superior education and fitness and ability, in the conduct of the affairs of our company was pressing. And discussion of the proposition to elevate me from the ranks to some official position wherein my services might be utilized in other more elevated spheres than that of guard and picket duty for the company continued; and over which I confess to a secret feeling of triumph and satisfaction. How I came to yield to these continued earnest solicitations I do not recall, for I rather enjoyed them, but suspect that the emoluments of the office, which would enable me to spare more pecuniary aid to my mother and the children at home, whom I never forgot, was perhaps the principal cause. Anyhow, I consented and was given the first lieutenancy of our company, in which office I served until by the death of our captain some time later I was promoted to that vacancy, and as capt. of Co. K. served to the close of the war. Having in years not yet attained my majority, I was a mere boy, and by far the youngest captain serving the Indian brigade.

After Gettsyburg

An obscure cavalryman, I. Norval Baker pondered the meaning of the war in the days immediately following the battle of Gettysburg. He served in Company F, Eighteenth Virginia Cavalry, which was part of Brig. Gen. John W. Imboden's brigade. Imboden escorted the wounded of Lee's army from the battlefield at Gettysburg back to Virginia. They were carried in a line of wagons that stretched for seventeen miles along the road, and were harassed by pursuing Union cavalry all the way. His experiences caused Baker to remind himself what the war was about. This selection is from Baker's unpublished diary, p. 24, which is in the Archives of the Virginia Military Institute at Lexington.

We all sat down or lay down on the ground to think about the last two months work. We learn we, or Lee's army have lost twenty to thirty thousand men since we crossed the river and invaded Maryland and Pennsylvania. What awful thing is war and what is this war for, anyway. Our poor men of the southern army say it is to free the negro and make the negro equal with the poor man of the southern states and have free mixed schools and a negro can marry a white girl and etc., and the men are saying they will wade in blood to their chins before such a thing shall happen to our people. Others say it is a money war, that some of the Yankee people up north have loaned their money to old Abe Lincoln to keep up the war and old Abe is paying them a big interest from the peoples crib, besides giving money loaners office and etc., the Yankee prisoners tell us it is to save the union and if they thought it is to free the negro they would lay down their arms and go home and others tell us they are in favor of having a labor union and the organization will not work well in the southern states where there are so many slaves and free negros, that the negros should be freed and sent back where they came from (Africa) and that will make this a white mans country.

Purchase Liberty for My Country

Henry Lea Graves, who was from Georgia, served in the fledgling Confederate Marine Corps and was stationed in Richmond when Maj. Gen. George McClellan's massive Army of the Potomac was slowly advancing on the Confederate capital. On May 17, 1862, he wrote to his family about the approaching danger and mulled over the reasons that impelled him to fight for the Confederacy. This selection is from Richard Harwell, ed., A Confederate Marine: A Sketch of Henry Lea Graves with Excerpts from the Graves Family Correspondence, 1861-1865 *(Tuscaloosa, 1963), 60-61.*

17th Tues.—Ma asks about my eating. I have so far got as much as was good for me. It is true we have not much to spare, but I do not feel inclined to complain and am only thankful that I fare as well as I do, and I shall be glad if we get off with the little hardship already suffered. I for one will feel willing to undergo any hardship if I can thereby purchase liberty for my country. I am by no means discouraged about the war and am sorry that any "Georgian" should talk of giving up the struggle. I for one, if God gives me strength, will never give up, and I hope and believe that our whole family, those in Georgia, Miss., Ala., Tex., and N. C., and wherever else they may be found will be the very last to consent to slavery. The idea of such monsters as Butler and Wool having control and power over my mother and relatives and friends is enough of itself, if nothing else would, to make me vow never to yield. I want my destiny and that of my kindred to be one and identical with the destiny of my country. Times are just beginning "to try men's souls" and I believe it is best that such times should come for I for one wish to know who are patriots and men and who are not. It is necessary for our land to be purged of its filth and now is the time, and dark times and gloom and trouble is the best thing to do it. We are in the right and as surely as I believe that God reigns, I believe we will accomplish our independence. Even let our armies be entirely dispersed and scattered in "guerrila bands" and the process of subjugation would be then but begun. The Southern people never can be conquered. . . . The talk of foreign "intervention" has been revived some little here for the last few days, caused by reports reaching Richmond that France had been so gracious as to recognize our independence. I have seen no notice of it in any of the papers, but noticed that it obtained what is called "pretty general belief." This is the greatest place for such rumors I ever saw. You hear a report of some important fact stated most positively on good authority and the next hour it is as positively contradicted. I have made up my mind to believe nothing but what I know to be true. With regard to "Foreign recognition," however, I believe it will eventually come at a time when we least expect it, but we will have to work out our own independence, and it is perfectly foolish to look and long so anxiously for it. I am consequently in favor of quitting begging abjectly for recognition, and go to work, invade and employ every other power we have and we will then soon be in a condition to demand it as a right.

Questions

1. *Think about Edward Porter Alexander's troubling decision to turn his back on his fellow officers in the U.S. Regulars and side with the South. How strong must the tug of loyalty to his home state have been to convince him it was right to fight against his old comrades? What does this say about the tension between the primacy of the state versus the primacy of the nation in nine-*

teenth-century American culture?

2. *William Thomas Poague gives primary emphasis to Lincoln's call for troops to suppress the rebellion, following the firing on Fort Sumter, as the cause of his decision to support the Confederacy. Think about the pivotal role of this decision by Lincoln in forcing thousands of residents of the Upper South out of their neutrality on the issue of secession. Four slave states, including Poague's native Virginia, left the Union rather than support Lincoln's war policy. What is the connection between this reason to fight and the issues of slavery and states' rights?*
3. *What was the primary reason George Washington Grayson gave for his decision to join the Confederate army? Does it have anything to do with the larger issues of the war, or is it a purely personal reason that was nevertheless shared by many other men?*
4. *I. Norval Baker seemed to put the issue of slavery, as it related to the war, in pretty blunt terms. Does this help to explain why even non-slaveowners in the South might be willing to fight to preserve the institution?*
5. *Henry Lea Graves was concerned about protecting his home from Yankee occupiers, but he also welcomed the trauma of war as a way to test the worth of the Southern people. If they could endure the sacrifices needed to win the war through their own strength, rather than through enlisting the aid of a foreign country, then they deserved to be independent much in the way that the Revolutionary soldiers had endured tremendous hardships to win the war against the British. Think about the willingness of men like Graves to endure suffering. Is there a relationship between this attitude and the enduring bitterness that the Civil War created for several generations following the end of the conflict? How difficult must it have been to give up these fervent hopes and fears that led the Confederate soldier to war, when he finally had to accept defeat in 1865?*

FURTHER READING

A number of historians have begun to enlighten us about the life and mind of the Civil War soldier. Reid Mitchell, Civil War Soldiers *(New York, 1988), offers a brilliant exploration of the impact of the war experience on the thinking of the Confederate soldier which emphasizes how the war tested his motivations to fight for independence. Gerald Linderman,* Embattled Courage: The Experience of Combat in the American Civil War *(New York, 1987), emphasizes the ideal of courage as a motivating factor in leading Southerners to battle. James M. McPherson,* For Cause and Comrades: Why Men Fought in the Civil War *(New York, 1997), stresses ideological reasons as the motivation of Confederate soldiers. Joseph Allan Frank,* With Ballot and Bayonet: The Political Socialization of American Civil War Soldiers *(Athens, Georgia 1998), examines the political awareness of the Southern soldier. And Larry M. Logue,* To Appomattox and Beyond: The Civil War Soldier in War and Peace *(Chicago, 1996), offers insight into how Confederate soldiers dealt with their defeat after the war ended.*

The Impeachment of Andrew Johnson

Michael Les Benedict

INTRODUCTION

The United States Constitution empowers the House of Representatives to impeach—that is, to bring charges against—government officials whom the House believes to be guilty of treason, bribery, or other "high crimes and misdemeanors," terms that the Constitution does not define. An impeached official is tried before the Senate. Conviction requires a two-thirds vote.

In 1868 the House of Representatives impeached President Andrew Johnson—one of only two presidents to have been impeached in the history of the United States. (President William J. Clinton was impeached in December 1998 and acquitted in 1999.) The impeachment was part of the most bitter conflict ever to take place between a president and Congress, made worse because it was part of the gravest crisis ever to threaten the nation as a whole—the Civil War and the Reconstruction of the Union. The Senate failed to convict Johnson by only one vote.

Impeachment was precipitated by the deep disagreement between Johnson and the Republican majority in Congress over how to restore the Union after the Civil War. Johnson's main goal was to restore loyalty among the masses of white southerners whom he believed had been misled into rebellion by the slaveowning elite. He was less concerned about securing basic rights to the former slaves (called "freedmen"), because he did not himself believe they should be treated as equals. Like most southerners, he expected African Americans to remain a subordinated labor force in the South.

To achieve his goals, Johnson established a Reconstruction program based on a tentative one that had been discussed in the cabinet shortly before Lincoln's death. It required white southern men to take oaths that they would henceforth be loyal to the United States. In return, Johnson proclaimed an amnesty and issued pardons. Johnson appointed provisional governors, who reorganized state governments. Once these governments accepted the end of slavery and met a few other requirements, they would be restored to normal relations in the Union.

Most Republicans objected that this program did not do enough to secure freedom and put control of the South back into the hands of former rebels. After failing to get President Johnson to cooperate in a moderate plan of Reconstruction, the Republican majority in Congress passed the Reconstruction Act of 1867, which established a new Reconstruction program. It instructed the United States Army to administer the South temporarily and supervise the reorganization of southern state governments on the basis of civil and political equality between the races. But Johnson continued his opposition, questioning the right of Congress to legislate on such issues while the South remained without representation. It was this continued conflict that finally led to impeachment.

Rejecting an impeachment resolution in December 1867, Congress finally impeached Johnson on 24 February 1868, after he tried to remove Secretary of War Edwin M. Stanton in apparent violation of the Tenure of Office Act, which required the Senate to agree to removals of government officers. The trial in the Senate went on through May. On 16 May, Johnson was acquitted on one of the counts of the impeachment by the margin of one vote. After a ten-day adjournment, he was acquitted on two other counts by the same margin, at which point the Republicans gave up and adjourned the trial.

The Johnson impeachment has remained a controversial episode of American history, raising questions about the authority and obligations of the president, the proper relations between Congress and the Executive Department of the government, and the nature of the impeachment power. Historians have disagreed about whether the impeachment of Johnson was justified, what motivated it, whether the trial itself was fair, and what the consequences would have been had the outcome been different.

Historians' Opinions of the Johnson Impeachment

Until the 1950s, few historians were sympathetic to the Reconstruction policy established by the Republican Congress after the Civil War. They believed it was designed primarily to punish southerners for the rebellion and to maintain Republican political power through the votes of the former slaves. This understanding led historians to view the impeachment of President Johnson as a dangerous act of extremism—an effort to secure the complete triumph of the Republican party and its Reconstruction program and at the same time to make Congress dominant over the presidency. However, in the 1950s and 1960s historians took a new look at the postwar period and concluded that Johnson had stood in the way of a fair Reconstruction in which the human and civil rights of the former slaves would be protected. Far more critical of Johnson, many historians reevaluated the impeachment. However, they continued to disagree about what motivated it, whether it was justified, and whether the trial was fair.

Impeachment: Response to Presidential Aggression

In the following selection, historian Michael Les Benedict describes the events leading to impeachment and argues that Johnson's aggressive behavior forced the Republicans to impeach him in order to defend Congress's Reconstruction policy. Abridged from Michael Les Benedict, The Impeachment and Trial of Andrew Johnson *(New York, 1973), 21–23, 26–27, 33–36, 39–43, 45–46, 48–49, 59–60, 73, 81, 95, 98–99, 101, 104, 126, 130, 142–43.*

While more conservative Republicans hoped for Johnson's cooperation, radicals shared no such illusions. In their opinion, the President had already demonstrated his capacity for destructiveness. His mild restoration policy had reawakened southern belligerence after Lee's surrender and was responsible for all the suffering that implied for southern loyalists. Republicans laid directly at his feet responsibility for the brutal New Orleans massacre of the summer of 1866, in which the city police killed 40 mainly black Republicans and injured 160 more in dispersing a peaceful convention of doubtful legality. They were equally convinced that the general mood of hostility to Union soldiers and blacks could be traced to the President's lenience.

Moreover, Johnson had already shown his willingness to nullify congressional legislation. Where it suited him, he had ignored the Senate's right to confirm government appointments, disregarded the Test Oath law, and emasculated the Freedmen's Bureau and Confiscation Acts. . . . He now proclaimed the Reconstruction Act "without precedent and without authority, in palpable conflict with the plainest provisions of the Constitution, and utterly destructive to those great principles of liberty and humanity for which our ancestors on both sides of the Atlantic have shed so much blood and expended so much treasure." Anyone who understood the President's character, radicals insisted, must recognize what lay ahead.

Fearing the worst, radicals had launched a movement to impeach Johnson during the second session of the 39th Congress. . . . Inside Congress, [George S.] Boutwell, [Thaddeus] Stevens, and [James M.] Ashley spearheaded efforts. . . . [Republicans] referred the [impeachment] resolutions to the Judiciary Committee, which began the long and tedious job of collecting evidence and taking testimony. . . .

As Americans for the first time seriously discussed the possibility of impeaching a president, they arrived at two opposing concepts of the law of impeachment. . . . Democrats, Republicans who opposed impeachment, and most lawyers argued that a government officer could be impeached only for an act actually criminal, a violation of a criminal statute. Many historians have ac-

---

Excerpts reprinted from *The Impeachment and Trial of Andrew Johnson* by Michael Les Benedict, published by W.W. Norton & Company, Inc., 1973.

Andrew Johnson (Courtesy of The Library of Congress.)

cepted this view as embodying the proper law of impeachment, accusing those who insisted on a broader interpretation of using impeachment wrongly in a purely political vendetta. But those who espoused the narrow view had an extremely difficult task in sustaining it, because in fact it was a novel argument, running counter to precedent, the overwhelming weight of American legal authority, and logic. . . .

Radicals argued that the "misdemeanors" the Constitution referred to as grounds for impeachment included misfeasance and malfeasance in office as well as crimes indictable before criminal courts. . . . [A]ll advocates of a broad impeachment power agreed that the place of impeachment in American constitutional law should be determined primarily by examining American precedents and American legal authorities.

. . . [T]hose who favored the broad conception of Congress's power to impeach turned to the line of precendents [precedents] established by the House in presenting impeachments rather than to those established by the Senate in deciding them. In every impeachment the House had presented to the Senate, at least some of the articles had alleged nonindictable offenses. . . . [T]he radicals also cited with special emphasis the convictions of [Judge John] Pickering and Judge West H. Humphries by the Senate.

But the radicals' greatest strength resided in the unanimity with which the great American constitutional commentators had upheld the broad view of the impeachment power. Those eminent legal writers had recognized that both English and American precedents were mixed. They had eschewed legal authority, therefore, and had appealed to reason instead. In an age accustomed to analyzing government primarily in terms of its theoretical and legal foundations rather than its practical workings, such "appeals to reason" offered scholars an opportunity for assessments based on the actual relationships between the various institutions of government. In short, the great constitutionalists for a moment left the realm of law and entered what is now called political science.

As a practical matter, American constitutional commentators [including the authors of *The Federalists*] . . . recognized that the maintenance of proper checks and balances in government, which they believed guaranteed liberty, depended upon the good faith and restraint of those entrusted with power. They recognized that the danger to liberty and the efficient workings of government lay not in the possibility that the president or lesser executive officers might act illegally, but rather that they might abuse the powers the Constitution *had* delegated to them. . . .

The abuses commentators feared were precisely those "too artful to be anticipated by positive law, and sometimes too subtle and mysterious to be fully detected in the limited period of an ordinary investigation." That the rules of evidence required for indictment and conviction were too rigid to serve in an area so dangerous to society worried William Rawle [author of one of the leading pre-Civil War commentaries on the Constitution]. Incriminating facts might be uncovered "which may be properly connected with others already known, but [which] would not form sufficient subjects of separate prosecution. Of these accounts a peculiar tribunal seems both useful and necessary," he reasoned, "a tribunal of a liberal and comprehensive character, confined as little as possible to strict forms, enabled to continue its session as long as the nature of the case may require, qualified to view the charge in all its bearings and dependencies, and to appreciate on sound principles of public policy the defense of the accused. . . ." With-out dissent, although often with less clarity and succinctness, the other major American constitutionalists echoed these opinions.

Had Republicans acted upon these doctrines, there can be no doubt that Andrew Johnson could have been impeached, tried, convicted, and removed at any time after December 1865, for his activities fitted precisely into the pattern . . . outlined.

. . . [Congress] had set rather specific parameters to the Reconstruction process when the 38th Congress adjourned. If Lincoln, and later Johnson, intended to continue the policy of administering conquered areas through provisional governors, those provisional governors, as officers of the United States, would have to take the "ironclad" test oath . . . [that they] had never endorsed or encouraged secession or resistance to national authority. Moreover, although former Rebels could take part in the reorganization after taking the amnesty oath, national patronage [federal jobs] could go only to those who could take the test oath. Republicans believed that the best security for a loyal Reconstruction would be a government politically allied to the Republican party, even if former Rebels served in it. With national patronage required by law to be put in the hands of loyalists, with the all-important provisional governors required always to have been loyal Union men, Republicans could expect that their allies would control the Reconstruction process in the South. This had been the case in Tennessee, Arkansas, and Louisiana, where Reconstruction had begun before the war ended.

Furthermore, a strong start had been made in solving the problem of transition from slave to free labor. The Freedmen's Bureau, funded by the income of abandoned, seized, and confiscated lands, would cooperate with missionary organizations in educating black people, guard freedmen's interests in the unaccustomed process of contracting for wages, and begin the process of distributing land to establish black homesteads.

But within a year of Andrew Johnson's elevation to the presidency, the preliminary Reconstruction program enacted by Congress lay in utter ruin. In pursuing his own policy, Johnson had destroyed it, without violating a law, using only his constitutional powers as president of the United States. Ignoring the Test Oath Act of Congress, he appointed former Rebels provisional governors in several southern states. He had excepted leading Confederates from his Amnesty Proclamation, but he willingly pardoned virtually any Rebel upon the recommendation of his provisional governors. The provisional governors were politicians, interested in political power, and they knew that their political futures would be more promising if they conciliated white southern leaders. When Johnson made it obvious that he would support such a policy by pardoning Rebel leaders, and when he made alternatives impossible by opposing black suffrage, most of the provisional governors began to work with former Confederates and to proscribe former Unionists who refused to cooperate. By December 1865, nearly every southern state had returned to Confederate leadership.

The Johnson administration had also ignored the congressional oath requirement in making ordinary appointments to the national civil service in the South. Postmaster General William Dennison and Attorney General James Speed found it possible to obey the law (although with difficulty), but Treasury Secretary [Hugh] McCulloch, encouraged by Secretary of the Navy [Gideon] Welles, had abandoned the oath requirement in August 1865, staffing the southern Treasury Department network with former Rebels. After the Post Office Department, the Treasury Department was the largest single source of national patronage within the states, and its positions were far more lucrative and sought after. In ignoring the oath requirement enacted by Congress, McCulloch abetted the pro-Rebel policy established at the state level by most of Johnson's provisional governors.

Johnson's decisions had been as disastrous to the race and labor policy of the Republicans as to their protean Reconstruction program. These decisions centered on enforcement of the Confiscation Act and the President's absolute right to pardon under the Constitution.

By late July 1865, Attorney General Speed began to restrict the enforcement of the Confiscation law. It is not clear that he did so at the direct order of the President, but there can be no doubt that the decision was part of a uniform administration program to restore the Union by conciliating white Southerners. . . . From September 1865 to December 1867, the Attorney General's office repeatedly ordered local officers to cease or suspend confiscation proceedings, bringing to a standstill nearly all the activity in this area. . . . In June 1866, Speed ordered a complete end to all proceedings.

At the same time the Attorney General acted to minimize enforcement of the Confiscation law, Johnson effectively destroyed the capacity of the Freedmen's Bureau to fulfill its congressional mandate. Former Confederates pardoned under the Amnesty Proclamation or by special presidential action immediately began to demand the return of their abandoned and seized property. When Bureau officials refused to accede to their demands, the pardoned Rebels appealed to the President. Commissioner Oliver Otis Howard argued that acquiescence in the Rebels' demands would completely disrupt the Bureau's activities and urged Johnson to consider property already condemned by the government to be beyond the reach of pardon. Instead, the President held that only confiscated land *already sold to third parties* should remain unreturned. Even land to which the government had received title under the Confiscation law would be restored to its former owners. Since little land had been subject to confiscation proceedings before the war's end because of the absence of courts, and since even land to which the government had received title had been turned over to the Freedmen's Bureau rather than sold, Johnson's order effectually nullified both the Confiscation and the Freedmen's Bureau laws. . . .

By May 1866, Johnson's interference on behalf of the South had become so blatant that many Republicans feared the President might attempt a *coup d'état*. This apprehension, fanned by Johnson's intemperate language and by the open advocacy of such a course by southern and northern Democratic organs, continued until the impeachment.

Finally, Johnson exercised the presidential power of removal and appointment in an effort to influence officeholders—and through them the public—to endorse his Reconstruction policy. . . .

. . . During the recess between the first and second sessions of the 39th Congress from July 28 to December 4, 1866, Johnson removed 1,664 postmasters, 1,283 of them for political reasons alone. Excluding the southern and border states, 1,352 of 12,836 postmasters were replaced—1,210, nearly 10 percent of the total, for political reasons only. And in many of those states—New York, Wisconsin, and Connecticut, for example—factions allied with Johnson had already controlled large amounts of the patronage before he began his assault.

The effect of these removals cannot be judged by their number alone. Johnson never intended to replace every federal officeholder; he meant to force them to endorse his policy of Reconstruction. As they saw their colleagues fall, they began grudgingly to do so. . . . Most patronage employees probably tried to remain strictly neutral between the contestants during the elections of 1866, but not until Congress passed the Tenure of Office Act, restricting Johnson's removal power, did some of them cautiously begin to speak out for their principles once more.

The President's course, none of the elements of which clearly violated law, had a staggering effect on the South. He converted a conquered people, bitter but ready to accept the consequences of defeat, into a hostile, aggressive, uncooperative unit. He restored to them political and economic power and through that power domination of the men and women they had recently held as slaves. He had set back the work of Reconstruction, as it turned out, two full years and had ensured that Southerners would resist the process instead of cooperating. To a large degree, the failure of Reconstruction could be blamed alone on President Johnson's abuse of his discretionary powers. . . .

But despite Republicans' violent reactions, Johnson continued the offensive, removing [General Daniel E.] Sickles [from his command in North Carolina] on August 27 and threatening the removal of General [John] Pope from his command in Georgia, Alabama, and Florida. As Johnson's rampage went on, Republicans began to fear more than ever that he might finally transcend the bounds of reason. "What does Johnson mean to do?" former Attorney General Speed begged [radical Republican Charles] Sumner. "Does he mean to have another rebellion on the question of Executive powers & duties?". . .

Yet Johnson had broken no law; he had limited himself strictly to the exercise of his constitutional powers. Confused constituents turned to their congressmen: "Is it possible that there can be a wrong without a remedy . . . ," one asked [Republican Senator Lyman] Trumbull. "Must the great people who patriotically saved the Republic remain chained by an arbitrary rule until a usurper at Washington overthrows our liberties?" . . .

After Congress passed the Reconstruction Acts in 1867, putting the South under the control of the army, Johnson obstructed their enforcement. On 12 August, 1867 he suspended from office Secretary of War Edwin M. Stanton, who was sympathetic to Congress's Reconstruction policy, replacing him temporarily with General Ulysses S. Grant. By suspending rather than removing Stanton, Johnson seemed to be acting according to the requirements of the Tenure of Office Act. Nonetheless, Republicans were furious at this clear effort to gain complete control of the army.

When Congress met, the impeachers appeared to be in a hopeless minority. The Judiciary Committee had kept its proceedings strictly confidential, and most congressmen believed the majority report would be against impeachment. . . . But when the committee published its report on November 25, Republicans learned that John C. Churchill had changed his mind as a result of Johnson's interference with the military. The majority report would favor impeachment. Churchill's reversal caused wild excitement, and radicals believed they could muster a fifteen- to thirty-vote majority. In the confusion, both sides predicted victory. . . .

. . . [But on 7 December 1867] the House defeated the majority resolution 57 to 108. . . . The radicals had not been able to muster a majority even of their own party. "You will see how Congress backed down on impeachment, & can guess the effect of it on the whole of the South . . . ," radical Representative George W. Julian wrote his wife. "It is pitiful!". . .

. . . Johnson continued the battle in Washington, D.C. On December 12, in compliance with the Tenure of Office Act, the President sent the Senate his reasons for suspending Secretary of War Stanton. Not questioning the Senate's right to restore Stanton to his office, Johnson argued that Stanton should have resigned when his opposition to the President's policy became irreconcilable. . . .

The Senate considered the resolution to refuse its consent to Stanton's removal on January 11 and 13. As a whole, the Republicans were determined to sustain the Secretary of War. But not all were zealous. . . . [James W.] Grimes, [John B.] Henderson, [Edmund G.] Ross, William Sprague, and [Peter G.] Van Winkle all abstained on the final vote. In this group were four of the seven Republicans who would vote to acquit Andrew Johnson of high crimes and misdemeanors after he removed Stanton in violation of the law. But two other Republicans who would vote for acquittal, [William P.] Fessenden and Trumbull, were among Stanton's most vigorous defenders.

The next day Grant turned the keys to the secretary of war's office over to Stanton. Furious, Johnson accused the General of double-dealing. A bitter wrangle ensued, which wedded Grant firmly and finally to the Republicans and reassured them of his position. . . . The President was determined to remove Stanton in violation of the Tenure of Office Act. . . .

The message appointing a new secretary of war ad interim in place of Stanton (the appointee was General Lorenzo Thomas, the nondescript Adjutant General of the Army) arrived at the Senate while it was debating the bill to repeal the absolute-majority requirement for ratifying new constitutions in the southern states. . . . As word spread through the chamber, representatives who had been on the floor rushed to their side of the Capitol to inform their colleagues, who had just received a message from Stanton telling them of the situation. Several senators hurried to Stanton's offices to urge him to hold on. . . .

The next day, February 22, the Reconstruction Committee reported an impeachment resolution to the House of Representatives. Every Republican member endorsed it, including both [John Armor] Bingham and Stevens. Citing as evidence only Johnson's order removing Stanton and his order to Thomas to take his place, the committee proposed: "That Andrew Johnson, President of the United States, be impeached of high crimes and misdemeanors in office." . . .

Most historians have interpreted the attempt to remove President Johnson as blatantly political, insupportable in law, a blunder from which the nation was saved by seven noble Republican senators who would not succumb to the political pressure around them. This is true even of those historians who have begun to recognize the circumstances in which impeachment took place and have debunked the idea that the President was an innocent victim unable any longer to disrupt the "radical" program. But such a view is naive in the extreme.

The managers of the impeachment. From left to right: Benjamin F. Butler, James F. Wilson, Thaddeus Stevens, George S. Boutwell, William Lawrence, John A. Logan, John A. Bingham. (Courtesy of The Library of Congress.)

Extralegal considerations did play a large part in the impeachment proceedings. But these considerations weighed not only upon the Republicans who voted for conviction. It goes almost without saying that the Democrats and the few "Johnsonized" Republicans who had been cooperating with them would under no circumstances have voted to remove the President and turn the office over to the Republicans. In fact, they were more consistently antipathetic to the entire proceeding than even the most hostile of the Republicans. . . . If one argues that Johnson's conviction would have resulted from votes motivated by political considerations, one must concede that the same considerations secured his acquittal.

. . . Most Republicans believed that impeachment was necessary for the future success of the Republican party and therefore for the security of southern black and white loyalists. The President had embarked on a bold offensive to defeat Reconstruction in the South. Before the House impeached him, he had removed every military commander in the South who was committed to carrying out the spirit of the Reconstruction Acts; he had twice replaced Stanton, quarreled with Grant, and begun to create a new military headquarters in Washington to be commanded by a more friendly general equal in rank to the General of the Army. If impeachment failed, Republicans believed, "the President will have schemes enough to endanger the peace of the country. It would open a Pandora's box.". . .

. . . [Despite these concerns, contemporaries] recognized most senators' commitment to impartial justice. Those who confidently expected conviction did so because they were certain of the President's guilt. And the violent reaction against the Republicans who acquitted him must be understood as the reaction of men who believed the President so patently guilty that they could not conceive of any impartial judge coming to a contrary conclusion unless influenced by extraneous and corrupt considerations.

Those who were not convinced of the President's guilt . . . believed most senators would judge fairly. The New York *Herald*'s Washington correspondent counted eleven Republicans certain to acquit the President and two more as doubtful. [James W.] Grimes, the first Republican to decide for acquittal, wrote before the trial began, "About a dozen men are determined to convict, about the same number are determined to acquit, and the balance intend to hear the evidence and weigh the law before they pronounce judgment."

Historians should view the trial of impeachment for what it was: not as an attempt by a violent majority to remove an innocent president for partisan purposes but as one of the great legal cases of history, in which American politicians demonstrated the strength of the nation's democratic institutions by attempting to do what no one could justifiably expect them to do—to give a political officer a full and fair trial in a time of political crisis.

An Effort to Establish Congressional Omnipotence

Not much more sympathetic to Johnson than Michael Les Benedict, legal scholar Raoul Berger nonetheless argues that the Johnson impeachment represented a misguided effort to establish congressional predominance in the federal government. The following selection is from Raoul Berger, Impeachment: The Constitutional Problems *(Cambridge, Massachusetts, 1973), 252, 259–62, 264, 295.*

MORE than one hundred years have passed since President Andrew Johnson escaped conviction by one vote, yet the record remains immediately relevant. His impeachment poses an issue which may again confront us: is the President impeachable for violating a statute . . . if in his judgment it invades his constitutional prerogatives? And Johnson's trial serves as a frightening reminder that in the hands of a passion-driven Congress the process may bring down the very pillars of our constitutional system. . . .

The key to enforcement of military reconstruction was in the hands of the Secretary of War and in the concomitant control of military commanders. The Secretary, Edwin M. Stanton, was a holdover from Lincoln's first term. By the Radicals' own testimony, he had close ties with them. . . . [A] provision of the Tenure of Office Act of March 2, 1867, aimed to make removal of the

Secretary of War dependent upon the Senate's consent. But Stanton had become a thorn in Johnson's side, and finally Johnson removed him, statute or no. At last Congress had a nail on which to hang an impeachment. . . .

It was high tragedy that by an accident of history a man whose will ran counter to that of the party which had elected him, and ultimately to that of the great majority in the North, became President at a time of tremendous national crisis. But once President, he was by the Constitution entitled to exercise his own judgment. . . . A President, however, is not to be removed merely for differing with Congress. Such differences were contemplated as part of the checks and balances of the Constitution, "designed to blunt the impact of majority rule." In the oft-quoted words of Justice [Louis] Brandeis, "The doctrine of the separation of powers was adopted by the Convention of 1787, not to promote efficiency but to preclude the exercise of arbitrary power. The purpose was, not to avoid friction, but, by means of inevitable friction incident to the distribution of the governmental powers among three departments, to save the people from autocracy."

Nothing is clearer than the intention of the Founders to repudiate and reject "legislative omnipotence." Notwithstanding, the Radical leaders, [historian Samuel Eliot] Morison justly states, "by a series of usurpations . . . intended to make the majority in Congress the ultimate judge of its own powers, and the President a mere chairman of a cabinet responsible to Congress." . . .

. . . What made the trial "disgraceful" was not that the charges were altogether without color of law but that the proceeding reeked with unfairness, with palpable prejudgment of guilt. The filing of impeachment charges against a President, however unjustified his differences with Congress, does not place him outside the pale. . . .

The impeachment and trial of Andrew Johnson, to my mind, represent a gross abuse of the impeachment process, an attempt to punish the President for differing with and obstructing the policy of Congress. It was the culmination of a sustained effort to make him subservient to Congress, to alter the place of a coordinate branch in the constitutional scheme. It undermined the separation of powers and constituted a long stride toward the very "legislative tyranny" feared and fenced in by the Founders.

Questions

1. *How did President Johnson obstruct the efforts of Congress to reconstruct the South? How successful does he seem to have been at the time the House of Representatives impeached him?*
2. *How united do Republicans seem to have been on the impeachment issue? How do you think you would have voted on impeachment in December 1867? How would you have voted in February 1868 when the impeachment resolution finally passed? Why?*
3. *Historians disagree over why the Republicans impeached Johnson. What are Benedict's and Berger's views? Whose view seems most persuasive to you? Why?*

The Impeachment and Trial of Andrew Johnson: Selections from the Documentary Record

The documents that follow illuminate the controversy over impeachment. They describe the story from the initial impeachment resolution that radical Republicans presented in January 1867 through Johnson's acquittal in June 1868 and give the flavor of the debates and the proceedings.

Impeachment Resolution of 7 January 1867

The following is the impeachment resolution that radical Republican James M. Ashley presented in the House of Representatives on 7 January 1867. How did Ashley's resolution reflect the broad view of impeachable offenses? Did any of the specifications charge a violation of law? What then was the basis of the proposed impeachment? Taken from The Congressional Globe, 39th Congress, 2d Session, *320.*

I do impeach Andrew Johnson, Vice President and acting President of the United States, of high crimes and misdemeanors.

I charge him with a usurpation of power and violation of law:

In that he has corruptly used the appointing power;

In that he has corruptly used the pardoning power;

In that he has corruptly used the veto power; . . .

. . . Therefore,

Be it resolved, That the Committee on the Judiciary be . . . authorized to inquire into the official conduct of Andrew Johnson . . . and to report to this House whether, in their opinion, . . . the said Andrew Johnson has been guilty of any act, or has conspired with others to do acts, which, in contemplation of the Constitution, are high crimes and misdemeanors.

Testimony Taken by the House Judiciary Committee

The House Judiciary Committee began to investigate charges that Johnson had abused his powers or used them corruptly. The following testimony from members of Johnson's cabinet related to charges that Johnson had wrongfully assumed authority to restore civil government in the South without first going to Congress, and that he had ignored the law requiring government officers to take the Test Oath when he made appointments in the South. Does it seem to you that Johnson's cabinet was trying to protect him? How? Did Stanton, whose removal would finally lead to Johnson's impeachment, seem any less protective of the president than Secretary of the Treasury Hugh McCulloch? Reprinted from House Report No. 7, 40th Congress, 1st Session, *401, 604, 607, 610–11.*

Testimony of Secretary of War Edwin M. Stanton, 18 May 1867

Q. Did any one of the Cabinet express a doubt of the power of the executive branch of the government to reorganize state governments which had been in rebellion without the aid of Congress?

A. None whatever. I had myself entertained no doubt of the authority of the President to take measures for the organization of the rebel States on the plan proposed during the vacation of Congress, and agreed in the plan specified. . . . It may be proper to add, in regard to the history of this subject, that . . . I had myself . . . prepared a rough draft of a form or mode by which the authority and laws of the United States should be re-established and governments reorganized in the rebel States. . . . [The project of Reconstruction] came under discussion in the Cabinet, the principal point of discussion being as to who should exercise the elective franchise. . . . The objections of the President to throwing the franchise open to the colored people appeared to be fixed, and I think every member of the Cabinet assented to the arrangement as it was specified in the proclamation. . . .

Testimony of Secretary of the Treasury Hugh McCulloch, 28 May 1867

Q. Have any persons been appointed to office in the southern States since the close of the rebellion . . . without taking what is commonly called the test oath?

A. A number of persons have been appointed to office in the southern States who were unable to take the test oath of 1862. . . .

Q. Were these appointments made by the President?

A. . . . I desire to state that this was considered a matter of so grave importance that, before any action was taken upon the subject of filling revenue offices at the South, it was a matter of Cabinet consultation; and, after a full and careful deliberation, it was agreed—as I recollect, unanimously—that, as it was important for the government that we should establish our revenue offices without delay, the Secretary of the Treasury would be justifiable in doing the best he could in regard to appointments, under the peculiar circumstances of the country. . . .

Q. In appointing men who could not take the test oath?

A. In appointing the best men we could find, and running the risk in reference to the oath. . . .

Q. The President assenting to that?

A. The President did not dissent, and I think he assented to the views of the Cabinet. On this subject, if I recollect right, we were a unit. . . .

Q. Do you hold that it is not your duty as an executive officer to take the law of Congress as declared and to obey it?

A. It is my opinion that an executive officer should obey the law literally.

Q. But still you acted on the notion that you had a right to exercise a dispensing power over the law, in the belief that Congress would modify it at the next session in accordance with your views.

A. . . . It was not my purpose to violate the law. I kept the law as nearly as I could. But I thought that the peculiar circumstances of the country and the necessities of the service would justify me in appointing, and recommending for appointment, men who might not be able to take the oath.

The Debate over Impeachment in the House

The majority of the Judiciary Committee reported in favor of impeachment on 25 November 1867. The House debated the issue on 5 and 6 December. Representative George S. Boutwell presented the majority view and Committee Chairman James F. Wilson that of the minority. After the debate, the House voted 108 to 57 to table the impeachment resolution. How did Boutwell and Wilson reflect two different understandings of the grounds for impeachment? Whose argument seems more persuasive to you? Boutwell's and Wilson's speeches are taken from The Congressional Globe, 40th Congress, 2d Session, Appendix, *55, 57–58, 60, 63–64.*

Speech of Representative Boutwell, 5 and 6 December 1867

[I]n this country a proceeding by impeachment is not a criminal proceeding. . . . The theory that . . . the President and other officers, as long as they do not violate the criminal statute laws of the country, may do any act or thing, however detrimental to the public interests, however contrary to the public morals, however heinous in its nature, and still retain their offices, is a theory so at variance with civilization, with the principles of law, and with the existence of the Government, that it ought not to receive our support or countenance unless the language of the Constitution imperatively requires us to yield to its authority. . . .

. . . [T]he phrase "bribery or other high crimes and misdemeanors" is used in the Constitution in accordance with and subject to the rule of reason, which lies at the foundation of the English common law. . . . Misconduct in office, misbehavior in office, misdemeanor in office, are equivalent terms. . . .

Chief Justice Story says, . . . "The offenses to which the power of impeachment has been and is ordinarily applied as a remedy are of a political character. . . . [Impeachment applies to] what are aptly termed political offenses, growing out of personal misconduct, or gross neglect, or usurpation, or habitual disregard of the public interests in the discharge of the duties of political office. . . ."

. . . [T]he President of the United States is bound to support the Constitution, the vital part of which . . . is that he shall take care that the laws be faithfully executed, and he violates that great provision of the Constitution especially when he himself disregards the law either by doing that which is forbidden or neglecting that which he is commanded to do. . . .

Speech of Representative James F. Wilson, 6 December 1867

The position which the minority of the committee occupy in this case may be summed up in these words: that no civil officer of the United States can be lawfully impeached except for a crime or misdemeanor known to the law; that this body must be guided by the law, and not by that indefinite something called its conscience, which may be one thing to-day and quite a different one to-morrow. If the case now before us, tested by the principles of criminal law, discloses high crimes or misdemeanors coming within the rule I have stated, then the gentleman is right in demanding that the President of the United States be impeached; and I here throw open to the gentleman the range of both statutory and common law impeachable crimes. If these cannot be found in the record of this case, then no amount of conscience in House and Senate can justify us in proceeding further with it. . . .

But the gentleman found in Story an authority to the effect that we may impeach for "political offenses." What is a "political offense?" . . . Is it the doing of something that the dominant political party in the country do not like? That, in one sense, is a political offense. Are we to impeach for that? We did not like the removal of our own friends from office by the present President. Are we to impeach for that? He has done many acts of political littleness, meanness, and treachery. Are these impeachable political offenses? Sir, it is unsafe for us to wander into the field of political or party action for offenses upon which to rest the impeaching power of this House. Disaster alone could result from such a course of procedure.

The Tenure of Office Act

The House did not impeach Johnson until he removed Secretary of War Edwin M. Stanton in apparent violation of the Tenure of Office Act, passed in 1867. As passed, the bill covered all important government officers, including the President's cabinet. The Senate version exempted the cabinet. The final language was a compromise. As you read the following document, consider whether or not the law covered Stanton. Excerpted from U.S. Statutes at Large *14:430–31.*

Be it enacted . . . , That every person holding any civil office to which he has been appointed by and with the advice and consent of the Senate, and every person who shall hereafter be appointed to any such office, and shall become duly qualified to act therein, is, and shall be entitled to hold such office until a successor shall have been in like manner appointed and duly qualified, except as herein otherwise provided: *Provided,* That the Secretaries of State, of the Treasury, of War, of the Navy, and of the Interior, the Postmaster-General, and the Attorney-General, shall hold their offices respectively for and during the term of the President by whom they may have been appointed and for one month thereafter, subject to removal by and with the advice and consent of the Senate. . . .

SEC. 6. *And be it further enacted,* That every removal, appointment, or employment, made, had, or exercised, contrary to the provisions of this act . . . shall be deemed, and are hereby declared to be, high misdemeanors.

Reprinted from *United States Statutes at Large; 39th Congress, Second Session,* Volume 14, edited by George P. Sanger, published by Dennis & Co., Inc., 1962. Originally printed in 1868 by Little, Brown, & Company.

A Conservative Republican Endorses Impeachment

When Johnson first suspended Secretary of War Stanton, he seemed to do so in conformity with the Tenure of Office Act. But when the Senate refused to agree to make the removal permanent, Johnson refused to concede his right to remove Stanton. On 21 February 1868, he precipitated impeachment by issuing an order removing Stanton and instructing General Lorenzo to replace him temporarily. This action was an apparent violation of the act, which Johnson denounced as unconstitutional. With this, the House passed a resolution of impeachment. Wilson, leader of the opposition to impeachment the previous December, was later named one of the managers of impeachment, responsible for presenting the case to the Senate. The following excerpt is taken from The Congressional Globe, 40th Congress, 2d Session, *1386.*

Deliberately, not to say defiantly, the President has violated a penal statute of the United States, and has thereby committed a high misdemeanor. . . . All of the circumstances attendent upon this case show that the President's action was deliberate and willful. There is not a shade of excuse or palliation in the case as it is presented to us. Perversely he has rushed upon his own destruction. Obstinately he has forced upon us an issue in which we must join or prove ourselves unworthy representatives of a free people. We have not sought this issue, but have resorted to every legitimate means to avoid it; we have manifested no undo desire to exercise the impeaching power which is vested in this House exclusively by the express terms of the Constitution.

Guided by a sincere desire to pass this cup from our lips, determined not to drink it if escape were not cut off by the presence of a palpable duty, we at last find ourselves compelled to take its very dregs. A decent respect for the executive office, a patriotic effort to avoid a collision between two departments of the Government, ever manifested by this House, seemed to have been most strangely misunderstood by the President. Our refusal to abuse a power or to resort to it even while a mere doubt as to our right to exercise it could be urged in opposition thereto seems to have been construed by him into a license to trample even the penal statutes of the nation. The result is before us. The President challenges the supremacy of the law and dishonors his constitutional obligation to "take care that the laws be faithfully executed." ... He defiantly ... declares that he will decide what laws are constitutional, and that such only as stand the test of his judgment will he respect, enforce, or obey. This is his case. He has elected to base it on penal statute. It is for us to traverse this case and put it to the country. Anything less than this would be a shameful abuse of our high trust and a criminal abandonment of duty.

The Articles of Impeachment

Most of the Articles presented to the Senate on 4 March 1868, were variations of Article I, reprinted below. Article XI tried to summarize the charges and put them in a broader context. Can you see why it proved to be the strongest article? How did the articles compare to the charges Representative Ashley levied in his impeachment resolution of January 1867? Which do you think provided the stronger basis for an impeachment? Why do you think the House framed the articles in this way? Abridged from Trial of Andrew Johnson, President of the United States, Before the Senate of the United States, on Impeachment by the House of Representatives for High Crimes and Misdemeanors *(Washington, 1868), 1:6, 10.*

ARTICLE I.

That said Andrew Johnson, . . . unmindful of the high duties of his office, of his oath of office, and of the requirement of the Constitution that he should take care that the laws be faithfully executed, did unlawfully, and in violation of the Constitution and laws of the United States issue an order in writing for the removal of Edwin M. Stanton from the office of Secretary for the Department of War. . . . Which order was unlawfully issued with intent then and there to violate the act entitled "An act regulating the tenure of certain civil offices,". . . .

ARTICLE XI.

That said Andrew Johnson, . . . [did] on the eighteenth day of August, A. D. eighteen hundred and sixty-six, . . . by public speech, declare and affirm, in substance, that the thirty-ninth Congress of the United States was not a Congress of the United States authorized by the Constitution to exercise legislative power under the same, but, on the contrary, was a Congress of only part of the States, thereby denying, and intending to deny, that the legislation of said Congress was valid or obligatory upon him . . . except in so far as he saw fit to approve the same . . . ; and, in pursuance of said declaration, the said Andrew Johnson, . . . did, unlawfully, and in disregard of the requirements of the Constitution, that he should take care that the laws be faithfully executed, attempt to prevent the execution of an act entitled "An act regulating the tenure of certain civil offices," . . . and, also, by further unlawfully devising and contriving . . . to prevent the execution of an act entitled "An act to provide for the more efficient government of the rebel States," . . . the said Andrew Johnson . . . [did] commit, and was guilty of, a high misdemeanor in office.

The President's Response

The president's lawyers responded to the articles on 6 March 1868. Can you succinctly summarize the president's defense? How did Johnson's explanation for his conduct differ from that alleged in the articles of impeachment? Do you find his explanation persuasive in light of everything that led up to the impeachment? Excerpted from Trial of Andrew Johnson . . . *1:38–39, 42.*

[T]his respondent [Andrew Johnson], the President of the United States, responsible for the conduct of the Secretary for the Department of War, and having the constitutional right to resort to and rely upon the person holding that office for advice concerning the great and difficult public duties enjoined on the President by the Constitution and laws of the United States, became satisfied that he could not allow the said Stanton to continue to hold the office of Secretary for the Department of War. . . .

This respondent . . . believed . . . that the Constitution of the United States conferred on the President . . . the power at any and all times of removing from office all executive officers for cause to be judged of by the President alone. . . .

. . . [T]his respondent . . . believes, that the said first section of the last mentioned act [Tenure of Office Act] was and is wholly inoperative and void by reason of its conflict with the Constitution of the United States. . . . [T]his respondent considered it to be proper to examine and decide whether the particular case of the said Stanton, on which it was this respondent's duty to act, was within or without the terms of that first section of the act. . . .

. . . [T]he President was compelled either to allow the said Stanton to resume the said office and remain therein contrary to the settled convictions of the President, formed as aforesaid respecting the powers confided to him and the duties required of him by the Constitution of the United States, and contrary to the opinion formed . . . that the first section of the last-mentioned act did not affect the case of the said Stanton, . . . or else he was compelled to take such steps as might, in the judgment of the President, be lawful and necessary to raise, for a judicial decision, the questions affecting the lawful right of the said Stanton to . . . persist in refusing to quit the said office . . . and to this end, and to this end only, this respondent did, . . . on the 21st day of February, 1868, issue the order for the removal of the said Stanton . . . and the order authorizing the said Lorenzo F. Thomas to act as Secretary of War *ad interim.*

Testimony before the Senate

Given the importance of Johnson's claim that he intended only to raise a court case testing his right to remove Stanton, a key question at the trial was whether the Senate would admit testimony evidencing his intent. The following testimony and the debate over its admissibility was typical of the proceedings. The president's counsel was William M. Evarts. House Manager of Impeachment Benjamin F. Butler raised the objections. Why did Butler insist that Welles's testimony was suspect? Would you have voted to admit it? Why or why not? To what degree did partisanship seem to determine how senators voted on admitting it?

Regardless of the merits, which side do you think came out of the exchange looking better? Why do you think so? Abridged from The Trial of Andrew Johnson . . . *1:675–76, 678–79, 693–97.*

Testimony of Secretary of the Navy Gideon Welles, Questioned by Mr. Evarts

Q. Were you present at any cabinet meeting at which, after the passage of that act [Tenure of Office Act], it became the subject of consideration?

A. Yes; on two occasions. . . .

Q. How was it brought to the attention of the cabinet?

A. By the President.

Q. As a matter of consideration in the cabinet?

A. For consultation; for the advice and the opinion of the members.

Q. How did he submit the matter to your consideration?

Mr. Manager Butler. If that involves anything that he said—

Mr. Evarts. Yes, it does.

The Senate organized as a court of impeachment. (Courtesy of The Library of Congress.)

Mr. Manager Butler. . . . [W]e object to anything that took place in the cabinet consultation, and in order to have this matter brought to a point, we desire to have the offer of proof put in writing.

Mr. Evarts. We will put the whole matter in writing.

The offer was reduced to writing and read by the Secretary, as follows:

> We offer to prove that the President, at a meeting of the cabinet while the bill was before the President for his approval, laid before the cabinet the tenure-of-civil-office bill for their consideration and advice to the President respecting his approval of the bill; and thereupon the members of the cabinet then present gave their advice to the President that the bill was unconstitutional. . . .

Mr. Manager Butler. . . . The question is whether, after a law has been passed, under the due forms of law, the President can show what his opinions were, and the opinions of his cabinet, before it was passed, as a justification for refusing to obey it and execute it. . . . [I]f that can be done, then impeachment is ended in this country for any breach of law, for there will be no President who cannot find cabinets subservient enough to advise him as he wants to be advised. . . .

Mr. Evarts. . . . [If the effort to remove Stanton constitutes a crime,] then the law imports an intent to do the thing done, and so to commit the crime, and that all else is inapplicable legally within the purview of an impeachment and its trial as much as it might or would be upon a question of a formal infraction of a statute under an indictment. . . . [T]his matter of evidence here touches that part of the case, and is to supply that portion of the evidence of what care, what deliberation, what advice attended the steps of the President as he proceeded. . . .

The Chief Justice. . . . The first article charges that on the 21st day of February, 1868, the President issued an order for the removal of Mr. Stanton from the office of Secretary of War, that this order was made unlawfully, and that it was made with intent to violate the tenure-of-office act. . . . The intent, then, is the subject to which much of the evidence on both sides has been directed; and the Chief Justice conceives that this testimony is admissible. . . .

Mr. Howard. I call for the yeas and nays. . . .

The question having been taken by yeas and nays, resulted—yeas 20, nays 29, not voting 5. The examination continued.

By Mr. Evarts:

Question. At the cabinet meetings . . . was the question whether Mr. Stanton was within the operation of the civil-tenure act the subject of consideration and determination?

Mr. Manager Butler. Stop a moment. We object.

The Chief Justice. The counsel will please propose their question in writing. . . .

The offer [the question] was reduced to writing and read by the chief clerk, as follows:

> We offer to prove that at the meetings of the cabinet at which Mr. Stanton was present, held while the tenure-of-office bill was before the President for approval, the advise of the cabinet in regard to the same was asked by the President and given by the cabinet; and thereupon the question whether Mr. Stanton and the other Secretaries who had received their appointment from Mr. Lincoln were within the restrictions upon the President's power of removal from office created by said act was considered, and the opinion expressed that the Secretaries appointed by Mr. Lincoln were not within such restrictions. . . .

Mr. Manager Butler. . . . I desire to call the attention of the Senate to Exhibit A . . . which is the veto message, wherein the President vetoes the bill expressly upon the ground that it does include all his cabinet. . . .

Mr. Manager Butler further argues that the allegations, made by Mr. Evarts, stating that the cabinet agreed with the President's interpretation of the Tenure of Office Act are "wholly illusory and deceptive."

The Chief Justice. Senators, the Chief Justice is of opinion that this testimony is proper to be taken into consideration by the Senate. . . .

Mr. Drake. On that I ask for the yeas and nays. . . .

The yeas and nays were ordered, and being taken resulted—yeas 22, nays 26; [not voting 6].

The Final Arguments

The trial took much longer, and the case was much more difficult to prove, than the Republicans had anticipated. Not until late April did the managers and defense counsel make their final arguments. Do you find Evarts's argument persuasive? Do you believe that Johnson's intentions were really so benign when he removed Stanton? How convincing do you find Bingham's response? Excerpted from Trial of Andrew Johnson . . . *2:273–74, 291–93, 395, 400, 407, 438.*

Argument for the Defense by William M. Evarts, 28 and 29 April 1868.

[T]he people . . . wish to know what the crime is that the President is accused of. They understand that treason and bribery are great offences, and that a ruler guilty of them should be brought into question and deposed. They are ready to believe that . . . there may be other great crimes and misdemeanors touching the conduct of government and the welfare of the state that may equally fall within the jurisdiction and the duty. But they wish to know what the crimes are. They wish to know whether the President has betrayed our liberties or our possessions to a foreign state. They wish to know whether he has delivered up a fortress or surrendered a fleet. They wish to know whether he has made merchandise of the public trust and turned authority to private gain. And when informed that none of these things are charged, imputed, or even declaimed about, they yet seek further information and are told that he has removed a member of his cabinet.

. . . That on its mere statement does not strike them as a grave offence needing the interposition of this special jurisdiction. . . . [I]t does not strike them as either an unprecedented occurrence or as one involving any great danger to the state.

"Well, but how comes it to be a crime?" they inquire. Why, Congress passed a law for the first time in the history of the government undertaking to control by law this matter of removal from office; and they provided that if the President should violate it it should be a misdemeanor, and a high misdemeanor; and now he has removed, or undertaken to remove, a member of his cabinet, and he is to be removed himself for that cause. . . .

That is the situation. "Was the Secretary of War removed?" they inquire. No; he was not removed, he is still Secretary, still in possession of the department. Was force used? Was violence meditated, prepared, attempted, applied? No; it was all on paper, and all went no further than making the official attitude out of which a judgment of the Supreme Court could be got. And here the Congress . . . has interposed the procedure of trial and impeachment of the President to settle by its own authority this question between it and the Executive. The people . . . are not slow to understand . . . that it is a question between the omnipotence of Congress and the supremacy of the Constitution of the United States. . . .

. . . What he did was all in writing. What he did was all public and official. What he did was communicated to all the authorities of the government having relation to the subject. . . . [Y]ou see at once that no rhetoric, that no argument, that no politics whatever can fix upon the offence, completed or attempted, any other quality than this: a violation of a law, if it shall be so held, in support of and in obedience to the higher obligation of the Constitution. . . .

. . . [N]obody ever violates an unconstitutional law. . . . Much has been said about the duty of the people to obey and of officers to execute unconstitutional laws. I claim for the President no greater right . . . than I claim for every citizen . . . when a law infringes upon his constitutional and civil and personal rights; for to say that Congress has no right to pass unconstitutional laws and yet that everybody is to obey them just as if they were constitutional . . . is, of course, trampling the Constitution and its defence of those who obey it in the dust. . . .

. . . [N]othing was done but the mere . . . exercise of right claimed under the Constitution without force, without violence, and making nothing but the attitude . . . which, if unquestioned, might raise the point for judicial determination. . . .

Final Argument of Manager John A. Bingham, 4 and 6 May 1868.

[T]he position assumed in this defence for the accused [is] that he may suspend the laws, dispense with their execution, and interpret and construe the Constitution for himself to the hurt of the republic, without peril to his official position, if he accompanies it either at the time or after the fact with a statement that his only object in violating the Constitution or in suspending the laws and dispensing with their execution was to obtain at some future day a . . . judicial decision upon the[ir] validity. . . .

. . . It is written in the Constitution that "he shall take care that the laws be faithfully executed." . . . [It] is thus written on the very fore-front of the instrument [Constitution], that he shall take care that the laws enacted by the people's representatives in Congress assembled shall be faithfully executed—not some of the laws; not the laws which he approves; but the laws shall be executed until the same shall have been duly repealed by the power that made them, or shall have been constitutionally reversed by the Supreme Court of the United States. . . .

If the President may dispense with one act of Congress upon his own discretion, may he not in like manner dispense with every act of Congress? . . .

. . . [H]e now comes with his answer and says that his only purpose was to test the validity of the law in the Supreme Court! If that was his sole purpose, how comes it that the President did not institute the proceeding? . . . The President simply utters another falsehood when he comes before the Senate and says that his purpose in violating his oath, in violating your Constitution, in violating your laws, was, that he might test the validity of the statute in the Supreme Court.

The Verdict

The Senate began to vote on the articles on 16 May 1868. They voted on Article XI first. Looking at the articles of impeachment, can you see why? Failing to secure a conviction by one vote, they then adjourned for ten days, with the supporters of impeachment pressuring the senators who voted for acquittal to change their minds. When they voted on Articles I and II, however, the result was the same. Can you see a relationship between the vote on conviction and the vote on whether to accept evidence relating to the president's intent? Taken from The Trial of Andrew Johnson *. . . 2:487.*

The Chief Justice. Upon this article [Article XI] 35 senators vote "Guilty," and 19 senators vote "Not guilty." Two-thirds not having pronounced guilty, the President is, therefore, acquitted upon this article.

Opinion of Senator William Pitt Fessenden

William Pitt Fessenden was the majority leader of the Republicans in the Senate. Like six other Republicans he voted to acquit Johnson. In the following selection, he explained his reasoning. Abridged from Trial of Andrew Johnson . . . *3:19–22.*

I did vote to overrule the President's veto [of the Tenure of Office Act], because I was not then, and am not now, convinced of its unconstitutionality. . . . The proper inquiry is, whether the President, in removing, or attempting to remove, Mr. Stanton from the office of Secretary of War, violated its provisions. . . .

. . . After the death of President Lincoln, . . . [Stanton] held at the pleasure of President Johnson, by his permission, up to the passage of the act of March 2, 1867, and might have been removed by him at any time. Did that act change his tenure of office without a new appointment, and transform what was before a tenure at will into a tenure for a fixed period? . . .

The word "term," . . . must, I think, refer to the period of actual service. . . . [T]he word "term" of the President, as used in the proviso, is inseparable from the individual, and dies with him.

If I am right in this conclusion, Mr. Stanton, as Secretary of War, comes neither within the body of the section nor within the proviso, unless he can be considered as having been *appointed* by Mr. Johnson. . . . As used in the Constitution, *appointment* implies a designation—an act. And with regard to certain officers, including the Secretary of War, it implies a nomination to the Senate and a confirmation by that body. A Secretary of War can be *appointed* in no other manner. . . . [I]t cannot be contended that Mr. Stanton was ever appointed Secretary of War by Mr. Johnson, and he cannot, therefore, be considered as included in the proviso. The result is, that he is excluded from the general provision because expressly excepted from its operation, and from the proviso by not coming within the terms of description. . . .

Even, however, if I were not satisfied of the construction given herein of the act of March 2, 1867, I should still hesitate to convict the President of a high misdemeanor for what was done by him on the 21st of February. . . . It was, at most, an attempt on the part of the President, which he might well believe he had a right to make. The evidence utterly fails to show any design on the part of the President to effect his purpose by force or violence. . . . To depose the constitutional chief magistrate of a great nation, elected by the people, on grounds so slight, would, in my judgment, be an abuse of the power conferred upon the Senate, which could not be justified to the country or the world. . . . Worse than this, it would inflict a wound upon the very structure of our government, which time would fail to cure, and which might eventually destroy it.

Questions

1. *Ashley's resolution for impeachment differed pretty radically from the articles that the House finally brought against Johnson. Which do you think better summarized the real basis of the charges against Johnson? Would the managers have had a better chance of winning a conviction if the articles had looked more like Ashley's?*
2. *In your opinion, did President Johnson's actions merit impeachment in 1867? How far do you think a president can go in refusing to enforce laws passed by Congress? Under what circumstances is impeachment an appropriate remedy?*
3. *What did the president's counsel try to make the central issue of the trial? Do you find their arguments convincing? How did the House managers of impeachment respond? What did they try to make the issue? How effective do you find their response? Was part of the problem in the articles of impeachment themselves?*

FURTHER READING

Eric Foner's Reconstruction: America's Unfinished Revolution, 1863–1877 *(New York, 1988) is the standard work on Reconstruction as a whole. Good brief introductions are Kenneth M. Stampp,* The Era of Reconstruction, 1865–1877 *(New York, 1965); John Hope Franklin,* Reconstruction: After the Civil War *(Chicago, 1961); Allen W. Trelease,* Reconstruction: The Great Experiment *(New York, 1971); and Michael Perman,* Emancipation and Reconstruction, 1862–1879 *(Arlington Heights, Illinois, 1987). The events leading to impeachment and the impeachment trial are best discussed in Hans L. Trefousse,* Impeachment of a President: Andrew Johnson, the Blacks, and Reconstruction *(Knoxville, 1975). Gene Smith,* High Crimes and Misdemeanors: The Impeachment and Trial of Andrew Johnson *(New York, 1985), is a well-written account aimed at a popular audience, but Smith's hostility toward the radical Republicans reflects old scholarship that is no longer accepted by historians. William H. Rehnquist, chief justice of the Supreme Court of the United States, has published* Grand Inquests: The Historic Impeachments of Justice Samuel Chase and President Andrew Johnson *(New York, 1992), which echoes Raoul Berger's criticism of the Republicans excerpted earlier in the chapter.*